To Armand,
with respect
and affection

The Italian-American Novel

Rose Basile Green

Chicago, Dec. 29, 1977

Other books by Rose Basile Green:

To Reason Why (Sonnets)
The Cabrinian Philosophy of Education

The Italian-American Novel

A Document of the Interaction of Two Cultures

Rose Basile Green

Rutherford · Madison · Teaneck
Fairleigh Dickinson University Press

Associated University Presses, Inc.
Cranbury, New Jersey 08512

Library of Congress Cataloging in Publication Data
Green, Rose Basile, 1914–
The Italian–American novel.
Bibliography: p.
1. American fiction—Italian authors—History and criticism. I. title.
PS153. I8G7 813'.03 72–11081
ISBN 0–8386–1287–3

PRINTED IN THE UNITED STATES OF AMERICA

DEDICATION

I deed to Italo-Americans
A precipice that trees the watershed
And feeds the stream. These last Acadians
The nymphs of lumbered forests now have wed.
First, in the pristine morning at the plow
The ancestors dug furrows deep and long
To plant the seedlings of the global bough
That pitched the hemispheres to wind their song.
Then, from the well of Rome the discipline
For law and spirit and the noble arts
Drained off the vintage fruit for bread and wine
And filtered to the soil of wildest parts.

Columbia restores their muse today
To sing all artists who flowed here to stay.

R. B. G.

CONTENTS

FOREWORD

History teaches some harsh lessons to those who care to sit at her feet and listen to her. One of the first such lessons is that a nation's political disunity and fragmentation carry heavy penalties.

The great voyages of exploration and discovery that began in the fifteenth century had as their protagonists western Europeans. Among these, none were more prominent than the Italians, as proved by such names as Columbus, Vespucci, Cabot, and Verrazzano. But they all sailed under the flags of other nations.

Discovery and exploration soon led to colonization, and here the Italians were not so fortunate. While the Spanish, Portuguese, French, and English, who had already achieved national unity, built up extensive colonial empires to which they carried their own languages and cultures, the Italians, still split into small and relatively weak city states, settled no new lands in their own name.

When the time came for them to emigrate in large numbers, in the nineteenth century, they found all newly discovered lands preempted by earlier settlers of other stocks and cultures. Nowhere (save in a few small and unimportant East African areas, since lost) were they able to run up their own flag and establish their own language and institutions.

The English of England had a might flowering in the new lands of America, Canada, Australia, and New Zealand. The Spanish of Spain was carried to lands that stretch from the Rio Grande to Cape Horn. Portugal's language became established in Brazil, a mighty country comprising nearly half of the South American continent. The tongue of France was carried to Canada, Haiti, Indochina, North Africa. The language of Dante could aspire to nothing more than a precarious existence, mainly in dialectal forms, in the midst of established speakers of other tongues.

American English developed a great and beautiful literature in its own right, side by side with that of England, and English writings received further notable contributions from Canda and the great English-speaking islands of the Pacific. Brazil produced a literature that bears comparison with that of Portugal. There is a whole series of Spanish-American literatures that flank that of the mother country. The language of France, in addition to receiving occasional literary contributions from former and present French possessions, is also the vehicle of a considerable Belgian and Swiss output.

In contrast, Italian literature stands alone. There are no offshoots. Only a very few Italians or people of Italian parentage have had the courage, in countries that were English-, French-, Spanish-, and Portuguese-speaking, to express their feelings, aspirations, and vicissitudes through the medium of their ancestral tongue.

Nevertheless, the feelings, aspirations, and vicissitudes were there, and had to find expression. It was natural that overseas Italians should use as their medium the majority language of their individual community, with which most of the aspiring writers were more familiar than with their ancestral Italian.

So there arose, in the lands of North and South America, a literary stream of works composed in English, Spanish, and Portuguese by writers bearing Italian names, sometimes changed to conform to the majority pattern, more often flaunting their Italian origin.

This was particularly true in the case of the United States of America, where the deeper discrepancy between Anglo-Saxon English and Latin-Romance Italian precluded the free-and-easy interchange that exists between Italian on the one hand, and Spanish and Portuguese on the other.

There is no question that an Italian-American literature, in English, exists. It has its own distinctive traits and bears its own peculiar imprint. While a few Italian-American writers have sought their inspiration in the general heritage of mankind, a far greater number have poured into their output their own individual and group experiences, telling what is in substance the story of the Italian immigrants in the great land that generously opened its doors to all comers, received them in its ample bosom, and by the power of its example rather than by any display of forceful persuasion converted them into members of an American nationality of which the overwhelming majority of us are happy and proud to form a part.

Yet the process of Americanization was not without its disturbing episodes: intolerance and even persecution here, overt discrimination there; a covert reluctance to accept the newcomers elsewhere. Both these sporadic occurrences and the broader, far more heartening picture of gradual assimilation are abundantly described in the pages of Italian-American writings.

To anyone who cares to examine these writings as a global contribution to American literature rather than as isolated works, the Italian-American output teaches far-reaching lessons: on the one hand, in the true spirit of tolerance and understanding that are required of the assimilating group; on the other, in the need for patience, forbearance, hard work that the assimilated group must display if it wishes the process to proceed smoothly and at maximum speed.

This emphatically does not mean turning the other cheek when one is unjustly slapped; nor does it mean losing contact with one's ancestral cultural heritage, and pride in that heritage. It does mean not losing heart or patience because all wrongs and injustices are not righted in one day; sticking to one's purpose through all adversity in order to better his own, his family's, and his community's lot, to reflect prestige and honor upon one's country of origin, and to offer a maximum contribution to the nation of which he is becoming a part.

While comparatively recent arrivals to the United States, the Italians nevertheless arrived decades before the organization of racial and ethnic groups into voting and pressure blocs, and before the advent of civil rights, open housing and fair employment movements; not to mention raucous and disorderly demonstrations and proposals to hire, promote, and admit, not on the basis of individual merit, but in accordance with quota systems worthy of the most obscurantistic practices of nineteenth-century European monarchies. Insofar as the American society lends itself to discriminatory practices, the Italians bore the full brunt of these, as the Germans and Irish had borne it at an earlier period, and as the Jews and east Europeans bore it in the same era. In my own pre-World War I experience I can recall newspaper ads that openly flaunted the message: "Apartment for rent; Negroes and Italians need not apply."

Yet the Italians, along with their contemporary fellow-immigrants, did not allow these episodes to sour them on the great American experience, or to discourage them from putting their best foot forward. Their experiences and example might perhaps be studied to good advantage by more recent additions to the great complex that constitutes America.

These experiences are best studied in the works of Italian-American writers, who occasionally sound a note of discouragement, even of rebellion, but who by and large point with optimism to the future development of their groups as it becomes absorbed into the mainstream of American life.

We have until now lacked a comprehensive study, historical, descriptive and bibliographic, of this particular current of American literature which, while it consists of isolated and separate works of uneven value, nevertheless sums up, in its entirety, the Italian experience in America. It was high time for a work such as the present one. To it the author has devoted years of painstaking, accurate research, bringing to light the existence of works which few of us, even of Italian background, knew about.

But this work is far more than a mere bibliography of Italian-American literature. The author, a distinguished writer and poet in her own right, has also undertaken a synoptical description and critical evaluation of the works she has discovered and studied. Her reasoned considerations and interpretations of these works are of the utmost value as literary criticism. Her summation of the Italian-American literary output in the larger framework of the life of the Italian-American communities in the United States transcends the merely literary and impinges upon the fields of history, sociology, and psychology. This is a work that will be read with entrancement by the millions of Italian Americans who want to learn of their own background and tradition; but it will be perused with equal interest by American students of the social, economic, historical, even religious currents that have shaped present-day America.

Mario Pei

ACKNOWLEDGMENTS

To Robert E. Spiller, literary historian, teacher, and friend, for encouragement, advice, and criticism.

To Roy F. Nichols, historian, teacher, and advisor, for his enlightenment in using history to understand the forces of literature.

To Peter Riccio, Howard Marraro, and Giuseppe Prezzolini of the Casa Italiana for their instruction in Italian literature and culture, but especially to Mario A. Pei for his inspiration in applying the discipline of research for clarifying propositions concerning the interaction of languages and culture.

To the members of the American Italian Historical Association and of the Italian-American Press for their faith and encouraging anticipation.

To the numerous Italian Americans who made possible records, materials, and personal illuminations not found in libraries.

The author wishes to thank the following publishers for permission to reprint copyrighted material:

Atheneum Publishers for the selections from *The Fortunate Pilgrim* by Mario Puzo, copyright © 1964 by Mario Puzo.

Brentano's for the selections from *Claudio Graziani, an Episode of War* by Silvio Villa, copyright © 1919 by Silvio Villa.

The John Day Company, Inc., for the selections from *Swords of Anjou* by Mario A. Pei, copyright © 1953 by Mario A. Pei.

Doubleday & Company, Inc., for the selections from *The Small Miracle*, by Paul Gallico, copyright © 1950 by Paul Gallico; copyright © 1952 by Doubleday & Company, Inc.; for the selections from *The View From Pompey's Head* by Hamilton Basso, copyright © 1954 by Hamilton Basso; for the selections from *Among Thieves* by George Cuomo, copyright © 1968 by George Cuomo; and for the selections from *Bright Day, Dark Runner* by George Cuomo, copyright © 1964 by George Cuomo.

Doubleday, Doran & Company, Inc., for the selections from *Olives on The Apple Tree* by Guido D'Agostino, copyright © 1940 by Guido D'Agostino.

E. P. Dutton & Company for selections from the book *The River Between* by Louis Forgione. Published by E. P. Dutton & Company, Inc., (1928) and used with their permission.

Frederick Fell, Inc., for selections from *The Seventh Month* by Frank Miceli, copyright © 1969 by Frank Miceli.

Grove Press, Inc., for selections from *Cain's Book* by Alexander Trocchi, copyright © 1960 by Grove Press, Inc.

Holt, Rienhart & Winston, Inc., for selections from *This World Is Mine*by Luigi Creatore, copyright © 1948 by Luigi Creatore.

Harper & Row for the selections from *The Eagle and The Rock* by Frances Winwar (Vinciguerra), copyright © 1953 by Frances Winwar.

Houghton Mifflin Company for selections from *Mountain Time* by Bernard DeVoto, copyright © 1946 by Bernard DeVoto. Reprinted by permission of Houghton Mifflin Company.

Kennikat Press, Inc., for selections from *The Literary Fallacy* by Bernard DeVoto, copyright © 1944 by Indiana University, reissued 1969 by Kennikat Press, Inc., and used with their permission.

Little, Brown & Company for selections from *Full of Life* by John Fante, copyright © 1952 by John Fante.

The Macmillan Publishing Co., Inc., for selections from *Americans By Choice*, by Angelo K. Pellegrini, copyright © 1956 by Angelo M. Pellegrini, reprinted with permission by Macmillan Publishing Co., Inc.; also for selections from *The Soul of an Immigrant* by Constantine M. Panunzio, copyright © 1924 by Constantine M. Panunzio; and for selections from *Son of Italy* by Pascal D'Angelo, copyright © 1924 by The Macmillan Company, Inc.

The Scott Meredith Agency for selections from *Three Circles of Light* by Pietro diDonato, copyright © 1960 by Pietro diDonato. Reprinted by permission of the author and his agent, Scott Meredith Literary Agency, 580 Fifth Avenue, New York, N.Y. 10036.

The Philosophical Library, Inc., for selections from *The Sparrows of Paris* by Mario A. Pei, copyright © 1958 by Mario A. Pei.

G. P. Putnam's Sons for selections from *The Godfather* by Mario Puzo, Copyright © 1969 by Mario Puzo; also for selections from *Excursion* by Francis Pollini, copyright © 1965 by Francis Pollini.

Random House, Inc., for selections from *The Dark Arena* by Mario Puzo, copyright © 1953 by Mario Puzo. Reprinted by permission of Robert Lantz-Candida Donadio, Literary Agency, Inc.; also for selections from *From the Academy Bridge* by P. M. Pasinetti, copyright © 1970 by P. M. Pasinetti.

Fleming H. Revell Company for selections from *The Story of Antonio, the Galley Slave* by Antonio Andrea Arrighi, copyright © 1911 by Fleming H. Revell Company.

Charles Scribner's Sons. Excerpts from *Days Before Lent*, 1939, by Hamilton Basso are reprinted by permission of Charles Scribner's Sons. Copyright 1939 Hamilton Basso.

The Vanguard Press, Inc., for selections from *The Grand Gennaro* by Garibaldi Marti Lapolla, copyright © 1935 by Garibaldi Marti Lapolla.

Walker and Company for selections from *The Grand Street Collector* by Joseph Arleo, coyright © 1970 by Joseph Arleo.

INTRODUCTION

Both the utopians of human equality and the resisters of the emergence of ethnic movements will challenge the idea of an Italian-American novel. The absolute egalitarian will insist that an American novel is an American novel, and that it matters not whether the materials are of Jewish, Negro, Italian, Lithuanian, or whatever reference. Furthermore, assured by an established formula in institutional scholarship and by fixed popular promotion, the devotee of an accepted tradition will probably maintain that an Italian or any other ethnic-American writer is successful only insofar as he meets the criteria for successful writing in the past. These standards, of course, are those which publishers maintained for works of fiction written prior to the cultural assimilation of the non-Anglo-Saxon minorities into the nation. Facetiously, therefore, the average American reader of novels may ask, "Is there a Burmese-American novel?" Why classify the Italian-American novel? Why classify the Italian-American?

In response to this challenge, there has mushroomed in many of our colleges and universities a wide diversity of ethnic studies, usually associated with programs in American Studies. Spurred by the phenomenal and, admittedly, pressured promotion of Black Studies, other minorites have been encouraged to stand up and be counted for their contribution to American civilization. Ethnic groups are actively seeking recognition of their "American experience," and perhaps their strongest impact has been made in their application for admission into America's literary mainstream of their own literature, both expository and imaginative. As for the Italians, their American experience is both universal and unique. Some of the incidents in the assimilation of the Italians into America were common to all imigrants; some of their encounters were exclusively their own because of their particular national reference.

Like the other immigrants, the Italians absorbed something from American civilization, and, in turn, contributed something to it. However, as Robert E. Spiller writes in the *Literary History of the United States*, "no competent study as yet been made of the Italian literary and cultural contribution to America."[1] To fill this void, several scholars have recently compiled works on the Italian experience in America, chiefly in the area of social studies. An exploration of the Italian-American novel, therefore, would feasibly consider the imaginative expression of the materials of these expository works. Furthermore, at this moment of our social history, when there is such a dynamic interest in ethnic studies, the contemporary literary pulse is responsive to information about this type of novel.

The writers of Italian-American fiction give a reasonably accurate record of the experiences of the Italian immigrants, the early specifics gradually extending to universalities. The Italian-American novelist, like any other artist, has had to achieve universality through a perceptive interpretation of his own cultural situation. Furthermore, since his inherited culture was historically both generic and long established as a source of the mainstream of European culture, the Italian who came to America had a unique problem. Finding it distasteful to settle underground in a subculture, his struggle was to find the points of identity between his sources and whatever these sources might already have contributed to the civilization of the established Americans. In the confrontation with the Anglo-Saxon society, the Italian in America worked to revive in that society 1) what referred to an ancient and classical harmony, and 2) what had been reaffirmed by Renaissance revision. This problem haunted even the most indigent peasant and made him inordinately sensitive to the abuse he felt he received from other ethnics. A ditch-digger might have been illiterate, but he knew about Dante. As a result, the writer who tells the ditch-digger's story is more than likely exposing the sufferings caused by affronts to personal dignity.

Coming to America in large groups between 1870 and 1914, the Italian immigrants sought here a better economic opportunity than they had found in their native country. That they arrived here in the wake of the great immigrations and that they were not able to communicate in a foreign language were two factors that intensified the normal problem of integration. Eventually, although they met with hostility at first, the Italians gradually made the change that established them as Americans. This change, however, was not implemented by legislation or by extended social assistance; it was effected only after years of economic struggle and social conflict. It is this conflict, intensified by the personal reactions of the immigrants to the American culture, that the autobiographies and novels record.

1. Robert E. Spiller *et al.*, eds. *Literary History of the United States.* Bibliography (New York: The Macmillan Company, 1948), p. 297.

A dual pattern appears to evolve in these writings. First is a development of the fiction through five stages before it identifies with the national literature. Second, interwoven in each of these stages of the dominant pattern is a minor, triple design, which underlies each phase of the integration experience: conflict, isolation, and assimilation. The following discussion is an attempt to provide the reader with representative works within this framework. The selected novels illustrate the process of each of these patterns in the development of the fiction as an interaction of two cultures. The end product of this interaction appears to be that, while the Italian-American writer is a depicter in realistic fiction of a segment of American life, he gives to that fiction a distinctive interpretation: the individual has the moral power to triumph in the struggle against a hostile environment. This positive treatment of material counteracts much in our modern writing that has presented American life as negative in spirit, materialistic in purpose, and nihilistic in achievement.

The development of Italian-American fiction is treated in this discussion, therefore, as a positive contribution to American civilization. An attempt is also made to analyze the materials of that contribution. If it is true that the United States of America is a repository of many immigrant strains, it is reasonable to believe that comprehension of the national culture is incomplete without inclusive knowledge of the contribution of each immigrant group. To acquire this knowledge, one area that may be explored for cultural concepts is that of the immigrant literature. Their own writings document how the immigrants felt about their American experience. In the case of the Italians in America, for example, their writing directly reflected the process of their assimilation. The evolution of these writings has produced two results: 1) a documentary of the interaction of two cultures, and 2) the evidence that the interaction is influenced by the writer of Italian ancestry in the direction of a return to a constructive optimism in our national literary themes. This optimism seems to have evolved from the immigrant's successful accomplishment of his immediate goals in America.

The validity of exploring a particular immigrant literature in order to understand better the general cultural concepts of American life receives substantial authority by making comparative studies in American literary criticism. Of the many celebrated critics of our literature, two representative examples are Van Wyck Brooks and Bernard DeVoto, who illustrate the variance of opinion that may exist between those who judge the same things. DeVoto, for example, writes in *The Literary Fallacy*[2] that literary critics of Brooks's coterie

2. Bernard DeVoto, *The Literary Fallacy* (Boston: Little, Brown & Company), 1944. Reissued by Kennikat Press, Inc. (Port Washington, N.Y., 1969), from which quotations are taken.

have misrepresented American literature and culture as a whole.[3] He contends, furthermore, that Brooks does not have the ability to translate "the resumption of specie payments" into terms of commerce, warfare, politics, brownstone houses, dispossessed farmers, corn burned for fuel, or the revolt of the uncultivated people. In other words, this type of literary critic knows only the history of writers, not the life of the American people; instead of reconstructing society, the critic requires that his opponent use technical terms correctly. Thus, says DeVoto, because criticism separated itself from American experience, the effort to appraise culture by means of literary materials was doomed to failure. It is in the attempt to bridge the gap between literary ideas and American experience that it is relevant to explore the writings of Italian-Americans as an ethnic group. Because standard authors have ignored the members of immigrant groups as subjects of human interest, they have only added another measure of distance between themselves as writers and the whole national culture.

Second in importance to the discovery of the existence and development of Italian-American fiction is the finding of any distinction in this particular writing. Taking the novels in their chronological order, the reader discovers a consistent theme running through them, a theme not always prevalent in other novels of the same time. Italian-American writers have nearly always used as a literary subject the alien, who, in turn, becomes an archetype for the isolated man in an established society. The treatment, however, is not one of repudiation of American experience; on the contrary, the Italian-American writer endows the literary protagonist with the faith to overcome obstacles by his struggles and to fulfill his destiny.

The individual has no such purpose in most of the "official literature," to borrow DeVoto's term, and characters like those in the novels of Sinclair Lewis,[4] for example, have little moral force. Because the people whom Lewis portrayed lived a life of such triviality, American

3. To Brooks's challenge that because of America's paralytic Puritanism and pursuit of wealth there have been no great artists, no great leaders, and no great men in the nation, DeVoto answers that this assertion is hortatory. DeVoto refutes the argument (p. 55) and defends America's growth in experience, architecture, painting, and design. He writes, "The great scholars and historians were busy at their jobs, with great work done and great work ahead of them. Yankee politicians were—not for the first time—remaking the domestic and foreign policies of the United States, were helping to give the nation the place in world organization which it maintained throughout the nineteenth century. In 'great affairs' Yankee business men, reformers, speculators, scientists, and educators were remaking the nation—and so were remaking the world. . . . This is one specimen of the literary misrepresentation of American life."

4. *Ibid.*, pp. 100–101. DeVoto maintains that the novels of Sinclair Lewis lack human profundity. He writes, "Leora Arrowsmith is emotionally undeveloped. Ann Vickers is an immature mind and her emotions are childlike. Dodsworth is so simple a personality that one doubts if he could have managed a corporation. . . . Maturity of mind, maturity of emotion, complexity of character of experience, profundity of aspiration, despair, achievement, or failure—they are not discoverable in these books. They are not present in America so far as these books try to be an index to America."

life in general was pictured as mediocre, and, in the end, contemptible. But mankind is otherwise, says DeVoto, who insists that American life of the early part of this century is not representatively described by writers like Mencken, Lewis, Hemingway, Dos Passos, and Wolfe. These writers apparently expressed no belief in the future and did not discuss men and women dedicated to the mature values of civilization. If one is to write about baseness and evil, the critic contends, he must recognize them as defections from the spirit of man.

According to this point of view, the writer of fiction must look to the democratic interpretation of life that upholds the dignity of man, any man, whether he be established or isolated. If the accepted coterie of novelists were indeed concerned with literary values apart from the real culture, the fact still remains that outside the fringe of this coterie there were writers who were expressing themselves directly from life. Among these were the Italian-American authors of fiction. But, even more important than acceptance of the historical fact of their existence is the urgency of recognizing that their writing is representative of and a contributing part of the national culture. To quote DeVoto once more, "If the national culture had been diversified by the incorporation of many European cultures, that increase necessarily weakened the inheritance of the early republican culture" (p. 159). Thus we find ourselves face to face with the interaction of two cultures.

In the definition of Italian-American writers in this discussion, the meaning is restricted to include: 1) those Italian immigrants who mastered the writing of English sufficiently to warrant publication, and 2) the descendants of Italian immigrants to the second and third generations whose writings earned some critical attention. No attempt has been made to include the works of other racial groups in America who wrote about Italian immigrants or who were influenced by either Italian culture or Italian literary subjects. In comparison with their numbers, the Italians in America produced a small quantity and a limited quality of fiction. In the census of 1940 there was a listing of 4,594,780 Italo-Americans, including those who were native of the first and second generations. If one were to include the third generation, the population stands at well over twenty million. Out of this number I have found over seventy published authors of fiction who have attracted any degree of critical attention. Only a few have achieved national fame.

This meagerness of literary output has apparently been owing to two causes: the limited education of the majority of the early immigrants and the concentration on the part of the immigrants and their immediate descendants on absorbing the structured mores of the United States. Furthermore, the English language and a difference in social concepts were two great barriers to the assimilation of the group. After mastering the language, the Italian-Americans, like other immigrants, faced the more difficult task of transmuting their own cultural traditions. The process of adjustment involved, therefore, a compromise between them and the established American community. It is this compromise that reveals itself when one explores what the Italian-Americans wrote about their experiences in becoming part of the nation.

To substantiate my exploration all available works have been consulted in order to make a selection of representative novels. Most of the volumes discussed here are available in the New York Public Library and the Library of Congress, Washington, D.C. Several, however, had to be traced over long distances. Pascal D'Angelo's *Pascal D'Angelo, Son of Italy,* for example, was recovered in California. The articles from American periodicals listed in the Bibliography serve as a referential measure for comparing the native reaction to the coming of the immigrants with the reaction of the immigrants to what they found in America.

In the process of selecting the novels, some were eliminated as either sub-literary or as thematically repetitive in content. The books discussed here were chosen for their aesthetic value and cultural documentation. Furthermore, to test the veracity and generality of the accounts in both the autobiographies and the novels, it was necessary to compare the incidents described in the books with the personal oral accounts of numerous older Italian immigrants who still remembered their early encounter with America.

The books that are analyzed here include autobiographies and novels, because the immigrants used both forms to relate their experiences, one form often being indistinguishable from the other. The limited number of autobiographies, however, attests to the lack of literacy among the early immigrants. The subsequent dividing line between these autobiographies and the later works of autobiographical fiction is very thin. The analysis of the autobiographies, however, does not serve as an outline or control for the discussion of the novels. On the contrary, the early works are presented as an introduction to the material out of which the fiction grew and then developed to broader cultural concepts.

From the output of each writer one work is generally sufficient as 1) most representative of the author's ability to present his themes, and 2) most relevant to the underlying process of the growth of his ethnic group. The arrangement of authors into progressive divisions corresponds to a pattern in the cultural growth of the Italian immigrant group in the United States. This pattern in Italian-American fiction seems to parallel a similar development in the national culture of America. In comparing the models, the chief problem is to determine the demarcation line between the stages of development in the Italian-American writing. Once these stages are clear, it is not difficult to establish the points of encounter in the interaction of Italian culture with that of America.

Social historians like Oscar Handlin[5] and Robert F. Foerster[6] have provided ample research materials on the subjects of the immigrants' assimilation of American culture and of America's assimilation of the immigrants. However one may consider the acculturation of an immigrant group as a political factor in the making of America, it is essential to agree with Robert E. Spiller that there could not be an American literature before there was an American race or nation in something more than a political sense. According to Spiller, the organic process of America's literary evolution follows four distinct stages, the literary growth corresponding to how the settlers adjusted to their new environment until they struck their "roots of national culture." These roots, however, have been generally represented by the literary historian as the result of the grafting of an old culture upon the growth of a fertile but primitive environment; whereas the roots of our national culture are becoming more clearly understood as the fixed product of cross-breeding an old culture with another one of stabilized form. The works of fiction written by Italian-Americans, therefore, document a process of interaction between two established cultures, each participating in the growth of the American race or nation.

The materials of this discussion are divided into three parts. Part I contains an analysis of representative autobiographies as a direct comment of the Italian immigrants, including the accounts of their background, their reasons for emigrating, their problems upon arrival, and their experiences in their first attempts at settling in a country new to them.

Part II contains an analysis of the immigrants' fictional treatment of American life up to the contemporary period. The materials in this second part present the weaving of the threads in the design of the interaction of the immigrant culture with the larger pattern of the development of the national culture. Five stages evolve in this process: 1) the early impact, the period of explanatory narratives describing the early problems of the first encounter of the Italian culture with that of established America; 2) the need for assimilation, an analysis of Italo-American life (as a co-culture) in communities separate from the national culture; 3) the revulsion into non-Italian-American themes, a reflection of the Italian-American's rejection of his immediate national heritage in an attempt to identify himself with the broader American culture; 4) the counter-revulsion, a return to old sources in which the Italian-American, like the frontier back-trailer, returns to his distinctive heritage and resumes Italian-American themes on a more artistic level of American fiction; and 5) the branching of an Italian culture

5. Oscar Handlin, *Immigration As A Factor In American History* (Englewood Cliffs, N. J.: Prentice-Hall, Inc., 1959).

6. Robert Franz Foerster, *The Italian Emigration of Our Times* (Cambridge: Harvard University Press, 1919).

rooted in American soil when the Italian-American writes mature fiction harmonizing the traditions of his distinctive heritage with those, generally, of his own nation.

Part III, the contemporary period, is a summary of the stages of the developments that led to the point of encounter in the interaction of the two cultures. The pattern of the works of Italian-American fiction shows a progressive direction in the point of view of the writers. Adding imaginative incidents to the autobiographies, the early novelists produced emotional and apologetic narratives in defense of themselves as an alien group. Later, other writers developed these self-conscious accounts into stories of more universal characters. Consistently, these characters represented the struggling members of the underprivileged and the misunderstood. Italian-American writers, however, nearly always use as literary subjects those individuals who had to struggle against their environment but succeeded in becoming reconciled to that environment. The important fact that emerges, therefore, is that in Italian-American fiction the individual is not treated as a victim of material determinism; on the contrary, he is the determiner of his own future, using his will power to achieve some measure of success.

This evolution in literary materials occurs at the same time that there is a change in the national literature from a genteel realism to naturalism. The struggle for articulation on the part of the immigrant appears as a factor in the national literature's progressive concern with the "common man." Therefore, while the Italian-American's writings became more universally American in themes, the notion of the immigrant as he had been conceived in American literature began to change. The alien became a member of the national group.

As the changing Italian immigrant lost his identifying ethnic characteristics, American society accepted him. The "alien" was transformed into the more inclusive—and now favorite—type, the underdog. But, distinctive of the Italian contribution was the consistent thread of affirmation with which the writers approached their literary subjects. Rejecting negativism and pessimism as unrepresentative of the real American spirit, Italian-American writers of fiction professed in their works the same optimism as that with which their ancestors had become a part of the American race and nation.

In the divisions of Part III an attempt is made to evaluate the Italian-American novel in contemporary American literature. The works in this section have been selected from the second half of the 1960s through 1970. In the discussion of each book in this section, a brief outline of plot serves to frame the identity of the characters as they set the themes in motion. An exploration of these themes occupies the greater part of each analysis, both as they are stated directly by the author and as he symbolizes them in the characters. The power with which the writer succeeds in communicating these ideas is the basis of judging the novel's function as a document and as a work of art. The novels have been selected, to a degree, for their sociological importance as well as for their aesthetic value.

Although a certain sociocultural emphasis has been essential in interpreting these books, I wish to avoid the Parrington tradition of using the novels primarily as social documents. In the final part particularly, I have placed more emphasis upon form and treated the novels as works of art in their own right. In the contemporary scene, the Italian-American novel, like all other works, must submit to literary judgments. In bringing the study of Italian-American novelists up to date as part of the whole American literary climate, I have, in the final treatment, allowed the nature of the material to determine my emphasis. In some cases, in order to communicate the particular writer's style and treatment, I have patterned my interpretations on the expressions of the given writer, even to inaccuracies that appear as ethnic characteristics.

In this survey my ultimate aim is to present the contribution of the Italian-American novelist to the mainstream of American literature. It is hoped that this presentation will compare with similar surveys of literary materials of other ethnic groups in the United States. Eventually, the amalgamation of the works of the literary artists of each ethnic group will serve to reorganize the present anthologies of American literature. With the integration of the writings of the various ethnic groups there will be a valid record of the literary art of the American people. It is in the spirit of assisting in the construction of such a record that the present book was written.

The Italian-American Novel

PART I

Autobiographical Accounts of the Early Italian Immigrants

In America they entered a world that was new both chronologically and ethically. It would not be an easy world. It would work them hard and relentlessly. It would be frequently and inexcusably cruel. It would be indifferent. . . . But it was a world in which hope would not be mocked by despair . . . a world in which they might aspire to their full dignity as man.

—Angelo M. Pellegrini, *Americans by Choice*

1

ENTERING A NEW WORLD

In their earliest writings, the Italian immigrants in America produced explanatory reports or autobiographies in which they attempted to define their unfavorable position in the nation's social and economic areas. As antecedents, these early works are a direct comment on the experiences that Italian-Americans developed later as subjects in fiction. An analysis of these early writings is useful, therefore, to evaluate the problems and to judge the verisimilitude of the subjects of Italian-American fiction. I have found that such an analysis authenticates certain consistencies in the various stages in the coming of the Italian to America as to 1) his background, the conditions in the mother country that fostered the need for emigration, 2) the exodus, the problems surrounding the physical act of immigration and the exploitations that accompanied this process, and 3) the arrival, the task of getting placed in a new country. After these stages, the immigrant experienced difficulty in his first attempts to adjust to a pluralistic society in its various areas—economic, educational, political, social, religious, and cultural.

Background Conditions in the Mother Country

Italians left their native country for any one of several reasons, social, economic, political. Invariably these reasons for their leaving were involved with some intolerable condition in their background from which the emigrants sought asylum. The political upheavals in Italy in the latter part of the nineteenth century, for example, dovetailed with America's need for laborers. After the Italian Revolution, the political escapee became a source of supply for America's labor market. In his autobiography, *The Story of Antonio, the Galley Slave,*[1]

1. Antonio A. Arrighi, *The Story of Antonio, the Galley Slave* (New York: F. H. Revell Company, 1911).

Antonio A. Arrighi confesses that he is an Italian exiled as a political criminal, and that he also seeks economic improvement. He had lived through the revolution of 1848–1849 in Italy and wanted to leave his impoverished home town, Barga, in the north of Italy.

Arrighi gives minute details of the several factors that contributed to his desire to leave his native country. He describes the spirit of revolution that preceded the unification of Italy, a revolution intended to free the country from

> the potentates who kept the country in turmoil and treated the people as though they were slaves. Several of these rulers were kept on their tottering thrones by Austrian bayonets, thus trampling upon the honour and prosperity of the land, and for this reason Austria was bitterly hated. (p. 23)

The author then extends this animosity to the Pope's spiritual power, which he identifies with temporal power; thus he assumes an anti-Papal attitude in politics, while he champions Garibaldi. Politically, Garibaldi was a rebel, and the Garibaldians were classified as outlaws. For this reason, the revolutionists who were caught were condemned to live as galley slaves in *galera* (jail). Prior to the account of his imprisonment, Arrighi describes the ancient timelessness and the primitive conditions that pervade the old village. All in all, from all these social, political, and economic conditions he sought to escape.

The urge to come to a fresh, new country may be more clearly understood after reading Arrighi's description of his slavery in *Cività Vecchia.* Furthermore, as he writes, to lose oneself in such a village is to know the soil of the spirit of rebellion. Arrighi describes *Cività Vecchia* as a strongly fortified town of twelve thousand inhabitants, whose citadel was designed and built by Michelangelo. At the time of the author's youth, the port was in the hands of French soldiers. The town "is so impregnated with sulphur that it gives its inhabitants an early appearance of old age," he writes; even the children look old. It is called "the city of old people" (p. 110).

To escape from such a forbidding antiquity is not easy. It was only because of an accident that befell a fellow-prisoner that Arrighi was able to leave, by hiding under a manure cart. Sympathizers helped him to arrive at Livorno (Leghorn), where, on the brigantine *Balena,* he was installed as a cabin boy. Sailing on May 25, 1855, he arrived in America on July 14, 1855.

Antiquity likewise dominates the background in Constantine M. Panunzio's autobiography, *The Soul of an Immigrant.*[2] in which the

2. Constantine M. Panunzio, *The Soul of an Immigrant* (New York: The Macmillan Company, 1924).

author graphically describes the remote Apulia. The high Byzantine towers of the early Christian era and the citadel dating back to ancient Rome are impetuses in reverse; the young man desires to wander. "This is a comparatively modern town," he writes (p. 5), because the streets are wide and the houses are built in the Roman style with their *atria,* or open courts, in the center. Furthermore, the streets offer shops, stores, offices, cafés, monuments to heroes, a cathedral, a municipal theater, and, at one end, a public garden. In judging the "modern" spirit of such a town, one need only consider that the most popular legend is of how one oversized centurion outwitted Hannibal in making him believe that Molfetta was a town of giants, thereby causing the Carthaginian to retreat from the outskirts of the town. Thus, the nineteenth century is not far removed from the first.

Panunzio, born to poverty, had a simple, happy childhood balanced by strict instruction in good manners, proper conduct, and correct catechism. He refers to the villas of the few wealthy people in his native town, but he insists that most of the citizenry lived in crude huts. The *contadini* (farmers) had to be satisfied with rude dwellings of rough stone or of a mixture of mud, with one doorway and one hole in the roof, the latter aperture serving as both window and chimney. He attests to the fact that most of the dwellings had earth floors, stone benches, and straw beds; but the *signori* occupied large buildings with elaborate furnishings. The town had a seminary, where Panunzio was educated. He says that it was because he rebelled against the tyranny of his teachers, who ruled by fear, that he first started to dream of larger horizons, and that dream meant America.

Moving from a native village in Italy to a city or town in America was an uprooting experience. In his book, *Americans by Choice,*[3] Angelo M. Pellegrini delineates six characters who made the move to various sections of the country. The first sketch is of his own mother, "La Bimbina," who left her native village in Tuscany to go to a frontier town in western Washington. La Bimbina was one among the many who fled "the denuded corners of the earth," driven by despair in her background and enticed by a new hope. Pellegrini writes that the immigrants came "positively and determined to our prodigal shores, where they knew there was work to do and the means to realize every peasant's dream: a permanent home" (p. 79). Since the circumstances of poverty were universal, those who had ambition looked to America. Of significance in these circumstances is the fact that these ambitious ones were optimistic and determined.

"They had followed the well-known pattern," maintains Pellegrini (p. 80). This pattern for most of them included service in the army,

3. Angelo M. Pellegrini, *Americans by Choice* (New York: The Macmillan Company, 1956).

marriage, and the discussion of the possibility of emigration. Would it be North America or South America? Would they settle permanently? The decision, as usual, was to go to the United States and to return for wives when they had earned enough money. The man Guido Sella, another of Pellegrini's six characters, and his brother, Armando, embarked at Genoa for the New World, arrived in New York, and were hired by an Italian labor contractor to go West to work with a railroad construction crew on the lower Columbia River. They arrived on the job "tagged as so much freight, and were immediately fitted out with the tools of their trade: the pick and shovel" (p. 81).

These conditions did not matter to the immigrants, however, whose chief aim was to find work. To many Americans at the turn of the century the infrequent statements written by Italian-Americans about their former conditions in Italy were "astonishing," as recorded in an article in the *Independent* magazine by Rocco Corresca on December 4, 1902.[4] As to his background, Corresca indicates that he had been one of the boys in Naples who were exploited in the dubious science of stealing. He was ready, therefore, to accept whatever amounted to economic survival.

As time went on, such desperate attitudes changed. In 1953, for example, Bernard J. Ficarra wrote *I Zappatori* (The Ditch Diggers) in which he propounds the theory that for many Italians the attraction of the United States was more than economic. It was "the invisible hand of the ancient Italian explorers which held an unseen grip upon the Italian for the land beyond the Atlantic."[5]

Corresca and Ficarra agree that the decision to leave the ancestral home in Italy to seek a new life in a strange country struck at the very roots of the emigrant. After the family discussions were exhausted and the final decision was made, the emigrant needed the emotional predisposition to act in making the change. Further complications depressed him when he had to raise the funds to implement the voyage. Also, he had to make contacts in the new country, either with a relative or with an immigrant "expert," who often proved to be an exploiter. The trip itself was long, hazardous, unpleasant, and humiliating. When the immigrants arrived at Ellis Island, they felt they they were not much more than herded commodities.[6] There were both psychological and emotional reactions to this exodus, the details of which are amply given by nearly all the early writers.

4. Rocco Corresca, "The Autobiography of a Boot-black," *Independent* (December 4, 1902), pp. 2863–67.

5. Bernard J. Ficarra, *I Zappatori* (Boston: Christopher Publishing House, 1953), p. 12.

6. In interviewing twelve immigrants in the vicinity of Torrington, Waterbury, and Bridgeport, Connecticut—all cities with large Italian-American population—I was told the repeated story of the herding of the immigrants at Ellis Island. All the persons interviewed (during the summer of 1960) were more than seventy-five years old.

The Exodus

Because he was a political escapee, Antonio Arrighi found sympathizers who helped his exodus. However, not all the immigrants were so fortunate. Because the physical act of leaving one country to go to another predisposes certain psychological attitudes on the part of the emigrant, it is important to know what these attitudes were. For example, Constantine Panunzio was typical of most Italian boys who had early recollections of reports in Italy about America. But these Italian ideas about America were vague. He said:

> We used to sing a song; it was about thirty stanzas long, and it told all the story of the famous voyage (of Columbus), but it had nothing in it about the continent he had found, or what was on that continent in our day.[7]

The famous Italian elementary school classic, DeAmici's *Il Cuore*, though referring to the story of going to America as "From the Appennines to the Andes," gives no details of the country. Furthermore, there is no distinction between North America and South America. Boston and New York were misty names in the mind of the Italian boy, whose cultural idea of America was confined to a dream of virgin islands inhabited by cannibalistic Indians and marauding pirates. People who returned to Italy from America spoke only of the money they had made; and the only Americans who visited Italian towns were like the raucous sailors who got drunk on Molfettese wine. Typically also, Panunzio believed that America was a continent of great forests and stretches of farm land; of its people, its government, and its institutions the boy knew nothing.

He arrived in America on July 3, 1902, after a stormy and difficult voyage that prompted his desire to return at once to Italy. Because the ship, however, was not scheduled to return for several months, the young immigrant decided to come ashore to savor the experience of "arriving." This experience actually proved far more satisfying than Pellegrini's, whose passage was more turbulent, more exhausting, and more frightening. The latter's crossing lasted ten days, a time of threatening danger endured by the frightened passengers who were crowded in the filthy steerage of an old ship where "the smell of vomit mingled with the odor of boiling cod in the galley."[8] The delay at Ellis Island was a brief, but welcome oasis prior to a long trek across the continent.

The exodus was equally difficult for the majority of the immigrants, according to both written and oral reports. Rocco Corresca worked for

7. Panunzio, p. 59.
8. Pellegrini, p. 12.

his passage to America by shoveling coal in steerage during the voyage. It was not uncommon for the immigrants to earn their passage in this manner, and the voyage to America was almost universally a hardship. Corresca affirms that knowledge of the difficulty of the crossing was, in fact, sufficient to restrain many who might have emigrated; they preferred the security of their familiar poverty. Many, however, proved their stamina by leaving their familiar environment and making the difficult crossing, but they confronted further hardships after their disembarkment.

The Arrival

The experience of Antonio Arrighi's arrival in America, for example, was not unusual. He writes that, stepping on the soil of the new country, he walks and walks the streets, not knowing where to go or what to do. Finally, completely exhausted, he stops in City Hall Park and goes to sleep. When he is awakened by a heavy club on the soles of his feet, he uses his first English words, "Hurry up; get out; fire." The irate policemen then strikes him to the ground, but the gathering crowd is sympathetic. At the courtroom Arrighi repeats his English vocabulary, which feat causes a commotion, with everyone's jumping up, running out of the room, and finding no fire. The judge calls everyone to order and calls in an interpreter. A physician who has witnessed the clubbing makes explanations and the prisoner is discharged.

Though Arrighi's story might be repeated with infinite variations, there is evidence that not all immigrants were so unattached upon their arrival. Corresca, for example, immediately made his way to the traditional "boarding-house," where fifteen men shared a room in Adams Street in Brooklyn. For him, as for many others, an offer of work came immediately through the usual "padrone."

Panunzio, however, after finding that he could not return immediately to Italy, started to wander. With fifty cents in his pocket, without friends, and with no knowledge of the English language or of the immigration laws, he set out in search of a job. He, too, followed the pattern of falling asleep on a bench, to be awakened by a heavy blow on the soles of his feet. Eventually, he gravitated to the inevitable Italian boarding house, which was already, as always, "full." He was forced to share a bed with three other men, a quadrupling that had no attraction for one who had always had his own bed. But, as he writes, "We had been taken in on trust, and the filth, the smells and the crowding together were part of the trust."[9] With these restrictions he began the process of becoming a citizen of the New World.

Not all the Italian immigrants who came to America remained in

9. Panunzio, p. 76.

New York, however. Some, like Angelo Pellegrini, went West, while others went South. Pellegrini writes that his group undertook the journey across the continent, over the plains, mountains, and rivers for six days, always with strangers among whom communication was impossible. The children were unhappily restless, plaintively hungry, and persistently asking questions that no one could answer.

Of all the available accounts, Pascal D'Angelo's *Son of Italy* is probably the most articulate autobiography in its treatment of the immigrants' arrival in a new country. Following his decision to remain here, D'Angelo refused to complain about the maltreatment that immigrants received as a general rule. His arrival was in 1910, however, when immigrant experts and labor foremen had developed improved methods of organizing the new immigrants. He writes that he and his father were met at the Battery by Mario Lancia, a construction foreman who could put them to work on state roads. Only a boy, D'Angelo was surprised and frightened at the sight of elevated trains, and he was confused by all the noise. He expresses bewilderment when he writes, "The marvelous foreman spoke some words in an unknown language to a uniformed man who received money. And the uniformed person looked sneeringly at the wonderful foreman."[10]

D'Angelo's impressions typify those of thousands who came from Italy to find themselves suddenly wandering in New York City. He describes his first ride in a trolley: "A most inconceivable vision was flashing past the car window" (p. 60). He observes the matronly woman sitting opposite to him, who scans him with a pitying gaze, but, who, like her husband and son, seems to the immigrant to be afflicted by some nervous disease, "for their mouths were in continuous motion, like cows chewing cud." Then, too, the foreman announces that they will not stay in New York. D'Angelo notices that the signs at the corners of the streets read "Ave! Ave! Ave!" (p. 61). How religious New York must be, he thinks, to express its devotion at every crossing. He wonders, however, why the "Ave" is not before the holy word, as in "Ave Maria." He thinks America is, indeed, a topsy-turvy country.

10. Pascal D'Angelo, *Son of Italy* (New York: The Macmillan Company, 1924), p. 61.

2

ADJUSTING TO A PLURALISTIC SOCIETY

Assimilation is a multiple-faceted process by which one group of people diffuses its characteristics into those of another in an interaction of culture. The process may be difficult, often painful, sometimes tragic. For the Italian immigrants, assimilation was both a necessity for functioning and a factor of survival. They had to assimilate; they had no alternative, if they were to remain in the country. Everywhere they settled, they found it imperative to make changes to implement their adjustment.

The several areas of immigrant assimilation include the economic, the educational, the religious, the social, the political, and the cultural. At first, the most important area was the economic one, since it constituted the main reason for the immigrants' coming; but the other areas eventually became significant.

Economic

Whatever their reactions were upon their arrival, Arrighi, Panunzio, Pellegrini, Corresca, and D'Angelo were each confronted by the fact that he was an alien in a land to which he must conform. Despite this urgency, however, before the immigrant could possibly start the process of assimilation he had to get settled; and this settling process was controlled usually by his economic need, a need that the men who wrote autobiographies met in various ways. For example, in his account of Guido Sella, who eventually became a racketeer, Pellegrini explains that here was an immigrant who sought opportunity, but "opportunities were implicit in the situation." These situations were sometimes misconstrued by men without business experience or without familiarity with the American process of the democratic law. Pellegrini observes that

> the immigrants left a world, where, by the accident of birth they and their ancestors had been permanently excluded from the possibility of self-realization. In America they entered a world that was new . . . chronologically and would work them hard and relentlessly. It would be frequently and inexcusably cruel. It would be indifferent. . . . But it was a world in which hope would not be mocked by despair . . . a world in which they might aspire to their full dignity as man.[1]

Sella flourished in the importing and exporting business. One day he wrote to his parents in Italy what he thought incredible, that the Congress was passing an amendment to the Constitution, prohibiting the manufacture and sale of alcoholic beverages. He wrote, "Can you imagine a law more stupid? You pour a glass of wine. You say *salute* to your friends. You lift it to your lips—and you are a criminal" (p. 104). With this interpretation, he saw nothing unethical about deciding with his business associates to invest thousands of dollars in liquor to supply the wants of his customers, "because," he said, as he observed among the most prominent citizens, "no one intends to stop drinking."

Rationalizing the character of Guido Sella, Pellegrini explains that

> of all the forms of delinquency into which the Italian immigrant was tempted, bootlegging taxed his conscience the least. For him prohibition had no inhibiting moral basis; hence, he had to make no adjustment of conscience in order to engage in the liquor traffic. Furthermore, he was perfectly at home in the techniques of fermentation and distillation. In the way of life to which he had been accustomed, these processes were salutary rather than criminal. The use of alcoholic beverages was completely integrated with his economy and his religion. Through barter or exchange he had often converted wine into bread. From time immemorial, he had set aside the best wine as a gift for his priest and to exalt the celebration of events such as the Nativity and the Resurrection. (p. 105)

Not all the immigrants who prospered in the making of beverages were lawbreakers, however. The wine-growers of California were men who enjoyed their work and made an art of manual labor. The economic thrust of this group of men transcended mere labor; they took real pride in work. Even the men who worked for the wine-growers were dedicated artisans who did not bother to carry a watch:

1. Pellegrini, p. 93.

> They go home when a job is done and not when a whistle blows . . . labor for these men—as indeed for artists—is a way of life. They enjoy what they are doing. (p. 48)

In 1900, at age thirteen, Louis Martini the wine-grower, another of Pellegrini's characters, had arrived in San Francisco from Pietra Ligure, a beach resort near Genoa, to join his father, a shoemaker, who had come in 1894. Pellegrini explains that father and son went into business together as wine merchants. By working assiduously and living thriftily, the Martini family accumulated an appreciable amount of money. Because the creation of things interested them more than the acquisition of money, they decided to become wine-makers. Although the making of wine was remunerative, for them its satisfying importance lay in the prestige of its "tradition and dignity." Like artists, they felt that one's whole lifetime was not sufficient to master the art of making a superb wine. The father, therefore, sent the son back to Italy to study the "art" of wine-making at Alba in one of the "finest . . . viticultural schools in the world." Since the wine-maker had to pass both the clinical and the organoleptic[2] tests, it was imperative for him to have an excellent palate as well as an educated mind. According to Pellegrini, pride in the wine-maker's craft extended to every detail of planting a new vine, naming a new grape, and finally saying, "This bottle is entirely the product of my labor."

This pride of work eventually extended to an aesthetic level; economics became the instrument to qualify for a cultural initiation into American social acceptance. As Pellegrini writes, Louis Martini was superior to the average immigrant of humble origins who tended to become abrasively aware of his wealth and, thereby, a social embarrassment. Martini never mentioned money; he would not say, "This is worth so much." He did talk of the perfect wine for the ideal moment, of how to improve the quality of his wine, of how to make his house more harmonious with its surroundings. To an appreciable number of judges of our society, when the process of earning a living acquires the lustre of quality, it has entered into the sphere of culture.

Like Pellegrini, Arrighi, too, made a satisfactory economic adjustment. After some preliminary struggles, he eventually found work with a Mr. Pasini, who sold bric-a-brac made of plaster-of-Paris. He learned to make statuary at the Pasini store, which was a rendezvous for the Italians in New York, who numbered "about three hundred at that time." He writes that most of the Italians were plaster-of-Paris toy vendors, or were employed in the manufacture of what he calls "ornamentals." One thing that all these Italian workmen had in common, Arrighi points out, was that they were happy to have work for which they were paid.

The same zestful pursuit of opportunity marked Panunzio, whose first act in America was to look for a job. He was immediately in-

2. The ability to receive a sense impression; in this case, the taste of the wine.

formed that he could find work anywhere with the "pick-and-shovel," the first English words he mastered. These words, incidentally, described the kind of labor that was predominantly available for Italians at this time, he learned. Panunzio explains that Italian immigrants preferred excavation to farm work because they were not acquainted with the implements of modern American farming. Furthermore, the isolation of working on an American farm repulsed these gregarious people; also, they were victims of the "padrone" system whereby a labor-exploiter made a profit per capita for securing and managing laborers for construction. Panunzio, however, did go to work on a farm owned by a George Annis, who subsequently refused to pay him more than five dollars after six months' work. He tried to get to Boston for a lawyer, but was incarcerated for attempting to board a train without a ticket. In due time, however, he was brought to a courtroom before a judge who, perceiving the situation, ordered him breakfast and bought him a return ticket home.

Panunzio writes of the judge's warmth and human consideration and makes the comment that

> I presume, however, that somewhere in the police records of the state of Vermont my name, alias "Frank Nardi," is to be found, along with thousands of other unfortunates, some of them doubtless as innocent as I. Doubtless, also, somewhere a careful student of the criminal tendencies of the foreign-born people of this country has counted my name along with thousands of others in his impersonal statistical study of the criminality of the immigrant groups in the United States.[3]

Although finding employment in the East was difficult, getting settled in the West was not always in accordance with the lyrical formula of a popular ballad. For the Pellegrinis, for example, their home was hardly the realization of the immigrants' dream of America. The author observes that the town that was to be their home had a "primitive and inhuman quality," even the external features of instability, as if it had been put together hastily by some nomadic tribe for temporary shelter. It appeared paradoxically undeveloped and decayed:

> Indeed, the entire setting has a quality of virginal primitivism to which her [his mother's] Italian eyes were unaccustomed. The forest at the back door, the ugly frame shacks, the grease covered street, and unstable board walks were such a contrast to the humanized Italian landscape that they gave an initial impression of poverty rather than of wealth.[4]

3. Panunzio, p. 128.
4. Pellegrini, p. 12.

The instinct for settlement was strong in Angelo Pellegrini's La Bimbina, however; she was quick to appraise the available possibilities and to accept their challenge. Pellegrini writes,

> The new environment was an invitation to work. There were board walks in disrepair, grass at the doorsteps, dwellings of wood hastily and carelessly put together because there was so much of everything that the natives had acquired neither the habit of work nor the idea of permanence in what they did. Because these were central attributes in her character, she accepted her new home with gratitude. She rolled up her sleeves and fell to the task. (p. 12)

Her work was with the cows, the chickens, the rabbits, the planting of seed in the soil, the reception of boarders to consume her abundant food. Meanwhile, her husband worked ten hours a day in the lumber camp. While he was away, she and the children did all the chores around the house. Of necessity, she "harnessed" the children's energy shrewdly and sternly; the boys kneaded the bread, worked in the garden, gathered wood, tended animals, and sold and delivered the surplus produce. The girls did the housework, willingly and enthusiastically. It was not difficult to drive the children to the immediate rewards of their labor. There was exhilaration over the fact that here there was work in which they might compete, with results they could relish. This delight impressed the frontier village in which La Bimbina was able to enjoy a new human dignity.

Pellegrini writes that La Bimbina's husband worked in the timber mills before the days of unionization. When he died in an industrial accident, his attending physician failed to report to the state the proof that death was caused by injury. For this reason, La Bimbina went to the state capitol, armed with a single argument, to call on the Commissioners of Industrial Insurance for the State of Washington:

> My husband worked at the mill for ten years. He was never sick. One day his chest was crushed between two railroad cars. He never returned to work. In six months he was dead. Who is to feed me and the children? Well? (p. 17)

Many of the early Italian immigrants had no Bimbina, however, either to care for them or to survive them. In fact, to find a place in which to live was one of the most pressing problems that confronted them in the process of getting settled. It was from this social need that these uprooted people fostered a distinctive type of boarding house. Pellegrini writes that

> the Italian immigrant boarding house . . . is a neglected bit of Americana.

It existed a relatively short time, about twenty-five years,

> but in its time it was as indigenous to, and as authentically of, America as were the saloon and the brothel of the frontier West. The saloon and the brothel thrived where there were men who needed liquor and women; the boarding house thrived where there were men who needed women to cook and wash for them. (p. 139)

Between 1900 and 1915, approximately three million Italians came to America. Some of these were family units, but most of them were men without women. Some of these men were too young to marry; others had left their wives and children behind; still others were hoping to earn enough money to return to the "Old Country" to marry. Pellegrini points out that all these men needed some type of female companionship and some form of familiar Italian environment. This psychological and physical need created the situation that nearly every Italian family in America offered room and board to men, a custom that disappeared by 1925. The universal characteristic of this institution was that the boarding house resembled a large, boisterous, vivacious family. In rare cases, writes Pellegrini, was it less than respectable. The burdens of its function, however, rested on the mother of the family, burdens worse than those she had had in Italy.

Was it greed that made these immigrants work so hard, or was it the peasants' love of productive labor? We ask this question with Pellegrini. He answers,

> For centuries they and their ancestors had suffered poverty. . . . They had worked from dawn to sunset; and they had worked in vain. They had come to America to seek relief from their misery . . . they found immediate relief from the most harrowing frustration that can strike a peasant: the frustration of fruitless toil. They discovered that in America every day of labor has its compensation in dollars and cents; that he who sows may expect to reap. The experience was novel and maddening in its effect. It is the fulfillment of every peasant's dream. (p. 140)

Keeping boarders was productive labor, a means of earning immediate dollars. It was also an act of compassion in making welcome those immigrant bachelors who yearned for a semblance of home life. Eventually, however, to fulfill this need, most families took in too many boarders and many problems ensued. Pellegrini writes,

> They rented large houses, put two or more men in a room, built huge dining tables and benches, procured extra-large tubs, bought wine by the barrel, groceries by the case—and put Mother to work. Six to twelve men in each home was the rule rather than

> the exception. Father kept his job at the mill or the mine. When he had time, and if he were perceptive and considerate, he helped his wife. But those were ten-hour days. . . . Perceptive and considerate or otherwise, Father was away from home twelve hours daily, and in no mood to wash dishes after dinner. (p. 141)

It may be asked why the mother agreed to such a harrowing physical burden in a day without electrical appliances; why she baked bread, made lunches, scrubbed floors, and scrubbed again at the washboard and did not send the clothes to the laundry. Pellegrini's answer to these questions lies in his analysis of the Italian concept of tradition. The immigrant mother was a creature of the Old World culture in which religion and superstition were powerful elements. In that culture, it was a women's sacred duty to keep her men clean and to wash for them, a duty that no healthy woman would dream of delegating to others. When the immigrant mother took men as boarders, she assumed the responsibilities of the mothers of these boarders.

Only rarely did the men help. Pellegrini emphasizes that Italian men were Old World males, who insisted on their prerogatives. They were not even aware of their inflicting cruelty in the services they demanded. Furthermore, in addition to the fact that these demands were unreasonable, dollars made the men fastidious. One refused pork, another fish, or lamb, or spaghetti. In any case, the author's friend Giovannina for five years prepared each evening nine separate dinners for nine different men.

Many psychological factors evolved in the attempt to rear children appropriately in the presence of all the men who boarded with the family. Countless women bore these conditions "while weeping in silence." Pellegrini gives an account of one such woman, Rose Mondavi, who was atypically aggressive. "With courage and uncompromising principle" she eventually dominated the boarding house and disciplined the boarders to her terms of order and decorum.

The immigrants displayed the same homogeneity in their work that they enjoyed in their living. Pascal D'Angelo, describing his experiences in becoming settled in America, writes, reiterating what the others record, that in this country the immigrants who originate from the same town "stick together like a swarm of bees from the same hive." They sought employment together as a group. When D'Angelo went to work in Hillsdale, he did so in the company of men who had known him and his father. This moral support of one's group made tolerable the exigency of living in a cold, foul cabin, and empowered him to work with enthusiasm.

Even within the larger metropolis, groups of immigrants sought the comfort of living with those who were their "paesani," their fellow-townsmen from Italy. Recalling this era in his novel *Three Circles of Light*, Pietro Di Donato emphasizes the fact that, though he lived in

Brooklyn, which teemed with Jews, Irish, Poles, and Italians, the Italians he knew were predominantly those who had come from Vasto, the Italian town whose chief skill was masonry. The Vastese who came to America, therefore, were masters of mortar and bricks. Di Donato writes,

> Masonry was the great, revered art of my people. To have been accepted and honored by them you had to be both Vastese and a master mason; otherwise, even if you were the King of England or the President of the United States you would have been contemptuously spurned.[5]

In the need for economic adjustment, therefore, the immigrants did not abandon their communal traditions. Joseph Caruso writes in *The Priest*[6] that, as the Irish left the neighborhood, Salem Street, Prince Street, and Copps Hill resounded with Sicilian yells and Neapolitan songs. Even the name of the church in this district of Boston was changed to St. Dominic, after the patron saint of the immigrants' native town of Augusta in Sicily. Traditions were, therefore, becoming constantly transplanted.

We have seen how the immigrants grasped at the first opportunities for labor. A few were prepared with a traditional skill; in most cases they were equipped with only the avid desire to work. At times, however, the initial work led the immigrant to other areas in assimilation. Arrighi, for example, who arrived in the early period, soon learned that his type of industry, making statuary, involved him in a cultural area which, in turn, promoted his social progress. He writes,

> During those days, the American people, especially those living in the country, had but a faint idea of ornamentation. Their homes contained little to beautify them. In their parlors almost nothing of an ornamental nature was to be seen, except some articles of necessary furniture, and I saw my opportunity. . . . I discovered that I was doing a work which tended to diffuse among the people a love for the beautiful and a desire to embellish their homes. . . . Families then generally lived in log cabins, for most of my time in this business was spent in western Illinois and Iowa.[7]

Returning from these isolated rural areas, Arrighi is challenged to increase and to extend his activity. He writes,

> Some had an idea that the work of selling plaster-of-Paris toys was degrading; but my experience tells me that it was both honour-

5. Pietro Di Donato, *Three Circles of Light* (New York: Julian Messner, 1960), p. 40.
6. Joseph Caruso, *The Priest* (New York: The Macmillan Company, 1956).
7. Arrighi, p. 194.

> able and useful. In this spirit a partnership was soon formed between myself and three countrymen to enter heartily into the business, each to have an equal share of the profits. We went from New York City to Mansfield, Ohio, where we opened a small store and sold toys and ornamental works. (p. 195)

It is feasible to conclude, then, that the economic endeavors of such a man as Arrighi did stimulate immigrant reception by native Americans, since he was successful enough as a traveling salesman to warrant his establishing a more permanent enterprise. It would be presumptuous to conclude, however, that men like him initiated in the Americans of the nineteenth century their love for bric-a-brac, but his success reveals the people's favorable response to the impact of the new, such as the cultural artifacts of non-Anglo-Saxon sources.

There is evidence that the Italian immigrants' eagerness to work earned the admiration of native Americans, who, in turn, helped them to improve their economic conditions. Panunzio, for example, functioned so well with the Richmond family that they soon treated him as an equal and recommended him to work for their relatives, the Butterfields, in Maine. The latter persuaded Panunzio to improve himself through education by going to college. A friendly policeman helped him to write the letter to Maine Wesleyan Seminary, which he subsequently attended. With unswerving tenacity he fought his social battle there and succeeded, even to winning a speaking contest. He writes,

> As the days passed, and I realized more and more the significance of the event, I became thoroughly convinced that, after all, with America's best people, foreign birth makes little or no difference.[8]

Commenting on this period of his academic life, he makes observation on how much better is the inspirational method of his American teachers in contrast to the coercion of the instructors he had survived in Italy.

Pascal D'Angelo's account, however, is more typical of the average immigrant's participation in the economic struggle. He tells of going from "gang to gang," in search of more endurable human treatment. Often the jobs did not pay enough for the men's railroad fares. Too often, again, the men were forced to live in crude hovels rented to them by their foremen at exorbitant fees. Furthermore, they had to buy food at competitive prices. As a result, the laborers could earn only enough to exist. D'Angelo explains, also, that most of the men preferred to stay in or around New York to work, because

8. Panunzio, p. 174.

> high railroad fares are usually what keeps laborers near this hell-hole metropolis. Going to a distant job is a gamble. A man may pay a large part of his scanty savings for fare. And when he gets there he may find living conditions impossible and the foreman too overbearing. Perhaps he will be fired at the end of the week. Where will he be then?[9]

The commissary system consumed most of a man's wages, and in extreme cases it ground the unfortunate laborers into perpetual peonage. Sometimes, lured by higher wages or free transportation, a laborer accepted work that was as far away as Florida. When he got there, he was greeted with inedible food and unspeakable living conditions. At this time, D'Angelo reports, Italian men were guarded in the South by "ferocious Negroes with guns which they used at the least excuse" (p. 111). D'Angelo writes, also, that in some instances the workmen received no wages at all and were told that they were in debt to the company.

The man in charge of the commissary always favored the acquaintance of that man who had a large number of friends among the workers and who could persuade these workers to go where he wanted them to go. This favorite got perhaps fifteen or twenty cents more a day, an increase that was an envied privilege; furthermore, his board bill was always lower than anyone else's. Another inequity harassed the immigrant laborer in that the commissary men kept a special book of prices of the objects the laborer bought. If a man tried to save money and spent very little, he was charged the same amount as those who had the greatest debts. The laborer had to buy at the camp store at the disposition of the profiteer. Foremen were helpless, since they, too, were subordinate to the commissary man.

D'Angelo describes the working conditions, the dangers, the daily accidents, the little value placed on the immigrant's life, the disregard for his dignity as a person. To overcome these difficulties required "immoderate tenacity and constant fortitude." Furthermore, brutality intensified the frustration of men like D'Angelo, who sought constantly the opportunity to educate himself in order to write.

It would be unnecessary to include here the numerous accounts of the difficulties of the immigrant laborers "on the job"; much has been written on this subject elsewhere. It is sufficient to conclude that the autobiographers generally tend to explain that the economic struggle was only one phase of their assimilation, a distinction that is of primary concern here. Of equal importance was their social acceptance, which was integrally involved with their improvement in education and in their eventual emergence into the cultural life of America.

9. D'Angelo, p. 100.

Education

Education, therefore, was a primary factor in Panunzio's assimilation. The men whom he met in his college environment removed his own prejudice that Americans were brusque, uncouth, and without compassion. He acquired a new view of life. He writes,

> Here in America I had earned my way through school and college; I had worked as janitor, tailor, woodsman, night watchman, mail clerk; and respectable people thought no less of me for so doing. I even courteously but firmly declined to accept the aid of a lady who had become interested in helping me financially. I hope I did not seem ungrateful; such was not the fact. I was simply enjoying my independence to the full. The American in me was unconsciously growing.[10]

Like Panunzio, Arrighi, too, eventually improved his status by studying for the ministry. But, as we observed in his economic pursuits, his entry into the world of culture came primarily through his work. While peddling his plaster-of-Paris objects he was accepted in homes, even to eat and to sleep. He would often sing for his hosts. He describes one particular incident, for example, when, after he had sung for his hospitable family, the delighted members invited him in to have supper and then to rest for the night. He found himself easily enjoying the American hospitality which, he says, was "as profuse as the country is great, and as sincere as big hearts could make manifest." He describes the abundance of food, and the friendliness of the neighbors who came to hear him sing. Later, he enjoyed a quiet room in which to sleep in a comfortable bed. After breakfast the next morning, he left his hosts, leaving with them his old address in Barga.

> Thus [he wrote] my first journey's experience ended in the pleasant and profitable occupation of educating people to appreciate the beautiful in art, even if its form came in the material of plaster-of-Paris.[11]

For him, then, his economic effort expanded into social integration, but the process of this expansion entailed a give-and-take between the itinerant immigrant and his receptive hosts.

On the other hand, Pascal D'Angelo, because of his more creative ambitions, had to struggle for his education and pursuit of culture against greater odds. At first his very innocence shielded him. Walking gaily on Broadway with his friends, he was blithe and his voice was resonant. As he passed through the noisy streets, he did not perceive

10. Panunzio, p. 179.
11. Arrighi, p. 200.

that many "unhealthy palefaced inhabitants of the city" glanced at him and his friends in disgust. He was not conscious to what degree the clothes that covered their bodies were shabby and degrading.

It was not until D'Angelo worked with some Mexicans that he discovered he could learn Spanish by using his friends' newspapers and selecting the words that resembled Italian. This practice led him to experiment with an English newspaper. At first there was little he could decipher, but gradually he learned more and more words. Then, one night, while watching an Italian vaudeville show in a theater in the Bowery, he decided he could write better farce himself. He decided to do so in English. He writes that

> After a few Sundays of hard work I had about three closely written pages of the most imposible English one could imagine.[12]

His companions around him laughed long and hard at what he wrote, both at the jokes and at the distorted English. Encouraged, he continued writing these "jokes" and offered five cents to anyone in his limited audience who could keep a straight face while he read. With this incentive, he launched his self-education.

He bought himself an old Webster's Dictionary for twenty-five cents and proceeded to memorize it. It became a game with him to use the most unfamiliar English words around the yard, and he became known as "that queer Italian laborer" (p. 146). It was difficult for D'Angelo, however, to master English without an organized program of learning. He acquired what he called an enormous knowledge of disjointed words and phrases, because he could not organize his words and relate them to his thoughts, and English grammar gave him excessive trouble. Although he read all types of poetry, rhyme confused him; but he eventually learned that "rhyme was not absolutely essential to poetic utterance" (p. 158). He came to the conclusion, also, that "much of what goes under the name of poetry is really trash." While he was so obsessed with his reading, he caused considerable discussion among his fellow-workers. Some insisted that a man who was born a laborer could never rise in status; others encouraged him to "advance in the world"; a few predicted that he might even become a foreman. Meanwhile, he decided upon a literary career.

He gave up his job and went to live in an indescribable, crumbling, malodorous room that had previously been a chicken coop and whose entrance was through a toilet that served ten families, aggressive strangers, and unwashed transients. The Public Library was his workshop; but away from that warm building, he became ill with the cold and lack of food. His poems traveled from publisher to publisher, and only after he wrote a particularly appealing letter to the editors of *Nation*

12. D'Angelo, p. 141.

did he finally attract attention. The editors read the poems, appraised them, and awarded him *Nation's* Poetry Prize. When the miracle happened, he attracted the interest of other influential editors, including Henry Seidel Canby. In this way, accepted by the literary men, he ascended the ladder to the discriminating social world.

Religion

D'Angelo's experience is an illustration of the progress an immigrant could make from the economic to the cultural areas of the fourth stage of development covered by the autobiographers, the reaction of the immigrants to their first encounter with a pluralistic society. Above all, his example implies a determination of will and an optimism that result from faith in oneself. This faith seems universal in the character of the Italians who decided to stay in America, and much of it apparently stems from their traditional religious practices. It is relevant, threfore, to note the experiences these immigrants had with religion in America. There were some interesting facts about their local problems with American Catholicism that are constantly reflected in the autobiographies and in the novels.

With rare exceptions, Italian immigrants came from Roman Catholic origins; but they encountered unexpected difficulties in America in practicing their traditional Catholicism in Irish-dominated churches. These difficulties, however, were not unusual between two groups of people with a language barrier. Furthermore, the Irish had the additional advantage of having immigrated a whole generation ahead of the Italians. Eventually, the passage of time gradually erased most of the difficulties, but not without pressures from other religious sources. Some of the more sensitive and socially ambitious Italian immigrants accepted the outstretched hands of Protestant evangelists. The latter approached the immigrants with a missionary zeal, and they profited from the friction between the two ethnic groups. Panunzio and Arrighi, for example, are two Italian immigrants who accepted "evangelical" aid in their education and who were encouraged to write their autobiographies. Their religious experience, therefore, was atypical.

Although admittedly Panunzio's religious assimilation was unique, it had some aspects that were typical of immigrant experience. It was unusual that he became a Protestant minister, but it was inevitable that in his religious area he would meet the same problems that impeded his cultural integration. In contrast to the fact that his decision to study for the ministry was influenced by the persuasion of native families for whom he worked and who made the contacts to educate him in the profession, he later made an ironic discovery. When he pursued his vocation in what he called "the Missions," he found that the instruction in classes in Americanization was in practice conceptually opposed to its theory. He learned that there was a social-religious attitude about Americanizing the foreigner. It was a religious duty to Americanize the foreigner, but the missionery did not fraternize with the proselyte. The task of socializing was always delegated; and when the "foreigners" got too near, the lines were sharply drawn.

The young minister was disturbed to discover that these lines were drawn equally as sharply within the church membership. In the once-prosperous church to which he was assigned in a suburb of Boston, the authorities now decided to proselytize among the Italians who were surrounding them. The officials of the church, however, informed Panunzio that they could not allow this prestigious house of worship, or even part of it, to be turned into an "Italian" church. Therefore they revoked his appointment.

Social Status

A similar frustration checked the efforts of those who attempted to Americanize their fellow-immigrants and to assist them in their social adjustment. Panunzio offered his services to teach an Americanization class supervised by a special factory committee whose chairman was the owner of the factory. English and Citizenship were the two courses through which the instructor would try to teach the principles of democracy and the history of the United States. Panunzio discovered that, for some unknown reason, while the people were eager to learn English, they were hostile to the courses in Citizenship. Puzzled, he interviewed the members of the class to explore their antagonistic attitude. The answers were substantially the same and were typified in the words of one who said,

> Look at us; we work long hours for only a pittance, and see the treatment they give us in the shop. The boss kicks us and calls us "damned dagoes," and *all that* in the shop of the man who gives you the money to run this class.[13]

When the teacher, questioned by the chairman, tried to clarify what the chairman called the immigrants' "lack of interest in America," he explained the feelings of these workmen (p. 209). Panunzio was stunned to hear the answer: "Damn the dagoes, let them go back to their rat holes" (p. 210). He observed,

> Please remember that when . . . you hear of I.W.W.'s and anarchism, of bombs, and the like, that it is the spirit back of our "damn the dagoes" that is responsible in no small measure for these difficulties. (p. 210)

13. Panunzio, p. 208.

Admitting futility, the Americanization class came to an end, and the position of the immigrant in this case became fixed as a fragmented commodity useful to industry.

The social status of these Italian immigrants received no advancement from the members of the community living in the shadow of America's historical monuments in Boston. There were no structured social forces in the city, and some of society's worst features poured systematically into the neighborhood. Panunzio writes that within a half-mile square flourished one hundred and eleven saloons (claimed to be needed for revenue) and fifty-three various institutions, which included poolrooms, bowling alleys, dance halls, gambling dens, and brothels (p. 231). He observes that these institutions were patronized to a large degree, not by people living in the vicinity, but by "out-of-towners or up-towners." He writes, also, that the community witnessed the most atrocious of crimes, and he refers to a study of the police records, which revealed that these crimes were committed mainly, not by inhabitants of the neighborhood, but by notorious criminals from obscure places, who came surreptitiously to the vicinity to perpetrate their crimes. The worst feature of the community, however, was that the people patterned their life-style according to Old World customs as if they were not a functioning part of America. This separation resulted from the lack of a constructive effort of any one group of people to promote effectively the education of the immigrants.

Inevitably, the immigrants as a group found that nearly all their social problems were intimately allied with their economic struggle. Panunzio gives a graphic description of the Steel Strike of 1919 in Pittsburgh, which revealed simultaneously the universal problems of all immigrants, Italian and non-Italian. The situation may be summarized in the remarks of a "leading citizen" in an interview that Panunzio reports:

> Ten or even five years ago we could have done anything we wished peacefully; a simple method of education would have prevented all this. But we are to blame; we have forced a feeling of separation upon these people. We needed them for the growth of our industries, we wanted them to come. . . . But we refused to admit them to our Civic and Social life; we gave them no access to our societies, our schools, and our churches. We called them undesirable aliens; we forced them to segregate into sections of their own and to organize into separate groups in which only their own language is used. First, they organized for the purpose of giving expression to their social cravings, and then those very groups served as centers of self-defense when we showed antagonism to their segregated life.[14]

14. *Ibid.*, pp. 243–44.

In Arrighi's case, his previous experiences as a political prisoner, which he identified as the result of Papal activity, developed his subsequent prejudices. The emotional emphasis of his opinions is obvious when he writes,

> In 1870, just as I graduated from Boston Seminary, the army of Victor Immanuel made a breach in the Porta Pia and entered the Eternal City. Thus the temporal power of the Pope was crushed, never again to disgrace civilization.[15]

He worked among the Italians of New York, starting June 21, 1881, at the chapel of Five Points House of Industry. By working hard he succeeded in activating some of his religious beliefs and in teaching a number of immigrants to understand their new society.

Political Field

While the educational and religious areas were extending the social assimilation of the immigrants, the political field of America was a scene of racial exploitation for many years. Rocco Corresca, in his article "The Autobiography of a Bootblack," implies the political situation when he writes,

> A man came and said that he would get us made Americans for fifty cents, and then we could get two dollars for our votes. I talked to some of our people and they told me that we should have to put a paper in a box, telling who we wanted to govern us.[16]

In the same article he reveals a popular Italian-American sentiment that the Republicans wanted a Republic and Democrats were against it. The Italians believed that the Democrats were for a king, whose name was Bryan, an Irishman. "There are some good Irishmen," he says. "But many of them insult Italians. They call us Dagoes. So I will be a Republican" (p. 2866).

There is no bitterness in the writing, however. Corresca confesses that he likes the country and that he does not want a king. Furthermore, "Garibaldi didn't want a king and he was the greatest man that ever lived." His spirit of hope, too, is expansive; and he often thinks of his former friends to whom he will write about his experiences in this country.

Bernard J. Ficarra says in *I Zappatori* that in the ultimate assimilation "the gradual growth of Italian influence is being woven into the silken pattern of American life" (p. 112). Politically, he makes the plausible observation that, because so many earlier immigrants had

15. Arrighi, p. 208.
16. Corresca, p. 2866.

returned to their Italian villages prior to World War I and gratefully remembered their indebtedness to America, one of the factors in World War II that aided our victory was Italian reluctance to fight against Americans. Furthermore, he writes, "Italians have been accused of many things; but no Italian has ever betrayed America, or sold her secrets to an enemy" (p. 104). He indicates, therefore, that the Italian immigrant's feeling for America is one of gratitude and loyalty, a feeling that the Italian-American would inherit with constructive ramifications.

Culture

As a result of the social and economic isolation of the early immigrant, his cultural integration was often marked by a corresponding dualism. Contradictory forces became serious obstacles to an integrated assimilation. As Panunzio writes,

> On the one hand, the youth of foreign birth finds himself confronting the inevitable difficulty of prejudice even on the part of good Americans, while, on the other hand, he is liable to be looked upon as a renegade by his own countrymen if he shows a desire to abandon the segregated life of immigrants and lose himself in the life of his new country.[17]

Since church officials feared the growth of an Italian institution, Panunzio turned to social work. Soon he learned that some officials preferred an American-born minister whereas others argued for him because of his Italian background. Still others claimed that as an Italian he had become too much of an American. The result was a paradox: too little American on the one hand, too little Italian on the other. This kind of conflict in the social, economic, and cultural position of the first-generation Italian-American is a cause for whatever has been tragic in his assimilation. The conflict, however, is a natural factor in the action of change, and the immigrant is a man who must eventually dispose himself to transformation. Feeling that he was neither Italian nor American, Panunzio found himself participating in what became a universal pattern in the process of assimilation. Because of conflict, he withdrew into isolation; he was a man *between* two cultures. This isolation, however, was essential as a plateau, a point of departure into change.

Making the first encounter, taking part in the conflict, and withdrawing into isolation, then, are seen as the preliminary steps to the integration of cultural concepts. The actual process of integration, however, was put into motion as the individual immigrant began to

17. Panunzio, p. 218.

change. Even the direction of the change was projected by the individual's need. For this reason, there were several possible outlines for this direction. Panunzio offers a fairly universal pattern of evolution from the point of view of the early immigrant. He makes the following neat categories of development: 1) a mobile and free attitude toward life, 2) a growth in the attitude toward the customary, 3) the control of thought regarding the opinions of others, 4) the conception of real as contrasted with what he calls inherited worth, 5) the adaptation to the practicability of American ways, 6) the achievement of self-reliance and independence as cardinal virtues, and 7) the progressive motivation in the vitality of optimism.

In this outline, as in those which are implied in the other autobiographies, what dominates the road to success is the development of self with the spirit of optimism. That road, however, was not always constructed with the approved materials that could insure a safe arrival at a desirable goal. It was a pitfall for the immigrant—newcomer that he was—to be ignorant of the historical framework that prescribed certain rules for that road. Guido Sella, for example, as Pellegrini reports, could not reconcile his limited knowledge of the written law with his own general beliefs of economic morality. Sella rather innocently continued his wine activity, which progressed into a traffic that induced moral degradation. Although he intended to earn only enough money to buy a gentleman's villa in Italy, his venture led him to speculation in raisins; raisins led to wine; wine needed retail bootlegging; bootlegging demanded protection; protection involved the formation of organizations, which devised the institution of the "bottle carrier"; and all this engendered the desire for more power, which was inevitably fed with involvements in vices that accompany the bootlegging milieu. The inevitable outcome of Sella's desire to flaunt his bootlegging success led to his becoming the victim of a woman engaged in the same illegal activities. In October, 1929, he was tried and convicted under the terms of the Mann Act. One of his former pick-and-shovel companions said, "There was a time when Guido Sella was worth half a million dollars."

Another friend replied,

> Perhaps that was the trouble. Many years ago, when he was a successful grocer, he let me read a letter his father had written him. It was an answer to one Guido had written to his parents telling them about the money he was making and urging them to join him in America. One sentence in that letter has stuck in my mind: "We (villagers) were made to understand and to endure pain and poverty; but we were not made to understand and to endure pleasure and riches."[18]

18. Pellegrini, p. 125.

Getting rich fast by any available means, then, was a dangerous temptation to the immigrant. Sella's case illustrates the deviant from the rule that assimilation is a slow, gradual, and cooperative process. The individual's adjustment to another culture must include the exploration and absorption of the sources and ramifications of the externals and superficialities of that culture. Reflecting this necessity, an example of a satisfactorily assimilated immigrant is given by Pellegrini in his description of the honest wine-grower, Martini. He writes,

> My final impression was of a man of quality, devoted to doing, to creating; a man to whom life is exciting and a constant challenge. Home and vineyard and winery are his laboratory where he works to bring things into being. *This is a beautiful day and a beautiful country and a beautiful vineyard.* . . . I should like to be twenty again, twenty years old, with the energy and vitality I have now. To what end? To improve further the quality of the day and the country and the vineyard. (p. 76)

In referring to this quality, Pellegrini comments on the foods in the restaurants in North Beach. He says that these essentials of living gracefully are a contribution to the way things are done in America and an expression of the matrix from which they are derived.

"I am interested in Italian immigrants," writes Pellegrini.

> I like to define that interest as aesthetic rather than statistical or sociological or economic. I want to feel the quality of the men and women who struck roots under the Mediterranean sun and then were transplanted to the North American continent. How did the uprooting affect them? . . . How many had been changed by the American experience? (pp. 151–52)

To summarize the information given by the autobiographers, we may conclude that the American experience changed the Italians by a gradual process. Having left an established but unsatisfactory background, the immigrants survived the shock of uprooting and arrived to face a completely new set of circumstances in their adopted environment. This encounter challenged them to exhaust the wellsprings of their humanity. After the struggle of getting settled was over, their battle for survival precipitated their need for identity. With this compulsion, they fought for delivery from debased conditions through manual labor. Socially, however, their problems were often insurmountable because of the nonacceptance that led them sometimes to societal starvation; starvation sometimes even led to crime.

Eventually, they extended their economic success to other areas; they became educated; they improved their status; they overcame their difficulties, including the religious ones. Acceptance, even distinction, came finally, when their improved economic conditions engendered those social and cultural achievements which could be constructively integrated into the national American character.

Integration, however, stimulated a restructuring of social dynamics in the nation, and was a precipitant in changing the accepted concepts, for example, of themes and types in creative literary activity. The Italian-Americans, therefore, felt the compulsion to identify with the national literature. Eventually, with the filter of their real experiences, they wrote their own stories to project a more truthful image representing them in American fiction.

PART II
The Emergence of the Italian-American Novel

Never in any country or age had writers so misrepresented their culture, or been so unanimously wrong. Never had they been so completely separated from the experiences that alone give life and validity to literature.

—Bernard DeVoto, *The Literary Fallacy*

I'm just the noisy "Americanized" brat of a plodding "Wop". . . . They call me Rose of Megara because my old man—peace to his soul—came from that town; but I was born in Union Hill. . . .

—Louis Forgione, *The River Between*

3

THE EARLY IMPACT

The gradual integration of the immigrants was accompanied by an equally gradual development of Italian-American fiction, a development that apparently also expanded the literary materials in biographies and autobiographies. There was no sudden transformation from writing autobiographies to constructing novels. Because the transition from autobiography to fiction was so imperceptible and so undefined, some of the autobiographies are furnished with the imaginative writing of fiction, while some of the novels are freighted with autobiographical detail. For this reason, in a study of fiction that would document the interaction of two cultures, some knowledge of the autobiographies is prerequisite to understanding to what degree the facts reported in those autobiographies authenticate the incidents in the novels.

This relationship between the autobiographies and the novels appears in the selection that the writers made of the contents of their works. The autobiographies, as we have seen, contain on-the-spot reports, as it were, of the actual experiences that the immigrants believed worthy of record; but, in making their choice of materials, the autobiographers were subjective in their selection. This subjectivism, entailing personal impressions and interpretations, brought the authors close to the borderline of fiction. Subsequently their materials, along with the oral accounts of other immigrants, became valuable sources for novels about Italian-American life or for subjects whose concepts were related to that life. As a result, the autobiographies serve as a measure of the verisimilitude of the novels and of the validity of the cultural concepts the novels contain.

That the two genres are similar in the selection of materials does not mean that the presentation of the contents of the autobiographies should set the outline for the development of the novels. From the available material, it appears that the two forms do not reveal a parallel development; chronologically and organically, one germinates the other. After the earliest Italian immigrants had told their story in autobiographical accounts, the tale was continued by the writers of Italian-American fiction. Substantially, it was in the work of the novelists that a design in the development of the cultural contents became apparent.

The evolution of Italian-American fiction reveals a pattern similar to that of the cultural growth of the nation. In discussing the organic process of America's literary cultural evolution, Robert E. Spiller outlines four distinct stages that correspond to the degree with which the settlers adjusted to their new environment until they struck their "roots of national culture."[1] However, while nationally an old culture had earlier imposed itself upon a primitive environment to strike the roots of its culture, in the case of the Italians their coming was an encounter of one traditional culture with another. What the Italian-Americans wrote in fiction, therefore, documents a process of the interaction of the two cultures.

Analysis of the works of fiction in which Italian-Americans treat American life reveals a growth process of five stages, which culminated in cultural interaction. Following closely the pattern of the national culture, the developing stages include: 1) the early impact, the period of explanatory narratives that describe the early problems the immigrants had when they first encountered American civilization; 2) the withdrawal into isolation, which revealed the need for assimilation, for an analysis of Italian-American "communities" as separate from the national culture; 3) the revulsion into non-Italian-American themes, a reflection of the Italian-American's rejection of his immediate national heritage in an attempt to identify himself with the broader "Americanism"; 4) the counter-revulsion, a return to old sources in which the Italian-American, like the frontier back trailer, returns to his distinctive heritage and resumes Italian-American themes on a more artistic level of American fiction; and 5) the branching of an Italian culture rooted in American soil, when the Italian-American writes mature fiction to harmonize the traditions of his racial heritage with those, generally, of the United States.

The works of fiction of the first stage were narratives that aimed to reveal the problems of assimilation from the immigrants' own point of view. In this group were Luigi Donato Ventura, Bernardino Ciambelli, Italo Stanco, Silvio Villa, Giuseppe Cautela, Garibaldi Marto Lapolla, and John A. Moroso. All born before the 1890s, these men

1. Robert E. Spiller, "The Roots of National Culture," *The Roots of National Culture: To 1830,* ed. Robert E. Spiller and Harold Blodgett (New York: The Macmillan Company, 1949), pp. 1–21.

participated in the first great flux of Italian immigration and were actively involved in that early impact. The problems they treat offer a variety of subjects.

LUIGI DONATO VENTURA (1845–1912)

Luigi Donato Ventura, for example, presents *Peppino*[2] in French, because many of the early Italian immigrants felt that it was to their advantage to pretend they were French. A number of Italians came to America after having lived in France for many years, so that they understood French as well as they did Italian. Some believed that the French people were more favorably accepted in America as a result of the American Revolutionary War.[3] *Peppino*, therefore, is an Italian story written in French by an Italian-American. In this story the author emphasizes the near brutality of the first encounter of one culture with another because the immigrant lacks knowledge of the new country's language and feels himself lost. Ventura writes "après avoir voté pour l'abolition des négres vous ne voudrez pas abolir l' Italien qui, pour cinq sous, noircit à la sueur de son front vos extrémités inférieures."[4] He introduces us to Peppino, a boy of twelve, who lives at the corner of Prince Street. One cannot resist him; he is a plaintive boy, one who dreams of a beautiful home in his native village.

Ventura tells us of Peppino's dreams, typical of the dreams of the immigrants who came to America, of coming to reap gold from the streets and carrying it away. Peppino reflects upon his contemporary American scene; he would not use his last five cents to see Jay Gould on Wall Street, but he would use it to ask the doorman at the *Herald* when Bennett, who was in Europe, "serait à son bureau."[5] He would also ask at the *Sun* when Dana would finish his lunch. The doorman does not understand him, but feels compassion for him. In this early Italian-American fictional comment there is already evident the comradeship of alienated men in misery.

When Ventura, with all his manuscripts rejected, admits that he does not have the five cents to pay Peppino for a shoe shine, the boy says, "No fa nient, la Madonna t'accompagni."[6] Later, when he is enjoying an active career in journalism, the author pursues his friendship with Peppino. He learns that the boy is living with his brothers "at a minimum" to send their money "al paese" (home). One of the

2. Luigi Donato Ventura, *Peppino* (New York: William R. Jenkins Company, 1913).
3. Eight men whom I interviewed in 1958 in Torrington, Waterbury, and New Haven, Connecticut, cited their own experiences in pretending to be French in order to get employment as cooks in New York City and Boston.
4. Ventura, p. 7.
5. When Bennett would be at his desk.
6. That's nothing. May the Madonna accompany you.

brothers, Antonio, earns good wages, but he gambles at *Mora*[7] and loses most of his earnings.

When Ventura goes to dinner at Peppino's home, he finds himself "en pleine Italie Meridionale." Here, children and women behave as they had in their Italian village; there is no attempt to become American in their way of life. The women wear their Abruzzi costume, while the men smoke and walk along the streets in a *dolce far niente* fashion. The group represents a level of peasant culture, because as the author approaches, one remarks, "È un signore che viene."[8] The exceptional attempt to behave like Americans is in the gesture of Peppino's brothers. Simultaneously they say, "Benvenuto!"[9] They then try to shake hands, but they do so with such force as almost to dislocate the arm of the guest. The gesture is symbolic of the over-eagerness with which Italians attempt to acquire American customs.

The author cannot resist the cordiality of his hosts and he must sit and eat spaghetti with them at nine o'clock in the morning. He observes that the room, though meager, is clean. He sees the pictures of Christ crucified and the Mother of the Rosary, and he senses the endemic quality of the religion of the group. He notices, too, the single geranium on the bare windowsill. The three brothers tell him that they come from Viggiano, a village in the province of Basilicata, a place from which immigrants have always come with a violin "sous le bras, sans un sou dans la poche."[10] The brothers explain that after they have earned four thousand dollars, they will return to Broadway, the Main Street of their native town, a street inhabited by all the people who have been to America.

Eventually, when Ventura is ejected from his living quarters for not paying his rent, Peppino and his brothers come to his aid. The boy's fidelity withstands many tests, and his great pride is his privilege of earning a living and winning the friendship of the men whose shoes he shines.

BERNARDINO CIAMBELLI (n.d.)

Because they could not read English, the early immigrants were a receptive audience for writers who could create entertaining fiction in Italian. The most widely acclaimed Italian writer in America was Bernardino Ciambelli, whose stories dramatize the experiences of the Italian immigrants in the New York area. His works are vividly melodramatic, but are indispensable social documents of the problems the

7. A popular Italian gambling game in which numbers are played by the simultaneous showing of the fingers on one or both hands.
8. It's a gentleman who comes.
9. Welcome!
10. Under their arm, without a sou in their pocket.

immigrants met in making an adjustment to the new environment. Ciambelli writes with a clear, uncomplicated Italian style, charged with emotion but as honestly realistic as Zola, with occasional digressions into fantasy in the manner of Poe. His works include: *I Misteri di Mulberry* (New York: Frugone & Balletto, 1893); *I Drammi dell'Emigrazione, Seguito ai Misteri* (1893); *I Misteri Della Polizia, Il Delitto di Water Street* (New York: Frugone & Balletto, 1895, 3 vols.); *I Misteri di Bleecker Street, Balletto, Romanzo Contemporaneo* (New York: Frugone & Balletto, 1899); *I Sotterranei di New York* (New York: Società Libreria Italiana, 1915); and *La Trovatella di Mulberry Street; ovvero La Stella dei Cinque Punti* (New York: Società Libreria Italiana, 1919).

SILVIO VILLA (1882–1927)

The innocence and optimism of a Peppino did not mark the mood of all the immigrants. Many of them carried in their minds the burden of the reflection of American attitudes toward historical incidents in the Italian mother country. At the beginning of the twentieth century they had to face, for example, the American notions concerning the Italian soldier and Italy's part in World War I.

In the review of Silvio Villa's *Claudio Graziani*[11] in the *Boston Transcript*, July 24, 1920, the book is classified as an American novel "done by a foreigner." This very definition makes *Claudio Graziani* useful as a testament of the ambiguity of the immigrant's position in the early encounter of the two cultures. Furthermore, the book already reveals that determined projection of will power on the part of the protagonist which evolved as a dominant theme with Italian-American writers. The reviewer writes,

> When the young of us listen fervidly to the rhythmical grumblings of our Siegfried Sassoons, a new pride and protest, with a deeper vision of underlying values will not come amiss. In the episode of the Italian front, Silvio Villa, an engineer in a Piedmont Alpini Corps, lays bare, with beautiful simplicity, the springs of human thought. Through a bare thirty pages, this little volume should stand among the masterpieces of the English language. In the first place it is written in English such as only foreigners nowadays can use. Secondly, it is merely a flash picture of the crucial moment in the life of a hero.[12]

Like many of the early Italian immigrants in America, Silvio Villa entered World War I by enlisting in the Italian army. A lieutenant of

11. Silvio Villa, *Claudio Graziani, an Episode of War* (New York: Brentano's [privately printed], 1919).
12. *Ibid.* Cut-out insert facing frontispiece.

the Engineers, he reported with a platoon of men at Edolo in Val Camonica to the headquarters of the Fifth Division, where he discovered that he was under the command of a captain of the Arditi.

In evaluating the military terms of other nations, Americans do so according to their own concepts, but these have not usually included a knowledge of the Arditi. These are the shock troops of the Alpines, "the pick of the best regiments, mostly volunteer." Villa writes,

> They don't stay in the trenches, but are held back of the line and just sent up at the last minute to replace the infantry for the attack. They must take the position or get killed. Once the position is taken, they are withdrawn, and again the infantry is put in their place to hold. . . . They don't use rifles, only hand bombs and poignards. They don't take prisoners. . . . If they fall into the hands of the Austrians, they'll be torn to shreds, so hated they are. (p. 6)

The Arditi, according to Villa, are the cruelest soldiers that this war produced, the most effective tools in the hands of a good leader, fighting "the good fight, none of the dirty gas business of now-a-days." The rest of the army admired them, because they played tricks as

> the cowboys out West play on the Eastern tenderfeet. They tickle you with their poignards, and wouldn't think anything of hitting you on the head with a club, as a joke. (p. 6)

Villa is surprised that his captain proves to be the close friend of his childhood years. He recalls with emotion his early years, when he and his friend used to sit in front of his father's house on a large terrace overlooking the plain. The erstwhile American has become Italian again.

> Below us was the city in a haze of mist. In front of us the chain of the Alps, like a great white wall, encircling the horizon. . . . The city lies astride of the Po, just at the foot of the hills, and then beyond is a great plain . . . with towns here and there, with streams and clusters of trees in blossom. In the distance the great white wall of the mountains. (p. 11)

As the two men meet, the encounter as related by Villa rectifies some misconceptions about the retreat from Caporetto, the withdrawal that impelled Graziani to join the Arditi.

> Line has been broken down between Canale and Caporetto—the second army is in retreat. The Austrians are coming down Val D'Resia and Val di Natisone. They are at Gemona, they are at Tolmezzo, we are shut in, caught in a trap. (p. 11)

The Captain gives a detailed account of how he returned all his men safely to Cornuda, where his Colonel, amazed, proposed for him one of the medals he is wearing. Graziani has wept for the dead soldiers. He can not forget how the third army crossed to Tagliamento, and how the enemy drove to Venice. He explains that the Italian soldiers were alone a long time on the desert of Carso, "forsaken by the rest of the world" after Piave, where "they fought like lions" (p. 15), and at Mount Grappa, "where Italy was saved" and where the Austrians were stopped by the worn and ragged Italians.

Graziani's question has been asked by numerous Italian World War I veterans who became immigrants to America.

> Whoever thought of our men in the remotest corner of the Carnic Alps? Everybody in the world was thinking of France, of the French front. They were left alone. . . . Now and then people saw pictures of them, those fake movies, made in Switzerland, where they were represented doing stunts. . . . People liked the show. . . . They didn't know. (p. 16)

The Germans, however, knew the tension of the arch of the eastern front, and knew how to snap it at the right time and at the right place. Graziani, the defender of his fighting men, says,

> "Who will have the right to condemn them? The people who stayed at home, perhaps, making money, hand over fist? Or the French that had all the support of England and America for their boys? Or the English who are safe beyond their channel? Or the Russians who have deserted? Or the Americans who haven't sent a man till yesterday?" (p. 17)

Before yesterday the Americans had not been involved. But our outgoing culture absorbed the Grazianis and, in the process, proved to the world à la Hemingway that no man is an island. America's Frederick Henry became a culture-hero of the disillusionment that breeds conceptual change in retelling the story of the retreat from Caporetto. This retreat, as John Aldridge has critically conceived it in *After the Lost Generation*, became the symbol of a whole literary group.

The clarification of the Caporetto incident is important, therefore, if only to emphasize that such an incident may have the latent potentiality of becoming a group symbol in American literature. It took a man like Hemingway to bridge the islands on which the deserted Grazianis stood, waiting to give their concepts to even the metaphors of our literature. But even if Hemingway had not used the incident in *A Farewell to Arms*, the memories of the retreat remained important enough to many Italian-Americans that Villa felt the need to tell the story for other Americans to read.

Other specific references in the Villa story are used to reveal human relationships within the two cultures as well as between them. These references are also valid comments on the Italian's evaluation of American life. One society's observation of another, for example, is often epitomized in the attitude that the men of one group take toward the women of the other. Graziani and Villa remember their early youth with "those girls of Turin that were our joy when we were students, so fine, so gentle, so graceful." When the Captain asks about American girls, Villa answers,

> They are great. . . . They are nice and strong, full of life, full of fun, good at all sort of sports, dance like angels! Know how to flirt! (p. 19)

In the end, Graziani becomes the symbol of the individual who is hopelessly pitted against inflexible authority. He receives an order to attack Col di Croce with his men, an impossible procedure since the Col is on a ridge perpendicular to the T-Bowl, where the Italian men are entrenched. Since the approach to the rock is a mass of wire entanglements, only a half-dozen men on the ridge could annihilate an entire regiment below. Graziani telephones the Colonel, a new officer unfamiliar with the terrain, and tries to explain that the position is untenable, but the commanding officer refuses to believe him. "Come and do it yourself," says Graziani, and waits for the Major to lead him to his execution. With this action, through which Graziani exerts his will for the victory of principle, he becomes an archetype for the numerous protagonists who champion the underprivileged individual in the Italian-American novel.

GIUSEPPE CAUTELA (1883– ?)

The interweaving of the reminiscences of the Italian background in these early writings was especially marked in the personal reactions of the immigrants to their new environment. In *Moon Harvest*,[13] Giuseppe Cautela recalls of Ortonova, Italy, that "the sweetness of spring seemed distilled in the cup of heaven" (p. 1) and that his uprooting was like that of a "tree by a cyclone." As a young man he rejected his life of little battles in the village, intending "to expand his ideas of human progress and emancipation." His intention, therefore, was something more than to escape; it became a need to extend into another culture. Even as a boy he had thought about how learned he would be some day, and that then people would respect him. But this fulfillment was as impossible for him in the static concepts of the old village as it had been for Arrighi and Panunzio, who gave such graphic accounts of their backgrounds in their autobiographies.

13. Giuseppe Cautela, *Moon Harvest* (New York: Lincoln MacVeagh, Dial Press, 1925).

Cautela's own life, along with his observations of the experiences of others around him, served as the raw material for his novels. Coming to America when he was fourteen years old, he became an apprentice to a barber, pursuing a specialized enough occupation that allowed him sufficient leisure for reading and writing in Italian. Then, after serving in the Italian infantry for three years during World War I, he returned to America, seriously intent upon learning English well enough to write in the language of his adopted country. With relentless persistence, he succeeded in breaking into print with some poetry, several essays, and a few short stories, all pertaining to Italian-American life and themes. Although he wrote several other novels, his major work, *Moon Harvest,* was the only one accepted for publication, and that was in 1925.

In *Moon Harvest* Cautela tells the story of Romualdo and his wife, Maria, who came to America already fixed socially by old traditions, community customs, and a growing family. In their attempts to adapt themselves to the new society, the young couple are challenged by unforeseen forces. Romualdo makes progress in his new environment, but Maria remains stationary. Eventually, Romualdo finds sympathetic compatibility with Vincenza DiDedda, a second-generation Italian-American who represents for him all the desirable goals in the new society. Maria, the incarnate symbol of the static old culture, must die, as all the former concepts that cannot be assimilated must expire. Ultimately, Romualdo, the man who finds himself isolated between two cultures, is compelled to move in the same direction as at the outset of his American experience.

Specifically, the struggle for Romualdo to assimilate American ideas begins with the visit to Uncle Flaminio DiLeo's house in Gravesend Bay in Brooklyn, where he sees how much can be acquired in the new country. When he attends night school to learn English, he refuses to continue because of the "stupidity of the method coupled with the irascibility of the teacher" (p. 53). Therefore, unlike Uncle DiLeo, Romualdo, "the intellectual, the aesthete, the poet, the man who delighted others" (p. 54), takes a job in a tin factory, cutting tin patterns by machine. He charms the other Italians in the factory by his fine, pure Tuscan dialect and his references to classic verse, but he must wear soiled clothing and his hands become grimy. He listens to people speaking English; he goes to see a performance of *Hamlet,* and then he reads only English because "three hours passed with Shakespeare's divine imaginings" is worth all his misery. He spends Sundays in the public library; he reads in the subway; he becomes acquainted with the best works of both English and American literature. Meanwhile, though her husband makes intellectual strides, Maria is satisfied with caring for her home and children. Concerned, Romualdo warns her that she must learn English or "you will remain a body without a soul here" (p. 58). But she is too exhausted, and, while she resigns herself to her unaccustomed surroundings, he identifies the restlessness of his own ambitions with a poignant homesickness for "his mother land."

What has really happened is that, in learning the new language, Romualdo has absorbed its cultural concepts. As he approaches new sociological value judgments, he becomes alternately charmed and terrified, depressed and exalted. He suffers a disturbance that no one can imagine, possessed as he is of a poet's sensitivity. As Cautela points out,

> Who would have thought that this poorly dressed immigrant saw all the gorgeous colors of the Orient if a lady passing by him wrapped his senses in her perfume? (p. 59)

He finds himself cursing the "terrible splendid city" that so stirs his emotions; he understands why others are satisfied with their new wealth, but he feels isolated from their achievements. He does not belong. Also, he feels that coarseness and bad taste are the penalty of newly acquired wealth. While he despairs of his idealism, he must face reality in Maria, who, heavy with pregnancy, fills him with a paradox of admiration and shame. His life has become dramatically representative of the large struggle of his group, the effort to survive the conflict of reality with dreams. There is a prophetic significance in the fact that when the new baby is born, Romualdo is glad that the boy resembles the mother; he does not want his children to be like him, and he admires his wife's character more than his own. Reality is too painful; he is not happy.

At the opera, he remarks that beauty is a gesture of the intellect, and he becomes aware of the fascinated response of Vincenza DiDedda at his side. At another time he discovers the "introspection" in her eyes. They discuss music and books, and Romualdo gradually becomes the victim of his peculiar situation. His position is further intensified when Vincenza starts taking lessons in Italian from him. Although she lives in the "Italian colony," her home is a reproduction of a villa, and she represents all the graces associated with a house designed by an architect to display the appointments of Italian Renaissance life.

Romualdo's life becomes a torturous contradiction. Although he attempts to transcend his group, he wants to remain a part of it; but his struggle inclines to favor the victory of the individual. Although he cannot believe that Vincenza, "so idealistic and pure" would betray the Italian code forbidding her to love a married man, his mind dwells on the great literary tragedies whose heroines put themselves above society. He anticipates the naturalistic protagonists who rationalize that "their act is not to be judged by ordinary moral standards, because of their great sincerity and sacrifice they make" (p. 117). But Romualdo is of a heroic mold in that his love had to be different, and that nothing should stain this ravishing dream. When he rationalizes that art has nothing to do with morals, he becomes conscience-stricken and cries, "God, illumine my mind!" (p. 143). It is Maria, his unchanging wife, who knows how things are, and who offers him black coffee, saying simply, "This will restore you, Romualdo" (p. 145). Then, as his love affair with Vincenza continues, Maria watches him silently.

Because Maria cannot endure expansiveness, she cannot complain of indifference. Cautela says that she is created simply, for things mild and durable, and that she retains a goddess-like serenity. But she, too, inevitably feels the fateful push in her surroundings. Intuitively, she senses chaos, just as she had felt the tremors of earthquakes as a child. Cautela writes, "Moreover it was useless to run, you cannot run; try if you will, the earth claims you." In her resignation, she accepts material determinism and lacks any will to help herself. The resignation, however, takes a toll, and she suffers from shock. She is able not to betray herself, as she shows when she urges Romualdo to dance with Vincenza at the DiLeo celebration. But it is she who remains extraneous and alone while all the romantic vaporings hover near her. What Cautela calls her Italian pride is her realization that endurance is an invariable fact in the quelling of illusion. In her quiet suffering is embodied the universal torment of the individual in a competitive and chaotic world. The new culture has given her, if not change, a new perception. She asks of her husband what all his knowledge is good for, if he cannot reconcile it with his family? Then, because she is a realist, she tests her doubt, and she discovers the facts of her husband's infidelity. As a result, she withdraws to her old sources and decides to visit Abruzzi. Her husband consents, expressing the hope that Maria will bring a "new message from their huts."

Romualdo is a man torn between two worlds, two cultures, two loves; and he cannot disassociate art from life, even in its worst circumstances. These dual struggles are the symbol of the members of this social group, who are neither Italian nor American, but who are tortured in the process of amalgamation. The tragic solution of Maria's has all the impact of reality, and, in the end, the romantic vapors are dissipated. Even if idealism momentarily buries reality in Maria's death—Cautela says she dies of a broken heart—it does so at the price of its own extinction, and Romualdo comes down to earth. He recognizes that beauty can be tragic and he rejects Vincenza's plea that he marry her, because Maria, in memory, is now more real than before. Vincenza must pursue her art as a singer, while, for the time being, Romualdo will renew himself. He will go back to Italy, but Cautela lets us feel that his protagonist must return. The old culture had helped to forge Vincenza, but the new culture became his only at the price of Maria's supreme sacrifice.

GARIBALDI MARTO LAPOLLA (1888–1954)

The sacrifice of the old culture was not always so dramatic or so heroic as the Italians became more Americanized. In Harlem, fronting the East River, with its poor and crowded conditions, the immigrants' first visible evidence of the changes they were making seemed to be their contribution to the deterioration of the landscape. Garibaldi Marto Lapolla writes in *The Grand Gennaro*[14] that now the red bricks are dirtier, the fire escapes are rustier, the narrow stoops are more worn, and the small grass plots are even barer than they were. Harlem now

> wears the bitter, humorous air of an old relation, once rich, now fallen in with the indigent members of the family assembled at a reunion in which beer and pretzels have taken the place of champagne and fancy sandwiches. (p. 3)

Life is the getting down to bare essentials, and only a backwash of the flood of the moonlight of the former romanticism can blur the sordid details; daylight reveals the change. The earlier German and Irish immigrants, who had prospered in business, had built the solid brownstones of dubious architecture and of minimal beauty. In one of the buildings, a "singularly narrow house, three stories high," three Italian families, the Accuci, the Dauri, and the Monterani, became "hopelessly entangled." Lapolla shows how these families, each from a different section of Italy, were "to meet, mingle, and separate, each bearing in charred burdens of memory the shock of their encounter" (p. 3).

The shock was omnipresent. The absorber of its impact, however, was innate in the immigrants' disposition "to make America," a rather curious concept. Lapolla explains that

> to make America, a nobody, a mere clodhopper, a good-for-nothing on the other side, had contrived by hook or crook in this new strange country with its queer ways and its lack of distinctions, to amass enough money to strut about and proclaim himself the equal of those who had been his superiors in the old country. (p. 5)

Obviously, the Italian immigrant applied this term derisively to his compatriot, but with a suggestion of envy tinging his contempt. "To make America" implies that the alien's struggle in America has little to do with his former position or virtue; it suggests that success is the reward of aggression, sometimes of dubious means, and even of violence. It is a peculiar interpretation of the frontier theory as the formulative material of democracy and the environmental explanation of Americanism.[15]

14. Garibaldi Marto Lapolla, *The Grand Gennaro* (New York: The Vanguard Press, Inc., 1935).

15. David M. Potter, *People of Plenty* (Chicago: The University of Chicago Press,

In his books, Lapolla shows that he is particularly well-qualified to interpret this singular concept of Italian-American culture. An educator as well as author, he is the social product of the American "Italian colony." Only two years old when his family migrated from Italy to New York City, he grew up in "Little Italy," attended the public schools, and eventually earned his professional degrees in education at Columbia University. While always finding time to do civic work among the immigrants, he concentrated on his educational work, especially as principal of Public School No. 174 in Brooklyn, New York. After successfully writing two textbooks on high school English, he completed three novels: *The Fire in the Flesh,* 1931; *Miss Rollins in Love,* 1932; and *The Grand Gennaro,* 1935. All three novels are detailed presentations of the social conditions of Italian-American life, but *The Grand Gennaro* best expresses the cultural problems of "Little Italy."

The Fire in the Flesh

In his first book, *The Fire in the Flesh,*[16] Lapolla writes with admirable competence and promising power. Although the plot is uneven in intensity, the book has educative value in its presentation of the Italian community in New York. The protagonist, Agnese, is a minor prototype of the more masterfully drawn Maria Santa in Mario Puzo's *Fortunate Pilgrim* (1964). Agnese, proud, attractive, and ambitious, has had the traumatic experience in her native land of having given birth to the child of a priest. Driven by the cultural taboos of her time and place, she marries a submissive and simple man, Michele Dantone, and escapes to America. Lapolla portrays effectively the years of hard work and suffering that Agnese and her associates endure. Agnese, however, remains independent and dominant, advantageously beautiful and desired by men, and correspondingly disdained by her moralistic neighbors. Using Michele as a pawn in her scheme, Agnese succeeds in negotiating with politicians. In the progression of events, several braggadocios emerge in Lapolla's characterizations. With detachment and with insight unblurred by chauvinism or buffoonery, the writer presents these characters in scene after scene of passion followed by murder, using the graphic formula that other writers have made typical of the crime novels of the sixties. Lapolla succeeds, furthermore, in lifting his characters above the stereotype; they have real life, and their actions, which may strike some readers as over-dramatic, are the actual performances of real, melodramatic people whom, we sense, the writer has known and observed in careful detail.

Phoenix Books, 1957), pp. 22–23. Potter is referring to Frederick Jackson Turner's essay, "The Significance of the Frontier in American History."

16. Garibaldi Marto Lapolla, *Fire in the Flesh* (New York: The Vanguard Press, Inc., 1931).

Miss Rollins in Love

In his second book, *Miss Rollins in Love*,[17] Lapolla continues with the Italian-American setting, which he grasps more aesthetically without sacrificing authenticity. Maturing away from the external props of torrid plot sequences, Lapolla is now subtle and masterful in handling human emotions and social relationships. Here his plot is brief: a typical American school teacher falls in love with an Italian-American student in her class. She is his guide and director in his quest to find himself and his purpose. She also stabilizes his ambitions and gives him a sense of values that helps him avoid a career in crime. Ostensibly, she personifies the best of the ideals of the American Dream as professed and lived by native Americans prior to the arrival of immigrants. Miss Rollins is the incarnation of the missionary zeal and sincerity of altruists who have helped immigrants to realize their own success. This exhilarating constructiveness Lapolla communicates with an almost Elizabethan ebullience of language. He is one of the first Italian-Americans to have mastered the rhetoric of fiction with literary distinction. After this book, with the tools of the craft so well in hand, he is ready for significant innovations in both content and form. His accurate eye catches a brilliant photograph from which he makes a memorable portrait of an ethnic in his next book.

The Grand Gennaro

Briefly, *The Grand Gennaro* is the story of an immigrant, Gennaro Accuci, who, though he had no social status in Italy, succeeds in twenty years in the United States in rising to the role of minor dictator in the Italian-American colony. In the end he is destroyed by his boyhood companion, Rocco Pagliamini, whom he has wronged.

Specifically, the story dramatizes the method by which Gennaro "made America"—dubiously, violently, and successfully. He exploited the trusting nature of his childhood friend by "moving into" Rocco's business, first by petty thievery and then by force. From his point of view, America offered nothing to the immigrant, who merely worked "like a beast of burden under the worst possible human conditions."[18] This was the time, in the 1890s, when laborers, especially immigrant laborers, were a "commodity" in industry, and Samuel Gompers was only beginning the battle for the recognition of the working man as an individual. A man like Lapolla's protagonist, therefore, with a driving compulsion to assert his individuality, would feel that he had to break the pattern of submission by whatever means he could. When

17. Garibaldi Marto Lapolla, *Miss Rollins in Love* (New York: The Vanguard Press, 1932).
18. *The Grand Gennaro*, p. 1.

Gennaro beats his former friend and forces him into obedience, Rocco numbly signs the contract forfeiting half of his business to Gennaro. Rocco voices all the nuances of the encounter when he concludes, "Well, you have made America, and made it quick. You were born an American!" (p. 12). To the Italian, then, being an American was being like Gennaro, who drove a bargain at the end of a knife. Paradoxically, it is curious that Americans at the time believed that such a posture was peculiarly Italian. But to Rocco, the average and typical Italian immigrant, Gennaro was atypical. Lapolla writes,

> This man in the room with him, who had come from the old country with the determination to pile up a stack in a short time, no matter how he did it, was outside the scope of his understanding. He had seen men like him . . . and giving way only under compulsion he could play an even game with them. But this man . . . was made of meaner stuff. (p. 14)

He was like a wolf out of the mountains, a starved dog with his tongue lolling. What Rocco did not know was that Gennaro was a not unusual "frontier" type, that he was not too different from the legendary prospector for gold.

When Rocco attempts to avert future trouble for himself by actually trying to use a knife, he stumbles, because this is not his way of doing things; and he loses completely any bargaining power he may have had with his menacing opponent. After his conquest of Rocco, Gennaro proceeds to crush others in subtler ways, and he emerges as the executive of a large rag-and-metal industry. His enterprises are not on the level of a Gould's or a Whitney's, but the pattern is similar. The author emphasizes, however, that Rocco reacts with the normal instincts of a man, and that his former gentleness and generosity now turn into hatred and the desire for revenge. Violence seems inevitable. Rocco makes one last attempt to regain his former dignity, when he says to Gennaro,

> The American fever is in you. The touch of gold in your hands has been too much. We [villagers] are not used to it. It does queer things to us—the good it makes mean, the mean it makes brutal. Give me the money that's mine, and you can have the business. You stay here; I'll go back to the old country. (p. 18)

But Gennaro needs him; it is Rocco who is the expert in the details of the business. Likewise, Lapolla shows, on a broader scale, powerful American entrepreneurs are dependent upon numerous Roccos.

Gennaro, too, becomes powerful. He makes all kinds of conquests, including not only his friend's business, but also his landlady's attentions in the absence of her husband. Although the years pass, he does not send for his family in Italy. Secretly, he has doubts about himself.

Lapolla asks, "Was it that, in spite of his money, his position among the *paesani*, he had not yet struck roots in the country to which he had come?" (p. 26). Thus, the author classifies the protagonist for us; he is an uprooted man whose rapid cultural conversion is a questionable achievement in any society. He is an Italian, and the Americans cannot accept him as one of them.

Lapolla uses the other men at the boarding house thematically to represent various degrees of ambition and zeal. Each one "wants to make all he can." Most of them, like Bartolomeo, the landlord, have in Italy "similar places and . . . wives and mothers are there and children waiting" (p. 36). Generally they believe they belong to their former country. Bartolomeo, the spokesman of the group, explains that he hates this country because it has changed them all. Lapolla writes,

> The clodhopper apes the man of education and good family; the man of good family and education becomes timid, or he's too well brought up to break the law and he loses out. The last are first, and the first are last and the whole world seems upside down and crazy. I'm going back where everyone knows his place and things are orderly and decent. (p. 37)

After Nuora (the landlady) and her husband depart, Gennaro would like to sit around and talk with the men, but he has little capacity for communication. He has also become aware of a new feeling, a

> sense of his having been roundly cuffed by someone he could not resist, a masterful overpowering person, and then left in a corner to weep out his shame by himself and wait for the departure of pain from his muscles and his heart. (p. 44)

For this reason, he sublimates his restlessness in a round of pleasures and orgies, but he finally decides to send for his family. Their joining him presents new problems, however, because the family is alien even to the limited amount of progress Gennaro has made in his cultural adjustment. He is repelled by the mannerisms of his dandified son, Domenico, and shows further irritation when he urges his wife to shop in "American districts," so that she may be transformed into the semblance of an American woman. Eventually his problem is solved with the death of his wife and the marriage of his son.

As Domenico, the son, becomes involved with the attractive and sympathetic Carmela Dauri, Don Anselmo, the priest, despairs of the moral and social dilemma that faces the second-generation Italian-Americans. The ethnic group as a whole, he claims, does not have the restraints of an orderly upper class with power and position, and the tendency of the younger people is to achieve wealth and follow their lowest instincts. He claims that these instincts for them have always "in the past been superinduced by culture, the training at the mother's knee, the dictates of the church" (p. 140). Here, in an uprooted society, the priest reasons, it has "become smart to be bad." He shudders when he visits the young people in their new apartment, and he is offended by the green plush furniture, the brass clock, and the fantastic mirrors.

For the "Italian colony" surrounding Gennaro, religious assimilation in America has been troublesome. The Italians have no church of their own, and only Gennaro's braggadocio generosity succeeds in giving them one. The socially conscious Signora Maria Monterano joins the Protestants, because Father Cassidy has felt he has done his duty by setting aside the basement of the Catholic Church for the Italians. Exploiting this discrimination, Miss Reddle, the social worker of the Harlem Baptist Church, becomes active among the Italian-Americans; but, after years of labor, her converts "sneak off and revert to the rites of their fathers."[19] Miss Reddle, however, is representative of the sincere attempt made by native Americans to ease the disgraceful social conditions and the unbearable poverty among the immigrants. As demonstrated in the autobiographies and other accounts by Italian-Americans, a multiplicity of Miss Reddles helped the strangers prepare to assume their responsibilities as citizens of the nation.

Lapolla states that other changes proceed slowly and surely in the Harlem group. At the end of the Spanish-American war, when Dewey returns to New York, the Italian settlement celebrates the "triumph of the American navy in a way they had hitherto reserved for their saints."[20] Gennaro is the center of all the activity, gathering together all the societies, each hoisting a patron saint, into a committee of welcome for the Admiral. The interweaving of Italian and American band music, the juxtaposition of the two nations' flags and buntings, and a local *festa* are all promoted by Gennaro, who is dressed as an officer of the *bersaglieri*.[21] The tragic irony of his situation is emphasized when, as he is about to lead the groups in the parade, he is given the news that his Domenico has died in a hospital in Santiago. There is dramatic weight to his comment, "We certainly made America. No?"[22]

Now Gennaro concentrates on becoming a ruthless business man, amassing a fortune. His preoccupation with building a church becomes a psychological necessity; he is seeking the aesthetic quality that he has missed in all his other activities. His engagement in this new mission leads him to discover a kindred spirit in his Carmela, who

19. The subject of the Italian's resistance to proselytizing is documented by Thomas T. McAvoy, O.S.C., ed., *Roman Catholicism and The American Way of Life* (Notre Dame, Ind.: University of Notre Dame Press, 1960), pp. 172–78. See also F. Aurelio Palmieri, O.S.A., D.D. "Italian Protestantism in the United States," *Catholic World* (May 1908), pp. 177–89.

20. *The Grand Gennaro*, p. 191.

21. The sharpshooters' corps of the Italian army.

22. *The Grand Gennaro*, p. 192.

becomes a mollifying influence on his way of life. The two attend the American classics that appear at the Harlem Opera House, and the children gradually absorb a new culture. Home becomes almost like an "American home," and the tactful Carmela, as its mother, discusses plans for college for Gennaro's children. He is almost lulled into a sense of security, serenity, and fulfillment. With his new dignity, he helps his old enemy, Rocco, by giving him a job; but Rocco has not changed and he organizes a strike against Gennaro. Rocco's relentless hatred seeks revenge and eventually wreaks violence upon the man who has lately become his benefactor.

Gennaro's funeral is symbolic of a group and of a nation. Here is not the sense of envy or the flair that made a cortege for Jim Fisk. Lapolla says that Gennaro

> is borne as a President might have been in the gold-encrusted coffin that was carried on the shoulders of Gennaro's most stalwart fellow-officers in the various societies he had headed. (p. 364)

This has not been a nameless foreign villager, nor has he been an ordinary citizen of the nation. There are a band, a procession, and a string of automobiles. Someone remarks that Gennaro himself would have said, looking at his own funeral, "I made America." The final symbol is in the gesture, later, of Carmela's giving Gennaro's personal effects to the son, Emilio. "They belonged to your father. They once belonged to his father." "And to his father," answers Emilio, who takes them and will keep them, "for luck" (p. 369).

In summary, the early impact deals with the problems the Italians encountered in the United States during the first great flux of their immigration. Luigi Donato Ventura makes an appealing case of *Peppino,* whose protagonist of the same name has great pride in his work, through which he strives with innocence and optimism to win the friendship of the men whose shoes he shines. His neighbors, however, are still only a group of transplanted Italians whose chief asset is an eagerness to become Americans. Like his neighbors and like the doormen of the commercial houses of the established society, Peppino finds comradeship with other people in economic straits. To the Italian-American writer these underprivileged people are symbols of his own forebears and their humble social position. An archetype of this symbol is created by Silvio Villa in Claudio Graziani, who, in explaining an episode in Italian history that has provoked much unfavorable comment in America, champions the subordinate who succeeds in principle. Villa's theme is expanded with diverse ramifications in later Italian-American fiction. As the symbol takes on a variety of forms, it is often found in the portrayal of the immigrant who, in his first encounter with the new culture, finds himself isolated as the result of the conflict of his progress in the new society with the inflexible inherited concepts that he is replacing. This struggle is illustrated in Giuseppe Cautela's *Moon Harvest.* Any success with this struggle, however, is usually limited to the confines of the Italian "colony," in which a man can attain leadership by applying the ruthless methods that in a small degree parallel the progress of individual enterprise on the national scale. The ambitious immigrant reaches for success at some dubious costs, as shown, for example, in the case of Gennaro Accuci, the main character of Garibaldi Marto Lapolla's *The Grand Gennaro.* All in all, it is apparent in these novels that the themes are structured on the struggle of the underprivileged individual to achieve success and his will to survive in a conflict with his environment.

Even the novelists of lesser literary stature employ similar themes. The plots of John Antonio Moroso, for example, consistently revolve around the problems of the unfortunate, the persecuted, and the errant. A newspaper reporter, Moroso tells a convincing tale of struggle, pursuit, or even crime, as is illustrated in one of his best novels, *The Stumbling Herd.*[23] This is a story of the "East Side," in which the melting-pot constituents of Jews, Italians, Irish, and others are rather loosely connected in the plot to reveal the squalor and the struggle of all the people involved. That they survive is owing only to their personal integrity and outgoing humanity.

In general, then, in their writings during this first phase of the immigrants' encounter with the civilization of the United States, the novelists, good or mediocre, write stories of cultural dualism and social conflict. This dualism, however, is a bridge to amalgamation, and the conflict already has visible constructive elements.

23. John Antonio Moroso, *The Stumbling Herd* (New York: The Macaulay Company, 1923).

4

THE NEED FOR ASSIMILATION

The narratives in which the Italian-Americans dramatized their first encounter were not embellished with songs and ballads of a new trail or frontier camp. On the contrary, with the nostalgic reminiscences of the old tunes of their native villages always sounding in the inner ear, these immigrants resisted giving up the distant beat of their former drum. However, like other pioneers, they now entered a second phase in their change; they had to make the effort to establish a home of some permanence for themselves in their new environment. In this phase, a time that generated an extension of themes, writers had a choice of two directions of structure—aggressive violence or lyrical optimism. Among others, Prosper Buranelli and Louis Forgione pursued the themes of violence, while Valenti Angelo became popular with more salubrious subjects.

Lapolla's Gennaro had revealed not only the favorable potentialities in assimilation, but also the factor of violence involved in the process. Violence, in fact, became as attractive a literary subject with Italian-Americans as it was with the more widely recognized writers of our national fiction. It offered a structural device for making a transition from the old themes to more complex ones, which authors could use to show that the immigrants were trying to escape their parochial restrictions. Furthermore, the ramification of experiences that dealt with conflict eventually made the use of violent themes inevitable. They seem to be the yeast of progressive action as Prosper Buranelli (1890–1960), for example, develops his detective plots in *You Gotta Be Rough* (1930); the underworld complication of *Big Nick* (1931); and the Big Money-Wall Street-gangster affiliations in *News Reel Murder* (1940). With Buranelli the old hatred and revenge motifs of Rocco against Gennaro have developed into the serious social problem of the emotionally maladjusted who have become criminals and who must be apprehended.

LOUIS FORGIONE (n.d.)

An exploration of the Italian-American's predisposition for certain criminal activities (which has developed a type in general American fiction, as in the example of gangster stories) is offered by Louis Forgione in his early novel, *The Men of Silence.*[1] The subject of the novel is an incident of the Camorra in Naples. Forgione draws on the annals of that institution between 1906–1921, after which came the end of the politico-criminal Neapolitan epoch. At first a philanthropic society to help the victims of the tyranny of the Bourbons in the old kingdom of Naples, the Camorra eventually became a political auxiliary of tyrannic misrule after the Bourbons had fled. Its

> life and object were entirely criminal, but colored more or less with the romance and mysticism of the past and still owing its safety to powerful social and political protectors. (p. xii)

Forgione portrays the famous trial at Viterbo. The murderers of the Cuocolo couple are tried and convicted, but there are forces that prevent the procedure from killing the organization itself. The trial is so maneuvered that the evidence of Captain Fabbroni and Maresciallo Farris is excluded because it implicates the police and the judiciary. The book is a revelation of a social community complex in Italy that has had repercussions in some facets of organized crime in America, where the complex has been fictionalized under a Mafia category of legendary proportions. *The Men of Silence* derives its title from *omertà*, which suggests the intrigue and code of that institution whose face appears as unfathomable innocence. Its portrayal has fascinated American films and television to a point that a number of semi-educated people believe that crime in America is an exclusively Italian importation. Statistics reveal, however, that the Italian immigrants have had no larger percentage of crime in America than any other immigrant group.[2]

On the whole, however, the writers of the second phase, during which time the Italian-Americans were making their first serious attempt at assimilation, had more subtle themes than those of crime to challenge them. Forgione himself, for example, removes his locale in *The River Between,*[3] to the heart of a Sicilian colony occupying the tenements on the edge of the Palisades. Socially he adjusts and extends the older themes to his immediate environment, reflecting that he is a second-generation Italian-American, born in New York City and educated in the public schools. After attending the City College of

1. Louis Forgione, *The Men of Silence,* with an introduction by Walter Littlefield (New York: E. P. Dutton & Co., Inc., 1928).
2. See Appendix, Table II.
3. Louis Forgione, *The River Between* (New York: E. P. Dutton & Company, 1928).

New York for three years, he went to work to assume the duties of his father, who became ill. Forgione continued to study, and in due time acquired two professions—writing and engineering. While he was educating himself, he became a friend of Pascal D'Angelo, the autobiographer who wrote *Son of Italy*, and his novel reflects many of D'Angelo's experiences.

The River Between is important not only because it is Forgione's best work, but because it is the most representative novel of the second phase in the development of Italian-American fiction. The characters, furthermore, are significant equally as symbols and as types. Demetrio, the father, who was once a powerful force in the Italian-American colony, is going blind; but he can see more by insight than can his less perceptive son, Oreste. The son is too insensitive to understand either the cultural values of his father or the conflicts with those values that disturb his wife, Rose. Inevitably, Rose quarrels with her father-in-law, leaves home, and sinks into depravity. Overcome by his frustrations over his failure to impose his traditional tenets of morality, Demetrio leaves home, now totally blind, and becomes a beggar. Eventually, Rose and Demetrio meet in the wretchedness of their degradation, and they become reconciled. The structural pattern is now clear: conflict, isolation, assimilation. Together, they ally themselves against the son and husband, who, alone, remains isolated because he undergoes no internal change from any conflict with himself.

Specifically, the story is embroidered with nuances of the theme. Old women discuss the powers of the Evil Eye possessed by the aged Demetrio, revealing an endemic superstition that is dynamic within them. Culture has become cult, and esteem is transferred from Demetrio to his son. For example, Oreste supervises the work on the foundations for the Marland Avenue power house. Forgione writes that the laborers work hard, "ceaselessly, mechanically, as only Italian laborers can." Like the worker of the previous generation, the laborer appears as a commodity for American industry, but the human spirit endures when "everyone was tired, flushed, grouchy, yet quick and alert with a reserve strength at this ending of the day's toil" (p. 2). Men now, however, are organized in work, and each participating man reflects his father. When Oreste fires one of his best laborers for disorderliness, and he resents the pleadings of the man's wife, he is disturbed by his own action. Forgione writes,

> For there was another man in Oreste, the son of Demetrio. There was a sense of gentleness, an insistent feeling of compassion which continually bewildered and startled him. (p. 9)

Oreste is even tempted to rescind his decision, but he must maintain discipline. He feels for the man, writes a letter of recommendation for him to a stevedore he knows, and overpays him ten dollars "by mistake." There is a new note, a baffled compassion, which has displaced the anger of the earlier novels. Forgione writes, "Demetrio's son threw himself on the bed, wondering whether he were a damned fool or not" (p. 10).

The son must accept his share of the hatred that the men have for his father, whom they suspect of demonic powers. He is one of the family from which the original immigrant had separated, the Emilio to Don Gennaro. Oreste barely knows his father, and shares little intimacy with him. This separateness does not, however, prevent his being concerned with whatever fear haunts the old man. His concern expresses itself in a term from the old culture as he addresses his father with "Sì, Signore." But suspicion becomes all pervasive; it surrounds the prowlings of Rose, Oreste's once-abandoned wife, another new type, the second-generation Italian-American woman.

Oreste and Rose are part of an era of American civilization as they seek the privacy of their own room, guided by the light of a kerosene lamp. She is markedly non-Sicilian as she addresses her husband, "old boy." As they find themselves in a dual cultural position, they learn that their problems have doubled. They must struggle to get along with each other to reconcile the marriage of a man and a woman, a marriage that has ostensibly failed. What were formerly only racial problems have become more universal now. Rose is no Maria to Romualdo, the submissive immigrant's wife, wide-eyed or dreamy. She says of herself,

> I'm just the noisy "Americanized" brat of a plodding "Wop". . . . They call me Rose of Megara because my old man—peace to his soul—came from that town; but I was born in Union Hill. (p. 39)

Her testimony accents her heritage, but a brittle new brass appears along with a disrespect for her inheritance. She uses exaggerated slang from a wide-open mouth in a metallic voice that jars everyone. Forgione compares her with a

> dark, defiant Amazon, tigerishly-rebellious, raising gold-weighted arms against the destiny of basic earth in this universe—against the tyranny of the seed!

She tries to imitate a common brand of Americanism with her slang and her cigarettes, and Oreste takes her at her own terms. Despite this deterioration, the former cultural ties rewind about them as the father hovers around the house "always spiting and sneering and spying" on his daughter-in-law. Oreste tries to shrug off this pressure simply by saying that his father is "old-fashioned and strict" and that the old man has the Sicilian's demand for respect. The father cannot tolerate a daughter who smokes and who goes out alone at night. He sincerely believes he is "guarding the honor of his family." With her American logic, Rose points out that if the father is so old-fashioned, he should go back where he came from, and that all his fussing about honor is only driving her away from the house. Oreste, although Sicilian enough to be angry at such lack of respect for his father, concludes that she is "an amusing girl of alien soul" (p. 46).

The father and son struggle for dominance in the business. This conflict is indicative of something deeper; it is the battle of survival between two ways of life. Legally, everything is Oreste's; that is as certain as his American citizenship. His security rests on his Americanism. The father, however, retreats more and more into an isolation, a brooding that develops into madness. He would revive his old sense of honor by demanding that he earn his place in the household. For example, he insists on working with the men, an act that has a tragic impact on his family. "It seemed as if the old man's footfalls still echoed, firm and measured, at long intervals from the outside hall" (p. 103). Rose, the American, admits that she has returned to the family because of her sense of personal failure. "I grabbed back at the old house, at the old life, at you," she tells Oreste (p. 104). But, because the old man is forcing his code of standards, she threatens to leave again; she knows that her presence disturbs her father-in-law's sanity. Then, when Demetrio disappears, the visible impediments of the old culture are removed and the young people are free to face their own problems. They now learn that what is at fault is something more universally and more inherently wrong; and the novel moves from symbols to reality when Rose and Oreste discover that their troubles are caused by their own weaknesses as people.

At this point, the human problems extend beyond the conflict of culture, and the process of assimilation in the characters reverts to personal evaluations. Rose realizes her husband's dullness and she now sees the squalor of the house that she had identified with security; she is faced with the "sweat of boarders, the deadening routine." She also begins to feel like a beggar in her husband's house. She recalls her former lover, Arthur Hallstead, and she plans to meet him again. She looks for happiness with Hallstead, because he represents her escape from the "Italian neighborhood, thick with people who know all about her, with scandal-mongers and spiteful enemies" (p. 136). In this unprecedented relationship her problem becomes less ethnically social as it becomes more intrinsically personal. Weary of her husband, she finds herself caught between two spheres, belonging nowhere. She has become the Mother Earth symbol of the Italian immigrant at the point when he, too, belongs nowhere. In frustration, she cries against the women who laugh at her. Finally, she feels that her only chance lies in open rebellion, because she identifies the "goody-goodies" with the old immigrant society; and her revolt is thus pitted against her husband, whose very virtues represent everything she hates. Her position is emphasized as she enters Hallstead's home with him. When she glances over the printed matter of the Sunday Magazine Section, she sees there what she thinks is America, the heterogeneous mixture of Grieg, Wagner, Irving Berlin, butterfly-girls, battle-axes, dragon ships, saxophones, and the Mazda Rhapsody. Forgione comments that

> civilization was crashing in Hallstead's snappy set! With a great leer it was toppling over. . . . Their desire for pep and snap had degenerated into civilized savagery. (p. 180)

This is the end of of the road for which Rose has turned her back on Oreste. She reflects that the river is between New Jersey and New York, and it is the division between the two sides of her life. After a "jazzy" evening with Hallstead, Rose looks across the river and she thinks of Oreste, "a veritable king out of the ancient days when their ancestors lived in the richness of a simple happiness!" (p. 189). Because she has human inconsistency, Jersey now seems more beautiful to her than the city had seemed from Oreste's window. Her question echoes that of all racially hyphenated immigrants' children, "Is there always a river between?" (p. 209).

She tries to run from her fate. When a man tries to seduce her into the world of vice, she has to run from him, too. The rebuffed procurer avenges her rejection by calling the police to track her down. Running still, she stumbles upon Demetrio, the father-figure of her abandoned past that now looms bigger than ever. Between them this is a second point of encounter, when the old and the "would-be-new" have a moment of truth. Rose and the blind old man stand still like statues, and then relent to understanding. His physical blindness had caused him to lose himself in the city, but his blighted insight has almost lost them all. And since she is the more democratic, New Worldly, and universal, life-generating woman, she starts to lead him home. Later on, from the city's side of the river, Rose sees Oreste's house in flames. The fire symbolizes the end of all the tortures that had existed in the house, which had stemmed from Demetrio's tormented mind and Oreste's stubborn will. At this moment, the rebel in Rose is conquered, and she bends herself to the "actualities of existence." She would stop running and give herself to "the river's motion." She would join the old Demetrio, ride over the dividing line, and welcome the old tradition. By being a good wife to Oreste she finds her way in a new world, and her change helps everyone in her immediate environment to survive.

VALENTI ANGELO (1897–)

The New World, in turn, becomes more and more receptive to newcomers, because it is more willing to give of itself. As a result, there are Italian-American writers who approach this compromise with grace and optimism, and they are willing to engage themselves almost entirely. In fiction this reaction is best revealed in the stories of Valenti Angelo, who, like Vaughn and Wordsworth, retreats into childhood in order to get closer to eternal truths. Angelo's creative extension is best illustrated in his own talents as author, painter, illustrator, and sculptor. A first-generation American, he came from his native Massarosa in Tuscany to live in a small town in California. Although his formal education was limited to two years of elementary school, he absorbed an eclectic knowledge of his environment from working in the fields, chemical industries, and rubber, glass, and steel mills. The libraries at night and the museums on Sundays supplied him with the educational materials for both his writing and his art work. After illustrating a book for the Grabhorn Press in 1926, he became established as a writer and illustrator. He has been most admired, however, for his illustrations in the folio edition of *Leaves of Grass.*

The delicate airiness of Angelo's illustrations harmonizes with the lyrical spirit of his writing. That he aims principally to entertain young readers accounts for the simplicity of his treatment. However, he deals with fundamental ideas, and he represents the experience and reaction of Italian immigrants as integral to the universal problems of all who have tried to become integrated in the New World. Of his books, *Golden Gate*[4] is the most typical of the theme of gradual adaptation by the immigrant of the customs and traditions of his former home life to his new environment. An autobiographical novel, the work is used by Angelo to describe the early years of the immigrant boy Nino as he settles in his new country and successfully assimilates while remembering his past.

In this book, Angelo shows his specific exuberance in the titles of the various chapters: "Voices Over the Sea," "Welcome to Liberty," "Nino Meets New Friends," "Invitation to a Party," "Celebration is Red, White and Blue." Nino, this more recent immigrant, remembers the land he has left; but he feels that there is only a little wall between him and the sea. He is not, however, devoid of all fear. As he compares the Statue of Liberty with the Trojan Horse, there swells in him the old Italian fear. But the fear is canceled by his regenerative imagination as he compares the tall buildings in New York with the pictures of his old fairy book. Later, as he progresses, he dramatizes his symbolic position; he wants to change his smock for American-styled trousers, and he is anxious to taste "wieners." We sense that he will never retain a *dolce far niente* method of walking in the afternoon in a displaced old-world village.

The sounds and smells of America engulf him. From the little house

4. Valenti Angelo, *Golden Gate,* A sequel to *Nino* (New York: The Viking Press, 1939).

in the California town he can hear the coyotes in the distance. As he listens, he is annoyed at the smell of kerosene, the olfactory symbol of that time in American economic industrial progress when the oil barons were revolutionizing the lighted hours of the American home. But as the boy Rocco absorbs his surroundings he must learn restraint; he finds out that it is not good to eat ten "wieners." Also, as he acquires sophistication in his new life, he does not forget his past. An excitement stirs memories of Italy in him, for example, when he discovers clay "just like Jacobo uses for making saints" (p. 97), and he takes the clay to his grandfather, who will use it with stones to build an oven for making bread. When the oven is ready, the family feels at home.

Getting along with the other boys at school is a parallel to the problem the old immigrants had on their jobs. There is the inevitable bullying by Red Dugan, who knows more English, and who is bigger in size. The scene depicting the small Nino tied to a tree and then heckled and struck by Red Dugan and Dizzy Smith is symbolic. Having first tied Nino's hands with wire and then the boy to a tree, the two older ones punch him while the sun beats down upon them. After they leave him, he asks an old question, "What have I done to make Red Dugan hate me so? Was it because I can't speak their language? I wish I knew" (p. 129). It is Lucy, whom he has worshiped, who finds him; she is the golden-haired girl in blue, the gentle figure of what is kind and compassionate in America. Lucy is a fresh drawing of Miss Reddle.[5]

Angelo projects this cultural problem in his narration of the incident with the hermit. Further ethnic extension is revealed when Father O'Brien tells of the difficulties of the early miners who had come before the churches were built; he is proud of how the miners built the churches with their own hands. Later, the workmen's struggles become one of the chief problems in the book. When Jim, one of the workmen, is lost in the shaft, his tragedy makes everyone aware of the constant presence of death. For the workmen, facing this kind of death is a parallel to the early immigrants' facing defeat. Now the subject is more universal, but the protagonist is still the underprivileged individual. Angelo reaches another cultural level when the Chinese Ha Young dies and Nino learns from his father that Buddha, the Chinese god, is "only another man's way in the search for truth."[6] The crux of his tale lies in his reflection that God is in all things that are good, but that there is another side to the story, the bad side, like the weeds that he and his father are pulling together.

Nature supplies further concrete symbols. Following the trials of the harsh winter, rounded out by a flood, the coming of spring, and the birth of his sister, new signs of stability and continuity in his home

5. See Lapolla, *The Grand Gennaro,* p. 140.
6. Angelo, *Golden Gate,* p. 216.

become apparent to Nino. "The earth seemed to palpitate as it spread new life over the soil that promised food in abundance" (p. 271). The book ends with the seed of happiness sprouting in the ground of hope.

In reaching for this promise of new life, the limping immigrant boy acquires further handicaps in Angelo's *Hill of Little Miracles.*[7] Ricco Santo is a boy of the "Latin Quarter" of San Francisco. Rinaldo Gambo, an aged remnant of the old culture, makes some shoes for Ricco and nails a prayer and a miraculous medal under the sole of the left one. The old man insists that this will help the boy's short leg to grow. While everyone prays for him, Ricco improves his walking by wearing the new shoes. At night he ties a rope around the ankle of his short leg, the rope supporting a hanging brick at the other end.

While minor incidents occur that are accepted as a matter of faith, tranquillity is pervasive among the people of the various ethnic groups in the "Quarter." Nina's baptism is celebrated with a feast attended by all the neighbors, including widow Finigan and Patrick O'Reilly, the neighborhood policeman. In the end it is Patrick who blesses them all in "his good-natured Irish brogue" and leaves them in happy spirits (p. 54). This neighborly feeling is further emphasized by the general compassion everyone feels for old Theresa, with her excessive flowers, Theresa whom people call "crazy" and for whom the Widow Finigan makes a big batch of vanilla snaps every week. Since everyone on Fisherman's Wharf knows everyone else, they keep a watch on old Theresa, who had once gone to the crest of the hill, waiting for her Leo, who had never returned from the sea.

The boys grow up in their usual "gangs." Danny O'Reilly leads the neighborhood boys against Mug Calahan's gang over an incident involving the disappearance of a piano case. Harmony reigns again when Uncle Luigi marries the Widow Finigan, but not without distress for little Ricco, whose painting has been effaced by old Jonah, the painting he intended as a wedding present. At the wedding, a dramatic symbol of the amalgamation of this society, Patrick O'Reilly tries to teach Mamma Santo the Irish jig, but his efforts are in vain. When the Italians dance the traditional tarentella, Danny comments, "The Eyetalians snitched that dance from the Irish" (p. 125), and much good-natured bantering follows. This harmony is a long step of progress from the original encounter of the first immigrants. The crucial moment comes when Ricco's gift is opened; he has painted the picture over from memory, another miracle of accomplishment. Then the general harmony is further extended by the boys—Tony, Danny, Mickey, Patsy, and Larry—who supply their own music with pots, pans, and a washtub.

In another incident of the book, Rinaldo makes a second pair of shoes for Ricco; as with the first pair, the left shoe of this one is too

7. Valenti Angelo, *Hill of Little Miracles* (New York: The Viking Press, Inc., 1942).

high. Prayer permeates the scene, and the larger meaning is reflected in smaller dimensions. The kitten, Sunshine, survives the burning of the club house, and Ricco does not believe that the survival is owing to the kitten's having nine lives. Life itself is a miracle. Although Angelo's concern is with struggles and handicaps, his subjects are constructively reaching everywhere. Optimism is the pervasive theme.

Assimilation now has made appreciable progress. In Angelo's *The Rooster Club*,[8] Nino has grown to Boy Scout age and is a full-fledged member of an organized environment. He "doubled-stepped along, trying to keep up with his older companions" (p. 16). He personifies the Italian-American immigrant (the adolescent stage of the ethnic) trying to acquire the American culture. His memories, however, stay with him, for as he walks with his companions at Mitchell Canyon, he notices that the woods are "just like the forest in Italy" (p. 23). He then learns his first lesson in American sportsmanship. After the boys seemingly have killed a snake, they pull straws for the keeper of the skin. When Nino wins the prize, he refuses it. While the boys argue, the wounded snake wriggles down a crevice.

Nino learns many things. He shares his life with the other boys; he learns to cook in camp-style with them; he sleeps in a sleeping bag; he joins in the group effort to ward off a family of skunks. Because the boys are not careful, their bacon is stolen by a raccoon, but they will not keep the captured animal because it is too small. Nino sees a fawn for the first time, and then a squirrel and a cotton-tailed rabbit. In this way he learns about many of the wild creatures of his adopted country. On the domestic level, when the boys protect Nino's dog from the belligerent O'Neil, he learns the democratic procedure for vanquishing a bully. With this knowledge, the once-alien boy has become integrated in the group.

The physical signs of integration are everywhere. Even at the bean field, the food is ham and eggs, preserved fruit, and toasted Italian bread. The boys compete with the Chinese students who pick beans to earn their tuition fees. It is inevitable that Wong, in the end, blinks his eyes, grins, and comments that the Rooster Club is "a nice bunch of fellows." Nino, "one of the boys," joins his companions to sing "For he's a jolly good fellow; that, nobody can deny" (p. 150).

At this point the maturing child-symbol represents the immigrant who has undergone some assimilation to his environment, although a great deal of growth lies ahead of him. Simultaneously, some of the associations in the ethnical background may have been transferred to new concepts of violence, as, for example, when the Camorra complex of Louis Forgione's *Men of Silence* is transmuted into the unwritten moral force of a Demetrio and his Sicilian cronies, a force that conflicts with the assimilation process in Rose in *The River Between*. Other

8. Valenti Angelo, *The Rooster Club* (New York: The Viking Press, Inc., 1944).

treatments of violence even go the way of the repetitious tales of pursuit that are so popular on the pulp level, as are, for example, the stories of Prosper Buranelli. But the more representative novels of violence treat chiefly those conflicts which are the leavening process for the mixed ingredients of assimilation. As Forgione implies, the immigrant must cross the river to the bank where the fire is consuming the past; the heat of that fire is the energy with which to bake the raw dough of integration.

Valenti Angelo's child is the promising material from which will come the man. Angelo leads his Nino (whom he calls Ricco in one book) to the point where he feels he is one with the other American boys. Passing through the *Golden Gate*, the boy overcomes his handicaps (aided by his traditionally bestowed faith) in the *Hill of Little Miracles*, and earns a membership in society in *The Rooster Club*. He anticipates maturity, but he will need to withdraw from his adolescent concepts to a plateau of introspection where he can reflect upon his identity.

5

REVULSION

According to Webster's Dictionary, revulsion is a sudden, violent change of feeling. Such a change occurred in Italian-American themes when the writers reached the plateau of introspection. This turnabout, however, had its model in the national literature. In their effort to make homes for themselves in a new environment, the pioneers of America expanded their narrations to include discussions of their political, social, and religious problems. Like other pioneers, the Italian-Americans reached the inevitable point in assimilation when, in the attempt to achieve identity, they experienced a sudden revulsion from the crudities of their new environment. Unlike the national pattern, however, the design in the development of this revulsion in the Italian-American writers went through two distinct, subsidiary phases. During the first phase these writers of fiction abandoned Italian-American themes; during the second phase, the younger group had a counter-revulsion, a return to the old sources, reiterating the Italian-American themes from a more highly developed integration with the native culture.

The first phase of the "revulsion" period is represented by such writers as Bernard DeVoto, Paul William Gallico, Frances Winwar (Francesca Vinciguerra), and Hamilton Basso. Although some of these writers were notably versatile in other fields, this group introduced in their fiction such literary themes as extended beyond the Italian-American life that former Italian-American writers had depicted. Bernard DeVoto and Frances Winwar, for example, are primarily nonfiction writers, but their novels are documents of the cultural change in imaginative themes. DeVoto, social historian, critic, and essayist, wrote mystery stories and tales of espionage and political intrigues. In *Mountain Time* (1917), his psychological realism is framed in the authentic American regionalism of a Western city far removed from any Eastern city's "Little Italy." Frances Winwar similarly develops a regional native-American treatment in *Gallows Hill* (1937), whose setting is seventeenth-century Massachusetts. One of her best novels is *The Eagle and the Rock* (1953), which is a slightly fictionalized narration of the life of Napoleon. The book may, in fact, be categorized as what Truman Capote calls nonfiction fiction. Miss Winwar turned eventually to the writing of biography, for which she has gained more distinction than for her novels.

BERNARD AUGUSTINE DEVOTO (1897–1955)

Bernard Augustine DeVoto was the first writer of Italian ancestry to become a major figure in American literature. As Orlan Sawey has written in his volume, *Bernard DeVoto*, in the *Twayne's United States Authors Series*, DeVoto's place in American letters needs a clearer definition. A versatile writer like DeVoto—novelist, historian, essayist, journalist, and critic—is bound to stir controversy among other critics. Like William Dean Howells, he was a commentator on American civilization in *Harper's* and other journals, and he is generally classified as a belletrist.

Born in Ogden, Utah, Bernard Augustine DeVoto was the son of Florian Bernard and Rhoda (Dye) DeVoto. His paternal grandfather was a Piedmontese cavalry officer, and his grandmother was of the Roman aristocracy. His mother's parents were Mormon pioneers. His childhood, DeVoto said, "oscillated between the poles of Rome and Deseret and found its own stability in adhering to neither." After attending both parochial and public schools in Ogden, he attended the University of Utah for one year and then went to Harvard in 1915. Between his junior and senior years he served two years as an infantry officer, and took his degree in 1920, along with Phi Beta Kappa membership. He and Helen Avis MacVivor were married in 1923, and he had his first novel published the following year. The DeVotos had two sons, Gordon King and Mark Bernard. To stabilize his income, he taught as Assistant Professor of English at Northwestern University from 1922 to 1927. At this time, also, he wrote articles for magazines, including *Mercury* and *Harper's*. In 1927, having sold two manuscripts, he went to Cape Cod for a vacation, where he continued to write, and, receiving $600 for a story in *The Saturday Evening Post,* he decided to resign from Northwestern to dedicate more of his time to writing. Two years later, in 1929, however, he took a position teaching English at Harvard University, where he stayed until 1936. He was the editor of *Saturday Review* between 1936 and 1938. Extending his talents in various directions, he taught several summers at the Breadloaf School of English; wrote novels; researched, edited, and evaluated the works of Mark Twain; worked as an editor of the *New England Quarterly*, (1942) and of *America in Books*, (1947–1948); was appointed member of the Advisory Board on National Books; edited the Easy Chair for *Harper's* (starting in 1935); and received honorary doctorates from Middlebury College (1937) and Kenyon College (1942). In 1947 he received the Pulitzer Prize in history for *Across the Wide Missouri*. After the publication of his final work, *The Easy Chair*, in 1955, he died on November 13. The book *Women and Children First* was posthumously published in 1956 under the pseudonym of Cady Hewes.

A prolific writer dedicated to realism, DeVoto pursued the facts in all his works; and, one of the best authorities on frontier history, he refused to romanticize the saga of the West. He was equally as merciless with the entrepreneurs who exploited the West as he was with the literary establishment of the East, which, he contended, has misrepresented the values of American democracy.

DeVoto connected the passing of the frontier to his theme of "dynamic equilibrium," the relation of creative production to historical fact. It is his idea that structures the basic premise of the present discussion of the Italian-American novel, with the logically ensuing thesis that American letters should reflect the writings of all the nation's representative groups. It was Bernard DeVoto who first used the phrase *the new frontier*. He wrote,

> Similarly, when told that the passing of the frontier has been a decisive change in the constituents of the equilibrium, a bystander's first comment is that a greater change shows in our current desire to solve questions politically rather than constitutionally. The new frontier is Washington, the new ethics are political, the new constituents are gangs—none of them wholly new but all of them stepped up by enormous induction.[1]

Although a balanced appraisal of DeVoto's works requires a separate volume, it is feasible to emphasize that he approaches all his work—the studies on Mark Twain, the histories, his critical tenets, and the novels—with the idea of the validity of the reality of the frontier. Despising sham, he attacks the status quo, and this attitude becomes the skeletal structure that he fleshes into the characters of his fictions. DeVoto's novels, therefore, are instruments for his explanation of the West and of the impact of the frontier on American civilization. Within this treatment is woven the latent idea of the influence of minority groups as an internal frontier of our national complex. His works of fiction include five novels; *The Crooked Mile* (1924); *The Chariot of Fire* (1926); *The House of Sun-Goes-Down* (1928); *We Accept with Pleasure* (1934); and *Mountain Time* (1947). Under the pseudonym of John Au-

1. Bernard DeVoto, "The Easy Chair," *Harpers* 176 (May 1938): 669–72.

gust, he wrote *Troubled Star* (1939); *Rain Before Seven* (1940); *Advanced Agent* (1942); and *The Woman in the Picture* (1944). His histories and books of essays include: *Mark Twain's America* (1932); *The World of Fiction* (1934); *Forays and Rebuttals* (1936); *Mark Twain in Eruption* (1940); *Minority Report* (1940); *Mark Twain at Work* (1942); *The Year of Decision, 1846* (1943); *The Literary Fallacy* (1944); *The Portable Mark Twain* (1946); *Across the Wide Missouri* (1947); *The Hour* (1951); *The Course of Empire* (1952); *The Journals of Lewis and Clark* (1953); *The Easy Chair* (1955). His numerous magazine articles are listed in *Four Portraits and One Subject: Bernard DeVoto* (Boston: Houghton Mifflin Company, 1963).

The Mystery Stories of John August

The novels of Bernard DeVoto are his imaginative application of the influence of the frontier concept on American institutions. Under the pseudonym of John August, however, DeVoto wrote four adventure stories that attracted popular readership. *Troubled Star* (1939), set on the campus of a Western university, is the story of Henry Zimmerman, the mayor of Benton, who is campaigning for the Senate. To win his election, Zimmerman must destroy the power of Stephen Bradford, the President of the University. Mysteriously, Bradford and his daughter, Susanna, receive threatening letters. For six years, Susanna has kept the secret of her marriage to and divorce from Dr. Alexander Cornish, and she is now in love with Dr. Gilson, who is an amatory opportunist. To secure his position at the University, Gilson is about to marry Susanna when she discovers that he has been writing the threatening letters. When he is found dead, suspicion points to various people, including Susanna. She is exonerated, however; she faces her situation maturely, and remarries her former husband. These people in the West are not romanticized; the spirit of raw competition is intensified by the isolation of the setting, which exposes fundamental human competition.

In *Rain Before Seven* (1940), DeVoto writes an espionage story, one of the first to be written during World War II. It has well-structured momentum, rapid pace, and uncluttered progression to exciting events. It does not, however, have the intricateness of *Advanced Agent* (1942), whose setting is in the United States. This book depicts the many entanglements of an investigation by federal agents of a wealthy Massachusetts man with Nazi prejudices. The plot involves two parallel developments that supply the kind of "cliff-hanger" episodic action that marks the successful adventure story.

In *The Woman in the Picture* (1944), DeVoto moves more ostensibly into his growing themes of American politics and ideology. Scott and Marta Warner lead a group of Americans to intercept Damon, a plotting American Fascist who is promoting Eugene Penfield to become President of the United States. Though the narration relies chiefly on action and episode, DeVoto's cerebral qualities manifest themselves in his rhetoric.

The Crooked Mile

With his first attested novel, Bernard DeVoto demonstrates his characterizing balance between his celebration of the West and his rejection of its degraders and exploiters. In *The Crooked Mile* he introduces us to the Abbey family, now in its third generation in the frontier town of Windsor. Gordon Abbey disdains the achievements of his deteriorated family, and through him the reader senses DeVoto's condemnation of the ruthless corporations that have raped the frontier.

The story, however, shows the continuity of a family's participation in the "Winning of the West," an engagement that reflects, not the pursuit of a dream, but the tenacious efforts to achieve economic independence. Gordon Abbey, defeated in his attempts for emancipation and power, returns to the old homestead and the old traditions.

The theme of the story is explicit in the metaphysical John Gale, a historian who has come to Windsor to write a history of the frontier. Using the device of sectional introductions and discussions of Gale's writings, DeVoto injects his philosophy of the frontier. Through Gale, DeVoto writes:

> There, till the end of time, Windsor woud have rested. The brief rebellion of Henry Clay Bryce, the farmers recrudescent, had shown that the frontier had constructed its own damnation. But Pemberton Abbey burrowed into the mountains and brought back his worthless copper salts, which in due time the Abbey Process transmuted into a new power. Here was the one chance that Windsor had ever had to break free. And Windsor, obeying the instinct of the Gadarene swine, had stampeded into the sea. Windsor, united, had crushed Pemberton's successors, the copper barons of the east. Windsor was doomed.[2]

The reader might assume that DeVoto is really pessimistic if he misconstrues the author's intention of justifying a myth only insofar as he believes it as a biography of the mind. In that case he would be making the error of which Gordon Abbey warns when he says to Hope Gale: "For you would have to pass judgment on your father's work. John Gale had only one idea . . . Last Days, the damnation of the human race, a damnation which either resulted from the landing of the Mayflower or was inherent in protoplasm when the original blobs coalesced in the sea" (p. 327). The conditional mood of this statement attests to DeVoto's belief in the validity of a realistic acceptance of the

2. Bernard DeVoto, *The Crooked Mile* (New York: Minton Balch & Company, 1924), pp. 309-10.

frontier experience and that the Puritan ethos in the West dispels romantic distortions, laying bare the facts, which will project operatively into the nation's future. Destruction lies in not facing reality: this is DeVoto's persistent, basic theme. A geographical frontier of courage and freedom is a myth that is dispelled by the compulsion of a man's necessity. This man, according to Gale, is a "hell-ridden calvinist" driven West from the East by economic pressure. The fact that Gale (DeVoto) believes that this frontiersman seeks land by which to repair his fortunes identifies the New England Puritan with every immigrant who has followed him. The reality of this pursuit is the dream of hope in the book DeVoto writes.

The Chariot of Fire

In his second novel, *The Chariot of Fire*, DeVoto explores the extremity of frustration that results from extended idealism as personified in the story of Ohio Boggs, a religious fanatic, who comes to believe that he is God. Boggs is really a drunkard who hypnotizes the unsophisticated Brashear family. The father and mother of the family persuade the reluctant daughters, Rose and Sue, to accept the mad "prophet," but they renounce him when he dies suddenly.

Several types of frontiersmen people the story: Jeff Brashear, the psychically resolved "best" log-roller, rail-splitter, roof-raiser, and timber-clearer, who seeks to expiate the sins of his drunkenness; Joe Stevens, who had been the type of riverman made legendary by Mark Twain; Thomas Chadbourne, the "infidel," who personifies the condemnation of the religious fanaticism of the camp meeting, which he calls an "orgy," the kind that led a pioneer family to burn their grandmother as a sacrifice. This extremity is what DeVoto is exposing as he writes:

> These people glorifying their creator had a striking similarity to the Winnebagoes in the dance before the warpath. They woo God by spasms and win him by delirium. They worship him by clattering their bones together in terror; they exalt him by rolling in agony through the mind.[3]

In emphasizing the frenzy of fanaticism by counterpointing the characters, DeVoto demonstrates dramatically his theories of the factual presentation of American civilization. The author shows through proletariat (alien) types the common man in search of the dream as Lias Whipple and his friend come to the settlement of Elam in search of religious freedom. DeVoto writes:

3. Bernard DeVoto, *The Chariot of Fire* (New York: The MacMillan Company, 1926), p. 47.

> They had the low forehead and the wide, stooped shoulders of the pioneer, the loose stride and the solemn mouth. They were of the race that was rising from the Mississippi to the Gulf to restore freedom and to bring the republic into being, to drive out the bootlicking Adams and to elevate Jackson the Liberator. They were the people; the New America. (p. 8)

The discovery the Americans make that the religion they seek is a cult is tantamount to the frontier-theory frenzy when it is exposed to the reality of the motives of the frontiersmen. DeVoto is aesthetically competent in using religious cults as symbols of the myth of the West. Familiar with the experience of the Mormons, he uses some of the aspects of the life of Joseph Smith as a frame for his Ohio Boggs. He succeeds in breathing life into the characters, to tell a story that engages the reader by its vigor and courage.

The House of Sun Goes Down

With his third book, *The House of Sun Goes Down*,[4] DeVoto continues his story of the Abbey family. When James Abbey leaves the South after the Civil War, he is intent on becoming a farmer dedicated to his own land. By his code, he suspects any enterprise that might enrich him. Ironically, when he goes into business with Herman Kleinfeld, his partner cheats him. Abbey leaves his son, Pemberton, little more than his dissatisfaction. Pemberton, however, educates himself to become a mining engineer. Reversing his father's pattern, he, in turn, extorts a million dollars from Mordecai Krug, because he discovers that Krug's title to a mine is defective. With further irony, Pemberton joins Herman Kleinfeld in a business to supply drinking water for Windsor. Kleinfeld, however, refuses to expand; so Pemberton sells his share to go into the smelting of low-grade ore by an original process. His business fails when his partner, the brother of his mistress, betrays him. Therefore, the third generation, represented by Pemberton Abbey, finds itself not much ahead of the first, except that now these Americans may apply themselves to the development of the land and fight off the growing syndicates that exploit it.

Although this story does not conform strictly to the conventions of the well-made novel, it is valid in its theme and characters. DeVoto's style does show an indulgence in some verbalization, a groping for the esoteric word; but the melodrama he sometimes excites demonstrates his theme about the frenzy and the cult of the mythical romanticizing of Western experience. The sharpness of detail he gives to his descriptions exemplifies DeVoto's fidelity to fact. Avoiding the puerile excita-

4. Bernard DeVoto, *The House of Sun Goes Down* (New York: The Macmillan Company, 1928).

tion of filling his pages with gunmen who rustle cattle, he disposes of the pulp version of the Western story and the stereotypes that have suppressed the truthful events of pioneering men and women. *The House of Sun Goes Down* is an authentic picture, graphically drawn by a selective reporter whose words are cinematic, stirring, and convincing.

We Accept With Pleasure

Bernard DeVoto's fourth novel, *We Accept With Pleasure,*[5] classifies him with Hemingway and Fitzgerald as a writer of the post-World War I era, although this book has neither the sentimentality nor the pessimism of the works of the other "lost generation" novelists. As Orlan Sawey points out, the book is DeVoto's definitive work in the combination of philosophy and characterization to communicate his theme that the exercise of the function of living that is required in the West is more sanative to American civilization than is the dilettante liberalism of the Brahmin establishment of the East.

We Accept With Pleasure is a long diagnostic novel covering sixteen months in the lives of a group of proper Bostonians in the post-World-War I period. The characters in the story are dramatized by a conflict in category: frontier historian John Gale's relatives in Boston, the Ewings and the Gales; the outsiders, Ted and Libby Grayson of the university world; and Ric Barreda, writer of popular plays and musicals. The catalyst that activates these characters is the dead Julian Gale, with whom the men had served and now remembered as a hero. The action of the story is counterpointed to the development of the Sacco-Vanzetti case and its ensuing events. The progression of this action is motivated by Loring Gale, who, having edited a radical journal in Chicago, returns East to edit and publish the letters of Julian Gale. From these letters, Loring learns that Julian was a fraud who had used his influence to become the commander of a squad, a sadist who had thrilled at the execution of an enlisted man. Loring, however, succumbs to the effete seduction of his surroundings, and popularizes his talents to journalism, procrastinating indefinitely his plans to write a real history on the importance of the West to American Civilization. His surrender is complete when he marries Beatrice Gale, whose amatory relationship he has shared with others, including the dead Julian.

The theme of the rejuvenation by the West of the destructive forces of the East is symbolized by Ted Grayson. Fired from his teaching post at Northwestern University because of his alleged pacifism, Ted has a nervous breakdown and goes East for treatment. Once more in

5. Bernard DeVoto, *We Accept With Pleasure* (Boston: Little Brown and Company, 1934).

control of himself, he sings the nostalgic songs of the West under the sponsorship of Ric Barreda; but his ballads are degraded into popular musical comedy by a composer, Misch Sachs, on another level of this theme in reverse. Ted informs Loring Gale that he had beaten Julian over the execution of the enlisted man, and that the memory of the incident had been a festering wound in Ted's mind. The chorus girl, Libby, who loves Ted, persuades him to return to teach history in the Midwest. DeVoto reiterates in this solution that the purity of the West is an escape from the suffocating debilitation of the East. To DeVoto the "lost generation" is made up of the intellectuals who succumb to the degradation of America's Eastern establishment. This theme extends to several levels of probabilities and political promises. Loring, Ric, and Jonathan make a speculative cult about what the synthetic Julian might have done if he had lived. DeVoto emphasizes that we tend to make idols of the dead even though they are egocentric and villainous, as long as they can be used as psychic crutches for our own failures and deceptions. These idols, like the characters of the writers of the lost generation, are false, destructive, and misrepresentative of the people of integrity who, like the real builders of the West and the dedicated workers (including other ethnics) of the East, are realistically pursuing the American Dream.

This novel is equal to many of the best in American literature, and it is one of the important books in which the author comments on our civilization. It is DeVoto's creative work that correlates with his thesis in *The Literary Fallacy* that our literature reflects more what the members of our critical coterie are saying to one another than what the writers are saying for the people. Although his psychological probings into the minds of his characters are sometimes contrived, in this book DeVoto reflects the same preference for the West that he shows in his histories, expecially in *Mark Twain's America* (1932). Since the portrayal of the Graysons is ostensibly autobiographical, DeVoto writes personally to the reader from the core of his belief. The book, therefore, has an intimate confessional sincerity and a profoundly human appeal.

Mountain Time

Mountain Time,[6] DeVoto's last and most popular novel, is one of the better works of fiction that followed World War II. Without the intricacy and profundity of *We Accept With Pleasure,* this book has freshness, vigor, psychological insight, intellectual stimulation, and historical authenticity. The story begins at Mercy Hospital in New York, where Cy Kinsman is the resident surgeon, and extends to a Twenty-third Street apartment where Josephine Caneday Willard lives with

6. Bernard DeVoto, *Mountain Time* (Boston: Little, Brown and Company, 1947.)

her husband, Sam, an unsuccessful writer, and their daughter, Deborah. Cy and Josephine have both come from the town of Custis, a mid-Western town. Cy has just returned from service in World War I, and, doggedly persisting in scientific accuracy in medical practice, he learns of the shortcomings of the head physician, Dr. Alexander McAllister, whom he worshiped in France and who is now the idolized physician of wealthy New York. Cy's bluntness and honesty do not endear him either to the head surgeon or to the other members of the hospital staff. McAllister, a ruthless, unethical butcher, knowing that Cy has discovered his duplicity and incompetence, forces the resident surgeon out of his position. Cy returns to Custis and becomes a garage mechanic and bootlegger, much to the unrestrained disgust of the townspeople, who have envisioned a greater future for the son of their revered Old Doc Kinsman. Cy's one saving interest is Josephine, who, psychologically disturbed from supporting her husband and tolerating his infidelities, has returned to Custis with her daughter. Treating Josephine's neurosis, Cy encourages her to sing, especially the Western religious ballads. When Sam Willard, who has finally written a successful novel and has become a literary poseur, visits her, she rejects him, and they are subsequently divorced. Eventually, after an idyllic interlude in the mountains which exhilarates them both, Cy and Josephine get married. Cy, compromising with reality, takes a position teaching physiology at the State University.

The theme of *Mountain Time* is consistent with DeVoto's belief that the sanative quality of the West under the influence of the simple virtues of the frontier is preferable to the sterility of the East, whose decadence is a potent force for the stagnation of intellectuals and their creative activity. At Mercy Hospital, for example, everyone is bedazzled by a supervisor who has obfuscated the exactness of medical science with poetic abstractions. Cy says of him that his work is a "fine poem," only it is twelve poems; that surgery with McAllister is "thinking with the fingers." Relentlessly, Cy insists that "if you guess that something's there and find it there, that was still a guess" (p. 9). Only his friend Pete respects Cy's unimpeachable "healing art." The theme of factual truth ramifies to the extenuating circumstances that distort that truth. Cy comments on Mac's lack of concern with the poor patients, that the supervisor extends himself only with the "colleagues" of wealth. When Cy and Pete discuss the supervisor's grandstanding performance of an operation on an ulcer and its diagnosis as "M'lignant or b'nign"—a reference that becomes a war trumpet—Cy asserts, "We've got to deliberate whether surgery is a science or an art" (p. 52). In the creative area, the dramatizing of success is the goal of another professed "little" man, Sam Willard, who would write a novel but says he cares nothing about success, which is a "false god." Josephine Willard knows, however, that Sam is absorbing Sherwood Anderson, aping him, and hoping for his success. DeVoto here is striking at the sham of poor writers who become structured into authors. Mac is equally structured at the hospital, where he makes certain that the audience sees skill at its utmost, the proved, inexplicable mastery that no one need challenge or explain. Cy, however, knows that something in Mac is dangerous. He himself will operate only on exhaustion of all attainable information, and not from an emotional belief in his own skill or the providential success that he calls the "Jesus factor." The belief is repeatedly counterpointed by the mediocre but expansive, dreaming Sam who, at one point, tells Josephine that she should find fulfillment in self-expression, after sarcastically asserting that everyone should "work for the great society" (p. 84). The conflicting tensions of the theme, therefore, are dramatized by DeVoto in a constant play over the application of intuitive belief or of empirical evidence. McAllister antagonizes Cy with his statement that "you can go through a hospital's records and find anything you want to look for . . . . You can prove that a saint's femur cured them or that they died because a hex slipped in the door. It's the good old game of library medicine" (p. 97). Eventually, when Mac's patient dies because his "thinking fingers" give a wrong diagnosis, it is Cy, who, knowing the truth, must leave. Ironically, Cy must eventually admit that the facts themselves are not the only truth. When he writes a recommendation for his friend Peter, he says, "Distrust everything till you can prove it, then trust it. But when you have to go ahead without knowing all you ought, go ahead on the basis you know. Disbelief has got to be your faith and you've got to dissect away illusion like old scar tissue, but if science is just skepticism working with care, it is also humility working in the awareness that the mystery is greater than the disbelief . . ." (p. 221). DeVoto would dissect away illusion like old scar tissue, as he would dissect the opaqueness, the effeteness of the Eastern establishment. Applied to the artist, this theme implies that "they had no right to make him feel ashamed" (p. 229). Applied to a smaller society like that in Custis, the dissection is the same in principle. The Brahmins of the East are the Canedays of Custis, "the office-holding caste, the Custis oligarchy" who pass judgment on Josephine's ambiguous relationship with Cy. The West, in toto, is a more lucid microscopic segment; men succeed on the frontier with the same mystique that moved Mercy Hospital. Gid Huntoon, the tycoon of Custis, is "not too fastidious in the ethics of turning a dollar." Running liquor with Art Ricco, too, is a way of surviving. It is only the old Puritan ethos that is transplanted to Custis that has the illusion of peace at the Congregational Church with its "Bible class, getting ready for Easter music, the voices of the Canadays, and the socials and the rummages and all the splendid sureness that this could never change" (p. 269).

There is, however, an underlying darkness, the blind opportunism common to humanity, which Mario Puzo, at a later date, analyzes so competently in *The Dark Arena.* In the clearing, Josephine says to Cy, "you're rotten with the disease of greatness, you had to be a great man, the greatest man of all. . . " (p. 273). This has an ironic twist when Cy is jailed on charges of drunkenness, charges that he knows are really that he has broken the "respectabilities of the ruling class." In the end, after their experience of "truth" on the mountain, Cy admits to Josephine that his rebellion is the summary of one great fear: "it was my father I was afraid of" (p. 304). DeVoto, therefore, admits that the aspiring artist is thwarted by the fear of those who have succeeded and who have organized themselves into a fixed establishment.

Mountain Time is a philosophic and aesthetic accomplishment. As an Italian-American writer, DeVoto in this book demonstrates his concern with the dedicated subordinate who eventually comes to terms with his circumstances through a compromise based on the discovery of self. The man on the frontier, geographical or within the culture, finds a constructive impetus in adjusting to the realities that discipline idealism: the West is to the East what the American dream is to the immigrant from the Old World. There are passages in *Mountain Time* that could show more than they tell for DeVoto; and sometimes his characters are scientifically clinical, especially his treatment of Josephine, but the writing in this book is generally sharp, convincing, and reportorially accurate. The atmospheric setting, especially in the mountain interlude, is truthful and stimulating, and the social attitudes of the time are authentically communicated. Bernard DeVoto's *Mountain Time* is a major contribution to the aesthetic performances within America's culture.

For a summary of the validity of DeVoto's fiction, it is feasible to refer again to Orlan Sawey's judgment, that these novels "have not received the place in literary history that they deserve."[7] These works of fiction have particular merit for their unity of theme concerning the verity of America's frontier influence and the healing quality of pioneer attitudes in contemporary society. DeVoto's dedication to his theme has disciplined his treatment of Mark Twain, his battle with the critics, the frame of reference of his histories, his litigation with the capitalistic exploiters of the West, and the cerebral techniques of his rhetoric in the novels. His works of fiction are major wellsprings of our literary mainstream.

FRANCES WINWAR (1900–)

Frances Winwar (Vinciguerra) is a widely acclaimed biographer, translator, and historian. Primarily disciplined by a sense of history, her works of fiction are classified as historical novels, a form that many

7. Orlan Sawey, *Bernard DeVoto*, Twayne's United States Authors Series (New York: Twayne Publishers, Inc., 1969), pp. 33–34.

readers hold suspect. As critics ascertain,[8] the accomplished writer of this genre has a fivefold problem: 1) the demonstration of a comprehensive understanding of his period, which entails intensive research, 2) a true plot that does more than replay history, 3) a plausible fictional character who transcends the known facts of history, a portrayal that may be challenged on every selected point, 4) the indifference of scholarly readers of both fiction and history, and 5) the equal indifference of the "best-seller" audience who cannot comprehend the relevance of historical reference. Capably undertaking this prodigious problem, Miss Winwar has succeeded in writing historical novels that the popular reading audience has accepted and that the academicians have approved. Demonstrating exhaustive documentation of material, Miss Winwar gives human significance to historical figures who come alive by the author's dramatic clarity and verbal simplicity in activating interior portraits.

Frances Winwar, the daughter of Domenico and Giovanna (Sciglio) Vinciguerra, was born in Taormina, Sicily, and was brought to the United States in 1907, where she was eventually naturalized in 1929. After one of her poems was published in a school magazine, she decided on a literary career, actively preparing herself by writing constantly during her high school, and, subsequently, her college years at Hunter College and Columbia University. In 1923 she was co-founder of the Leonardo da Vinci Art School in New York City. That same year the *Freeman* published her article on Giovanni Verga, and she attracted the attention of Lawrence Stallings, the literary editor of the *New York World*, who committed her to write weekly book reviews for the following two years. In 1925, she was married to Bernard D. N. Grebanier, Professor of English Literature at Brooklyn College. After the birth of their son, Francis, she dedicated herself to a literary career. She won the Atlantic nonfiction award in 1933 for *Poor Splendid Wings*, and went on a two-year lecture tour on Victorian literary figures. Having divorced Grebanier, she was married in 1943 to Richard Wilson Webb, a writer of fiction. She then devoted herself to writing novels.

Miss Winwar's books of fiction include: *The Ardent Flame* (1927), *The Golden Round* (1928), *Pagan Interval* (1929), *Gallows Hill* (1937), *The Sentimentalist* (1943), *The Eagle and the Rock* (1953), and *The Last Love of Camille* (1955). In addition to her works of fiction, she has written ten biographies, three histories, several translations, and an art monograph.[9] During all this production, she has continued making numerous contributions to national magazines and newspapers on historical and literary subjects.

The first book published under the pseudonym of Frances Winwar

8. See, for example, Peter S. Prescott, "Books," *Newsweek*, September 20, 1971, p. 93.
9. See Bibliography.

was *The Ardent Flame*[10] which, set in thirteenth-century Italy, is a romance about Francesca da Rimini. The familiar story, evoked with highly styled, luxuriant prose, has been well acclaimed by the critics. In her second book, *The Golden Round*,[11] Miss Winwar demonstrates her growing facility in handling plot. Also set in thirteenth-century Italy, this narrative elucidates the struggle between the Roman Catholic Church and the Court of Emperor Frederic. The conflict is dramatized through the characters of Pier, the Chancelor to the Emperor, and his wife, Candida, who had once been Frederic's mistress. As they plot to gain the throne, Pier and Candida augment the tension by supporting the Pope against the Emperor. With clear, uncomplicated narration and firmly honed dialogue, Miss Winwar tells a brisk and engaging story of the human intrigue that generates historical events. This book stirs the imagination and rewards the quest for information.

Her third novel, *Pagan Interval*,[12] is a more imaginative, aesthetic work, a decided interruption in her characteristic use of historical background. Unfreighted by familiar situations, the story is a weaving of fantasy in which the author dramatizes the designs of love and intrigue to plot the events. For this story, Miss Winwar uses an exotic setting on the Mediterranean island of Ennios, where myth and legend supply a background of various pagan traditions evoked from Greek, Roman, and Saracenic sources. On the island are marooned two Americans, Mark Blake, an archeologist, and the attractive Clarice Arlan, who has come to regain her health. The two become involved with the Baron von Schonhof, a collector, and events come to a climax during a providential earthquake.

In *Pagan Interval*, Miss Winwar manipulates competently the tenuous area of emotional analysis, relying on the use of pathos in human relationships and the salubrious effects of idyllic atmosphere. Her withdrawal from realistic dialogue into mythical reflection is appropriate to her departure here from the realistic episodes of the historical events that discipline her other novels. This book attests to her poetic disposition despite her preference for history.

In *Gallows Hill*,[13] for example, Miss Winwar is firmly entrenched once more in the frame of history. In this novel she treats of seventeenth-century Massachusetts, giving a frightening authentication to the sinister quality of the practice of witchcraft as the result of the misinterpretation of the most innocent external facts. Characters in whose integrity the author believes are subjected to brutal atrocities and ruthless executions. She re-creates the ethos and hysteria of the times, supplying a literary antecedent for more formally dramatic works like Arthur Miller's *The Crucible*.

10. Frances Winwar, *The Ardent Flame* (New York: The Century Company, 1927).
11. Frances Winwar, *The Golden Round* (New York and London: The Century Company, 1928).
12. Frances Winwar, *Pagan Interval* (Indianapolis: Bobbs-Merrill, 1929).
13. Frances Winwar, *Gallows Hill* (New York: Henry Holt & Co., 1937).

Frances Winwar's fifth novel, *The Sentimentalist,*[14] is another creation of imaginative plot that depends upon regional situation and stunting parochialism. Donald Harlan, a disbarred lawyer and disciple of Tammany, goes to the little town of Deerfield, Vermont, to bide his time while outliving his disgrace. He meets the beautiful Abbey Page, an eighteen-year-old girl of charm and integrity, whom he believes he can force to adulate him. As she matures in strength and capacity, he matches her growth with his corresponding degeneration. In a dramatic episode, Donald Harlan is ironically proclaimed a hero, while Abbey is falsely condemned as immoral. Lacking any positive qualities, even of an attractive villain, Harlan personifies the extreme degradation of the human being. Abbey suffers in the reader's judgment, because she is portrayed only externally in the situation. In another age saturated with the Puritan ethos, a Hester Prynne evolved with transcendental proportions as she was counterpointed by the intricately suffering Rev. Arthur Dimmesdale. Hawthorne, however, was psychologically interpreting a metaphysical age in American social history. On the other hand, Miss Winwar ostensibly creates an innocent Abbey Page as a victim not only of less analytical writing, but of an extroverted age that applauds cardboard images.

The Eagle and the Rock

When Miss Winwar uses familiar, historical figures, she is on firmer ground. Therefore, with *The Eagle and the Rock,*[15] which is usually classified as a romantic novel, the author tells a biographical story with discernment and insight. To narrate the events of Napoleon's life with the causal factors of his rise and fall risks the author's raking of a battlefield where every inch of ground has already been analyzed ad infinitum. Despite the danger, Miss Winwar succeeds in creating a tale in which event leads to event, and the motivations of the characters engender the dramatic progression of these events. She demonstrates what Francis Mauriac has claimed, that no novel "genuinely portrays the indetermination of human life as we know it." In *The Eagle and the Rock,* Miss Winwar shows that the maker of history is a human being and that events relate to the thoughts and actions of projected personality.

The point of the book is that the political and social changes in Europe at the first half of the nineteenth century were generated by revolution and then implemented through the machinery of war by the exercise of a traumatically obsessed personality with a fanatically applied will. Paradoxically, this will, in seeking to destroy established power, is blindly intent on monopolizing all power for itself. According to Miss Winwar, the psychological force behind this determination

14. Frances Winwar, *The Sentimentalist* (New York: Harper & Brothers, 1943).
15. Frances Winwar, *The Eagle and The Rock* (New York: Harper & Brothers, 1953).

lies in Napoleon's beginnings, in circumstances and deprivations that demand compensation. In the book, the thematic device of "the little Corporal's" success, therefore, is the machinery of personal ambition. Miss Winwar succeeds in creating a paradox. She incorporates this terrifying compulsion in a man who appeals to the reader's sympathy. We see Napoleon as an extension of ourselves, manipulating the mood and morals of environment to a justification of our own complaints. Once generated, the force of this manipulation changes the environment; as Pascal wrote, "The whole sea changes by a stone cast into it."

Using a circular device to narrate the events, Miss Winwar begins with Napoleon's death on St. Helena. The story is written in the first person by a disinterested bystander named Laurestan, who, the author tells us, was Napoleon's boyhood companion and lifelong friend. Using the reportorial technique of following the recollected journal of this witness, Miss Winwar evokes the detailed personal and familiar anecdotes of the protagonist's life. She gives a human dimension to the historically documented anecdotes, which are the authentic frame for her work. To the detailed accounts of Ludwig and Zweig, as well as to the memoirs of Madame Junot, Meneval, and Constant, the reader may add Miss Winwar's dimension of an engaged imagination, which ensures dramatic participation in the events. Although the author describes no battle scenes, she creates a compelling commentary on history and warfare as motivated by people acting on their own terms.

Miss Winwar explores the many ramifications of man's pursuit for power. This power, the extreme of fulfillment of life, is ironically related to man's death wish, she shows, as she states that all heroes are dead heroes and "It is death that confers immortality" (p. 3). In his death, Napoleon's face is beautiful, erased of his ambition, pride, and vainglory, and his features attest only his youth, the hero, the maker of republics, and the First Consul. Life has left only the "contraction of a bitter smile," which detail epitomizes the man's concepts.

One of Napoleon's beliefs, as reported by Victor Laurestan, was that institutions, like people, decay and die. Napoleon changes history because events have changed. When the rabble becomes an uncontrolled mob, government must have unity. For this reason, Napoleon calls the intimidated King Louis a *coglione*, a fool who has produced anarchy in place of trained soldiers. Not the time for "Plutarch's men," the murder of the Archbishops is only one example of the prevalence of assassins. It is Napoleon, "the lean Corsican, uncommunicative, ambitious strategist," who gets what he wants and never counts the cost, who knows the need of organized power. To him the enemies are the royalists, rebels, and traitors, while the "National Convention happened to be the government of France" (p. 70). Any means of acquiring the unity to strengthen this government is feasible. Love is part of these politics; if Josephine marries Bonaparte, Barras will have the command of the Army of Italy; and this move sets a policy. Policy, therefore, is a personal act. As Napoleon asks, "But can I have any being without glory and France? Which reduces my victories to a pedestal for the elevation of Napoleon Bonaparte—the great General, five-foot-five!" (p. 99).

The attainment of personal glory is also what Tallyrand seeks as he shrewdly plans a grand ball to display the intimacy of husband and wife, and calculates the influence of Citizen Bonaparte in the strategy of using her as intermediary with former aristocrats for honors and influence. To the victims of this rapacious power, the campaigners, by "combining poetry and historical imagination," interpret their conquests as liberation. Laurestan recalls the boy who, silent and lonely, had amused himself by throwing pebbles to make eddies in a rain puddle. Miss Winwar writes,

> "Nabuliune, the stone, the pool, the ocean of humanity of which myself, Josephine, the soldiers who were following him, the English who were pursuing, the Egyptians still ignorant of his coming were a part, together with the rest of mankind present and to come, whose lives would never be the same because of him." (p. 120)

Furthermore, Napoleon's practical device for making eddies was charlatanism. When the Moslems are almost convinced that they have converted Napoleon, he writes and confesses to his friend that a little masquerade does nobody any harm and may bring about good results. He says, "It was by becoming Italian that I won over the Italians" (p. 135). Thereafter he constantly refers to his statement, "C'est un peu charlatan, eh?" His flexibility of personality, however, changes into fixation, an obsessive belief in fate and destiny. It is his vision that creates the myths that become fact through the engineers of science; later, his generals call him the "wisdom of the nation." But he knows that it is victory that makes him a liberator instead of a traitor to the Revolution. He rationalizes the extravagances of the Tuilleries, saying that "Governments and rulers should speak to the eyes" (p. 168). He believes in setting up a dynasty because "The French like continuity." Underlying the externalization of his power, however, is his complete detachment from the human factor, which Miss Winwar communicates effectively in describing the corpses of the French soldiers on the field at Marengo where, at daybreak, the bodies are white mounds. The nation, meanwhile, delights in the splendor of the new monarch. Miss Winwar here injects the recurrent theme that only art can survive the ironic discrepancies and immoralities of politics. As Canova describes the statue he has sculpted of Napoleon, he warns that "death will change that beauty to a banquet for worms. Art will go on" (p. 217). One other constant remains—political intrigue, along with the manipulation of women within this network. Never far from personal motives, the affairs of states move on Napoleon's idée fixe over Josephine's barrenness. This obsession leads him to his marriage to Marie Louise and the international betrayal that ensues. Flattered by Murat, he gives the crown of the Kingdom of the Two Sicilies to his marshal and sister; and following the historical events, his final concern is, "To whom shall I leave all this?" (p. 314). The lust for power carries him on, whatever his stated reason; and Moscow and Waterloo follow. It is because he will not dishonor himself that he does not want to give Warsaw to the Czar. Napoleon says, "I am not a born king. A born king, no matter how often he runs away before the enemy, can always crawl back to his palace. But I cannot, being merely the child of fortune. The day I cease to be strong, the day I cease to be feared—that day I shall be lost" (p. 327). This basic insecurity, then, shapes him as much as do his swift battles and his supreme confidence in himself. In the end, the reader is convinced of the eddies in history that the personal psyche creates and of the play of this psyche, the play of person upon person. In Napoleon's defeat, Miss Winwar tells us in the words of Caulaincout, "He knows that everyone he trusted has played the part of Judas. He also knows that his wife and child are safe" (p. 341).

That Frances Winwar has the Italian-American frame of reference in her treatment of this familiar material is demonstrated in several ways. She introduces the Corsican to us as "Nabulune," the son of Letizia Ramolino, who scoffs at the legend of having given birth to Napoleon on tapestries. "Gesù, Giuseppe e Maria!" she cries as she affirms that penniless people like them have no tapestries. Miss Winwar retains the Italian names of Vittorino and Antommarchi; and she attests that the "u" was removed from the Italian *Buonaparte* in order to gallicize the name. Furthermore, the relics of civilization in Corsica are emphasized as Greek and Etruscan. At school, the French boys mock the boy Napoleon's "foreignness," so that he cries, "How I hate those French. . . . I'll make them pay for it some day" (p. 24). The author's attitude toward Italy is one of enthusiastic privilege. When Laurestan is to be sent to Italy to study Archeology, he considers it an unmerited reward. However, Miss Winwar is cautiously expository when she states that the Directoire looks upon the Italian expedition as a raid that would fill the state coffers and their individual pockets. She lets the reader infer that the exploitation of Italy is an example of similar exploitation in other situations. On personal terms, when she characterizes the notorious Josephine, Miss Winwar emphasizes the wantonness of the Creole when compared with the loyalty of Desdemona, implying the superiority of Venetian integrity. Likewise, in the course of the battle, the narrator exuberates when the men approach the peninsula; for example, "We had crossed the great Saint Bernard. We were in Italy!" (p. 176). An extension of this exhilaration fills Laurestan as he is in his study overlooking the Borghese gardens,

"Where the Roman swallows fly up in joyous clouds at twilight, the France of 1803 appears more remote than Aladdin's realm" (p. 183), providing an example of point of view. At the Emperor's court, again, the reference to Italianism is one of high esteem when Miss Winwar describes Prince Camillo, with whom the ladies are "rapturously co-quetting . . . this real, this blooded aristocrat, the head of the most illustrious Roman family that owned principalities, estates and an incomparable art museum" (p. 212). While such a reference might even be disregarded by a modern Italian, the Italian-American writer cites it with pride-in-inheritance. This kind of pride is manifested in the contempt with which Canova reacts to Pauline's innuendoes in the discussion over Napoleon's statue. He had refused to give the statue a face or Napoleon's name, admitting to Pauline that the man who took Venice is not to be forgiven. "Your hero is no hero to me. He raped the Queen of the Adriatic in his lust for conquest. He ravished Italy. Yet I must make him immortal with my art!" (p. 216). Napoleon, however, knows that he should do something for Italy. He says to Laurestan, "She must become an independent state and that independence must be my work." Miss Winwar credits him with the intention. She extends this credit to include a certain idealism in Napoleon, the kind of integrity with which he loves the patriotic Marie Walewski. The author writes, "Courted as she was, she could have sold her influence as Josephine had done and was still doing. But she had the rectitude of a Roman matron" (p. 250).

Miss Winwar accents Napoleon's most lyrical moments with references to his Italianism. At Campiegne, watching the rain from the window of the castle, he says, "*Il vento sbuffa, la pioggia precipitasi*" (p. 299). She shows that the Italian words forecast a menace, and she presses them with melancholy. Matured in an America that has isolated so much of the Italian culture, the author seems to retain in her subconscious an accumulation of specifics, demonstrated in the singing before Napoleon of Grassini, whose "rich contralto was nobly suited to those grand arias of the Italian school that wed spirit and sensuousness in their sublime slow melodic lines" (p. 301). Grassini's amorous touch is given so lightly that "only those who knew that for an ecstatic interval she had given herself to him with all the ardor of her Italian soul caught the message she conveyed." In this language, Miss Winwar has adapted Italian lyricism to American idiom and thus given an aesthetic finesse to phrases that might otherwise be suggestive, coarse, or ridiculous.

The themes of *The Eagle and the Rock* are effectually dramatized in other characters that shaped and affected Napoleon's destiny. The pursuit of power for personal gratification in all its predatory nuances, as history proves, is exaggerated in the extravagances and opportunistic intrigues of Josephine. Miss Winwar, however, magnifies the character of Josephine, emphasizing her suffering, fears, and frustrations, which stir the reader's pity. On the other hand, Marie Louise is a spatial entity of pliable and insensate material for the structure of political betrayal. The theme of betrayal is perhaps most pathetically dramatized in the machinations of Napoleon's own family, especially in the detailed portrayal of Pauline. Joseph, however, who is usually an absurd caricature, comes into focus with dignity and stature. Napoleon, as the protagonist, is more than a two-dimensional madman. The minutiae Miss Winwar supplies in conversations and scenes bring to life the driving passions of a frustrated human being hurtled on by the force of his psychological need, even though it infects a continent.

Frances Winwar, in writing this historical novel, has created an interior portrait with a fresh and new approach. In treating of Napoleon from the educated view of an Italian-American, she gives a solidity and verisimilitude to the characterization that is detached from either gallic chauvinism or Anglo-Saxon resentment. Furthermore, she witnesses to the characteristic Italian-American emphasis on the importance of the human factor in evaluating the personal strength or weakness of those who attempt to subdue the environment. Emphasizing personal motivation, Miss Winwar has given us familiar history heightened by the pace and progressive momentum of fiction. Into the story of an age of revolutionary action she has injected emotion and concrete details.

The Last Love of Camille

In her final novel, *The Last Love of Camille*,[16] Frances Winwar uses the concept of romanticism as her basic theme. To dramatize the principles of this spirit she fictionalizes the love affair of Franz Liszt and Delphine DePlessis, better known as the Lady of the Camellias. To the cursory reader, the narrative might seem to be a distortion of Franz Liszt's dedication to art and humanity; actually, the portrayal of the artist is symbolic of the permanence of real art as it resists the temporary vacuities and pressures of exaggerated passion and overextended emotion. Miss Winwar's book is tantamount to the sacrificial fires that blaze before the temple of the creative spirit, while the vigil light of the work of art endures. The author's rhetoric tells and shows the luxuriant extravagance of romanticism, and the reader responds emotionally to the impassioned style that engages him in identification with the attitudes of nineteenth-century Paris.

The story begins as Delphine, or Alphonsine Duplessis, is at the height of a career as the most adulated society prostitute in Paris. The granddaughter of an unfrocked priest, and the daughter of an inebriate, la Duplessis now has a circle of lovers, which includes the senile Prince Stacklyn—who confuses her with one of his former mistresses

16. Frances Winwar, *The Last Love of Camille* (London: Alven Redman, 1955).

—and the puerile, Don Quixotish Édouard, Vicomte de Perregaux, the only man who offers her marriage. Miss Winwar tells a convincing story of Alphonsine's dependence upon her lovers, details of which are drawn in scenes at the Boulevards, conversations at the Jockey Club, meetings at the Café de Paris, attendance at the concert halls, and the intimate developments in the dressing-room. Alphonsine falls in love with Franz Liszt, who adores her with an almost abstract passion, which he identifies with his art. Struggling with her tuberculosis and fighting the competition of Liszt's musical commitments, she impulsively marries Perregaux, a climactic event to which unavoidable reactions carry the story to its tragic end.

Romanticism as a fatal corruption is the dramatized idea of *The Last Love of Camille,* and Alphonsine Duplessis's consumptive disease is its pervading symbol. The concept of romanticism is older than its devotees, as Alphonsine is older than Edouard. The construct always has its poets, as in the novel it has Ronceval, who sees in the affair between the great Liszt and the "little waif of the Pont Neuf" a subject for a Murger romance and a theme for Balzac. He senses the witchcraft in the pianist's magnetism, a demonic super-expression of the delirium of Romanticism. Miss Winwar weaves this supernatural dimension into the chapter "A Midnight Fantasy" as she creates the mythical gargoyle as a remnant of the evil that had vanquished the revolutionaries. She says for the artist, "How else could the evil breed of critics remain in power, slashing the throat of innocent poets with their sharpened quills?" (p. 64). This same evil spirit, the author shows, has la Duplessis fall in love. In the courting of this love, Franz Liszt gives to Alphonsine Napoleon's jeweled apple tree, a symbol of art similar to that of the golden bird of Yeats, the artifice of eternity that will survive the natural lives of all the characters. Alphonsine is kept informed by her dressmaker, however, that there are live factors of concern, like the writer Madame d'Agoult, who has been Liszt's mistress and who has now written a book about their affair. Miss Winwar makes critical observation that there is nothing to worry about with brainy women. This is a thrust of realism that might be easily dismissed. Liszt himself has moments of reverting to his real situation, as he does in "The Love Theme." Examining the initials *E. de P.* on the gifts in Alphonsine's boudoir, he has a sudden revulsion, asking himself what he, the Hofkapellmeister at the Ducal Court of Weimar, the composer of church music, the honored guest of the most exalted houses, is doing here? But when she enters, he forgets his questions, and is exalted in his emotions. She, however, as the passion that consumes, cannot understand a whole spectrum of emotions. In her extremity she must have an apt symbol, and she and Franz decide upon the star over the churchyard of the Madeleine. From this extended point of lyricism, the underlying theme asserts itself to a resolution. As Alexei Stacklyn recounts his hashish dream of the doomed Annette, who had died at twenty-two, Delphine has a foreboding of her own death. This threat is doubled by the fear that she will lose Franz. When she admits this fear to Édouard, he assures her that Liszt is a man whose heart can not be held for long, because "Artists are like that" (p. 136). Against the doctor's orders to leave Paris for her health, she insists on waiting for the chance of Liszt's return. She has time, therefore, to think of death. Liszt, in his turn, agonizes with desire and rebellion over his obsession. Having identified her with the lady of the Campo Santo in Pisa, he romanticizes Delphine with the beauty of death. Miss Winwar explains that his whole generation had been overshadowed by death, and that they were all in love with Death and with her handmaids, violence and suffering. She writes:

> What were these works of the imagination but the recurrent nightmares of a generation conceived in darkness and terror on the cold slabs of a tomb? Romanticism was the name they gave to their spiritual rebellion, and he, Liszt, was one of its leaders. (p. 147)

The duality of the conflict between the spiritual and the physical nature of man found its apt monument for a continent in the romance between a great artist and "the great courtesan." Under her sentence of death, Camille is the romantic symbol supreme. Liszt, who, in turning from Marie d'Agoult, had gone to a professional courtesan to harden him against the "lure of women," finds that Camille is at heart an ingenuous girl with fierce pride of self-respect; thus he is an embodiment of another tenet of Romanticism, that men love "the lost woman with the heart of gold." The reality that ensues from this romantic concept is the fixed abode of the realm of the imagination. Liszt, the artist, creates from his identity with the dying Camille his composition the "Dance of Death," whose genesis is in the love theme inspired by her. Miss Winwar insists that Alphonsine was the restless spirit in the music of Liszt waiting for the incarnation of sound. When Alphonsine doubts Franz's love for her, she remembers that he has said, "The fount of art is eternal. You will last in me as long as my music, and my music is immortal because it springs from the eternal fount" (p. 177). Camille, therefore, is inextricably identified with Liszt's music, and she cannot escape Death. As Miss Winwar comments, "All living ends. All joys as all sorrows must die. That was the Romantic credo" (p. 241). It is appropriate, finally, that Alphonsine looks loveliest when she is dead. Her head, with its halo of point d'Alençon lace, looked like that of a pure young girl. In her hands she held a bouquet of camellias to which a crucifix "lent the grace of final indulgence" (p. 267). It is equally appropriate to interpret the Mephistophelian mockery in Liszt's Concerto in which the "crazed demonic cackle stormed the ear and stilled the heart, till calm returned to the spirit which, in the resignation of the piano, told of the fugacity of love and beauty and of all things born to die" (p. 270).

As an Italian-American writer, Frances Winwar has approached her conceptual theme with inherited Italian symbols. The chief symbol is Franz Liszt's compulsive obsession with the stone face at the Campo Santo of Pisa at the time when he begins to compose the "Dance of Death." He identifies this obsession with Alphonsine Duplessis, whom the reader pictures, in Miss Winwar's words, with Leonardo's women, those of the smiling-sad eyes and equivocal lips, and that angelic purity. It is a face of the Renaissance, "preserving its disturbing mystery." A literary reference is in Liszt's comment on Marie d'Agoult's book, asserting that the author has been his Beatrice and that "It is the Dantes who make the Beatrices!" (p. 148). There is enough implied criticism of the European male's arrogance here to conclude that an Italian-descended woman has the courage to write the statement only out of her American affirmation. Then, when Miss Winwar describes Liszt as having "clear blue pupils as darkly compelling as the hypnotic eyes of an Italian," she uses the comparison of an Italian-American woman. She drops phrases in Italian like *il velo greco,* which she says Liszt uses, that lack the ornateness of the Italian writer but have the insistent Italian terms that Italian-Americans use with American precision. Conceptually, also, Miss Winwar embodies an Italian-American attitude toward her story in her method of extolling art. While luxuriating linguistically to give by use of rhetoric the feeling of the period, Miss Winwar controls any extravagance of superimposing ethics upon the situation. She neither condemns nor approves; but she lifts human relations to aesthetic levels. This kind of treatment is significantly Italian-American, as is demonstrated from the academic arenas portrayed by Bernard DeVoto to the social explorations of the writers of the sixties. The most significant factor, however, is in the question that Miss Winwar asks, "But if the beloved dies, does all love die?" (p. 270).

The Last Love of Camille is suitably the definitive novel by Frances Winwar. It is a book of proper scope enhanced by visionary rhetoric. While the author writes biographical history better in *The Eagle and the Rock,* in this novel she shows her most assured talent with the conventions of fiction in treating a familiar situation illumined by unusual people. Whereas she has narrated much of the detail in her previous novels, in this book she has the characters act out more of the drama. The language communicates both the time and the setting, and Miss Winwar's use of irony is subtle and uncontrived. That men should believe that this courtesan is the embodiment of innocence and integrity, and that such a woman should fall in love with complete dedication are two assumptions that are made simply plausible and aesthetically acceptable. Among other things, Miss Winwar is saying to the reader that women have levels of virtue that exceed sexual predicaments in their historical environments. The plausibility of Camille's passion depends, however, on the reader's understanding of Miss Winwar's structure, an analysis of the theory of the art of literature itself. As a symbol of Romanticism, the author has in Camille an ideal image of a consuming, destructive, and distorted concept that carries within itself the seeds of its own destruction. Only great art such as that embodied in Liszt—although he was inspired by the ideals of Romanticism—can survive the death-dealing consumptiveness of its exaggerations. As Edmund Wilson, exploring the concept in *Axel's Castle*, points out, the inner direction of Romanticism is suicidal. It evaporates when it comes in contact with reality, just as la Duplessis, who has extorted and distorted love, dies when she, with a diseased body, cannot survive real emotion. With poetic insight and historic immediacy, Miss Winwar has romanticized Romanticism.

PAUL WILLIAM GALLICO (1897–)

Paul William Gallico is perhaps the most representative Italian-American writer of fiction who does not treat of the immediate problems of adjustment confronting the immigrant, but rather transforms the themes to recognizable and already familiar American materials. A second-generation American, Gallico is the son of Paolo Gallico, the Italian concert pianist. Paul was born in New York City, where he grew up and went to school. He earned a B.S. degree at Columbia University in 1921; then he studied medicine for a short while, and finally decided upon a literary career. With his years of experience as a sports writer and editor for the *New York Daily News*, Gallico has written many stories which deal with sports. He speaks not only of an ethnic group, but of the whole "American world." He writes of the years when "It was an era, when spending was wild, and emotions were geared to a dizzy pitch, to which only the sensational brought appeasement" (Farewell to Sports).[17] The range of his subjects is revealed in some of his titles: *Farewell to Sports, Golf is a Friendly Game, Lou Gehrig: Pride of the Yankees,* and such stories as "Oh Them Golden Mittens" and "Quick and Dirty." The unassuming individual who would lead a more exciting life is his constant theme, a theme that reaches romantic proportions in *Adventures of Hiram Holiday* (1939) and its sequel, *The Secret Front* (1940). Although he has enjoyed popularity with such titles as *Mrs. 'Arris Goes to Paris, The Hurricane Story,* and *Mrs. 'Arris Goes to New York,* he is more aesthetically representative in *The Snow Goose* and *The Small Miracle.* His internationally popular *The Snow Goose* is a definitive completion of the broad theme of men in conflict,

17. Mentioned in Olga Peragallo, *Italian-American Authors and Their Contributions to American Literature* (New York: S. F. Vanni, 1949), p. 113.

with its treatment of the rescue at Dunkirk. In *The Small Miracle*[18] the author lifts the Italian-American subject away from "Little Italy" to the level of a universal theme.

The Small Miracle is a story that makes poetic the period of revulsion in the development of Italian-American fiction. Its subject might have been treated by a member of any ethnic group traveling in Italy, but its distinction as a product of an Italian-American lies in its lack of either groundless condescension or gratuitous sentimentality. The author handles his subject with an indigenous understanding, and this is a new note in the American's writing of things Italian. Gallico has none of the culture-exploration of James, nor has he the irreverence of Mark Twain, or the irresponsibility of lesser Twains. There is a subconscious racial identity as he describes the orphan:

> The combination of Pepino's dark lustrous eyes and Violetta's smile was so harmonious that people favoured them and they were able not only to earn enough for their keep but, aided and advised by Father Damico, the priest of their parish, to save a little as well. (p. 17)

The theme concerns itself again with the isolated individual in conflict with the world. Gallico writes,

> Since the mountainside was a rough world for a small boy, he was sometimes beaten or injured and Violetta would gently nuzzle his bruises. When there was joy in his heart, he shouted songs into her waving ears; when he was lonely and hurt, he could lean his head against her soft, warm flank and cry out his tears. (p. 18)

Pepino's belief in St. Francis is as natural to him as breathing. Furthermore, there is neither quibbling nor apology for his faith on the part of the author.

> And besides, there was a precedent. Giani, his friend, the son of Niccolo, the stableman, had taken his sick kitten into the crypt and asked St. Francis to heal her, and the cat had got well—at least half well, anyway, for her hind legs still dragged a little; but at least she had not died. (pp. 22–23)

The "precedent" is a symbol of the Italian's acceptance of his religious beliefs, and acceptance that in the Italian-American became not a factor of belligerence, but an innocent indifference to anything or anyone that questions his religion, which is a part of his Italianism. In his lack of apology for his religion, the Italian-American has con-

18. Paul Gallico, *The Small Miracle* (Garden City, New York: Doubleday and Company, 1952).

tributed to religious understanding in the nation from a cultural rather than from a racial area. Like Pepino, he usually does not question the validity of his religion, nor does he expect others to do so. The reader senses this in Gallico's treatment of Pepino.

Pepino's putting his religious beliefs into practice has been encouraged by his former G.I. friend, Francis Xavier O'Halloran, who taught him, "If you want to get ahead in this world, kid, don't never take no for an answer. Get it?" (p. 24). Pepino's character, forged out of the sources of faith, thus gains its practicality from a member of his religion who has been molded in the American school. Cultural relationship at this point has reached beyond the malice bred by racial tensions and arrived at personal understanding.

The pathos of the human situation in Gallico's treatment is revealed when he writes,

> Never had any small boy looked quite so infinitesimal and forlorn as Pepino standing in the boundless and almost deserted . . . St. Peter's Square. Everything towered over him—the massive dome of St. Peter's, the obelisk of Caligula, the Bernini colonnades. Everything contrived to make him look pinched and miserable in his bare feet, torn trousers, and ragged jacket. (p. 37)

In these words there is a casual assumption of a long tradition of culture, so much a part of the marrow of the bone in the writer's hand that there is no embarrassment in the presentation of fear, humility, or poverty. He is not merely a detached observer, a writer on an "Italian holiday," but one who can now identify himself with Pepino. Thus, while Gallico has not chosen to write about an Italian immigrant boy in America, in turning away from such a subject he ends squarely by identifying himself with the boy's ethnical roots. He is equally at home in describing Pepino's poverty as he is in quoting Pepino's question to the Swiss guard, "Please, will you take me to see the Pope? I wish to speak to him about my donkey Violetta, who is very ill and may die unless the Pope will help me" (p. 37).

The device of using the flowers to bring about the "small miracle" is an externalization of the springs of the universal human heart. A Swiss guard may recall Luzern; the Pope remembers the Alban Hills; a boy stricken by the plight of his only friend, an animal, provides the one common key to the crypt of St. Francis. The legacy of the Saint, which they all, from Bishop to workman, find, is, as the Bishop says, "Poverty, love, faith. This is his bequest to all of us" (p. 57).

The bequest of Italian themes to the literary types in the American scene, therefore, can be more easily understood after considering Gallico's universal application of these themes. An author's honest and unbiased treatment of ordinary characters has been the proposed method of most American novelists; but with the Italian-American writers the treatment persists in a stated sympathetic attitude toward the downtrodden, a seeking to find an adjustment that will serve as an achievement for the struggling individual. It becomes more and more obvious that the environment need not be the result of material determinism; it may well be the structured accomplishment of the degree of willed effort on the part of the individual. Therefore, while these writers contribute to the rise of the "common man" theme, their attitude either reveals or implies, not a naturalistic pessimism, but an optimism based on faith in the human being.

HAMILTON BASSO (1904–1964)

It is to be remembered that Bernard DeVoto was preoccupied in *The Literary Fallacy* (1944) with his quarrel with the American writers of the 1920s, of whom he wrote,

> Never in any country or age had writers so misrepresented their culture, or been so unanimously wrong. Never had they been so completely separated from the experiences that alone give life and validity to literature. (p. 167)

In my attempt to amalgamate the parts of this internal separatism described by DeVoto, Hamilton Basso represents the Italian-American writer who contributes to the completion of a comprehensive American character.

The son of Dominick and Louise (Calamari) Basso, Hamilton was born in New Orleans, the birthplace of both his parents. A third-generation American, he spent a normal boyhood and attended the public school in his native city. After nearly completing four years at Tulane University, he launched into his literary career as a reporter. He has since become one of the nation's most distinguished writers of the South, but the national growth of America as an entity has been his consistent underlying theme. In *Mainstream* (1943), Basso writes that the men who played a prominent part in our political and economic pattern are "tributaries" that swell the mainstream of today's America. He contends that the making of an American culture has been a vast and complicated process, and that many springs flow into the mainstream. Furthermore, to make an adequate analysis of that stream, the other springs must be explored.

Days Before Lent

Basso makes in his works an exploration of those springs which flow into our general cultural stream. In *Days Before Lent,*[19] he provides an example not only of a balancing force in his presentation of the South,

19. Hamilton Basso, *Days Before Lent* (New York: Charles Scribner's Sons, 1939).

but of the amplifying details in the treatment of the individual who seeks completion despite the pressures of his society. For this novel he received, in 1939, the Southern Author's Award, which is given yearly for the most distinguished book on a Southern subject by a Southern author. His theme concerns the hero, Dr. Jason Kent, a bacteriologist, whose conflict torments him. He must decide whether to do research in India or to work at home. His involvement with the pathetic ex-pugilist Joe Piavi, a criminal victim of insensitive exploiters, offers him the opportunity to withdraw into himself, through which he finds his own identity. He finally decides to improve the environmental conditions that have created the Piavis of the world.

His "alien" is in reverse, but his theme is particularly recognizable as he writes,

> Jason was alien to them at first, his reddish hair and blue-gray eyes were strange in their brunette world, but that was soon forgotten.[20]

Jason Kent is, therefore, another Pascal D'Angelo,[21] but writing with a title,

> but behind the title, behind the exact impersonal language, would lie the whole tangled story of his life, Jason Kent, M.D., his life and many others, with notes and comments on the life of his time.[22]

This new extension of relating his life to that of others as part of the "life of his time" is what is important.

The young doctor's relationship with his peers is sound; in fact, Dr. Hunt wants Jason to accompany him on the research project in India, but Jason senses that the others have learned to like him because he has been a "joke-maker." When Hunt contends that there has been something unscientific in his own acceptance of Freud for having effected cures, that so had Dubois, Rasputin, and Cagliostro, Jason answers, "So could Marie Laveau." When the German Doctor Muller asks him who Marie Laveau was, Jason enlightens him with, "She was a voo-doo doctor who thrived here in New Orleans not so very long ago" (p. 11). The seriously professional Muller does not appreciate his humor.

Hunt, whose "youth had been relatively normal," is attracted by Jason's irregular contacts with streets and wharves. Basso explains that "Jason came from a part of society of which Hunt knew little and he liked to hear Jason tell of it: a world inhabited by priests and prizefighters and peddlars and just people who worked with their hands" (p.

20. *Ibid.*, p. 4.
21. See Pascal D'Angelo, *Son of Italy*.
22. Basso, *Days Before Lent*, p. 4.

17). This world is represented in the book by Father Victor Carducci, Jason's constant friend, and the ex-prizefighter, Joe Piavi, his equally constant burden.

Symbolically, Jason is a spring to the mainstream where Hunt resides. He has difficulty in telling Hunt that he hopes to be married and is thinking of taking a remunerative position with a concern that manufactures insecticides. He wants to tell Hunt, but he cannot. Basso writes:

> He knew that Hunt, without saying anything, would in some way indicate, possibly by screwing up his eye, that that was the end of that. In the secret part of himself, behind the barbed-wire entanglements that kept out the world, he was proud he had won Hunt's respect. He was anxious to keep it, he was not brave enough to face Hunt's scorn—understanding, perhaps even affection, but scorn: an outer reflection of the rankling unadmitted scorn he felt for himself. (p. 23)

As he explains to Susanna, Jason has inherited from his father the doctrine of the "surprisables" (the individuals) as opposed to the "unsurprisables" (the automatons). In his exhortation we sense his isolation, and he himself has admitted that the isolation is inherited. He believes that American society is made up of people who, like Pavlov's dogs, are conditioned to any given situation, growing up in cages—suburbanite cages, Maine-in-the-summer-Florida-in-the winter cages, all ending up like buttons stamped by the same machine. "They live alike, dress alike, play alike, hope alike, fear alike and, above all, they think alike" (p. 27).

Despite this explanation, Jason's attitude is not a cynical one. Just as science is never cynical, neither is he; for, he says, "every time I'm about ready to give in, I meet one of the surprisables" (p. 28). They're to be found everywhere. He is certain, he continues, that "more people escape from cages than we think. For every one you meet, there must be thousands you don't meet. That's what gives you hope."

He admits that most of the "surprisables" he has known have been among the poor: Victor's grandmother, Mr. Schmidt in the bakery, old Piavi, and the Negro stevedores on the wharves. This does not mean that the poor do not live in cages. He says,

> The stimuli presented to them by life, however, are of greater variety and are administered at very irregular intervals. Their conditioning has not been so severe. They are more free, less afflicted by what Pavlov calls "inhibition by extinction." (p. 28)

The "surprisables," therefore, are wells of springs that swell the mainstream of American culture.

Speaking of his childhood, Jason recalls having read books about poor neighborhoods, "with all the people rather foul and degraded, and my own recollections don't fit into the picture at all" (p. 39). He admits there were smells, and that some people didn't mince words, "but the foulness and degradation simply were not there." In this reiteration, Basso emphasizes DeVoto's theory.

Later, when the drug-maddened ex-prizefighter Joe Piavi finally turns on the source of his degradation, Nick Weinstein, his manager, who has exploited him beyond his means, Jason tries to understand his own involvement with Joe. Basso writes,

> He only knew, with the terrifying urgency of murder pressing against every moment, that he must get to him as quickly as possible. Murderer. Pug, muggle-head, bum—now murderer. The blood-stained word made no difference. It strengthened, rather, the bond between them. The exact nature of their relationship was beyond description, but at its core lay a blind feeling on Jason's part, pulsing along the heart-beats of his blood, that Joe's life, Joe's destiny, was fatefully bound to his own. (p. 260).

He cannot get to the police, however, before Weinstein's mob do the inevitable. Nick's trigger-men are efficient. Meanwhile, arguing with the police and bolting through the Mardi Gras crowds (the unsurprisables) have proved too much. Joe becomes Jason's alter-ego in the final conflict. Jason suffers for the insensible Joe, as he realizes that the murderer is being hunted down. Joe, therefore, becomes the symbol of every man who is an unfortunate.

Basso explains that the symbolic Joe, the individual, albeit unfortunate, has welded, by his act of murder

> this whole scattered Mardi Gras crowd into a oneness it would not have otherwise had. By murder, and by his escape making it necessary for the police to hunt for him, he had forged a swarming collection of individuals into closer and more vital unity of the mass: vesting it with an awareness, even in its holiday mood, of life and death. (p. 281)

Basso shows in several ways that men need a unifying faith by which to live, as in the cases of Victor, who goes through a crisis successfully, and of Tyrrell, who defeated by the tub-thumping and propaganda of the day, commits suicide. When Jason finally sees the murdered bodies of Joe and Danny, his friend, he realizes that "some obscure justice had been done" (p. 346).

Alone in his room, he understands, at last, the nature of his bond with Joe. He remembers that he had once lived with his father in a world of people, "the living world of human beings. It was this world he cherished most, the world of man as against the world of ideas, the open world of humanity as against the world of the laboratory" (p. 351). This, then, was the world where he wanted to do his work. While

Joe was alive, that world was not entirely gone. It is true that he felt no real affection for the dead man; for Jason, Joe's value and importance lies in his symbol—

> a symbol of the old street, and all those who lived in it, and that swarming world of smell and sound of which his father had been so integral a part. . . . Therein lay the simple happiness and splendor of his life. He was fond of his kind and lived with them and the world of his own making was larger, and far warmer, than the greater world of wealth, or success, or fame. (p. 352)

The author makes it clear that Jason does not wish to recapture the past; he seeks to lead no life but his own. His alter-ego remains now with Victor, the other live member of the group of three old friends. The universality of the theme is revealed in Basso's description of the regenerated priest, who now felt

> as if he were walking in the midst of all humanity. All the children of Christ, All the sons of God. Yet in his turmoil, he was deeply conscious of his own oneness, his own agonized separateness. The one and the many. The individual and the multitude. The man and the mass. (p. 237)

The paradox is the same as that which permeates so much of modern writing, but with Basso, as with others in this group, it keeps its equilibrium through optimism.

In *Days Before Lent,* therefore, the author presents an individual who successfully finds a place in his environment. Jason Kent, in finding such a place, revives the tenets of his father, who had cherished the world of man against the world of ideas. By *world of ideas* Basso means the world as it lies, in little and only potentially, in a laboratory, as compared with the arena of humanity. This concept is similar to that of the alien pitted against a locked structure of social values. In a parallel transmutation, the alien has become the universal individual in conflict with an established idea in society. Basso's novel, in which he turns away from Italian-American life as a setting, still contains the struggles of the immigrant scene. What was an alien culture to the immigrant has now become the fixed laboratory (or any confined and exclusive area of life), which the individual rejects in favor of the broader environment of humanity.

The View From Pompey's Head

The structure that Basso rejects he calls "Shintoism" in his novel *The View From Pompey's Head.*[23] In this popular book he is more specific

23. Hamilton Basso, *The View From Pompey's Head* (Garden City, N.Y.: Doubleday & Company, Inc., 1954).

in delineating an established culture as a form of ancestor worship. The quality of the progenitors is not always important; the mark of the gods at the shrine is their antiquity. The "first" families that founded Pompey's Head retained for themselves all the keys to the doors of their temples, and these keys were not readily accessible to newcomers.

Anson Page, the protagonist of *The View From Pompey's Head,* left his native Southern city after his father, a lawyer, had won a token victory in court for a Negro handyman who had been assaulted by Mr. Pettibone, a local "Shintoist." Fifteen years later, as the younger partner of a well-known New York law firm, young Page is sent back to Pompey's Head to investigate the charges made by the unpopular wife of Garvin Wales, the nationally famous novelist of the South. Mrs. Wales claims that her husband's former agent, Phillip Greene, had embezzled twenty thousand dollars of the novelist's income at regular intervals over a set period of time. Page welcomes the assignment because he has always felt a stranger in New York and is anxious to see his old home again. Back in Pompey's Head, he visits his former friends, particularly Dinah Blackford, his former "girl," whom his wife, Meg, has advised him to "get out of his system." Interwoven with the threads of the attempts to get the interview with Garvin Wales are the details of Page's finally possessing Dinah, an act that symbolizes his conquest of his obsessions about the South. By means of flashbacks, Basso gives the details of Page's background to the point of his going for his interview with Wales. Page learns that Wales has approved of the payments of the money to Greene, who, in turn, had made checks to a certain Anna Jones. Wales admits that Anna Jones, an octoroon, was his mother, whom he had paid to keep her identity secret from everyone, including his wife. This admission dramatizes Basso's theme that everyone is striving equally to create his own ancestral shrines and that the individual must confront and conquer his past in order to find his identity.

Much that Basso writes in this book is specific about the growth of Italian-American fiction. He uses many symbols of the struggle of the alien as the "outsider" of an accepted culture. The novel is one of the revulsion phase because the materials are turned away from actual Italian-American life, but the old themes are there.

The author introduces Anson Page to the reader as a "slender, dark-haired man with serious brown eyes and a grave expression in his thin, well moulded face" (p. 8), distinctly a Latin type. Then, not only is he different from the in-group American type of culture hero, but Page is also an outsider of his firm. Basso writes,

> Mr. Barlowe the head of the firm was St. Mark's, Princeton, and Far Hills, New Jersey, and Anson could never forget that he was Montague High, South Carolina State, and Pompey's Head. . . . The distance that separated him from Mr. Barlowe might have

> been less had he, too, been a bright, well-connected boy from one of the leading law schools, but he had come into the office under circumstances so peculiar that he had been as strange as a savage in church. (p. 23)

In examining his past in Pompey's Head, Page realizes that he has no ancestors there. Although his mother had been one of the Lawrences of the state, his father had been a New Hampshire man,

> at a time when all Northern men were lumped together as carpetbaggers, and his portrait would never be hung on the walls of the Pompey's Head Historical Museum. (p. 42)

This isolation has many physical symbols for him. He remembers an Italian restaurant in New York, for example—a place with "homesick murals." Basso writes,

> These little restaurants always seemed very insubstantial to him, tied to New York by the slenderest kind of mooring, and he never went into one without thinking that, if left to the pull of its own particular gravity, it would rise above the city and float back to whatever Italian town or village it was that the proprietor had come from. (p. 127)

The portrait, which is a secondary presentation of a real man, and the restaurant, which is a substitute for the refuge of a man's own home environment—both of these outward projections are attempts to seek the proper place, the culture to which a man "belongs."

Basso shows that it is quite normal for any man, not only Page, but also Wales—to all outward appearances a national success—to proceed from the feeling of being an "outsider" to that of being simply inferior. Furthermore, he points out, all inferiority feelings are alike. To illustrate this point he says that the man from the South (place symbol of alien environment) is always treated with condescension by a Northerner. He writes,

> Once the South came into a conversation and it was learned or remembered that you were from that part of the country, people always tried to say something agreeable. It was a commendable display of good manners, but it didn't always work. Although nobody intended to be superior, it invariably tended to sound that way, and, much as you didn't want to get your back up, you found yourself asking what it was that they had to be superior about. (p. 143)

Because being out of one's element sometimes causes one to be treated as inferior, the isolated person attempts to return to his own "proper place." Hence, while Basso and the other writers of this group have turned their backs on specific Italian-American subjects, they find that in becoming involved with broader materials there is a latent pull for them to return to their traditional subjects. The return, however, is not easy. When Anson Page listens to all the local chatter at the party given in his honor, he wonders (and we feel Basso wondering with him) if "this was what they meant when they say that you can't go home again." While he has been away, he has changed, and Mulberry (the plantation of the Blackford's, the shrine) has also changed. He continues to observe,

> In the old days at Mulberry the talk used to be about purple finches and cedar waxwings and what fish were running in the river and whether the ducks and quail were coming back, and now the talk was about targets and morality and whether we should use the bomb. He supposed it was inevitable. (p. 349)

It is clear, then, from how he displaces his hero, that the author, though he emphasizes the need to go back, believes that this going back is a difficult thing to do. Without the agony and wistfulness of Thomas Wolfe, Basso sets his protagonist in motion, an action which follows the familiar pattern—from conflict, through isolation, to assimilation. Anson Page reaches the point when he feels completely out of things. Basso writes,

> He wanted to be away from those people and out of that room. It was not that he thought he was better than they, or more intelligent, or endowed with deeper sensibilities. He simply did not belong with them. . . . He asked himself where *did* he belong, did he belong anywhere, and then he saw Dinah, watching him, perched on the edge of a chair. (pp. 356–57)

Dinah Blackford, married now to Mico Higgins, is the corporeal symbol of the lost culture of the South; and, with her, Page shares a "curious kind of isolation." He does not want to fall in love with her, however, because he feels that he has found a sound reality with his own wife. Dinah, he senses, is an illusion like Mulberry and the whole South. He knows, too, that with Dinah, "the man and woman thing . . . is colored by the unreality, the moonlight-and-magnolia dream. . . . And life isn't" (p. 378). Page, therefore, finds himself in the same dilemma that had caught Romualdo.[24]

Discovering that the lost culture is an illusion, Page must move back to what is real. He realizes what Meg, his wife, meant when she had urged him to go back to Pompey's Head and that "girl," and get them both out of his system. He therefore succumbs to Dinah and "when

24. See Cautela, *Moon Harvest.*

at last he possessed her . . . past and present came thundering together and he was master and owner of it all."[25]

After he overcomes his personal obsessions, Page is free to solve the problem of Garvin Wales, the once great novelist of the South, whose wife is now threatening to sue the publisher for embezzlement. Page is amazed to learn from Wales why so great an author has written with so much hate. Wales, admitting that his mother had Negro blood and that his father had been a share-cropper, confesses that he has always hated the people of the socially accepted world. He says, identifying even Page with "the right people," "I hated you for not knowing! I wanted to rub your faces in that dirt and filth, just as mine was" (p. 394). He has written of sordid themes, therefore, because he has resented his lack of a real background. Page recognizes him as a veiled Shintoist, after all.

Basso reveals that Garvin Wales is a composite picture of the accepted writers of contemporary American novels. As Wales raves on, Page thinks,

> The truth is that this man doesn't believe in anything. Perhaps he once did, but not for a long time. It's been a kind of vengeful nihilism he's lived for . . . he does hate himself. . . . The real destruction came from within. (p. 396)

The key to Wales is, then, that he is crippled by the same cult of "belonging" that has injured the entire South. Page, thinking for the author, asks what were all the rapes, miscegenations, feuds, murders, fratricides—the swarming coilings as in a snake pit—but a wild, senseless striking out at that which Wales had always longed for, and because of Anna Jones, his mother, could never have. The writer, then, is fallacious because he has lost control of his resentments, and we are squarely faced by DeVoto's theory.

Page finally realizes that he, too, has been crippled by the cult and that he has been walking with a moral limp. When he had first left the South, it was because his "gentility" had been hurt; he had lost his sense of belonging. But reality, completion, and, for the alien, assimilation, effect the cure of this "limp," and prove that ancestor worship is a place, a view from Pompey's Head.

To summarize the third phase of the emergence of Italian-American fiction, it is essential to keep in mind that at this point the writers turned away from Italian-American subjects. Frances Winwar and Bernard DeVoto set their stories in new regions; but since they are not writers of fiction only, their works, although indicative of this phase

25. Basso, *The View From Pompey's Head,* p. 382.

of the development of Italian-American fiction, are not so exclusively representative as those of Paul Gallico and Hamilton Basso, both of whom are primarily novelists.

Bernard DeVoto is the major figure of the Italian-American writers who have not used the geographically restricted settings of an ethnical community for telling a story. Making use of a diversity of forms, he has developed a consistent theme, which emerges from the subconscious of one who is a member of a minority. Stressing the importance of the frontier as a continuing influence on American civilization, he demonstrates the significance of the fresh impetus generated by the continuing flow of immigrants other than those who established the New England Puritan coterie. He dramatizes this theme through the characterization of dissenters, pioneers, and realists. Persistently analytic, he professes that American letters should represent more honestly the complexion and the aspirations of the American people. Neither a blind romantic, nor a destructive iconoclast, he insists that the mainstream of American life and letters should cleanse itself of muddy idealism and reveal the sanative substance of its tributaries. In his novels, histories, and critical works, his ideas, based on sound research and knowledge, are a refutation of the artistic distortion that he reveals in *The Literary Fallacy.* He is the prime witness of the material for this discussion, demonstrating that American literature has suffered from a deliberate fault.

A testament to this fault is Frances Winwar, a prodigious writer-scholar whose works merit far more attention and acclaim than they have received. Critic, novelist, biographer, and historian, she shows the endowments of quality and application that give substance and validity to her works. Furthermore, because of the dramatic charge and luxurious imagination of her language, her books are aesthetically rewarding and readable. With refined wit of discernment and good taste, she creates historical events and personalities that engage both the scholar and the cursory reader. She has a keen perception of human nature, and is disciplined by her always reliable historic sense. As an Italian-American, she informs our attitudes with an analytical objectivity toward familiar subjects, sometimes using romanticism as a cloak, as she does in *The Last Love of Camille.* Her biographies, especially, demonstrate that behind familiar attitudes lie the lives of real people. In *The Eagle and The Rock,* for example, she dispels both prejudice and chauvinism. Her works illuminate the dark rooms of our distortions, and bring the balanced vision of daylight to all the corners of our literary house.

Paul Gallico has consistently used for his themes the unassuming individual who seeks happiness in trying to reconcile his dreams with his environment. In his novels he writes of men and women in many settings. Numerous heroes of his are sportsmen, since his incubation for the literary profession was as a sports writer. As an illustration of the third phase in the development of Italian-American fiction, *The Small Miracle* is as representative as any of his books because of its popularity and its relationship in subject to Italianism from a reversed point of view. This point of view, furthermore, has the added dimension of identity of the author with his materials. Although the subject of the novel is not of Italian-American life, it is obviously treated with a latent Italian-American attitude.

The greatest amount of revulsion from erstwhile environmental subjects is found in the books of Hamilton Basso. He discusses the cultural values of America on a national scale, using the South as a symbol of a minority within those values. This symbol, therefore, is the internal application of the alien concept. While Jason Kent, the hero of *Days Before Lent*, is a "tributary" to the mainstream of society, he finds his identity in his involvement with Joe Piavi, the unfortunate victim of circumstances, and in his final decision to live—as his father had advocated—in the world of human beings as against a world of abstract ideas.

In his definitive novel, *The View From Pompey's Head*, Basso illustrates the struggle of the individual who seeks his identity while conflicting with the rigid frame of the fixed ideas in an established society dedicated to ancestor worship. Anson Page, the "outsider," must go back to the South to possess both it and its symbol, Dinah Blackford, in order to find himself. Established environment, therefore, is often the geographical dimension of place; and the isolation of the individual is dependent upon his relation to that place, whether he is inside or outside of it. Sensitivity about his position in that place is apt to give the individual a moral "limp," as Basso defines it. To rid himself of this limp, this sense of inferiority because of the injury to one's traditional gentility, the Italian-American writer must likewise return to reality. He must face again the fact that his tradition lies in an Italian-American "place," the section of life in America that now contains ancestors for him. As a result, he undergoes a counterrevulsion and changes his subjects again, consults his progenitors, and takes another view of Italian-American life.

6

COUNTERREVULSION

When they discovered both the inadequacy and the distortion in the themes that represented our national literature, American writers of Italian descent returned to Italian-American subjects for their fictional materials. This phase corresponds more exactly to Robert E. Spiller's third division in which the settler, homesick for his racial past, went back to the "old sources of wisdom and beauty" in order to improve his condition. Because they were for the most part second- and third-generation Americans, the writers during this phase, in their looking backward, were able to do so with the advantage of a more firmly achieved cultural integration than that exercised by those who went before them. Born at the beginning of the twentieth century, they identified their views with those who were not only of a different age, but also of a more advanced technological period, making possible an extended cultural attitude in the national scene. Among others, the group includes Guido D'Agostino, Jo Pagano, Mari Tomasi, Jerre Mangione, George Panetta, Jimmy Savo, Pietro DiDonato, and John Fante.

GUIDO D'AGOSTINO (1906–)

The struggle of action out-of-place is, generally, the applied attempt to overcome isolation; and it is this theme that occupies many of the writers who have returned to Italian-American subjects. Guido D'Agostino, a second-generation American, for example, was born on January 20, 1906, in the heart of "Little Italy" in New York City, where he grew up and was educated in local public schools. As an amateur boxer he learned a great deal about the problems that other sons of immigrants had with social adjustment, and he finally decided to write about these problems. In his short stories, he treats with humor the various aspects of immigrant life in the United States, but he elaborates his themes more seriously in *Olives on the Apple Tree* (1940), and *Hills Beyond Manhatten* (1942). In the latter novel he uses French characters, but they are only a variation of the people he portrays in his first and more fundamentally thematic book. His other books include *My Enemy the World* (1947) and *The Barking of a Lonely Fox* (1952).

D'Agostino treats specifically the problem of isolation in *Olives on the Apple Tree.* In this book the Gardellas are the separated force; they have intensified their isolation by removing themselves from the "Wop-Roost" and by attempting to approach too hastily the set patterns of a more cosmopolitan area. Frederico and Giustinia have prospered; and their son Emile (baptized Emilio), M.D., attempts to find favor with the medical staff controlled by Dr. Stone. Emile is also contriving to "break into" the staid country club by courting a girl in society. He is counterpointed by Marco, the immigrant who makes no attempt to change.

As the Gardellas represent the new Italian-Americans, Marco is the back-trailer, the character whom the author presents as the isolated reject of an interactive culture. America, Marco thinks, is not the ideal of which he had dreamed. D'Agostino writes,

> I have seen this country from bottom to top. I have worked at every kind of job and I have found nothing to make me stay in one place. I see a big . . . country—rich, beautiful, like never I seen anything before and all I feel is I want to keep moving. Everybody I find like your doctor here, and Nick over there—mad, sore like hell about something. Nobody satisfied with anything, and I have become so that I sick myself with this American sickness.[1]

It is obvious, however, that the author is writing from the level of a more socially integrated generation; he is able to reproduce Marco's cry that he has constantly looked for people like himself, Italians who have traditionally loved their work, the soil, the good crops.

> The love of the grapes and the good wine. The love of the food and the table and the conversation, the laughing and everything else that makes the life worth while. I was so sure to find all this here . . . because here the man is free and can do what he wants and say what he wants—and the country so big and so rich, with plenty for everybody. (p. 294)

In Marco, D'Agostino is reaching back to an old desire and the early reason for the Italians' coming to America, but the writer is concerned

1. Guido D'Agostino, *Olives on the Apple Tree* (New York: Doubleday, Doran and Company, 1940), p. 26.

with the desire of a person other than himself. The author looks back; he reflects, and Marco becomes the precursor of the modern, universally frustrated man,

> Everything is all mixed up. The farmer is no more farmer, he has become the businessman. The man who was good to handle stone, now he is a slave in the laundry. . . . I look for the Italian. What have I found? No more the Italian but a bastard Italian. Quick he forgets everything from the old country to make money and have a car and buy food in cans and become just like the American he is working for. But he does not become the American and he is no more the Italian. Something in the middle—no good for himself and no good for the country. A real bastardo. (p. 294)

In this process of becoming an anomaly hovering between two cultures, the Italian-American who tries to save himself develops into Emile, who would turn his back on everything Italian, or, at his best, would angrily sneer at the old ideals. With his sneer, however, he becomes the victim of his own weakness. In him, the writer represents neither a straw man nor a hero. Emile is an individual, a human being, frail and devoid of heroic virtues. He is a pedestrian man, like Dreiser's men, responding to his surroundings and adjusting to an economically constructed society. He promotes his relationship with Dr. Stone only to the extent of trying to set up a false victory for the elder man in a hunting expedition, an attempt that is thwarted by the more honest intentions of the Italians on "Wop Roost." Emile finds his salvation, finally, in returning to the "Italian colony" and in making Angelina his wife.

On reflection, contends D'Agostino, the assimilation process is never successful if its outward pace is faster than the people's ability to change. The cultural give-and-take between two groups takes time. As Marco says,

> If the minute you land here you want to rush to become American, then little by little you kill yourself—and you cheat the land that gives you a home because what you brought with you from your own country to make it richer and better, you have thrown away and forgotten. (p. 295)

This reflection, however, is made from a new level of experience and from another generation's practice at living. Emile might have succeeded in "breaking into society" if he had not gone too fast. His entry was ascertained; he already had Dr. Stone under obligation to him, but, as his druggist friend warned him, "You're never satisfied. You gotta push a thing and push it until it snaps back in your face" (p. 262).

Emilio and Marco are, therefore, two sides of one coin that is rolling back. Marco walks to his niche, but Emilio must be pushed back. He has been thrown too suddenly into a Darwinian world in which he is still an alien. He makes the mistake of being over-sure. "You've got to be realistic," he says; but he talks without realism. "This is a world of dog-eat-dog, a survival of the fittest. If we can't cut a niche for ourselves it's just too bad. We don't belong" (p. 279). As a matter of fact, he does not belong. The author emphasizes repeatedly that his subjects do not belong in a pessimistic world. There is a way out, however, a method that is right; and Marco explains it as he picks up an olive:

> The olive that jumps to the apple tree. The olive that shouts that it is an apple. There is the mistake. There is the whole trouble. . . . The worry of the immigrant is not to be American. The worry is to work, to produce what you can produce and that is what makes you an American. (p. 295)

JO PAGANO (1906–   )

Jo Pagano, a second-generation American, was born on February 5, 1906, in Denver, Colorado, where he attended the public schools and eventually turned to art and writing. After successfully selling a series of short stories, he collected some of the episodes of these stories, most of which were autobiographical, and used them in the novels *The Paesanos* (1940) and *Golden Wedding* (1943). His experience as a scenario writer for Warner Brothers Studio served him well in dramatizing the typical events of Italian-American life.

The series of events in *The Paesanos* are continued, and culminated in *Golden Wedding,* in which the author reviews the married life of the Simones, who are now celebrating their golden wedding anniversary. Jo Pagano tells of his parents' background in Italy in *Golden Wedding,* and his method is objective as he refers to the citizenry in Europe who regarded America as a "fabulous domain." His father and mother met in America; the accounts of other courtships and marriages do not involve his immediate concern. When he later makes some references to these clumsy courtships, Pagano does not reduce his story to the account of erotic functions and of primitive compulsions, which marked so much of the fiction of the period. It is because Pagano as a second-generation American probably found himself often explaining the marriage customs of the early immigrants that he writes at all of the making of the "ambasciata," the informal overture for marriage.

The description of the golden wedding is a eulogy on the completion of fifty years, during which two people have shared their labor and dependency, a recall on the part of the author. "The great-wheel of their life had turned a full half-circle, and, in turning, had crossed the orbit of a universe. The history of their life was the history of an era, of a dozen eras."[2] Pagano identifies the development of this Italian-American life with the normal growth of the nation. He writes that at the turn of the century the family moved to Rockton; in 1903, the "Black Hands" sent them the horror-striking letter sketched with a skull and bones; in 1914, the daughter, Rose, had her first baby; in 1918, Lou, "Figlio mio," was "sacrificed to democracy." Because this large scope of treatment controls the unity of the book, the golden wedding is the focal point, the coming to rest of the wheel of a lifetime. The celebration is like the "old Italian ones," with music, flowers, the savory foods, the dancing of the tarantella—all the concrete details are recalled. The episode is intensified by the implications in the urgency of Stella's words that Bob and Carl are returning to Spain to fight off the "Fascist menace" that is trying to stamp out "everything that people like your mother and father mean in this world (p. 298). In the end, the author saves the story from becoming a propaganda piece by his reiteration that the golden wedding is the symbol of the courage of the future and that the young must "do what is in your heart to do."

The Condemned

Like other modern novelists carrying the banner for social justice, Pagano freights his next work, *The Condemned*,[3] with embellishments of erudition. The traditional, assured, but casual references to the classics are replaced here by the deliberately inflected recitation of names like Kretschmer and Janet, Strecker and Ebaugh, Rosanoff, Charcot, Jung, and Freud. The lucid simplicity of the pioneer and of the villager has given way to the complexity and jargon of the pedant. This change in verbal treatment is a demonstration of the writer's return to his sources in an attempt at counterrevulsion with a surfeit of subtleties, some of which adhere to him like borrowed tentacles. However, there are many connotations in such a remark as Pagano makes in "God is a world with many meanings, but man is man" (p. 18). The return, therefore, despite the verbalizations, is to fundamentals.

The Condemned does not, like *Golden Wedding*, have Italian-Americans as subjects; but the themes are similar. The author is concerned with various types of nonconformists and misfits who are trying to make an adjustment to a society whose fixed standards will inevitably convict them. In this story about the causes of violence, Pagano reasons that the criminals, Howard Tyler and Jerry Slocum, are victims of circumstances—Tyler, of his traumatic experiences in the slums; Slocum, of his mental disability caused by a brain tumor. Tyler becomes the accomplice of Jerry Slocum's crime, although he has not anticipated being involved in a murder. It is, however, because of Tyler's confes-

2. Jo Pagano, *The Golden Wedding* (New York: Random House, 1943), p. 284.
3. Jo Pagano, *The Condemned* (Englewood Cliffs, N. J.: Prentice Hall, Inc., 1947).

sion of guilt that the murderers are apprehended. Slocum's plan to kidnap and to kill Robert Wineberg is organized consciously and executed sadistically, but Pagano argues that the action is the exercise of an unbalanced mind. When a group of men of the community lynch the murderers, the question is asked, "Who is really to be condemned, the murderers or the community?"

Conceptually, it is because society is made up of Basso's "unsurprisables," that Howard Tyler and Jerry Slocum do violence to each other and to their victim, Robert Wineberg. The narrated backtrack to Howard's childhood reveals him as a poor boy in a mill town, whose marriage and expenses create in him an endless circle of fear, a fear that leads to drunkenness, a weakness that puts him into the hands of Jerry Slocum. Jerry, of course, symbolizes the abnormality of aggression that corrupts weakness into criminality: he is the visible sign of hatred in mankind, the kind of hatred that must vent itself upon a scapegoat. Wineberg is symbolic of the cerebral "alien," altruistic and philanthropic, who must suffer at the hands of the radical elements of what Pagano calls a "reactionary bourgeosie." Parodoxically, the author insists that the killer is really of the "under-privileged masses," the group that has been isolated from the country's wealth. Wineberg says, for the author, "It's the social duty of the fortunate few like myself to help" (p. 112).

As Pagano asks his question about who is responsible for a criminal's act, he is implying the question of why society makes an "alien" of a person because of his race. In this question lies the new dimension of the old treatments. He asks, "Are we all inseparable, mutually dependent, therefore co-responsible?" (p. 169). In seeking an answer, he analyzes the lynchings of Howard and Jerry, and reveals that this mass crime has been performed because of various sexual perversions in all of the participants. Jonathan Holmes, for example, needs the sight of blood for sexual satisfaction; Mike Riorden and Robert Lawson expiate their own alcoholism by killing alcoholics.

The true victim of the criminals is Wineberg, the American Jew (representative of racial minorities), who symbolizes persecuted humanity at the hands of unbalanced brutality. Gil Stanton, the American intellectual, seeks retribution by taking work in a social-welfare agency. Pagano explains that as each facet of society resumes its fixed place, the author probes into economics (class warfare), psychology (crime as action out-of-place), ethics (we are all sinners), mysticism (astrologers' belief that all events are always there); and he questions whether anyone has the right to condemn or to isolate anyone else. Structurally, therefore, the novel is an analysis of the fragmentation caused by action out-of-place, showing that harmony lies only in a rational entirety. The story is a contemporary articulation of the desirability of assimilation. Although it is obviously polemical, the novel has authenticity and power.

MARI TOMASI (1895–1968)

Gradually the themes of Italian-American writers of the second generation have come to deal with a firmer implantation in the native American soil. Mari Tomasi reflects the earth and granite of Vermont in *Like Lesser Gods*[4] after having explored the ancestors of her characters in her account of the hill people of Ibena, Piedmont, in *Deep Grow the Roots.*[5] George Panetta draws a contrasting illustration in *We Ride a White Donkey,*[6] in which there is much hilarity when a group of Americans go on a Calabrian picnic.

With Miss Tomasi, especially, there is a convincing and aesthetic presentation of the process by which Italian mores and culture may become throughly absorbed in the most ostensibly restricted Anglo-American locale. Miss Tomasi, born on February 1, 1895, in Montpelier, Vermont, where she was educated before attending Wheaton and Trinity Colleges, absorbed in depth the local atmosphere of granite-surfaced New England. Restricted by a long illness pursuant to an accident during her infancy, Miss Tomasi found time to teach, and to work with *The Montpelier Evening Argus.* In 1942 she was awarded a fellowship at the Breadloaf Writers Conference at Middlebury College, and in 1944 she was awarded honorary membership in the International Mark Twain Society. Her books demonstrate a firm interaction of the cultural concepts of her Piedmontese parents and the established labor society of Vermont.

Like Lesser Gods

Examiners of literary Americana are paying increasing attention to the realistic story of regional interest that Mari Tomasi tells in *Like Lesser Gods.*[7] With an almost ingenuous reverence for simple life and rugged art, Miss Tomasi weaves a clearly outlined tapestry of strong fibres and primary colors from the lives of the granite workers of Vermont. She uses characters unashamedly as symbols in their relationship with the established inhabitants of Granitetown, her fictionalized title for Barre, Vermont. Her special appeal, however, is in her dramatization of daily routines, which are occasionally heightened by achievement or depressed by frustration in the lives of dedicated people in the pursuit of a particularly difficult craft. Mari Tomasi engages the reader pleasurably by her fluid, easy narration, which she controls in a language of simple strength stretched by poetic evocation. Her characters approach the reader without artifice, with an instant invita-

4. Mari Tomasi, *Like Lesser Gods* (Milwaukee: Bruce Publishing Company, 1949).
5. Mari Tomasi, *Deep Grow the Roots* (Philadelphia: J. B. Lippincott Company, 1940).
6. George Panetta, *We Ride a White Donkey* (New York: Harcourt Brace, 1944).
7. Mari Tomasi, *Like Lesser Gods* (Milwaukee: Bruce Publishing Company, 1949).

tion to their moods and thoughts, and an enduring involvement in their problems.

The point of *Like Lesser Gods* is that the work men do is their participation in the divine order of creation, the work of human beings appearing as only slightly less in importance to that of the divinities. Mari Tomasi's granite workers, descendents of craftsmen of medieval days, are like lesser gods when they create memorials in stone. The veneration that these laborers have for their craft is demonstrated, for example, when the freshly graduated physician, Gino Tosti, son of Lucia, tells Pietro Dalli, the stonecutter, of his fatal occupational disease; and Pietro comments that the *Dio* creates new life and takes it away, but the stonecutters take up where He left off—they make a lasting memory of a man's life. Gino concedes that Pietro incorporates the old mythology that "on Olympus lived the greater gods; and below, the lesser."

Pietro Dalli is himself an earth-rock monument on a miniature but thoroughly crafted scale. With an artist's dedication to his art, he is happily absorbed in his work and his family. At the crowning point of his achievement, in an unprecedented burst of animation, he writes to his old uncle and teacher in Italy that two united affirmatives can only result in a "more positive affirmative." In another flow of articulation, he admits his formerly secret dream of performing his "best job," a cross he is carving with his distinctively elaborate sign of vines smothering other vines. The stone, wreathed by the leaves of the grapes that are the source of wine, represents Pietro's faith in the universe; but it is his tragedy that his well-meaning wife, Maria, despises that very stone, which she plans to destroy because she believes it is consuming her husband's life. When Pietro achieves his American pursuit of happiness in his well-adjusted family, a comfortable home, and a convivial relationship with his fellow-workers, his damaged cross becomes the external memorial of his body, which the chalk dust is claiming. Unrelenting in his affirmation of life, he sees his daughter, Petra, as the continuity of his vision of "the beauty of stone," a beauty that must be carved with awesome reverence and unstinted labor. His son, Americo, is that part of him which has been realistically materialized by the concerned and affectionate Maria. But, for the greater part of his dream of an industrious and rewarding life, Pietro remains grateful to his uncle and teacher who not only hovers in the memories of his subconscious, but has come to live with the family. As he approaches death, Pietro Dalli views the panorama of his life in Italy and in Granitetown. His friendships, his love, his family's loyalty, the power of his work, the resilience of a faith imbued by old Italian priests are all contained in the deathbed plea of the Old-World *paesani* to the Divinity. He dies, finally, when he hears the four o'clock whistle, while he is envisioning himself in the Shed, eager to finish his cross before the end of the day's work. The smile on his face attests to his belief in a future of hope.

Pietro's old teacher, affectionately called "Mr. Tiff," is a symbol of the old frame of culture in Italy, the religious and social morality of southern Europe, the persistent criterion of conscience, which disciplines the behavorial patterns of even some contemporary Italian-Americans. Significantly, as a nomenclatural symbol of Americanization, the former instructor's pseudonym is derived from his bona fide name, Maestro Michele Pio Vittorini Giuseppe Tiffone. This erstwhile maestro is now an umbrella mender, his new role emphasizing the material aspect of the rectifier of errors. Meanwhile, everyone around him gravitates to him for advice on making the decisions engendered by trivial or important events. Mr. Tiff is a refuge in the storms of love, hate, revenge, conciliation, and tolerance. Efficient in his role, he is instrumental in Petra's "integrated" marriage to Danny Douglas, the most eligible member of the town's formidable "Wasp" establishment; he maneuvers the successful solution to the local political chief's illicit love; and he implements (to the bafflement of the parish priest) the purchase of a stained-glass window for St. Michael's. He thus personifies Mari Tomasi's theme that the strength of endemic concepts in Italian character regenerates what might be corrupted in America. Their durability, however, depends upon cooperative ingenuity and indifference to danger. Mr. Tiff is a functioning symbol of Mari Tomasi's idea that man's creative genius is immortalized when the artist carves his ideas into a lasting medium: in this case, stone.

Miss Tomasi extends this theme to another level in the characterization of Maria Dalli, whose stoic strength matches spiritually the granite that she resents bitterly as her husband's killer. Fiercely loyal to Pietro, she attacks his masterpiece as she would strike the body of a menacing pagan earth-god who feeds on the blood of her lover. It is Maria Dalli's strength, eventually, that supports the family in their grief when Pietro dies. In Maria, Miss Tomasi has carved her own symbol of endurance. When Maria learns that no threats, or pleas, or violent act will change Pietro's attachment to his work, she becomes grimly reconciled to the facts. Likewise, she is reconciled to his death. She demonstrates on her creator's behalf that the ultimate enduring achievement is human reconciliation.

This providential reconciliation is the amalgam of the behavior of the young people in the story, which covers two phases of social history in Graniteville, one in 1924 and one in 1941. Americo, the younger generation's edition of Pietro, applies himself to his books in the same manner that his father had pursued his craft. We observe the determined son, after his father's funeral, leaving for the university in Burlington, urged by his mother's sagacity, driving into the dawn of a bright future. Petra, who has loved Mr. Tiff and never defied his instructions, reflects the same determination in her applied strategy to adjust to the inner-directed establishment into which she marries. Furthermore, this process of assimilation is repeated in numerous ways by the neighbors and friends who people the story. The population, like Ronato, rings a chorus of approval around the circle of the Dallis as everyone insists upon the proper artistry for Pietro's memorial.

Mari Tomasi has used both themes and events to demonstrate Italian-Americanism in labor. She insists that this laborer is a model of honesty and integrity, parched with a thirst for beauty, and driven by a passion for artistic perfectionism. Her protagonist dominates many scenes, selling home-made wine "illegally," singing with his friends at the annual lavish Italian picnic, insisting on quality as prior to quantity in his production of labor, approaching the saints as members of the family, reacting with sudden confusion to the arguments of his children in a world unknown to him, insisting on strict moral conduct, and always enjoying to the utmost his Italian diversions of hunting mushrooms, playing bocce, distilling grappa, and exercising his born right as head of the family. Mari Tomasi has given a rapid pulse to this Italian-American; and, while she indulges in ethnical images like "the look of Pompeii" on Ronato's ominous face, she pictures her themes of endurance and continuity as perpetrated through assimilation. Both her skill and her objectives are symbolized in the scene where Danny shows Petra the sketch he has made of Petra holding in her hands the spread-winged figurine of St. Michael. He had made the figurine before his accident; but the sketch he managed afterward, using the mutilated hand to create this tribute of crippled love he was now offering her in his need of her.

As Maria Dalli discovers, stone is not always the victor. Stone can not reason; nor can it plot as the brain does. Mari Tomasi tells us that reason must implement the compromises of rigidity; flexibility presupposes the reconciliation that results in assimilation. *Like Lesser Gods* is a refreshing ground swell of the pre-cultures beneath the stones in the walls of American social stratification. More than a document of regional history, Miss Tomasi's book is an evocative and symbolic story, a lucid picture of America at work, a colorful weaving of the Italian ethnic experience into the American tapestry.

As a novel, *Like Lesser Gods* is a celebration of life and an affirmation of man's capacity to resist hostile forces. It is Mari Tomasi's attitude of positiveness that draws the smile on Pietro Dalli's face as he dies. Admittedly, she often motivates events providentially, but the action is consistently plausible. Her symbols are obvious; she makes of Pietro the rock upon which Mr. Tiff, the transcendental figure, builds the intangible monument to Italian character in America. Miss Tomasi demonstrates by repetition and emphasis that Italian-American people are serious and constructive; but she lauds all women as she depicts the Mona Lisa wisdom of Maria as the amalgam of family unity. Her characterizations have universal applications also in the poised virginal projection of Petra to the receptiveness of the once confident but now realistically wounded Danny. These characters are also symbols, Petra being the recent contribution to a fixed American civilization that must nurse its flaws. As a novelist, Miss Tomasi depicts her scenes with authentic vitality, inviting engagement. The reader becomes nostalgic, urged to climb the hilly streets of Graniteville, to roam over the surrounding "camp"-studded mountains and then return to Main Street to the unpretentious restaurant that specializes in authentic Northern-Italian cooking. Miss Tomasi informs, instructs, and delights, while her narrative structure is successfully held together by the progressive continuity of Mr. Tiff's influence, the Italian-American conscience flowing into the mainstream.

JERRE MANGIONE (1909–)

The theme of social fragmentation persists in the novels of Jerre Mangione, especially in *Mount Allegro.*[8] Mangione, a second-generation Italian-American, the son of Sicilian parents, Gaspare and Josephine (Polizzi), was born on March 20, 1909, and grew up in a heterogeneously ethnic community in Rochester, New York. A graduate of Syracuse University, he is an experienced editor, reviewer, feature-writer, and educator. After successive years of employment in publicity, advertising, and government service, he became the administrator of the creative writing program at the University of Pennsylvania, from which base he continues to write. His novels include, besides *Mount Allegro, The Ship and the Flame* (1948) and *Night Search* (1965). In addition to short stories and magazine articles, his other works include *Reunion in Sicily* (1950); *Life Sentences For Everybody,* (1965); *A Passion For Sicilians,* (1968); and *America is Also Italian,* (1969). He is presently working on a book on the Federal Writer's Project.

Mount Allegro

Of all his works, Jerre Mangione's most significant example of return to the Italian-American life as a recalled literary subject is found in *Mount Allegro,* which is autobiographical in material and presentation. Giustinia, the sister, says, "When I grow up I want to be an American." As the author and his brother Joe argue as to whether or not they are Americans, their father assures them that it will be their children who will be *Americani.* "But you, my son, are half-and-half," the older man comments and poses the problem of the back-trailer.

8. Jerre Mangione, *Mount Allegro* (Boston: Houghton, Mifflin Company, Riverside Press, 1942).

There is little comfort for the writer when he "talks it over with the gang," shows them a globe, and asks them where their parents came from. They answer that they don't know and that they don't care.

Things do not become easier in the Amoroso household when the parents insist that the children speak Italian at home. This requirement emphasizes the line of demarcation between their life at home and that in the world outside. It is significant that Mangione marks the dichotomy of the Italian-American world, but that he does not identify himself with it completely. He indicates that the differences affected his "relatives," thus placing himself in the group whose better assimilation helps them to make an objective evaluation.

His relatives have difficulty in understanding American concepts. For example, the author's father cannot conceive of using the George Washington hatchet legend as a moral lesson because he feels that the story encourages boys to use hatchets. This reasoning leads to a rampage against American education, a system that apparently produces neither manners nor tact. With equal concern, the parents argue against "movies" whose characters win their arguments by the use of knives.

It is the American women, however, that present the greatest enigma to the old Sicilians, whose strict code of etiquette does not allow for smoking, flirting, or the wearing of scant clothing. Mangione asserts that it was a foregone conclusion among Sicilians that a non-Italian wife could not be faithful to her husband. American women believed in divorce, the Sicilians argued; therefore, a man shouldn't marry an American woman. A man was allowed sexual freedom, but it was up to a woman to resist him. Most Sicilians believed, says Mangione, that America is a "crazy land" where women worked in factories with men, and where women walked down the street with men. Also, they could not understand why children married without consulting their parents. They blamed America for the disrespect that children had for parents, and for the apparent fact that money was more valuable than family honor. The author's comments recall the concepts of Louis Forgione's old Demetrio in his conflict with Rose.[9]

The Sicilians, in turn, had concepts that Americans have found difficult to understand. For example, the group on Mount Allegro had the not-unusual Italian attitude toward religion, whose external observances indicated that many of them did not attend Mass. Mangione reiterates the usual point that there was no Italian church where they lived and that his parents' attitude was not unique. Italians have such an ingrained Catholicism, he says, that they can violate some of the strictest rules without a feeling of guilt. "Unlike their Irish-Catholic neighbors, they had almost no fear of God and felt as much at home with Him as they did with each other" (p. 71).

9. In *The River Between.*

One concept among Sicilians, which was common to many other Italians, was that of belief in the Evil Eye. Mangione stresses that even in Mount Allegro this superstition admitted the functioning presence of the devil. These agents of the devil are, willing or otherwise, conveyers of ill-fortune and must be thwarted by would-be victims by carrying something pointed, either a horn or amulet, or by forming the hand in the shape of two horns. Sicilians believe that people possessing the "mal'occhio" have definite physical features: a cadaverous body, olive-skinned face, and eyebrows coming together in an unbroken line.[10]

Mangione affirms Louis Forgione's explanation of the Camorra[11] when he explains that his "relatives" did not always believe that justice and law meant the same thing. He writes that Sicilians held sacred the unwritten laws of the people, which opposed the written laws of tyrannic force. Mangione makes the point that it was because written law had never protected the people against the politically protected brigands that honor and respect were the really sacred laws. To the Sicilians in America these legacies were as real as health and disease, but they were more important because health can be restored, while the man who loses his honor can never retrieve it.

The children's dream in the Sicilian household was, according to Mangione, that their parents would drop all their old ideas and customs. He admits, however, that, much as they desired that their parents live an American life, they did not have the vaguest notion as to how this was to be done. Assimilation, however, was taking place successfully within the neighborhood, despite the children's impatience. Many Polish and Jewish people lived in Mount Allegro. Symbolically, Mr. Solomon and Mr. Michelangelo were great friends and spent many hours together, although Mr. Michelangelo spoke no English and Mr. Solomon no Italian.

The children of the Sicilians, however, grew up in the face of the conflict of misunderstood concepts. Mangione reflects that the more aware he became of the real differences between the "Latin world" and the "Anglo-Saxon world," the more disturbed he became. However, he admits that he feels the pattern of America; that, with the passing of time, he is able to see his "relatives more objectively"; and that he has begun to forget his childhood resentments. He asks a significant question, "Was it in the chemistry of human life for my relatives to become Anglo-Saxonized—the apparent goal of the melting-pot theorists? So long as they believed in freedom and democracy and their long history showed those ideals to be as ingrained in them as their religion—was it necessary that they try to change themselves?

10. See the definitive study in Edward S. Gifford, M.D., *The Evil Eye* (New York: The Macmillan Company, 1958).
11. See *The Men of Silence.*

Didn't America need their wisdom and their warmth, just as they and their children needed America's youth and vigor?"[12]

The question implies the course that cultural interaction was taking in the pursuit of human values. The process, however, even in a more integrated generation, produces a dual personality. Marco and Emilio had to bide their time; and Mangione, too, has had to make compromises. When he goes to Italy, he is accepted as the "son of Peppino," as though his father had left Sicily a few weeks before. Then, when he tries to share the expenses of his poor relatives there, they become offended and forgive him, "only on the ground that [he] was an American and must have been brought up among a lot of Indians" (p. 260).

The feeling of not belonging, the universal cause of the conflict between the individual and his environment, is what makes the Italian-American go back to the sources of his tradition. Jerre Mangione's physical return is a symbol of this need in his book *Reunion In Sicily*.[13] The return, however, emphasizes the doubt as to where he belongs, if anywhere. He expresses the fear he had in Sicily of being mistaken for a native Italian, for even the American tourists did make this mistake about him. He began to feel "like a character in a Pirandello play who feels he is losing his identity" (p. 2).

The Ship and the Flame

With *The Ship and the Flame*,[14] Jerre Mangione proceeds from anecdotal autobiography to more imaginative progressive action, with which he illuminates his characters and brings them into dramatic focus. Thematically, he has extended the treatment of fragmentation to an international area, staging the idea that flight from a hostile environment may not be assurance of freedom for an individual. Escaping from one sociopolitically inimical arena, the pilgrim may sail directly into the fire of another nation's battle line of human greed and intrigue. Beneath all destructive institutions, according to Mangione in this book, lie the tyrannic forces that are bred by the devious, evil, or impotent traits of human nature. Among these consuming forces, the spirit of man floats, often without direction, to an unknown harbor, at whose port the navigators may or may not negotiate to disembark for safety.

The Ship and the Flame is a day-by-day report of a shipload of refugees from Nazi concentration camps, who are hoping to settle in America. It develops that the passengers have been deluded; their Mexican transit visas are invalid and they are threatened by the terror of returning to the concentration camps. This fear and the attempts to validate

12. *Mount Allegro*, p. 246.
13. Jerre Mangione, *Reunion In Sicily* (Boston: Houghton Mifflin Company, 1950).
14. Jerre Mangione, *The Ship and the Flame* (New York: A. A. Wyn, 1948).

the visas create the dramatic tensions of the plot, which is further complicated by the developments of personal relationships among various passengers. Confronted with the need of animating the tiresome passing of time, these dislocated people on the seas ply their emotions on one another. Josef Renner, the exiled Austrian radical, is an ideological hero, while Stiano Argento attempts to live by reason in a world of passion. Mangione structures Argento's problem in the polarization of the voluptuous Teresa Lenska and the loyal wife, Margarita, both of whom love Argento, who eventually finds himself faced with the dilemma of choosing between them. There is also the deserter, Paul Kalinka, whose erotic relationship with the lustful Simone Brasson is drawn with graphic, detailed attention.

Mangione writes in this book that "The handwriting on the wall had taken flame and was devouring the world" (p. 34). The reason for its igniting, he says, lies in the fetish for superficiality. He incorporates this idea in the personality of Protocki, whom Paul Kalinka finds offensive and intolerable. Anyone who resists, by demonstrating his ethical or political philosophy, is implementing suicide. When Paul finds Renner dead, he reads in the suicide note the words, "I am weary of fighting and you must admit there is some satisfaction in cheating the enemy with a little pill" (p. 83). Mangione extends this theme of the destructive quality of spinal inertia to the consideration of the breakdown of the "backbone" of the United States. He has Captain Cabral say to Teresa that, speaking psychologically, America, in his opinion, is on the verge of a nervous breakdown. Later, this idea is extended to global dimensions. Stiano, reading the words of Mazzini, is amazed to find how well the Italian revolutionary summarized the conditions that permeate the world today. Mazzini's words are the point of Jerre Mangione's book, suitably communicated in the overall metaphor of the ship. Later, Stiano, reflecting on Renner's death, thinks about the flame which, he says, he has watched develop over many years, while he has kept his hands folded like those of men in despair. He wonders if the flame might be striking again in the distance. Attempting to put his thoughts into action, he urges the passengers to send radiograms to the captain. Warning them, he says, "We have allowed ourselves to be victimized by the same sort of inertia that brought disaster to Europe" (p. 261). Galvanizing the theme of lethargic isolation, Mangione says through Sadona that he does not fit anywhere in this modern world. "Other people," he says, "do not know what they want or where they are going" (p. 298). The immigrating individual, therefore, according to the author, may coordinate his fragmentation by concentrating on what he wants and on where he is going.

The Ship and the Flame is a thought-provoking novel. Mangione handles with professional competence the motivated action of his characters and the progressive movement of the plot. The atmosphere of fear and impending terror is mitigated by the control manifested in the reasoning of strong persons like Stiano and Sadona, who philosophize on inertia and its application both to world politics and to the future of the passengers on the S.S. *Setubal.* Mangione has an ethical insistence that the reader observe the message, which is not only verbally articulated, but also effectively symbolized in the novel's architecture. The ship is the individual; the person is, particularly, the ethnic who is drifting between the shores of social categories. Mangione is a consciously skilled writer who exercises both care and balance in composition. He is also the creator of characters who, while acting as cultural symbols, portray the strengths and weaknesses of people aptly classified in a suitable political allegory. The individualistic philosophy of a Mazzini is affirmed by Mangione as an inherited cultural animus, which the Italian-American writer must assert. This spirit must work in concert on the ship of a culture, however, or the entire structure will be consumed in the fire of the tyranny that feeds on the brute power of dissension.

Night Search

The affirmation of Mazzini's philosophy propelled into heroics the actions of men like Giuseppe Garibaldi. With the red scarf of the Italian revolutionary spiritually binding his right arm, Jerre Mangione creates Paolo Polizzi, the spirit who walked America's immigrant track of labor and whose controversial death is the incentive of the book *Night Search.*[15] Years later, Polizzi's illegitimate son, Michael Malory, accidentally discovers a clue to his father's murder, and resolves, like Hamlet, to avenge his parent by demonstrating the truth.

Michael's quest carries him from Provincetown to New York, and eventually to the small town of Nightingale-on-the-Hudson, his frustrating search dramatically counterpointed by the anxiety and love of Lucy Hawthorne, the woman who symbolizes his future. Michael has been married to the insane Lucy, who committed suicide and compounded his psychic need to avenge the forces of violence. As Mangione directs his protagonist from place to place, describing Michael's motivation by flash-backs and chronological expositions, he tells the story of Paolo Polizzi's revolutionary activities and amatory incidents. The reader learns that Polizzi had spared little time for his son because, as a public figure, active in the labor movement, he had consumed his years and talents as a controversial editor of an antifascist newspaper in New York. When he was murdered, neither the newspapers nor the police pursued the case to discover either who the murderers were or what their motives had been for killing Polizzi. Michael Malory, educated in the proper schools and bred in the social environ-

15. Jerre Mangione, *Night Search* (New York: Crown Publishers, Inc., 1965).

ment of the Eastern establishment, a veteran of World War II, and a cooperative American, needs to discover his natural father in his soul-searching. The intensity with which he seeks justice gives impetus to the progressive action of the book, and the revelation of truth dramatizes the theme. When Michael finds the killer, he discovers that revenge in the traditional "eye-for-an-eye" concept of his father's people is neither a just nor rational solution of nor expiation for problems engendered by human beings.

Michael Malory protests that his life cannot be separated from his father's. He says, "I'm not just another man from Scarsdale. I'm my father's son, and I can't forget that he is dead while the man who killed him is alive and free" (p. 142). Mangione, however, is writing his book above the level of an indignant son's quest for justice. Conceptually, the son is the writer's generation of artists who would rectify the injustices of their milieu.

There are numerous ramifications of Mangione's major theme. After he states the thesis that to ignore the crime is a gross repudiation of the ideals for which Paolo Polizzi fought, the author emphasizes that the speakers at various meetings "all agreed that the assassination was politically motivated, but there was considerable disagreement as to whether Paolo was the victim of the fascists or of the communists" (p. 16). The problem that evolves from this disagreement is based on the question of why the murderer had not been found after so many years. Michael might even accept an explanation based on expedience; after all, he has accepted the fact that it was not because Paolo and Mrs. Malory considered marriage a capitalistic bourgeois institution that his mother had remained married to Malory; rather, "his mother would have found it financially inconvenient to divorce Malory, her millionaire husband, and marry a penniless radical" (p. 18). Cynical as this conclusion may be, it is indicative of Michael's facing of truth. Furthermore, his affluent surroundings have served to accent Michael's fascination with Paolo's surviving friends—whom he meets through Eva Berger—the "elite" of the American Left-wing movement, including authors, professors, union organizers, ministers, and poets like Arturo Giovannitti. Paolo had been an agitating Pied Piper on whom people tried to pin labels—"anarchist, socialist, syndicalist, Trotskyite . . . but no label ever sticks because he belongs only to himself." The genius of his prophetic power was in the social evils of his native village. Paolo had denounced his roommate, a co-worker of Mussolini's in the Socialist Party, as a charlatan and potential traitor to the Socialist Party, left Europe, and became "the Established hero of the American underdog" (p. 53). Paolo engaged actively against Mussolini sympathizers, disrupting their meetings and writing incendiary editorials about them. Michael realizes that his father had an innate distrust of the obvious, that he had been a man like Pirandello, who could not operate with conventional logic, and he sees Paolo loom like a mountain of elusive subtleties, a person whom he could never fully understand. Later, as his search continues with apparent futility, a planted seductress comments to Michael that he is a lonely dreamer "always searching for something that is missing." It is this missing factor that he gropes for relentlessly, but he must face the fact that the truth will not atone for his righteousness. Mrs. D'Amico, sister of the assassin, Vincent Russo, warns Michael that truth can be cruel and destructive, especially when, as in her case, it is impossible to tell all of it. When he learns the facts, Michael is finally able to reason that, had he killed Russo as he had planned, he would have thrown away his life for an act of pride. To Russo, Paolo has been as much a father figure as he has been a haunting possibility to Michael. Each man has to destroy his obsession in his own way to find himself. Deciding to accept his father, not as an idol, but as the faulty man he was, Michael can come to terms with the future and know "that his only hope for a valid life was to find and cultivate the solid ground of his own identity" (p. 282).

Michael's identity is that of Jerre Mangione and that of all the Italian-American writers who have come to terms with the facts of their relationship to their environment. To destroy themselves because they have learned that the autonomy of a fragmented concept has died would be tantamount to committing a Hamlet's suicide, whereas, by accepting their innate concepts, they continue to travel determinedly with a receptive vehicle.

Mangione has an appreciable grasp of his materials, a steady narrative rhythm, an even pace, and a command of disciplined prose. With the help of smooth flashbacks, the story flows plausibly even when it depends upon providential solutions. The art of *Night Search* demonstrates not the agonized surge of a transcendental idol, but the pedestrian progress of a relentless gadfly who shares his nature with a flawed humanity.

GEORGE PANETTA (1910–)

The ear best attuned to the voice of the Italian dialect in America belongs to George Panetta, whose parents emigrated from Reggio Calabria in 1900. He was born on August 6, 1910, in Brooklyn, New York, where, in time, he went through high school and then studied for one year at City College, New York. Forced to rest in bed for six weeks when was twenty years old, Panetta developed a passion for reading, which helped him to decide upon a literary career. If his reading preference ranges from short-story writers through Shakespeare, the nineteenth-century poets and essayists, and the great European novelists, the setting of his own writing still is what he knows best, the Italian-American community, with its accent and its eloquence. He was able to mine rich material while he worked for the Works Progress Administration in the Harlem and Chinese districts of New York, and writing commercials for Young & Rubicam helped him to a crisp, lucid style. Even his novels, in their episodic treatment, reveal his preference for the conventions of the short story. A number of his short stories have appeared in national magazines, including *Story*, *Harper's Bazaar*, *Mademoiselle*, and *Fantasy*. His novels include: *We Ride a White Donkey*, 1944; *Jimmy Potts Gets a Haircut*, 1947; *Viva Madison Avenue*, 1957; and *Sea Beach Express*, 1966.

We Ride a White Donkey

Panetta's first book, *We Ride a White Donkey*,[16] is a series of sketches of the activities of the Caparuta family in the East side of Manhattan. With no attempt at subtlety, Mr. Panetta portrays with the emphasis of caricature the exaggerated, overt antics that dramatize the theme of conspicuousness. In the Calabrian idiom, to "ride a white donkey" means that one is attracting undue attention, as though he were riding an unknown animal. At times Panetta ridicules his characters; a chapter like "The Picnic" demonstrates his talent with successful, if ribald, humor.

Panetta has effectively mastered the dialect and should be as memorable for his portrayals as are corresponding writers of Yiddish stories. The device gives effective tone to his writings, which gain substance by the author's balancing hilarity with tragic elements.

Jimmy Potts Gets a Haircut. Viva Madison Avenue!

In his second book, *Jimmy Potts Gets a Haircut*,[17] Panetta tones down the farcical exposure of character to the level of pathos. The tale concerns Jimmy Potts, a four-year-old who goes to Romani's barbershop to get a haircut. The explicit note that Jimmy's mother has written is eaten by a horse. Therefore, Jimmy has bizarre instructions for the barber, which supply the dramatic impetus for the rest of the story.

Panetta's command of Italianized English is so letter-perfect that his caricatures are masterful portrayals. He gives them added dimension by contrasting them with Irish and Jewish people whose prototypes are still living on Bleecker Street. A brilliant satire on the melting-pot drama begins with Mayor LaGuardia's entry into the story. Panetta's rhetoric is simple and sharp, sometimes bordering on carping com-

16. George Panetta, *We Ride a White Donkey* (New York: Harcourt Brace & Company, 1944).

17. George Panetta, *Jimmy Potts Gets a Haircut* Illustrated by Reisie Lonette (New York: Doubleday & Company, 1947).

ment, but he cannot resist intruding himself with comments on Catholicism and child psychology. He is at his best when his characters are talking and acting true to form.

In his third book, *Viva Madison Avenue!*[18] Panetta, in telling the experiences of two Italian-Americans, George and Joe, in the advertising business in New York, relies heavily on short-story technique. With its lapses into the extravagance of burlesque, the narration loses the control that convinces the reader of verity.

Sea Beach Express

Panetta writes his fourth book, *Sea Beach Express*,[19] from nine-year-old Tony Boccaro's point of view. Whatever exaggeration there is is acceptable, because the reader is reminded of the wonder of a child's thinking. Tony and his father and mother take their little Puerto Rican neighbor, Pedro Lopez, along with them on the Sea Beach Express to get off at Coney Island. It is a gentle story, portraying the New York Italian neighborhood and emphasizing the importance of a day's outing to people who are huddled within the geographic limitations of residential sections of large cities. Although the book, written in simple prose, is particularly appealing to readers of the middle elementary grades, it is good social documentation for the mature observer of American culture. The ethnic idiom is authentic, and the ebullience of the characters correctly reflects the verve of Italian-Americans. Panetta has here created a veritable sound-track for a record of this group.

JIMMY SAVO (1910–1960)

The degree of the Italian-American's integration is tested at times most dramatically in his reactions when he returns, as we have seen in several other instances, to the soil of his ancestors. As an example, Jimmy Savo reveals a native-American maturity in his sojourn to Italy in *Little World "Hello!"*.[20]

Savo, a thorough New Yorker, was born in 1910 on East 97th Street of poor Italian immigrants. While he helped to support his family by selling newspapers on street corners and in saloons, he discovered that he could earn money by singing, dancing, and juggling. When he was nine years old, he began playing the amateur night circuits; when he was thirteen, he made his debut as a juggler in a New Bedford vaude-

18. George Panetta, *Viva Madison Avenue* (New York: Harcourt, Brace & Company, 1957).
19. George Panetta, *The Sea Beach Express* (New York: Harper & Row, 1960).
20. Jimmy Savo, *Little World "Hello!"* (New York: Simon and Schuster, 1947).

ville house. A living Horatio Alger legend, he was ranked by reputable critics as one of the country's outstanding mimes. Brooks Atkinson wrote, "Jimmy belongs in the company of aristocrats of the profession with Charlie Chaplin, Joe Jackson, the Frères Fratellini."[21] Portraits of Jimmy by several artists hang in museums, and E. E. Cummings celebrated his genius in a poem.

A confirmed American who has struck his roots, Savo returns to his sources with an attitude similar to Gallico's, as though pulled by a magnet to an integral part of his own being. The story relates his first visit to Italy, where his parents had been born, sixty miles from Rome. His wife, a native of Rome, inherited an old castle that her father had bought. What the Italians think of these returning Italian-Americans they speak only in whispers, because, he writes, "we were foreigners and they were all excited because only foreigners would have the idea of living in the castle with ghosts in it. Foreigners and pazzi" (p. 6).

Nevertheless, the people of LaRocca di Poggio are all waiting at the gate of the town to greet them. Savo's ideas about Italian castles are confused. He recalls that as a boy he had tried to sell puppies on the street near the Hotel Plaza "with all the rich, well-dressed men and women going in and out past the doorman in his grand uniform" (p. 11). He is not prepared for the reality in Italy. On the way, he and his wife pass an iron cross, a symbol of the past; he learns that St. Francis had lived for ten years at the foot of this mountain. He is touched when the twin boys who accompany them take off their shoes because they have decided that the sound of their walking may bother him. He learns about the people's affection for donkeys and also about their superstitions. As he recalls what he has seen in the paintings in the museums in New York and in Rome, he sees the reality of memory here.

He perceives the natural dignity of man in some of the simplest types. "Hello! Hello, everybody," he says, and he notices a tall thin man with twinkling eyes, who sweeps both arms out wide and makes a deep bow. This is Temistocle, known as the "baron."

They finally reach the castle (symbol of the old tradition) on the highest point of the town. The fortress is a welcome to their past. To them it seems to hold out its arms and squeeze the whole village into one snug, jagged little bunch; it is a rugged, tight-fisted place. As Savo further reflects that the whole town could have been set down in Columbus Circle, his ideas go back and forth and he is pulled back again. He studies the medieval well in the courtyard. It, too, is a symbol of tradition, and, he says, "We were in the middle of poetry; a kind of soft gray-green poetry" (p. 52). His world has become misty, but the American in him will not accept the fact that he should dismount from the donkey by using the backs of men.

21.*Ibid.*, "About the Author," p. 182.

The people's cordiality and generosity are overwhelming. When Savo suggests that he is hungry, the villagers come back to him loaded with supplies: figs, spring water, legs of lamb, jugs of wine, cooking kettles, and bundles of wood for a fire. They bring oil lamps, too, and other pieces of furniture "a bit worse for wear."

To Savo, the past begins to come alive. He discovers that the castle is painted with various coats-of-arms, those of a marquis, a Pope, and of the Countess di Cervara. Effusively, the people tell him the legends associated with these symbols, and the past becomes one with the present. The recollections of the people make their conversation timeless. The "baron" raises a glass of wine to toast:

> I drink to Cristoforo Colombo, and also to Amerigo Vespucci, who had the great privilege of giving America its name, to John Caboto, and to all the great explorers born in this sweet land of Italy, for having discovered the country from which a new lord comes to the Rock of Poggio. (p. 38)

The actions of the people dramatize the reality of the situation. Little Marcellina is caught "stealing" what proves to be three of Nina's cigarette butts, which the child is hoarding for her father. Gradually, Savo begins to realize the implications of being the "boss of this diminutive town," a term that has been a joke to him. Suddenly, it assumes a different meaning. He reflects that in this small town in that roofless house, a baby is going to be born, and he, after all, is the landlord. When he decides to put new shingles on the castle itself, his action is accepted as a great gift to the townspeople. "The roofs of the Rock of Poggio are going to be repaired. Viva! Viva!" (p. 52). In this way, his American practicality builds a monument to local pride.

Savo finds that his interest increases as the human problems unfold around him. Carefully, he wins the trust of the boy Alfreduzzo whom the townspeople have condemned as evil with the "curse of his ancestors." He asks Alfreduzzo to buy him eggs, proving that the boy, by carrying the eggs without breaking them, can dispel the superstition. Likewise, his American tolerance and expansiveness further reveal to the villagers how narrow their attitude has been toward the attractive Veneranda, whom the local women call "bad" out of envy. Savo's mother-in-law takes Veneranda to Rome as a maid, but the girl prefers to return to the village to prove her status, and to marry the local shepherd. Savo and Nina (his wife) have salvaged her "good name."

He discovers that the villagers have odd ideas about America. Old Joe asks Savo if he can curse in America without paying a fine. When Joe is assured that Savo has this privilege, he is convinced that America is a land of freedom. Later on, a villager, Gian-Domenico, is hurt while working for the new "lord." When Savo takes the injured man's sheep to pasture, the villagers begin to understand democracy in practice.

They do not, however, think much of some of his economic ventures. When he pays large sums of money for antiques for the castle, the people decide that the Americans are queer people who buy things that other people are ready to discard.

Savo's prime achievement is his breaking the legend of the woman whose husband had thrown her to the bottom of the well and whose face appears there on moonlight nights. He investigates the bottom of the well and there he finds a rare Etruscan statue, which he places in the cortile with the other antique stones. There is a hint of American domesticity when he writes that with the geraniums around her, she looked "prettier than ever."

As time goes by, he becomes more and more preoccupied with the village life. He helps to look for the lost Cheemy; he and his wife take part in the festa (celebration); life teems around them. When he helps the bell-ringer, the villagers note that he "kept time with the band." In fact, he has become in tune with everything about him.

Then, in the middle of all this absorbing activity, America summons him home; he gets a call from his agent in New York to play in George Abbott's *The Boys from Syracuse.* Therefore, as he watches Andrea place the last shingle on Veneranda's future home, he feels that his work is done. His purpose in returning to Italy has been accomplished; the old culture has repaired its frayed edges with the resources of the new.

When the Savos leave, as Veneranda releases to her father the rope pulled taut around the neck of the white cow the Americans have given her as a wedding gift, the shepherd gives the departing "lord" a flute. The musical instrument, the symbol of the spirit, is exchanged for the creature, the source of sustenance. Prophetically, Gian-Domenico, who has not uttered a word for twenty years, says, "We live for your return" (p. 181).

PIETRO DIDONATO (1911-)

The return to the "old sources of wisdom and beauty" was not always so tangible as it was for Jimmy Savo. For him his personal involvement was so complete that his counter-reaction to revulsion made an entire circle. Underlying themes rolled back through Italian-American subjects to the farthest point—the racial sources in Italy. For most Italian-American writers, however, the perceptive skill of "looking backward" came only after a prolonged period of growth; maturity brought them the detachment necessary for reconsideration, and the way to return to their original sources was opened to them only through a more complete cultural integration with the American scene. This does not mean that the subsequent results of the return were always a healthy fructification of concepts—a first novel was often a too-rapidly plucked green fruit, like Pietro DiDonato's autobiographical *Christ in Concrete* in 1939. But if the branch is productive the next yield is not only more delectable, but much richer in the distinctive characteristics of its bearer.

Pietro DiDonato was born in April, 1911, in the Italian tenement district of West Hoboken, New Jersey, the son of Annunziata and Domenic DiDonato, both of whom were born in Abruzzi, Italy. When Pietro was twelve years old, his father, a bricklayer, met with a violent death on a construction project. Because of faulty material used in its construction, the building collapsed and buried Domenic in stone and mortar. Young DiDonato had to assume the dead father's burden of supporting the mother and her seven other children. Pursuing his father's trade, he matured rapidly in competition with experienced and skillful masons. When, a few years later, Pietro's mother died, he left school in the seventh grade, but he continued to attend night classes in engineering after days of heavy manual labor. Eventually, with the cooperative support of his brothers and sisters, he moved the family to Northport, Long Island. At this time he decided to write, and he sold his first short story to *Esquire* in 1938, which subsequently was selected as O'Brien's best short story. The same story developed into *Christ in Concrete* (1939). Mr. DiDonato's other works include: "It's Cheaper to Be" *(Esquire,* March, 1939); a play; *The Love of Annunziata (American Scenes,* 1941); the novels *This Woman* (1958), and *Three Circles of Light* (1960); the biographical *Immigrant Saint* (1960) and *The Penitent* (1962); and the collection of selections from his large works, which he has entitled *Naked Author* (1970).

Christ in Concrete

With his book *Christ in Concrete,*[22] Pietro DiDonato was the first Italian-American writer to stir the American reading public to recognize fully the Italian-American experience. A significant documentation of America's social history, DiDonato's novel, appearing almost simultaneously with John Fante's *Wait Until Spring, Bandini,* is a theatrical presentation of the circumscribed world of Italian-American construction workers in New York City prior to the 1940s. Autobiographical in material, this first novel is creatively illumined by poetic speech, progressing with telegraphic action in episodes. DiDonato writes a story that educates by visual presentation, and shocks his readers into analyzing causes of the problems dramatized. Following the first chapter, which had appeared as a short story in *Esquire,* the book-length version develops through an impressionistic rhetoric reminiscent of Joyce. The characters, intelligent proletarians, go through a precisely

22. Pietro DiDonato. *Christ in Concrete* (New York: Bobbs Merrill, 1939).

developed revolutionary process as they respond to the duplicity and injustices of the established society that controls their environment.

Christ in Concrete is DiDonato's own story presented through the character Paulie. When the boy is twelve years old his father, Geremio, is killed in the collapse of a building flimsily constructed with imperfect materials because of the builder's profiteering. Geremio is the Italian bricklayer in America. He is of Abruzzi stock—the ancient "Brutie," Italy's mountaineers, "the Highlanders of the Peninsula." These mountains generate a hard-work ethos, not exclusively manual, since it has had its masters of aesthetics like Gabriele D'Annunzio. In this tradition of strength, Paul shoulders the duties of a man, shielded only by his determination to follow his father's trade in order to support his mother and his seven younger brothers and sisters. In chronological episodes, Paul experiences Veblen's philosophy, immediate sex, fortune-telling, expanding Russia, and religious crisis. Eventually he discards the superstitious myths that had sustained his parents and their friends in their passive acceptance of the inequities of their environment. Paulie is able to visualize a better world by diciplining his natural intelligence in night classes and by conversing with the men he meets at work. His sense of responsibility grows as the result of his mother's dependence upon him.

DiDonato, in re-creating his own story, succeeds in dramatizing the condition of the exploited immigrant worker. By intensification, he portrays the situation, prior to the current welfare structure, of a woman like Annunziata, Paul's mother, who is refused any aid at the municipal social-service agency. With deliberately sensuous language, he relates the problems of the family to the pressures of the construction-workers' world. As a result of the specific setting, the theme of the struggle for social humanism is circumscribed, but DiDonato's resolution is visionary and optimistic. Having shocked the reader's sensibility with scenes depicting Geremio's demise, Nasone's smashed body, and Paulie's breaking of his devout mother's crucifix, in the end the reader is left with the young protagonist and the prophecy and promise of the dying Annunziata. DiDonato writes:

> . . . son . . . everything in my world is for thee. For thee I desire the fullest gifts of Heaven—To thee must the good Dio bestow the world—and lasting health. He must bless thee with the flower of womankind and many-many children as yourself . . . and joy and peace without measure—for to me—thou art most precious. (p. 311)

DiDonato has created in Paulie a symbolic figure for the Italian-American experience, one who will transcend both the value system that his parents brought with them from Italy and the concepts that impinge on working people from their immediate environment. The luxuriant dialogue is refreshingly effective in its masterful sound, a translated Italian-into-English that is lyrical, onomatopoetic, crude, and reverent. DiDonato does not write English with an Italian accent, as George Panetta does; his is a different achievement—an English that conveys robust Italian conversation and lyrical colloquialism through natural American speech. He also demonstrates a story-telling gift that is real and appealing. What might cursorily seem to be an immature fondness for experimenting with words is, rather, an effective method of communicating the gropings of the boy-protagonist. It is to the author's credit that the rhetoric demonstrates the truth that dignity and intelligence are not the social prerogative of just any articulate group. With this book DiDonato has struck bluntly into America's social conscience.

This Woman

In his second novel, *This Woman,*[23] Pietro DiDonato explores in personal and intimate terms the depths of a man's conflict with himself as he struggles between the seduction of his senses and the persistence of his ideals. The latter he classifies also as spirit or soul.

DiDonato tells the story of Paolo, son of Geremio, who meets an attractive widow, Isa Tromm. Isa, the daughter of fundamentalist Southerners, balances her present isolated status against that which she formerly enjoyed as the wife of Jack Tromm, a much older man who had been a hotel manager of some substance. Sparing no details, DiDonato traces the progress of the love-making of Paolo and Isa as they dodge the voyeuristic watchfulness of Isa's tyrannical mother, Mrs. Latham, who insists that Isa had caused Jack's heart attack. After considerable turmoil, the love affair culminates in marriage, but Paolo is obsessed by the imagined presence of the dead ex-husband. With compelling intensification, the momentum grows to a crisis. Paolo insists on exhuming Jack Tromm's body in order to assuage his irrational, comsuming jealousy, constantly aroused by the presence of the dead man's clothing, pictures, and sundry personal possessions that Isa has refused to destroy. The mother-in-law's goading is the device by which DiDonato creates the dramatic tension of the action, especially with the details heightening to the scene of the desecration, the mad act of expiation that restores Paolo's sanity while it deranges Isa. Gradually, in the resolution of the story, Isa regains her lucidity and reveals to Paolo the traumatic shocks in her past and the truth about her child, Jacky. Eventually, with the birth of their son, Isa and Paolo attain sufficient equanimity to look forward to happiness and a rewarding future together.

In this book, Pietro DiDonato explores a man's obsession with three

23. Pietro DiDonato, *This Woman* (New York: Ballantine Books, Inc., 1958).

things: brickwork, women, and his soul. He writes that the protagonist's "mental theatre" starts with the factual solidity of building construction, reverts to the mercury of sex, and culminates with the balm of spiritual judgment. This triad of experience spans Paolo's moral growth as he marks time. His artisanship in bricklaying is an external projection of his cultural past, which he uses as a criterion to judge the values in his American environment, as he does with "the grimy structure of the Hotel Modern," which revolts him. The idea of having inherited values of physical structure is personified on one level as Paolo struggles with his real nemesis, that his father was crushed to death in the collapse of a building under construction. With the catalytic experience of his attachment to Isa, he is thwarted in his search for either vengeance or peace, realizing that this woman is a "wife-stranger, grinning, gloating." She is physically what America has been apparently to all Italian immigrants. His mother appears to him in a dream, speaking to him in Italian, saying of his wife, ". . . the secret service [men] of God are looking for her; for this you deserted your father and mother!" (p. 183). However, he is married to Isa and he has tried to make her "one with him." That she has not been willing to part with Jack Tromm's effects appears to him a refusal to take the sacrament of repentence. In the sociocultural area, Jack Tromm is to Paolo the symbol of the old American industrialist, a product of the Germanic ethos that was able to control the mind of America at the end of the nineteenth century. During her marriage to Jack, Isa's illicit love-making with Reilly was a thematic application of the symbol of the Anglo-Saxon's puritanic ethic as it broke down upon the corrosive challenge of the Irish. Now, Paolo, in analyzing Isa, judges her pejoratively, especially when he compares her with his Madonna-like sister. He wonders why he has been crucified with the presence and the need of this woman.

The identification of "this woman" is a categorizing of ethnicity in miniature. Paolo is a second-generation Italian-American wedded to a nation that has served others before him.The country is symbolized by Isa, with whom he has fallen in love, "his mate with his name, his confidante, his friend, his great romance, the chosen, the blessed in the temple, the sharing receptacle and fountain-head-to-be . . ." (p. 138). Gradually, like the immigrants lost in American society, he finds that he is chained "in an alien house," and that he will participate in the future in an "identity-forfeiting" communion of his body and soul. Paolo, like many Italian-Americans, has what DiDonato terms a "Catholic necessity" for the purification of the Confessional in order to consummate the unity of the body, "flesh and soul." Furthermore, he feels that Isa's smile masks the mocking that Italian-Americans have perceived in the smiles of an Anglo-Saxon establishment. When Isa, seeing him in a rage, says that she is afraid of him, he tells her that she has brought her fear with her, long before she met him. At the climax of the story, the final burial of Jack's body is the symbolic rooting of ethnics who preceded the Italian-American, and the act is representatively violent. With the expiation of this necessary act, Paolo concludes that idealism is a functioning illusion, that even oneness with a woman is a romantic dream. The reader senses that DiDonato is saying, on another level, that the American Dream is an inspiring but romantic idea. However, his endemic Italianism is his salvation, and he feels he is God's agent. He is regenerated with the "Confessional-leaving newness," and he reconciles himself to his identity. He feels that it is good to know he is still alive and, "Romanly," to wear this life like well-fitting armor.

The novel is a sensational exposure of obsessive desire and a probing analysis of the human being's disposition either to transformation or to destruction by love. DiDonato is a sensitive explorer of the socially layered conditions of people reacting in personal trials and in their group relationships. His characters in *This Woman* are cultural symbols. Paolo, for example, is the expiating son of an economically frustrated father, whose work had been imposed upon him because of his ethnic limitations. Aesthetically, this book is disturbing and unbalanced, externalizing as it does the mental torture of the protagonist. DiDonato uses traditional words and phrases in very untraditional ways; ideas are sometimes submerged by catalogues of terms through which, somehow, the author hopes to find a precise point of communication. The tumbling turmoil of the words reflects poetically the agony of the protagonist's mind.

Three Circles of Light

After his popular first novel and his probing second novel, *This Woman,* Pietro DiDonato revamped his value judgments about some concepts of Italian-American culture in *Three Circles of Light.*[24] In his mature reflection, DiDonato recalls the background of his father's death, which was the subject of his first book, *Christ in Concrete.*[25] In the retelling he becomes reconciled with his traditional religion. He faces the dual nature of Italian-American religion with an honesty that enlightens the reader, especially in the treatment of what is termed "folk religion," that substratum of faith that exists below the level of organized religion.

In *Three Circles of Light,* DiDonato shows that many Italians in America retained their belief in faith healers, especially in what they felt was their need to counteract the Evil Eye. DiDonato describes, for example, the powers of La Smorfia, who is the high priestess of healing to the "paesanos." The victories that LaSmorfia scores over the local Dr.

24. Pietro DiDonato, *Three Circles of Light* (New York: Julian Messner, Inc., 1960).
25. *Christ in Concrete* (Indianapolis: Bobbs-Merrill Company, 1939).

Episodio rankle him. When the physician tries to treat the daughter of one of the "paesanos" for a "tumor," without success, La Smorfia steps in and delivers a ten-pound baby. When a young wife, complying with Dr. Episodio's advice, puts her baby out in its carriage in wintry weather and the baby is turning stiff and blue, LaSmorfia comes by and breathes life back into him with mouth-to-mouth resuscitation.

The old woman's power in the neighborhood is as great as a saint's. Superstition mingles with faith, and some of the people see no distinction between the two. When La Smorfia offers her primitive Mass to break the summer heat in 1918, the ensuing bolt of lightning is accepted as a real effect of a direct cause. It is the task of the local priest to expel the imported superstitions, which he calls "spiritism, animalism, the imitative and certain so-forths" (p. 80).

DiDonato's reflection is concerned not only with the primitive among the Italian-Americans, however. He is equally concerned with reconciling the attitude, not uncommon among Italians, that the mother of a family had to remain loyal to a faithless husband. The main plot of the novel deals with the familiar story of an Italian immigrant—in this case Geremio diAlva—who takes an "American" mistress, Delia Dunn, but finds it inconceivable either to give up his wife, Annunziata, and family, or to have his wife and family condemn him. The story is told from the point of view of the growing boy, Paolino, who speaks for the author. Paolino's mother is the symbol of womanly endurance, which DiDonato extends further to stand for her whole ethnic group as it endures adversity. When the father dies, the fourteen-year-old Paolino matures; he has learned the fear of God and a sense of sin. That the father's affairs may have brought down the judgment of God is what the author dramatizes through the feelings of the boy. Morality pervades the characters and their motivations. When Geremio's deception is discovered, a neighbor, Filomena, warns the betrayed wife,

> Annunziata . . . the American heart and soul feels not for our kind. Have Geremio discard Delia Dunn and those Americans who look down upon us as an inferior race. Remember seriously, when darkness strikes one of our homes, it is the paesano who brings the order of strength, and the sacred taper of care and love. (p. 191)

With these words, the woman makes Annunziata the symbol of the problem of a whole culture that tolerates the corruption of a dream.

DiDonato is not merely reiterating the theme of the laborer frustrated by overwhelming odds; he is also crystallizing the moment when the immigrant realizes that he is confronting the challenge of the new world. He reflects that it was not the American Dream that championed the family of the dead Geremio. "Present were the members of the parish of San Rocco, the fathers and mothers of my people" (p. 229). Whatever pursuit of the "Dream" they may have planned, they know they have to do it by themselves.

The author's return to his own is complete as he embraces not only his people's religion, cleared of superstition, but also the true sense of belonging that his being identified with them gives him. At his father's wake, Grazia LaCafone, a neighbor, literally grabs Paolino's hands, symbolically snatching him back into the racial group. She says to him:

> Wouldst Americanize yourself like "Jerry Phillips"? Who lies, in the box of the dead, here, "Jerry Phillips" or the Vasteso Geremio diAlva? . . . Cheek to jowl, lip and trowel with the "Americans" he would be, eh? We Vastesi from centuries before Christ know who we are, but when will the "Americans" know who they are? Are the "Americans" here to lament. . . . No! As true as the wounds of the Savior, to the "Americans" Geremio is a useless and dead "wop!" (p. 281)

Although he writes that the happiness of illusion is sacrificed to the darkness of truth, DiDonato looks forward to the time when he will remember the "distant dreamings." His reflection, therefore, is extended to the future, along with his conviction, which is emphasized by his mother's words, that his father has preceded them to immortality.

JOHN FANTE (1911–   )

As DiDonato rediscovered his identity by developing his religious faith, other writers sought to find themselves in different ways. John Fante, for example, became absorbed in a Freudian search for an ideal, which he eventually identified with his mother. Born in Denver, Colorado, on April 16, 1911, he started his self-probing while he was a high school boy at the Jesuit Regis High School, from which he was graduated before he attended the University of Colorado. Leaving the university, he went to California to look for work. After a succession of attempts to settle himself as a cannery hand, a hotel clerk, a stevedore, and a grocery salesman, he tried once more to program himself to academic life by enrolling at Long Beach Junior College. Expelled for his "general laxity" and disruptive behavior, but inspired to write, he concentrated with success on selling short stories to magazines. Encouraged, he decided upon writing as a career. When his first book was not accepted for publication in 1934, he rewrote it as the widely acclaimed *Wait Until Spring, Bandini* (1938). Partially autobiographical and representative of a wide spectrum of the search-for-identity theme, his other books include: *Ask the Dust* (1939), *Dago Red* (1940), and

Full of Life (1952). Most of Fante's material deals with people who are caught in the urban environment. In his themes he comes closer than any of his predecessors among Italian-American writers to a realistic treatment of the psychological.

Dago Red

In the collection of stories in *Dago Red*,[26] Fante discusses, particularly in "A Kidnaping in the Family," his urgent desire to know his mother as she had been when she was as young and beautiful as she was in her picture. Because he desires to marry his mother, his incestuous reflections confuse the concepts of his religious training. He rationalizes that if divorce is impossible, he will wait for his father to die. Searching his catechism, he is relieved to find no law forbidding mothers to marry their own sons. A growing boy who nurses such ideas grows up, not surprisingly, into a man of passion and resentment.

In his maturity, Fante's resentment grows as he thinks of the past. The "back-trailer" is sometimes apt, therefore, to turn his search into a quest for security, the security that he feels he has lost by "not belonging." When he tells of Paul Carnati's rejection by Maria Scarpi (the author's mother) and his rushing furiously into marriage with someone else, the writer says, "Italians called this a spite marriage" (p. 5). Such a comment is possible only because he is overconsciously Italian, for obviously, anyone of any other nationality would also call such an arrangement a spite marriage.

His resentment would build a fence around everything he recalls. When he describes the feast of Saint Rocco, he observes that all the important people attended, "including a lot of Americans who didn't count but who came down just to look and laugh, because they thought feast days on the North Side were amusing" (p. 6). His subjective attitude carries the reader from this festive scene through the pathos of a whole winter's anguish, during which time the father attempts to maintain some dignity under the burden of another of the hard winters of unemployment in Colorado.

Psychological analysis assists the author's incisive description of the interior growth of an Italian-American boy. The reader feels the author's personal identification with the boy's troubled conscience when he goes to his first confession, and feels the impact of his intense relief after making it. The author, speaking as "I," feels happy; he says his penance and goes into the sunshine of a serene afternoon. His style glows with youthful lyricism. "I never felt so clean," he writes, "I was a bar of soap. I was bright tin-foil. I was a new suit of clothes. I was

26. John Fante, *Dago Red* (New York: The Viking Press, 1940). This series of stories appeared previously in *The Atlantic Monthly*, *The American Mercury*, *Story*, and *Harper's Bazaar*.

a haircut. I was Christmas Eve and a box of candy. I floated. I whistled."[27]

Inevitably, Fante's reactions to racial antagonism become strong. Carrying his emotions to their logical conclusion, he is involved in brutal physical combat over use of the words "wop" and "dago" in the story "The Odyssey of a Wop." When O'Neill, the grocer, greets him with "Hello, you little Dago!" he says, "So I detest him and never enter his store if other customers are to be seen, for to be called a Dago before others is a ghastly, almost a physical humiliation. My stomach expands and contracts and I feel naked" (p. 165).

The use of these words gives rise to a double-edged conflict. The author paradoxically loves his heritage more, while he hates it for this embarrassment it causes him. He tries to hide his lack of "American things." At school he does not listen to the priest who urges him to be proud of great Italian-Americans like Columbus, Vespucci, and John Cabot. He would turn against everything that reminds him of his father, mother, and grandmother. But he admits that, away from home, he can "sense the Italians." It is an encounter and a conflict. "We look at one another and our eyes meet in an irresistible amalgamation, a suffusive consanguinity; I look away." When he looks away, he returns to the obsessive experience, the hearing of the hated term that was used even by the non-Italian priests. His search for identity then continues; he follows the Plaza man, who, he says, "doesn't know he's as good as a god in his waiter's apron" (p. 171). In the waiter's mistaken self-effacement the author recognizes his "own corpse" and realizes that he has "come home" quickly and quietly to a rational comprehension of even the term "wop."

Later on, out of violence and apostasy, the writer undergoes the counter-revulsion that leads him to need a confession like that first childhood one. Tired of illicit love, he actually welcomes, with a renewed rational control, the physical danger of a real earthquake. When he is aware of the survival of St. Vincent's golden cross, he reminds himself that this is a coincidence; Aquinas would call it that, and so would Augustine, and St. Ignatius, and Father Driscoll, and so must he. He remembers what Aquinas wrote about superstition and repeats that he must be rational. "And I laughed because I was so scared, and I was praying with instant familiarity a prayer I hadn't remembered for fifteen years" (p. 197). The act of returning to his faith is symbolic of his returning to his heritage.

The religious theme in the stories, therefore, supplies the path for Fante's racial regeneration. The final story, "Hail Mary," is replete with symbols. Willie Cox, the assailant of the author's Catholicism, is the symbol of everything the author must overcome; he knocks Willie's teeth out. Fante is also aware of a slump in Hollywood, which empha-

27. *Ibid.*, "First Communion," p. 34.

sizes the low ebb of morality around him. He identifies with others as a victim of the depression; he owes the landlady for his rent. All this represents the externalization in his environment of what has recently been an inner conflict. Then, with renewed faith, he ends his account on a note of optimism, as he is about to mail out his story.

Wait Until Spring, Bandini

Fante used psychological realism more and more as he developed his former themes. From the short stories, he extended his themes to a full-length novel, *Wait Until Spring, Bandini.*[28] In this novel Fante's protagonist is seen to mature through the device of monologue. From the reflections in Bandini's mind the reader gets an impression of Maria's personality, also. When she talks about Frederic's cold, Bandini immediately frets about the "cold in his soul," and the reader is invited into the depths of that soul. Likewise, Fante involves the reader with the mind of the adolescent Arturo, who yearns for a girl named Rosa, and the author lets us share the boy's reverie when he visits the Blessed Sacrament. To understand the characters, therefore, the reader must see them through the eyes of Bandini, who, looking at Maria, sees that "She was so white, that Maria, and looking at her was seeing her through a film of olive oil" (p. 13).

Fante's work demonstrates that a general solution through optimism is still blurred by the trauma of ethnic isolation. The confusion resulting from the sense of not belonging finds its symbol in the writer's constantly mistaking his love for Rosa Pinelli for his love for his mother. The trouble here is psychologically analogous to "action out-of-place" in the author's difficulty in differentiating his loves. His very identification is blurred, since, as his character Arturo, he prefers to be known as John Jones. Arturo's misery increases and he seeks comfort in daydreams. When the boy is shocked at the sight of his mother scratching his faithless father's face, he sublimates his hurt in a daydream about Rosa's death. Finally, Arturo is able to mature.

With his maturity, he acquires courage. When Mrs. Heldegarde, a widow, loses her argument about dogs, she descends to common name-calling. She yells, "You peasants! . . . You foreigners! You're all alike, you and your dogs and all of you." Arturo, who has never answered her before, shouts back, "Brutta Animale! . . . Puttana!"[29] As his words give him release, he turns from a tongue-tied silence to an articulate encounter with a basic problem. The fact that he has become articulate indicates that hope lies ahead for ending his confusion and for illuminating the place where he belongs. That place gains firmer rooting in a constantly changing America.

28. John Fante, *Wait Until Spring, Bandini* (New York: Stackpole Sons, 1938).
29. Ugly animal! . . . Harlot.

Full of Life

Humor attests to adjustment, and John Fante's next book, *Full of Life,*[30] is a joyful comedy of domesticity. It exudes mature serenity and comfortable acceptance. Fante identifies his own creative instinct with his wife's giving birth to his son. In this narration of human achievement, Fante charts his own change from the agonized themes of uncertainty and quest to those of tangible reality and immediate fulfillment. He is now, as a man who owns a home, economically involved, and, now that he is about to become a father of a family, is also involved socially. No longer concerned only with the struggles of the ethnic worker, Fante here tells the story of an Italian-American who is now part of the mainstream of American life.

John Fante tells this story simply, directly, and lightly. The uncomplicated plot hinges on the domestic problem of the discovery of termites in the kitchen floor. Because the narrator's purse is slim and because his father, Nick Fante, is the "best bricklayer in California," Papa, always available, becomes a functioning member of the young Fante's enlarging household. Papa and Mama Fante are adamant that Joyce will have a son, and the author makes an amusing narrative device of the old Italian superstition that garlic in the keyhole and salt in the bed will assure the birth of a male child. When Papa Fante arrives with his wine jugs, salami, cheese, and tool kit, he forms an immediate alliance with Joyce. They forget why Papa has come; the floor, which caves in under Joyce's weight, is not so important as the more aesthetic construction of a fireplace. John feels that he is a superfluous appendage in all the anticipation; his role extends to absurd proportions when Joyce must be rushed to the hospital. After the birth, the new father feels trapped, with futile language and "miserable inadequacies," but he rallies in restored faith and a shared emotional identity with Papa.

The point of this book is symbolized in Fante's wife, Joyce, who changes from being a calm and rational partner to reigning like the legendary pregnant earth-woman, demanding fulfillment of her compulsions and attention to her obsessions. Fante externalizes this transformation by Joyce's substitution for her customary exotic scent, "Fernery at Twilight," of a plain cologne that sanitizes her presence with the smell of laundry soap and household alcohol. The author pursues the theme of change on many levels. For example, Joyce insists that John promise he will never treat their child as Papa had treated John, beating him with a trowel. John, allowing that Papa had been right because the boy had sold the concrete mixer to buy a bicycle, agrees to read books on how to rear children. It is Papa, however, who cannot change, whose loneliness is irradicable, and who remains "all the way

30. John Fante, *Full of Life* (Boston: Little, Brown and Company, 1952).

from Abruzzi, a peasant to the end, sitting on the bench, alone in the world" (p. 101). A symbol of many Italian-American writers, John promises Papa that he will write the story about Uncle Mingo for the baby to read. John's adjustment to his environment is shown to be unstable on the way to the hospital; he feels hysteria like a shapeless, smoky, and unexplained explosion. It is significant at this point, however, that the hysteria is due not to ethnic fragmentation, but to a universal experience. This universality marks Joyce's change, also; she punctuates her religious conversion with a maturity, a "quality of womanhood not associated with her pregnancy; a tradition, rather, an identification . . . with the church's high reverence for women, an elevation of her to that state I felt for the Virgin Mary as a boy" (p. 152). After Joyce goes into the delivery room, John runs into the chapel, and his contrition restores his lost religious faith. After the birth, feeling that it is women who are full of life, John and Papa share the "loneliness of man and the sweetness of all men and the aching haunting beauty of the living" (p. 176). In the end, the sound of Papa's singing as he is packing his things provides the theme music for a hope-filled future created by a constructive past.

There are specific Italian applications of the theme in this story. In San Juan, for example, although Papa admires the "non-Italian girls his sons had married," he suspects them of trickery or of ignorance of how procreation works. He, without grandsons, scowls at the four grandchildren who accompany Joe Muto on his visits. When John comes to get him, Papa is excited, a patriarch surrounded by the ancient aroma of "ambrosial redolence, fresh green peppers sizzling in golden olive oil, charmed with the fragrance of garlic and the balm of rosemary, all of it mingled with the scent of magnolias and the deep green richness of vineyards in the back country" (p. 37). John realizes how much he has changed. Later, when Papa chides him about his "over-educated immaturity," John recalls the "priceless learning handed down from generations of Abruzzian forebears." He finds much of this knowledge difficult to use, however, because it is imported primitive superstition. Again, when Papa engages the pregnant Joyce's assistance in shoveling sand into the mortar box, John objects, reminding him that his wife is not in Italy and is not used to this kind of work. But Papa obstinately insists that the child is his grandson, and that he is going to be fine. This paternal obstinacy extends its force to Joyce as she exercises her new Roman Catholicism which, in a circling progress, rests upon John in a reconcilation with an important dimension of his inherited culture. Fante writes,

> Somehow I would capture the old feeling, the reaching out with the fingers of my soul and grasping the rich fine joy of belief. Somehow I had felt it was always there, that I had but to move toward it with only a murmur of desire and it would cloak me in

> the vast comfort of God's womb. There was the scent of incense, the creaking of pews, the play of sunlight through stained-glass windows, the cool touch of holy water, the laughter of little candles, the stupendous reaching back into antiquity, the baffling realization that countless millions before me had been here and gone, that other billions would come and go through a million tomorrows.[31]

Ultimately the strength of Italian antiquity reaches Papa, himself. Going to confession for the first time in fifty-five years, he reestablishes the spiritual thread linking him to his son and his grandchild. The confession is in Italian, and it is a rambling discussion, "indistinct and intense," retaining the strength of Papa's individuality; but he makes his personal adjustment, from which exercise both he and the priest emerge "tired and perspiring." On a cultural level, this adjustment demands a similar effort.

Full of Life is an unassuming and unashamed testament of optimism. The exuberant tone of the book carries into the style, which pulses on with clarity and airy rhythm. Colloquialisms now and then alert the reader to listen to the family conversation. There are ethnic overtones, but the focal drama is universal. And Fante has evoked a plausible human experience with a comic sense that both delights and relieves the reader, for this domestic tale might have been treated clinically or journalistically. Aesthetically, and from a distinctly male point of view, Fante achieves a satisfactory parallel between the fulfillment of natural reproduction and the sustenance of the human spirit. While his characters pleasantly dramatize ideas, they are primarily people engaged in the most genetic and galvanizing experience of mankind. As a novelist, John Fante is, with this book, an author of universal American experience.

In summary, then, the fourth phase of the development of Italian-American fiction is the period when the writers reacted against the group immediately preceding them, who had turned away from Italian-American subjects. Now the authors experienced counterrevulsion, a return to their original sources and racial traditions in recognizable materials as well as in basic themes. In so doing, the novelists became more realistic, because they were now attempting to understand themselves by exploring the road back to their own ancestors in a search for their "place" as a solution in overcoming their isolation. This phase of counterrevulsion may, therefore, be further defined as a back-trailing, a taking another look at Italian-American life to see where it stood in the panorama of the national scene. Above all, the

31. *Ibid.*, pp. 148–49.

writers in this period of return had an advantage over those of the first and second phases, the advantage of their being native Americans whose assimilation to the national culture gave their presentation the added dimension of objectivity.

Jo Pagano in *Golden Wedding* gives the history of his parents' life, fifty years of shared living as the "history of an era," and he integrates the development of Italian-American activities with the normal growth process of the nation. In this novel the author looks to the future with hope, but in *The Condemned* he poses questions about the problems inherent in the conflicts within our society. Pagano says, for example, that being criminal is synonymous with being underprivileged, and he thinly veils his characters whom he presents as the "aliens" within the complex of the nation. *Aliens* he now defines as those who are isolated from the country's wealth or from the accepted levels of status. He writes extensively on the fragmentation of the individual as being due to "action out-of-place," and he contends that the community must be held responsible for the lack of the integration of its members.

Most of the novelists narrowed *action out-of-place* to mean the struggle to overcome isolation. One of the most lucid presentations of this conflict is Guido D'Agostino's *Olives on the Apple Tree*, in which the author directs attention to the danger of attempts at too-rapid assimilation. D'Agostino insists that the chief concern of the immigrant is not that he should worry constantly about being an American, but that he should work to become the best man he can possibly be; in so doing, he will become an American. In the process of "breaking into society," a man, like the protagonist Emile, must allow himself time to give as well as to take. The world, says D'Agostino, offers more than the survival of the fittest; a man must make the effort to make himself fit.

That the Italian-American must fit into the American complex like an instrument in an orchestra is a persistent theme of Jerre Mangione, especially in *Mount Allegro*. To analyze this "fit," he recalls the incidents of Italian-American life in his old neighborhood in Rochester, and he concludes that the isolation of the individual in that community was due to his being caught between the two parts of a dual society. Mangione himself differs from the writers of the second phase of the development of Italian-American fiction in that he has become more assimilated than those writers and correspondingly less isolated. He contrasts the cultural values of Sicilians and Americans and observes that assimilation is the result of compromise between human beings. In the attempt to overcome the feeling of "not belonging" lies the individual's greatest struggle. So baffling may this struggle become that the writer seeks contact with people who may offer a solution simply by being the original source of the concepts of the participants in compromise. Mangione, for example, pursued the elaboration of his theme by going to the land of his ancestors. Writing of his experiences in *Reunion in Sicily*, he emphasizes the dual nature of the Italian-American, but he is also able to evaluate more clearly how much he is an American. In *The Ship and The Flame*, characters are floating on the high seas of international concepts and their ensuing conflicts. Life goes on, Mangione shows, with an American exuberance, pursuing a dream that will never fully escape its European frame of reference. It is quite possible, eventually, for the dream to solidify into a functioning reality, as Mangione shows in *Night Search*.

Some writers, however, restrict their observations to the native environment and prefer to demonstrate to what degree Italian-American life has changed in the United States. For example, Italians become like other Vermonters in Mari Tomasi's *Deep Grow the Roots*, and Vermont absorbs the Italians in *Like Lesser Gods*, while Calabrians learn to laugh at themselves in George Panetta's *We Ride a White Donkey*. But the degree of adjustment made by the European-tested Italian-American is perhaps best illustrated in Jimmy Savo's *Little World, "Hello!"* Savo makes his visit to Italy not to define the twofold nature of his racial condition, but to clarify what he, an American, has inherited from his ancestral soil. A clear, physical symbol is cast before him: he is made the lord of the castle of an Italian village. This tangible liaison puts him squarely between the two cultures, and he is responsible for any action that may result from his position. In this book the author emphasizes as clearly as any writer before him the importance of the differences in the minor cultural concepts of two races and the influence of individual human behavior on the fusion of those concepts. Savo indicates that it is only because he is so much an American that he is able to be "in tune with everything about him" in Poggio. Counterrevulsion in him has, therefore, made a complete circle, rounding out Italian-American life with the return to its original sources.

Although Mangione and Savo emphasize the picture of the integration of the Italians in America by the contrasts they make with the original sources, other writers have added dimension to the picture by offering more specific perspectives in the American setting. Pietro DiDonato, for example, recalls the frustrated immigrant workmen in the story of his father in *Christ in Concrete*. Later, with the detachment acquired with greater maturity, he overcomes some of his former resentments and reconciles himself with his personal desires in *This Woman* and with his traditional religious faith in *Three Circles of Light*. In these novels the author arrives at the constantly recurring theme in Italian-American fiction: the moral power of the individual to overcome adversity and to use his will to adjust satisfactorily to the environment. DiDonato illustrates this theme especially with the character of Paolino, the boy who rids himself of illusions but looks to the future with optimism.

The reaffirmation of his religious convictions preoccupies John Fante, also, but he "back-trails" to old subjects through psychological probings not found in previous Italian-American writers. Much of the conflict in Fante's plots is the activity of the "out-of-place" emotionalism that supplies the themes of his short stories in *Dago Red.* He achieves optimism through religious faith, but he does so only after extensive introspective monologues like those in the novel *Wait Until Spring, Bandini.* Finally, the transition from internal struggle to vocal articulation brings him face to face with reality and humor, as he shows in *Full of Life.*

Reality, therefore, is the goal for which this group of writers is striving, a reality they achieve by an objective evaluation of the conflict between and within the two cultures they have been exploring. Looking backward, studying the sources, analyzing "place" and "out-of-place" with relation to the isolation of the individual, recognizing the need of "belonging," and breaking away from internal repression to articulation, the writers of the counterrevulsion view the future with hope. Without any illusions of rapid escape into the American Dream, they anticipate the integration of the hyphenated Italian-American into a distinctive American in literature.

7

ROOTING

When a civilization strikes its roots in a new soil and eventually extends its branches, it grafts its culture into that of the land in which it has planted itself, blending into patterns of harmony. This harmony marks the fourth phase of the development of the national immigrant culture of the United States, the level at which the new environment is understood and the assimilated culture finds its expression in accord with tradition. To reach this phase, the Italian-American requires a further step of development because of his particular racial inheritance. His alien (non-Anglo-Saxon) background has increased for him the degree of conflict which, in turn, has produced his greater isolation and, now, as a result, complicates the process of his integration. This additional difficulty, however, rewards him with a supplementary quality—an optimism engendered by increased challenge and honed by the test of his indomitable faith.

This quality of optimism is revealed in the books of modern Italian-American novelists who have written works that may properly be included in the anthologized national literature. This particular ethnic American fiction, however, has some distinctive features that appear consistently in the novels of newer members of the group up to 1965, writers including Michael DeCapite, Luigi Creatore, Joseph Petracca, and Lawrence Madalena, Raymond DeCapite, Charles Calitri, Joseph Caruso, and Rocco Fumento.

MICHAEL DECAPITE (1915–1958)

Michael DeCapite was born on April 13, 1915, in Cleveland, Ohio, where he was educated, and eventually graduated from Ohio State

University. He pursued graduate studies in philosophy and architecture at New York University, but floundered for a while as a laborer, a clerk, and, significantly, as a reporter. Gravitating to a writing career, he wrote short stories and magazine articles. Finally, he decided to concentrate on longer works. His books include *Maria* (1943), *No Bright Banner* (1944), and *The Bennett Place* (1948). The succession of Michael DeCapite's books reveals a development away from autobiographical materials to more universal and objective treatment. He remains discursive in method, however, and his characters are symbols of ideas.

Maria

In his first novel, *Maria*,[1] DeCapite relies heavily on autobiographical materials covering a span of three generations. Setting the narrative in his familiar Cleveland, he tells the story of the protagonist, Maria, an American (like DeCapite's mother) born of Italian parents. Dutifully, Maria consents to a family-arranged marriage, and subsequently leads a difficult life with Domenic, the husband who fails and eventually abandons her. Tenaciously determined to rear her children as exemplary Americans, she withstands the series of misfortunes that constitute the episodic structure of the book. The events are viewed through the eyes of Paul, Maria's eldest child, who is confused by and resentful of his parents' and grandparents' mode of living.

DeCapite writes this book ostensibly from his own experiences; the reader senses that the author is subjectively engaged in the narration. For this reason, the tensions of immigrant life in America that the writer is dramatizing have a personal and authentic vitality. Although much of the action is external, the characters are not artificial. DeCapite has successfully portrayed real people, unfamiliar types in American literature, like Bernardino, an amiable man whose emotional ties are with his mother country and who suffers particular misery in the difficult task of transplanting his roots to this country. The point DeCapite is emphasizing is that his people are not without roots, and that they are faced with a replanting of what is already mature. The process of this transplanting requires strength, whether it result in success or defeat. With Domenic, Maria's husband, it spells defeat, because his financial failure shames him so that he cannot face his friends and relatives. However, the reader senses that Domenic is not so representative of the author's theme as are the other characters, who are stronger, more appealing, and more prophetic of a better future. DeCapite has painted a sensitive and sympathetic portrait of the Italian-American's rooting process.

1. Michael DeCapite, *Maria* (New York: John Day Company, 1943).

No Bright Banner

Everything is firmly rooted in the scenes of Michael DeCapite's *No Bright Banner*[2] In this novel, he develops Paul Barone's coming-of-age in the context of America's coming-of-age. Paul gropes through his overstimulated adolescence at the same time that the nation is haphazardly seeking to shape itself from the amorphous materials of its burgeoning industries. A second-generation Italian-American whose grandparents came, respectively, from Abruzzi and Naples, DeCapite sets his novel in the South Side of his native Cleveland during the 1920s. His studies in philosophy and architecture help him to look at the South Side of his city, and he sees not a "Little Italy," but a place alive with work, expansion, prosperity, and feverish optimism. Because the steel mills are the economic spinal cord of the city, the workers have built their flimsy, two-story houses near the factories, which houses have become ugly with dirt and smoke. DeCapite observes that, in his memory, the Flats have not had the features of a particular country or of one ethnic group. Everywhere are elusive landmarks of the coming and going of past immigrant groups, but the remnants are feeble. The South Side, he says, is the same everywhere in America today; it is made up of citizens and a few noncitizens, nearly all of them working people. It is a section of the city that has been built by Polish, Russian, Irish, Greek, German, and Italian communities, each interweaving with the other. Children of all complexions roam about, and they bear names of various national origins; Barone, Kelly, Livitsky, Schultz, Meliki. Only the street names recall the Scots and the English who were the first settlers. This South Side had not been part of the early settlers' dreams, but its evolution was inevitable. DeCapite says that "without form, slapdash, expedient, destructive and constructive, merciless and vital, the South Side was peculiarly American" (p. 4).

When you grew up, recalls the author, you remembered your father as set apart and different from the father of your friends; but there had been a positiveness in that difference, a determination that was direct and decisive. Remembering was a romanticizing of the past, and the "old man" was part of that past. The often-repeated story of the father's leaving the South of Italy for a new world, the incidents of the hostility of this new world—these are now intangible reminiscences in a tangible present. As the author gives details of his father's conditions, he recalls them, not discretely as his father would have, but with the totality of his own growth as an American. He feels that his father, Carlo, had left not a beloved country, but a social idea, an unchanging

2. Michael DeCapite, *No Bright Banner* (New York: The John Day Company, Inc., 1944).

land where an instituted aristocracy would not recognize the individual personality of the members of the peasantry.

Although Michael DeCapite was born in the South Side, he does not devote the entire book to the Italian-American struggle in America, as he did in his first novel, *Maria.* The narration has another level, the author's probing of the character, the delving below the surface of events. *No Bright Banner* is, therefore, the story of a universal human being, Paul, who happens to be the son of an Italian immigrant. No longer a stereotyped character, this boy grows up, goes to college, and then roams from job to job—a young man looking for his "place" in a mature world. In his quest to find himself, Paul joins a leftist group of aspiring literati in New York, is disillusioned by their collective fragmentation, and joins the army to fight overseas. DeCapite portrays his protagonist as one of the many who hope that the future may yet contain the salvation of a stumbling humanity. The strength of the integration of the cultural concepts of two nations is symbolized by the author in the warm father-and-son relationship.

Paul's optimism is the reward for surviving many minor tests. In what might have been a typical description of a boy making his first Holy Communion, DeCapite adds the rather disconcerting note that, in his mind, the boy reflects that it is amazing how easy it seems to be good: "all you had to do was to keep yourself strong and not be tempted by the gang" (p. 26). In this simplistic conclusion ironically lies the crux of his life in connection with others. When the members of the gang do tempt him, he learns that the victory lies in fighting and in giving the "other fellow" a black eye.

The boy continues to grow. DeCapite says, "The corner was the city and the South Side, and it changed as you changed" (p. 38). It is no longer a matter of juxtaposition. The writer becomes a part of his environment, and the important thing is that both he and the environment change simultaneously. The boys have a clubhouse, and the difference between the author and Lefty is not that he is a "Dago," as Lefty calls him, but that there are different kinds of boys. Lefty is the sort who wants to go to poolrooms, while Paul is the kind who wants to help build the clubhouse. In this difference lies the symbol of a change in social attitudes. The individual seeks his peers according to the disposition of his own personality.

Paul is not like the men of his father's generation, whose members had read Dante and the nineteenth-century nationalistic writers of Italy. His mind is fired with Tom Swift, Dick Merriwell, King Arthur, Robin Hood, Tom Sawyer, and Huckleberry Finn. Significantly, he dreams of the Mississippi, and wishes he might join Huck on the raft with Jim. He has done some hand ploughing in the American soil.

The clubhouse becomes more his home than the place where his family lives. Spring is the time for baseball, but the passing of the season brings with it a maturity measured by violence. As the boy grows up in the brutality and upheaval of the South Side, he learns discretion, and his life takes on direction and purpose. DeCapite's story of this boy is not merely a rambling reminiscence; it is the recalled presentation of the facts in the development of an American. The episodes in this boy's life become typical of those of any boy. When, for example, his teacher catches him giving another pupil the answers in a test, Paul becomes aware of an insecurity that upsets his usual equilibrium. He becomes a demon at studying, and he allows his teacher to believe that his learning is the result of her teaching. He has applied a practical lesson in policy.

Later on, he learns about steel; he works in this industry into manhood. Then, while he is at the university, social convulsions shake the nation. In his corner of the world, he discovers that he is dissatisfied with the university because he must spend hours paginating books in the library in exchange for room and board, while the other students dance and go to games. Despite his wretchedness, he must study because he needs desperately to succeed. In his loneliness, he becomes independent, and the hill beyond Claremont University becomes his haven for observation and introspection. From this hill he tries to envision the horizons beyond his existence—the "old man," his experience with steel, the South Side. Where do they fit into this new scheme? He wonders. Then things fall into place. While reading Sherwood Anderson's "I Want to Know Why," he finds himself. For him, now, all his impressions, his childhood incidents, and his growing maturity compress into a "moment of beauty." This moment is the point of harmony at which his isolation ends, and, in tune with himself, he can proceed with assurance. He satiates himself with the "puzzling elegiac sadness of Americans, the profound uprooting of individuals" (p. 87), and he devours *Dark Laughter*, *Poor White*, and *Winesburg, Ohio*. He goes on to *Main Street*, *An American Tragedy*, and *A Farewell to Arms*; and in the fall he realizes that "it was America" that has been in his thoughts, and he feels comfortably at home.

Now his college friends become his peers. With them he shares the emotion from the past, which he identifies in the present with his friend Steve's account of having seen a boy crushed under a railroad train. Life vibrates with a new tension, a different awareness of violence. The journalistic defense he helps to prepare on the death of the boy, Tom Brewster, is misrepresented as subversion. The faculty, most of whom DeCapite reveals as having lived by compromise, do not come to Paul's defense, and his expulsion presents him once more with the specter of isolation and struggle. He thinks of all his friends, each frustrated in his own way, and he finds it difficult either to hold onto his dream or to discard it.

New York and a group of uprooted "free-thinking intellectuals" open new vistas. He meets members of the "Party"; some write plays, some, novels; they all discuss literature.

Paul goes to a "meeting," and he is nauseated "at the spectacle of Americans following a line, carrying around a dialectic bludgeon, without any critical judgment of their own" (p. 196). At twenty-five, he looks around at his fellow-Americans, all exploring and searching. A new frustration grips his undefined spirit; but it is a shared feeling and it becomes an amalgamating force. Suddenly, Paul finds himself "at home again," and hurries away from his confused acquaintances to the security of his Aunt Mary's.

Reality compels him to go to work, and it is good to do so, even in the city Street Department. His maturing cognizance is dramatized when he defends his co-worker, Buck, against the police officer who calls his friend a "nigger." He goes to Chicago and becomes a reporter on the *Record*, a position that puts him into active contact with violence. In time, he becomes friendly with another reporter, Jiggs, a counterpart of himself. When Brandon, his old friend, dies for the "cause" in Spain, Jiggs speaks for both of them: "I'm beginning to feel like a Hemingway character" (p. 282). Jiggs, Paul's alter ego, becomes his conscience everywhere, the liberal critic and the nonconformist to the creed of "they shall take who have the power and they shall keep who can" (p. 288). It is the shared-by-growth experience that makes the two men alike, but Paul must eventually write that "even from a distance, I was battling with you, Jiggs" (p. 289).

In his own regeneration he recognizes that the many who are lost in alcohol and sex "were lost before they got these," and that the war would bring direction to a rudderless crew. Believing that futility and cynicism are on the way out, he fights in the war because he hates the lie of fascism more than the half-truths of our own society. There is something of old Carlo's positiveness engrained in him. In his final letter to Jiggs, a testament, he says that as he sees it now, he does not think it was Communism or Marxism that Brandon and Lillian (his bohemian "girl") had believed in so much as it was the "order" their minds were after; it gave them a lifeline in a world that only pretended to be moral, but really was not. He confesses that he is looking for this order, too, and the search makes him think of his "old man," the positive personality. "He gave me confidence because he believed in himself; he had a kind of integrity in everything he did and said; more, he left me with the impression it was possible to have integrity" (p. 291). He explains how reason without heart has taught us inhuman techniques and ends his long letter, significantly, with a universal note: "We need a fuller truth and in seeking it, I think we are finding ourselves; . . . let enough of our humanity be left to us, let enough of our youth and energy remain so that we may go on with the struggle after this is over" (p. 294). Finally, this struggle identifies Paul with his father, Carlo, and his friend, Jiggs: the past and the present. He is now the assimilated man whose roots are firmly grounded, but sprouting new growth. At the conclusion of the novel, Paul, like America in her mission, has gained confidence in himself, anticipating a future of progress in the betterment of the interrelationships of all humanity.

The Bennett Place

DeCapite demonstrates professional expertise in his next work, *The Bennett Place,*[3] a mature book that he handles with caution and psychological perception. The writing is lucid, vigorous, and unpretentious. The reader feels that the author identifies himself with the character George Mather, who (just as in the past DeCapite had been stimulated by the memory of the "old man") is needled by the older professor, Cherrington. The essential thing for Mather is to get his book finished and published in order to receive a pension. The protagonist, therefore, must make an adjustment; he must continue to compromise to earn his pension, his place.

The novel is a thoroughly American one in subject, and, like many of its contemporary works, it is developed with introspective monologues of psychological realism. Mather is a lover of nature; but the woods, flora, and roads that he describes are always intimately connected with the memories of incidents past or present. As he studies the buttonwoods and cedars, he remembers Katharine's conversation about the great walnut's being rubbed smooth by deer shedding their horns. He reflects that it is amazing what a place or a note can evoke. Without too many nuances, he interprets externals in a Jamesian manner. Ideas spring into action through the association of objects as he contemplates the manner in which comprehensive minds synthesize ideas into concrete symbols. For him, the teaching of history is something more than lecturing about scholarly data, because, like more than a scholar, he wants to bring to life the great seminal minds that made the country—Williams, Paine, Jefferson, and others.

The immigrant archetype has become an American type among other Americans. What has formerly been isolation with a sense of not belonging has subsequently evolved into psychological detachment and self-control. George Mather is the descendent of the Emilios, Geremios, and Carlos. While his prototypes had struggled with racial issues, Mather must work to find stability and continuity in order to produce anything or to make a contribution, "especially these days when the ways of men were tortuous indeed and culture was crumpling everywhere" (p. 39). He senses, however, that the culture is "crumpling" because it is changing, like Shelley's dead leaves, to hold and protect the seeds for the next season.

3. Michael DeCapite, *The Bennett Place* (New York: The John Day Company, Inc., 1948).

The old society's deterioration is symbolized in Katharine's suicide; and the unraveling of the causes of the dead girl's loneliness is the exploration of society's sickness. Symbolically, another form of alienism projects itself in the analysis of the stuttering revelations of Johnny O'Malley, whose mother had done the Bennetts' washing; while the native conscience is incorporated in Dr. Henry Benson, who "wanted to sound an alarm, break through the thin smugness and send it reeling with reproach, with its sins, snobbery, monumental dullness, with all the incestuous secrets learned through forty years" (p. 180). Benson had known the truth without being told, "for the moving finger that released her (Katharine) was not compelled by a moment's insanity—it had been trained for years" (p. 181), in the moral duel between the girl and her grandmother. This duel represents American society as it strikes a death blow to its decaying traditions in an action the reverse of that of the growth of aliens from a decaying tradition to a robust regeneration. The story of the breakdown of the Bennetts is symbolic of a national malaise. The conflict between the sterile arrogance of the grandmother and the soft elusiveness of Katharine is the struggle between the generations of "native" Americans. The doctor warns Mrs. Bennett, "The world's moving . . . and she doesn't belong to you."

The key to a void in American culture lies in Katharine's words, after her grandmother's death, "Sturdy American stock, wasn't she? . . . One more speech and I would have screamed. I loathed every minute of it, just as I hated, yes, hated her!" (p. 197). The significant fact is that now that the grandmother has died, the surviving descendant is afraid; she feels that she is shipwrecked and drifting. Dr. Benson listens to her cries of desperation that she is sick of nothingness—doing nothing, being nothing, facing nothing. Symbolically, he turns from her to the presence of Stan, the "second-generation alien" who now is the real world. Benson (the residue of the American culture that survives the crumpling) feels that he has awakened from the "abstract state he has been in since yesterday afternoon; he felt a need for the very sanity and life he doubted" (p. 208).

Hope, optimism, and sanity, then, are the distinctive features that mark the rooting of the Italian-American contribution in the national fiction. Modern writers, no longer on the defensive, return to old themes with the enthusiasm and verve of rediscovery. Joseph Caruso, for example, again describes the West End, in his case the one in Boston, retelling the story of the teeming life of the Sicilians in *The Priest.*[4] Raymond DeCapite reiterates the autobiographical approach

4. Joseph Caruso, *The Priest* (New York: The Macmillan Company, 1956).

in *The Coming of Fabrizze,*[5] and *A Lost King.*[6] Charles Calitri extends his subjects beyond Italian-American themes, but characteristically retains the struggling-hero subject in *Strike Heaven On the Face.*[7] Calitri tells the story of Walter Davis, modern liberal American, a dean who cares enough about his students to help them to solve their problems even if it means fighting his principal, his school board, and his wife. The themes are diverse; they take the direction of exploration of those forces which drive individuals against authority, and of the isolated "aliens" in their conflict with established norms. Significant is the fact, for example, that Calitri writes his story for constructive aims, to help both teachers and students toward fulfillment.

LUIGI CREATORE (1921–)

The pattern of the interaction of cultures is dramatically illustrated by Luigi Creatore's *This World Is Mine.*[8] The psychopathic ward is an objective correlative for the modern world; the Navy man suffering from amnesia is the contemporary individual, the human being who in his subconscious has retained the trauma of isolation, the pains of "not belonging," and the thwarted struggles for fulfillment. Escapism is a balm for this individual who cannot find his place in the real world, a community of pluralistic forces, an America made of many cultures. Amnesia is Victor Blake's escape, and his struggle lies between his impulse to return to the conscious world and his desire for the comforting isolation of the dream world with which his amnesia protects him. There is a magnetic pull for him to remain in the ward, not having to face what he really is, a being whom he no longer knows. All he does know is that he left a theater, went into the sunlight, and forgot where he was going. To him "realization that you are sealed in comes as quickly as you can turn your eyes from one blank wall to another" (p. 3).

As he stumbles to find out more about who he is, Victor Blake (the name on his identification card) eventually finds himself in a ward of the Navy hospital in California. He sometimes cooperates with the doctor; sometimes he does not. Soon he identifies himself with a friend, Lee Benson, who becomes a character in an escape story in his dreams. He plans a real escape with another inmate, the quiet Carter, from whom he will somehow abscond in the future. It is an endless pattern

5. Raymond DeCapite, *The Coming of Fabrizze* (New York: David McKay Company, Inc., 1960).
6. Raymond DeCapite, *A Lost King* (New York: David McKay Company, Inc., 1961).
7. Charles Calitri, *Strike Heaven On the Face* (New York: Crown Publishers, Inc., 1958).
8. Luigi Creatore, *This World Is Mine* (New York: Rinehart and Company, 1942).

because, according to Creatore, this is a sick world. When the men in the ward are playing poker, they symbolize men everywhere. Reynolds hates Cohen because he is a Jew; this hatred starts a fight that involves seven men, while Victor remains an observer. The doctor, the voice of sanity, warns them,

> We're all in uniform to fight and win the same war. One man is just as good to his country as the next man. . . . There's no place for hatred in our own ranks because a man has a different religion or comes from a different section of the country. Didn't you learn anything in school? Didn't they teach that your country was built by a hundred different peoples with different creeds? (p. 114)

With this book, Creatore is a modern American writer, an Italian-American whose roots have now, indeed, struck deep in his national soil, and his subjects are those which concern many other writers of American novels. Creatore, however, is especially concerned with the man whose action is "out-of-place," a theme that appears with increasing frequency with Italian-American writers. His man with amnesia must help himself; he must not remain endangered by satisfaction as he says, "No choosing of sides, no responsibilities, no puffed eye and cracked lip for me" (p. 117). Hemingway reminded the twentieth-century world that "No man is an island," and these words inherited from John Donne seem to be the key to the thrust of modern existence. To withdraw to the island is to turn away from the rhythm of the globe.

The saving grace in Victor Blake is that he operates with no hate and no pessimism; but it is hardly a sanctifying grace, because he admits that he would not know whom to hate. His philosophically naïve realism isolates him. He says, "Against whom should I direct my wrath? Against the Jews? I could be a Jew. Against the Negroes? . . . one drop of Negro blood in my veins would damn any feeling I might develop against the black-skinned people" (p. 117). Victor Blake is, therefore, the abstraction of the American whose memory of all prejudices has been removed. He is, of course, not in a real state, because he is an anomaly; he does not know what he is; he could be anyone and it does not become him to hate his own kind. He admits that he is the living proof of the fallacy of intolerance. Dramatically, his unreality endows him with the particular flaw that he does not like other people's contests, including the war. It begins to become clear, therefore, what has caused the amnesia; the doctor's probings slowly reveal that Blake has had a delayed shock as a result of his experiences with violence in active battle.

Normally, the man who escapes from reality fights the man who tries to force him back to it. Victor would like to shake Dr. Mader from his pedestal; he tries to trick the doctor. But the application of sanity is the only method with which to handle the sickness of others, and the doctor knows what his patient is doing. Blake is Creatore's modern American. He therefore extends Blake's escapism to the multitude that will not confront the facts. People only say that they wish to better themselves and the world. In practice, it is easier to destroy entire religions and make thousands of people inferior by legalizing one totally organized thought. Creatore writes,

> And merely by keeping our original positions, we rise above the people we push steadily down into the mud. . . . Then we can call them filthy kikes, and filthy dagos, and filthy niggers—and we escape with clean hands. Clean minds, too. Clean of anything resembling thought, understanding, or decency . . . one morning the world will wake up with amnesia. (p. 124)

Blake enjoys the irresponsibility of his position. He dreams of a girl; he later wonders if she is his wife, since he knows he has one because of the gold band on the finger on his left hand. When Carter first suggests physical escape from the hospital, Blake stalls for time to think about this alternative. Gradually, the thoughts of freedom outside the institution seduce him. Perhaps there would be a price to pay. Finally, he resolves that freedom could not be any more torture than this imprisonment of the mind and body. His dream-memories of Lee Benson help him to decide; the ward becomes a magnet for memories. He knows, however, that a magnet has only so much power and that it can attract only the things that are close to it.

The idea of returning to a real world of broader horizons attracts him. With this objective in mind, he ends his cooperation with the doctor, who represents truth; he would follow his own sickly way. Remembering the bombings, he admits a general disgust with the world that has soured and retched its insides all over a seemingly innocent earth, a condition that had made him look to escape. However, he still does not want to find out who he is, because the merits of his dream world seem rich. He must not look at his records, which the doctor finally suggests he may see. Then, gradually, under sedation, he hears a voice he has not heard before, the voice of his conscience, which tells him he must cooperate with the doctor, the way to the truth. The struggle continues; he must fight the sedation; he must stay awake to escape with Carter, who looks at him whenever he closes his eyes. He makes an observation that systems are not good; they should all be abolished, even this system of Carter's watching him. This observation helps to strengthen his will to fight the medicine, another system. When Carter approaches him and talks to him, Blake cannot answer him audibly, and he succumbs to the sedation, the means to truth. Later, when Carter is discovered a suicide, Blake makes the provocative comment that the knife was Carter's weapon for escape and that everyone has just such a weapon. He returns to his own dreams of Lee Benson.

The war is filled with uniformed men supposedly fighting for freedom. Since militarism is universal, Creatore is writing not about the problems of one racial group, but of those of the entire nation. He asks not "Why is the heart of the Italian-American breaking?" He asks instead, "What good did it do to gain land, to win battles, if the soul of Democracy was dying?" (p. 223). This recalls the questions of Gennaro and Demetrio, and all the players who are shuffling their cards with all other men. It becomes clearer to the amnesia victim that the escapists all escape to death—Lee Benson, Carter. He decides finally that "I would think this thing out. I was strong. I always had been strong" (p. 237). Dr. Mader, who has forced him back into this reliance upon his will power, then leads him to his waiting wife, Connie. Approaching her physical reality was like walking into a darkened room and suddenly turning on the lights. The light symbolizes the return to will power, a constructive reality in a world darkened by the pessimism of intolerance and materialism.

Creatore's novel is a well-constructed story of the individual's struggle with his own isolation, the withdrawal going deep into his own mental world. This situation is not uncommon in contemporary fiction, but the significance of Creatore's Victor Blake is that the author does not let him disappear into darkness, nor does he watch him wander away into the rain of fate. On the contrary, the writer has led the protagonist to will himself from darkness into light.

JOSEPH PETRACCA (1914–1963)

While some Italian-American writers were successfully rooting their concepts in apparently native American characterizations, there were others who continued to portray the circumscribed ethnic communities. One of these is Joseph Petracca, the author of *Come Back To Sorrento,*[9] a series of stories without chronological continuity.

Petracca ties his stories together with the character of Patsy Esposito, an Italian who works on the Brooklyn docks, saves his money in a boot, and plans to return to Sorrento where he will buy the land to nurture an olive grove. All this careful planning is disrupted, however, when Patsy (Papa) meets the attractive woman who becomes Mama, the convincing persuader and excellent cook, who pleasantly commits Papa's life to settling in America. Upon his marriage, he assumes the responsibility of taking care of Nonno, the grandfather. In time, the birth of five children increases his immobility, both dutifully and emotionally. Finally, he gives himself completely to becoming a naturalized citizen of the United States. He becomes a voter, choosing to support Al Smith because the candidate is a Catholic. He has, indeed, become a part of the American scene.

9. Joseph Petracca, *Come Back to Sorrento* (Boston: Little, Brown & Company, 1952).

Patsy Esposito is a familiar Italian-American father-type, a tragicomic figure who is haunted by a frustrated dream. Petracca has made his protagonist move with life and authentic sound. The Italian-American vernacular is evocative, and the lively incidents rekindle the memory of struggles that once appeared tragic but now are recalled with nostalgic amusement. The author has contributed a significant work to our ethnic artifacts.

LAWRENCE (LORENZO) MADALENA (n.d.)

Lawrence Madalena's *Confetti For Gino*,[10] likewise demonstrates the persistence of a fragmented section of American life in its portrayal of transplanted Sicilians in the tuna-fishing colony in San Diego. While the author has drawn a detailed picture of an entire community and its resisting folkways, he tells a sentimental story of a second-generation American-Sicilian, Gino DeMarino, who falls in love with a non-Italian girl. Intermittently with the development of Gino's romance, Madalena dramatizes Gino's devotion to his midget brother. Much of the tension of the events is created by Gino's reluctance to accept the fixed mores of his people. The plot is not the essential strength of the book; Madalena has emphasized the environment and its pressures.

Confetti For Gino is worthwhile as a detailed and solid documentary; Madalena has caught the primitive sturdiness of a transplanted people, unashamedly functioning with all their convivial, social, and sexual idiosyncracies. Gino's resistence to the dramatic activities of his people is symbolic of the difficulty of replanting roots in a new soil. The Italianized American phrases throughout the book orchestrate the disparate incidents into a completely authentic communication of sound. The author achieves a certain unity, also, in his representation of this particular close-knit Italian colony in California. The book supplies a terse chapter in our American social history.

RAYMOND DECAPITE (1924–)

Raymond DeCapite was born in Cleveland, where he lives with his family. His father and his grandparents were born in Italy. After he was graduated from high school, he served three years in the United States Coast Guard during World War II. After the war, DeCapite worked as a shipping clerk and in a restaurant. Entering Ohio State University in 1947, he subsequently earned his college degree at Cleveland College and an M.A. degree in English from Western Reserve University. While he was an undergraduate, he started to write, con-

10. Lawrence Madalena, *Confetti For Gino* (New York: Doubleday & Company, 1959).

tinuing to do so while he worked at various posts as a sales-order clerk, cashier, and crane oiler. He then became a rewriter, first for a Cleveland shipping magazine, and then with the Ohio News Bureau Company. *The Coming of Fabrizze*[11] is his first novel.

The Coming of Fabrizze

There are writers who direct their protagonists into such light that their focus is poetically evocative of the heroes of past romantic movements. Raymond De Capite creates such an ethnic hero with *The Coming of Fabrizze*, whom he draws with easy, broad strokes, simply sketched on a brightly visible canvas with a background of the Italian "colony" in Cleveland in the 1920s. DeCapite, exuberantly manipulating his main character, galvanizes the many hopes and ambitions that the immigrants looked to fulfill in that decade, when America was to them a legendary Eldorado, strange, enchanting, promising, and possible. The book is a story of the daily events of this group of people, of how they exert the greater part of their energies to accomplishing their hopes, and how they achieve a measure of success. DeCapite also explores the conflicts that temper this success, while the characters rally from defeat to pin new hope on the image of a man who has integrity and bravura.

Following his Uncle Augustine, the charismatic Cennino Fabrizze comes to America and charms the community of Italian immigrants in Cleveland, where he goes to work on the railroad. In a short time, his natural leadership helps to elevate him to foreman of the laborers. Fabrizze also becomes the successful storekeeper around whom the other workers center their activities. His magnetism draws to him all the other characters, the conniving Rombone, the convivial Antonio, and the sage Mendone, the father of the beautiful Grace. All the people in the neighborhood adulate the vibrant, zestful, and capable Fabrizze, and they all concentrate on promoting his courtship and marriage. As life proceeds with a crescendo of success, Fabrizze and his neighbors launch on the critical adventure that climaxes the plot, their investment of their earnings in the rising stock market. Guided by the equivocal Vivolo, they are all caught in the suspenseful momentum and fascination of the ticker-tape, which hurtles them all into brief, heady success and the inevitable crash. Totally involved, the reader rides the crest of the story, and, with the neighborhood, anxiously awaits the following year for the sound of the music that is the announcement of Fabrizze's name up and down the street.

The point of this novel is the portrayal of the Italian immigrants in America during the nineteen twenties and the participation of their experience in the national socioeconomic structure. DeCapite shows

11. Raymond De Capite, *The Coming of Fabrizze* (New York: David McKay Company, Inc., 1960).

that success or failure is often measured by personal criteria; and, often, for a group, the conflicts are generated among themselves as well as from their environment. There are many levels of the theme of the pursuit of economic happiness; Augustine, for example, has lived in America as though he were in a cocoon, working for the railroad and hoarding his money. When he, like many other immigrants, returns to Italy, he discovers America in himself. However, while he is there in Rivisondoli, the villagers ask him if he has seen in America the hundreds of people who leave Naples each month. He gives his *paesani* the message that America is a good place for people, but that for the young, it is better. He says, "But it means work. It means work" (p. 17). Once established in the new country, Augustine's nephew, Fabrizze, starts at the "beginning" with a shovel, the universal initiating instrument of the Italian man in America. Reaction equals opportunity; when the men are asked why they have left the Abruzzi, they have a "strange moment" of silence. Augustine tells Fabrizze that he will come and go to and from Italy until he has no home at all. Fabrizze, however, by applying himself, builds a reputation for Italian workmanship. As McGuire, the foreman, rides a smooth stretch, he knows that it is a bed put in by Fabrizze. He says that when the engine pounds and shakes, it is "a stretch by Gallagher" (p. 104). While he has unmatched skill at work, Fabrizze is exploited in the stock market investment. The neighbors feel, with Grace, that there is talk of thousands, but they see less money than ever. DeCapite then turns to the source of the trouble, the man who has come among them, Vivolo, who admits that he is the only one who could guess that the stock market would break. While everyone's fortune falls, Vivolo earns over a million, and he has already packed his bags to leave. It is a time of trouble for everyone, and Fabrizze, the honest man who sells everything he owns to pay his debts, moves away to invest his small earnings. Spiritually, he never leaves the neighborhood; his presence is kept alive mysteriously, because he personifies the hope that is in the people themselves. He sends word to them that, after their barrel of trouble, there will come their time for happiness. His letters to the neighborhood are epistles of hope for their future. Raymond DeCapite transcends the prosaic as he makes the reader hear the music of this hope.

Fabrizze is a folk-hero of the Italian-American zest for life, personifying the theme of regenerative experience that DeCapite evokes with skill and verve. On his first job, Fabrizze is recognized as the "man who'll set fire to this row" (p. 30). One of his co-workers calls him "the piper." When Rossi asks Fabrizze how he gets such work out of the men, the young foreman answers that the men were saving the work and he challenged them to spend it. He is irresistible. DeCapite writes,

> They came to fetch him for work. Shouts were heard as they swept him like a prize into the railroad yard. His success was startling evidence of the opportunity in America. (p. 36)

Even his courtship shows his executive ability. When he addresses Grace Mendone, he admits to her that he has been looking for her and that he has been gathering information about her, a pleasant task "like gathering flowers." After Fabrizze has married Grace, one of the men, Penza, comments "They were telling me that Fabrizze needed a wife. He married the most beautiful girl in the city. They were telling me he was too young to be a foreman. Now he's the supervisor. They were telling me I had a hole in my shoe. Now I have a hole in the other shoe" (p. 63). Distinction follows Fabrizze. His child inherits his blue eyes and reddish-gold hair, and the neighborhood adulates this atypical beauty. Fabrizze's success is above average, too; therefore, his losses represent a greater tragedy for all of them. Because they have depended upon him, he sells his house and land, divides the money among them, and leaves them. After he is gone, everyone is dejected. The neighborhood feels his loss like a sickness; he has been their shining hope. Now he is their lost child.

One of the neighbors, the wise old Rumbone, magnifies the legend by suggesting that Fabrizze has gone to Italy. In this way, he intensifies his usual insistence that "he belongs with us." They all agree that the lost savings do not matter; they can all start saving again. They want Fabrizze to come back. When Fabrizze's letter arrives from Chicago, the entire neighborhood is elated; and, in passing the letter around among them, they feel that he belongs to them again. DeCapite indicates that of such expansively personal communication are heroes made. The tiny neighborhood has every nuance of the human ability to structure common aspirations into the transcendental dimensions of an ideal man.

Raymond DeCapite writes with the direct impact and evocative lyricism of poetry. Many of his phrases have resonance and the precision of *le mot juste.* His dialogue is crisp, vigorous, and instantly communicative, like the compressed lines in a rapidly paced drama. Economical with description and exposition, DeCapite has the magnetism of the born story-teller.

Personal struggle, the continuing involvement of the human being, is the theme, also, of DeCapite's *A Lost King* (1961), in which the son, Paul Christopher, cannot adjust to the pressures of modern living in his father's household. On the whole, DeCapite makes a fair success of his protagonist's problem, using the father-and-son relationship as the framework of his story. In this novel, in which "wit is the ache of unexpressed love,"[12] the author anticipates the treatment of family emotional problems without sentimentality, an approach that has been reached almost simultaneously by other Italian-American writers.

This kind of treatment, for example, marks the maturity of Charles

12. Anne Ross, "Books," *New York Herald Tribune,* December 31, 1961, p. 7.

Calitri's third novel, *Father* (1962), in which he explores the theme of a son's need to know his father before he can know himself. The Italian-American-Jewish narrator must remove the sense of guilt he has in knowing that his father had once been a Roman Catholic priest in Italy. By conquering himself, he is able to make the psychological adjustment that engenders love and admiration between the Jewish son and the Catholic father. In this situation, therefore, what has once been treated as action out-of-place because of racial differences has now become intensified in a more universal human relationship. Hence, the final mastery of the isolation that separates two worlds, two cultures, and two generations rests on the pivotal point of the encounter between two human beings.

ROCCO FUMENTO (1923-)

This point of encounter, this victory over isolation, is adequately represented by Rocco Fumento in *Tree of Dark Reflection*[13] in which the author treats the father-and-son relationship on a more universally applicable psychological level. The interfusion of love and hate is identified as the workings of a guilt complex inherited by the son from the father. Between them, religion is not a difference of form; it is the underlying factor whose quality and degree of importance differentiate the internal disposition from which each of the men responds to his environment. Fumento has learned from his own background the multiple human problems that involve the Italian-American Catholic family. Born in North Adams, Massachusetts, in 1923, he was educated there in the public schools. After serving two and a half years in the Army in World War II, he went to Columbia University, graduating magna cum laude, after which he did graduate work at the State University of Iowa. A teacher of the techniques of writing, he skillfully presents in his book the story of Daniele Faustino. Daniele searches two worlds and two generations in the struggle to rid himself of a guilt complex that he cannot expiate until he knows the background of his father.

Daniele Faustino grows up in an Italian-American neighborhood in Wakely, Massachusetts, the only boy in a family of four children ruled by the iron hand of a blasphemous and lecherous father, Domenico. The family is tenuously held together by the pious and ineffectual mother, whose love for and loyalty to the father serve only to strengthen the male parent's tyranny. Of the sisters, Guilia hates the father, Theresa fears him, and Florence despises him. After Domenico abuses his family beyond endurance, a doctor advises the family to have him committed to a mental hospital. When he is eventually

13. Rocco Fumento, *Tree of Dark Reflection* (New York: Alfred A. Knopf, 1962).

released, the still unsubdued father returns home, but immediately abandons his family. In the interim, Guilia marries to get away from home, Theresa runs off to New York for an ill-fated future, and Florence marries a local mill hand. Daniele grows up in the bitter poverty, the hatred, and the unhappiness bequeathed by his father, finding his only comfort with Mark and Miriam Stern, two Jewish companions whom he admires and loves. Eventually he goes into the army and is sent to Italy. Going to Limotola, his father's birthplace, he visits the old woman who had reared Domenico. From her he learns about his father's childhood, and from his Uncle Guido, a priest who is his mother's brother, he learns that his father had once studied for the priesthood. Domenico, however, had not taken his vows because he had fallen in love with Guido's sister. Daniele understands that his father's brutality stems from a sense of guilt, because Domenico had really believed in his vocation. When Daniele returns to America he seeks Miriam, who is the only one who has kept in contact with Domenico. Miriam reveals that she is about to become a Catholic nun. Fumento uses her as the catalyst to reunite the father and son. She points out to Daniele that his intense hatred for his father has always been closely allied to love and that Daniele, who has apparently lost his own religious faith in his obsessive pursuit of his father's background, has substituted the devil for God. On reflection, while uncovering his father's secret, he reveals to himself his own faults and eventually recovers his faith.

Specifically, Daniele's psychological involvement with his father escapes him at first; but Fumento warns the reader. "He'd punish me, but always through my mother. It was as though in my mother he'd found a scapegoat for me" (p. 41). In his puerile innocence, he cannot understand his father's behavior, but he can see in Giulia's eyes the hatred of Domenico, who drives even the parish priest to his death. Giulia refuses to have her father at her wedding, and the other sisters withdraw from him in time. In all this, Daniele can only sense what is wrong, and he is disturbed that he cannot find a plausible reason for these tragic developments.

Since each member of the family is eventually left alone, Daniele seeks the friendship of Miriam and Mark Stern. Symbolically, this relationship represents the assimilation of opposing cultures. Daniele wonders why, if they were so different, so cruel, he was unable to tell these Jews from all the gentiles on Appleton Avenue. As their relationship grows with their childish pursuit of a haven of "unchartered Eden" in a spot beyond the railroad tracks, Daniele arrives at the moment when he feels the dichotomy of excitement and peace at the same time. He senses that Miriam seems to understand his silence and is pleased by it.

Meanwhile, as he finds peace with the Sterns, he is tormented by his father. When Daniele explains that he cannot play with Miriam on the Sabbath, his father tells him that God has come between them, that man creates God, and sooner or later his creation becomes his enemy, and then man struggles to destroy God. Daniele cannot understand what his father means. He is even more baffled later, when he visits his father at the hospital for the mentally disturbed. His parent greets him with "I prayed to God, but no one came, and then . . . I prayed to the devil" (p. 147). The only certainty the boy feels now is that his father is a madman, and that the sight of his father in this state is a sign of his own damnation.

Meanwhile, the ties holding together the rest of the family have begun to disintegrate. Because Theresa cannot bear the father's presence, she leaves home. When, as a result, Florence, who alone does not fear the father, asks him if he'd peacefully go to hell, he answers, that he can not go because he is already there. Daniele notices the father's mirthless laugh and, later, his frenzied outpourings in his sleep. When he visits his father at the asylum, the boy notices that the old man sheds constant, involuntary tears. Then, when Domenico returns home only to increase his former blasphemies, the family is horrified. Finally, to their relief, the father leaves home.

Daniele, however, finds no freedom. One night he meets his father, who tells the boy that he has stayed in the same town only to be close to his son. Domenico has fled from Florence, who pities him, and he feels he has had too much pity from the mother. "It's better to have you—even with your hate" (p. 192). With these words the broken man speaks for the culture that accepts its rootings in the new soil, however that soil may have resisted it. Furthermore, he accepts the condition of his future even if the old world, as symbolized by his wife's love, would cling to him at any cost.

To accept such a relationship shocks Daniele. As a result, he must go to a psychiatrist, and he becomes a symbol of the universal sickness of maladjustment in our modern society. The physician constantly probes his fear, repeatedly asking him what his father is like. Socially and personally, this question evokes responses in him. He begins to understand that, because the father has abandoned them, the family must go on relief for food; because the father has given them only hatred, they are all disturbed.

The effects of this hatred increase in proportion to its causes. At Theresa's funeral, Daniele is repelled at the sight of his father, whom he has not seen for some time. Despite this revulsion, Daniele has confused feelings later on when he must leave for the Army. Although he cannot understand why, he cannot resist visiting his father. He confesses to Miriam, with whom he spends his last weekend as a civilian, that he does not know why he is seeking his father, but he is full of questions about him. He finds no answer to these questions, nor does he derive any comfort from seeing his father. To rid himself of his increasing hatred he would, in fact, rid himself of all emotion and all belief. He cries out desperately to Miriam,

> Help me not to believe, to destroy Him, and then perhaps I'll find peace; then I needn't shake my fist at God because there'd be no God. (p. 293)

In these words we find another variation of the old pattern: conflict, isolation, assimilation. If Daniele can isolate himself completely, he may arrive at some solution later; and his assimilation is implied as being connected somehow with the confusion of his image of his father with his belief in God.

He discovers, however, that he can rid himself neither of his father nor of God. His need directs him to the Italian village, Limotola, his father's birthplace, and to his Uncle Guido, who knows about Domenico's past. He is impressed with the wisdom of his uncle, who seems even more learned than the average Jesuit; and he is amazed that this Italian priest is a scholarly professor of English and American literature. Significantly, the priest comments, "Faulkner, Hemingway. But I'm afraid I don't see the seeds of greatness in them. They write only from the surface of their minds" (p. 399). His most overwhelming surprise, however, is at Uncle Guido's revelation that Domenico had had religious training. The priest says,

> he was so good, . . . not only religious, but truly spiritual. . . . I was always rather envious of him because I felt he was in direct communication with God and I was not. (p. 410)

Having learned the truth about his father, Daniele returns, and, when he is released from the army, he goes to Columbia University to study writing. In his subsequent intellectual conflicts with his religious faith he arrives at some temporary conclusions. When a pervert who is trying to seduce him is killed by accident, he accepts this tragedy as a warning and becomes once more articulate in prayer. Finally, during his parting visit with Miriam, who is leaving for the nunnery, he learns the details of the final period of his father's life. Miriam, who had never had any serious religion at all, has discovered her vocation through her knowing Domenico. She makes Daniele understand that the father's perversity was an instrument to force them all to defend themselves and their faith. Thus, Domenico conquers the adversity of a hostile environment, an obstacle that the individual must overcome in order to find identity.

When Fomento writes that the story of Christ is the only story he can write, he creates a conclusive, comprehensive symbol for the Italian-American novelists who have integrated their two cultures. Their plots may vary, but the novels they write are architectural structurings along the lines of struggle, sacrifice, isolation (or temporary defeat), compassion (or compromise), and eventual moral victory. In general, then, these works reflect what Fomento reveals, a tradition that is deep-seated in the Italian ancestry, an optimism for which the writer finds some symbol related to spirituality as the basis of ethical humanism.

In reviewing what directed the creation of such a symbol, the reader may find its outline in the fifth phase in the development of Italian-American fiction, the final rooting of Italian culture in the national complex as revealed in the writings of American authors of Italian ancestry. In the first place, there are novels like Michael DeCapite's *No Bright Banner,* in which the writer tells the story of the Italian-American segments of the national population, not as fragmented sections on the fringes of society, but as contributing parts of the society. The growth of the individual's personality within these groups is no longer confined to the problem of an alien in our midst; it is the struggle of an individual who is a component of the American nation. This individual is drawn in the writing not along stereotyped racial outlines, but with the depth and perception of psychological probings into personality, as DeCapite is with Paul. This author treats of human problems like the father-and-son relationship, in contrast to the earlier themes of Italians versus other racial groups, or of class groupings of the underprivileged who are opposed to the established order of society. Paul, for example, becomes adjusted when he absorbs the philosophy of his father, Carlo, who has taught him the positive attitude that seeks order, for which goal the struggle is never ended.

Applying this constructive principle to the story of more generally recognizable characters of American society, DeCapite contends in *The Bennett Place* that the established society in America, as symbolized in the suicidal Katharine Bennett, must continue to struggle to adjust itself to the changes in the culture that are due to the presence of "aliens." The breakdown of the Bennetts illustrates the void created by the "ancestral" local culture when it makes no compromises and hence leads its own descendants to destruction. Dr. Benson, the sane representative of the native culture, expresses the positive values of hope and optimism. In his delineation of the physician, DeCapite demonstrates the attitude of the firmly rooted American writer of Italian ancestry, the artist working to remove the fallacy of our literary representation theorized by Bernard DeVoto.

No longer on the defensive and no longer appealing predominantly to emotions, the members of this group of writers return to old themes with a sense of self-discovery. The psychological probings that identify these writers with many of their other American contemporaries now function as a preferred method of treating the subjects of their novels. A man learns about himself by studying his personal relationship with other people, as does, for example, Father Octavio Scarpi in Joseph Caruso's *The Priest.* A boy grows into manhood and is able to discover himself only when he understands his father, as Paul Christopher does in Raymond DeCapite's books *The Coming of Fabrizze* and *A Lost King*. Charles Calitri, too, moves from the defense of a principle in opposition to tyrannic forces in *Strike Heaven On the Face* to the more confined personal struggle within the father-and-son relationship in *Father*. The older themes, therefore, of the conflicts in the encounter of two cultures change to the narrower field of the psychological impact of one human being upon another. The treatment is refined still further when the author restricts the themes to the specific problem of one individual who seeks to discover himself by knowing his father. Symbolically, American culture can be understood only by knowing the contributing factors of each and all of its persons.

For reasons of emphasis this confinement of treatment may become so extreme that the author may limit his subject to the internal life of one individual. The writer may portray this individual as one who can overcome his isolation through an inordinate effort to use his own forces. Such a character is shown to be separated completely from society, as is Victor Blake in Luigi Creatore's *This World is Mine*. But Blake, too, needs someone like the father archetype—in his case, Dr. Mader—to lead him back to sanity. Blake's amnesia is symbolic of modern America, an ironic symbol of an America without prejudice only when it is a nation without any awareness. Such a withdrawal as Blake's, however, lacks verisimilitude; and, despite the temptation to escape into deadly prejudices, the modern American must achieve real freedom and equality through an effort of will, as Victor Blake does to see the light that helps in fighting intolerance and materialism.

The concepts in these novels, therefore, are universal and representative of the whole American culture. Just as a nation may trace its "soul" to its source in a plurality of ethnic contributions, so, in these novels, the protagonists discover themselves through an analysis of their own fathers. As a definitive example, this process of self-discovery is thoroughly probed by Rocco Fumento in *Tree of Dark Reflection*. The son, Daniele, *is* the father, Domenico Faustino, and only when he sacrifices himself to absorb his father's past is he able to identify himself. Fumento, thus, creates another Christ figure as the archetype for the solution of the struggle in every man.

In this solution appears again the constant pattern of conflict withdrawing into isolation which, in turn, must compromise or transubstantiate into integration. Revealed in the early novels, in which the writers depicted community fragmentation, were conflicts which, out of their very nature as the encounter of two alien cultures, created the withdrawal into isolation. As assimilation increased and gradually dispelled this isolation, the Italian-American novelists contributed a new and valid maturity to American fiction. These writers have come of age by exploring their own tradition as represented in their fathers, and now present universal problems in human relations.

As they construct their stories, Italian-Americans who are now writing novels convey, as do their fellow-artists, much poetry in their comments on contemporary American life. As they make their investigations, they are imaginative, and references to their ethnic background abound. These references are not always conscious; they may grow out of latent attitudes with which the writers explore those forces which make an individual more than his circumstances and abilities had indicated he could be. It is these forces that appear to dominate the themes of today's Italian-American novelists.

PART III

Contemporary Italian-American Novelists

"He wondered why he had this urge for self-abasement, once almost thrilling as a scholastic virtue, a way of coping with all those Anglo-Saxon teachers . . . all of it now seemed only another tired excuse for the essential failures of his life, his inability to accept his roots, his nationality, his language and lack of it, his father and mother who were to him total strangers."

—Frank Miceli, *The Seventh Month*

"Audacity had liberated them. They were pioneers, though they never walked an American plain and never felt real soil beneath their feet. They moved in a sadder wilderness, where the language was strange, where their children became members of a different race. It was a price that must be paid."

"Where were those wretches who cursed America and its dream?"

—Mario Puzo, *The Fortunate Pilgrim*

"I have no intention of placing my fate in the hands of men whose only qualification is that they managed to con a block of people to vote for them."

"But his children would grow in a different world.

They would be doctors, artists, Governors, Presidents. Anything at all. He would see to it that they joined the general family of humanity, but he, as a powerful and prudent parent would most certainly keep a wary eye on that general family."

—Mario Puzo, *The Godfather*

8

NOVELS OF RECALL

During the years between 1960 and 1970 the Italian-American novel made a great leap into the stronghold of American letters. The list is long of those writers who have published one promising book with the projection of more to come. There are also the creditable works of recent immigrants like P.M. Pasinetti, Niccolo Tucci, and Arturo Vivante. I must emphasize, however, those novelists who have continued to develop the concepts that occupied the previous authors, who were writing from their American experience and who reflected an ethnic orientation. Allowing for differences in treatment, the current group includes George Cuomo, Eugene Mirabelli, Robert Canzoneri, Frank Miceli, Robert Cenedella, Joseph Papaleo, Francis Pollini, and Mario Puzo. There are, however, others who predictably will cast a bright light on the horizon of the 70s.

Because of so many authors and titles, selectiveness is both desirable and imperative; it is hoped that the reader may be led to further exploration on his own through introduction to some representative novels. The books dicussed here have been chosen both for their aesthetic value and their representation of a trend.

The writings of the early Italian-Americans were unashamedly autobiographical, and the theme of personal recall persists in many of the imaginative works of authors in the second and third generations. Admittedly, some of these reminiscent books are sentimentally nostalgic, but they remain authentic documents of historical events from a sociological perspective. Furthermore, the various authors demonstrate differing points of view, reflecting their particular Italian origins, depending on the region in Italy from which their ancestors came. Each particular story in the American setting appropriates the organic factors of the inherited customs and traits of its respective writer.

In the recent autobiographical novels, the basic impulse to search for identity precipitates the resulting self-discovery as the writer both recalls and shares the experiences of the parental home. Having survived, however, the alienation and the fragmentation of a childhood ethnically separated from that of other authors, the Italian-American writer has matured with sufficient assurance to tell his experiences with humor, detachment, and objectivity. Several writers are socially conscious to the extent that they have related these experiences universally to the "vertical frontier" life in America, experiences common to all ethnic groups that are minorities in the mainstream. Among these creative composers of recall, some have produced works that are sound sociological documents that are, at the same time, aesthetically valid in the development of characters intensified through dramatic experiences.

MARION BENASUTTI (1908–)

Marion Benasutti, the daughter of Joseph E. and Elvira (Serafini) Gosette, was born in Philadelphia on August 2, 1908. The wife of Frank J. Benasutti, builder, she has had two children, Noel (deceased) and Frank J., Jr. Inspired by her writing courses at Temple University, Mrs. Benasutti has devoted her time to writing and related literary activities. After serving as the woman's editor for the *Italian-American Herald*, 1960–1962, she became the editor of the *Pen Woman* Magazine. An administrative member of the National League of *American Pen Women*, she has contributed various articles and short stories to newspapers and magazines.

No Steady Job for Papa[1] is Mrs. Benasutti's first novel, an intimate account of the experiences of her large, closely knit family in Philadelphia during World War I. A story of personal loyalties, the book is a presentation of the self-respecting American ethnic who celebrates the opportunity for hard work. Thematically, Mrs. Benasutti gives this ethnic a wide human dimension, exploring the truth that the pursuit of the American Eldorado is not necessarily the definition of happiness. She activates her characters by "It's love for each other and striving towards goals." This idea pervades Mrs. Benasutti's story, but her dramatization of characters has not only the diorama of Italian-American life in an Anglo-Saxon neighborhood, but the recurring echo of a Tyrolean frame of reference. The various members of the

1. Marion Benasutti, *No Steady Job For Papa* (New York: The Vanguard Press, Inc., 1966).

family, furthermore, are romantic symbols of levels of aesthetics and functions with which the author operates to give exhilaration to the realism of necessity.

The story, therefore, is not strictly Papa's, but of Papa's engendering the emergence into womanhood of Rosemary, the narrator and protagonist. Like Louisa May Alcott's Jo, Mrs. Benasutti's Rosemary grows in the book from childhood to the brink of womanhood. The second of five daughters, Rosemary tells of this Italian-American family as it is first settled in a western Pennsylvania coal-mining town and later moves to "Back Street" in South Philadelphia. Contrasting the levels of life in Back Street and Front Street with the Tennis Courts that are symbolic of the established Anglo-Saxon society, the course of action follows Papa's quest for work. Rosemary narrates how Papa, when he was thirteen years old, had come to live with his half sister. At twenty-two, he returned to Fiave, where he met the barmaid whom he married and left briefly to return to America, dreaming of earning enough money to send for his bride. Three years later, Mamma's determination and a baby, Trina, are reasons enough for her to follow him, despite the lack of the promised wealth. Papa's unsteady odyssey with employment, however, is not a matter of indolence. Following an injury in a soft-coal mine, he goes to work in the Navy Yard in Philadelphia. A frail man, temperamentally unsuited to hard labor, he is only the residue of his vanquished hope of becoming a scholar or an artist. The maneuvers of the Italian village power structure having forced him out of his intended career, he sublimates his frustration in America into the determined exuberance of a "sunshine" philosophy. A seasonal laborer, he builds the brick and stone steps of other people's homes, while the other members of the family work to supplement his income. His once-beautiful wife drudges away at her sewing as she competes with his possessive mother for his love. Encouraging the educational and career progress of the daughters, Mamma eventually realizes her determination to own a "nice house" in Germantown.

The point that Mrs. Benasutti is making in this book is that people should celebrate the spirit that seeks some kind of fortune "beneath the dirt of the mythical golden pavements." Poverty, she insists, is a quality of the mind. However, although the family on Back Street does not think of itself as poor, Rosemary is resolved that some day she will explore the "other-world place" of the Tennis Courts, and that she will do so through her own efforts. Mrs. Benasutti shows that this self-determination is an extension of the will in Mamma, the traditional disposition of *fare la bella figura,* to appear well in the eyes of others. The writer intensifies Mamma's emotions in scenes of conflict, each episode consuming a part of her: the departure from her native country, the moving from the "nice house" in the mining town, the eventual death of friends, the successive departures of Rosemary from her jobs, the repeated sacrifices to start over again. The cardinal sin, according to Mamma, is committed by that person who is pessimistic and consequently accomplishes nothing. Outward appearance is an important support of determination, and Mamma insists that the daughters dress as beautifully as possible. She personifies the code that indigence need wave no banners, because beauty is the staff of the inner spirit. The theme of success as an interweaving of work and beauty operates on other levels in the family relations. Because Papa has built for Mr. Corning a set of steps "with such a beautiful nose," Rosemary is offered a position as a typist at the Philadelphia Rapid Trust Company, of which Mr. Corning is president. This fulfillment of her role is for Rosemary a practical application of optimism. What the father externalizes as perfectionism, the people around him harvest productively, regarding Papa's sacrificial attitude toward beauty as "God's purpose in all things." This theme of faith extends to less happy incidents, like the time of the grandmother's death, which results in the reconciliation with Mrs. Lacey. On a fundamentally societal level, Mrs. Lacey, who "lays out" the dead grandmother, is an instrument of racial harmony and assimilation, which are implemented by a universal tragedy. The visible beauty of the grandmother is now a memory of the old culture made permanent in the rituals of death through cosmetics graciously applied by an enlightened neighbor. It is Papa, the tragic-comic hero, who cannot stop crying; his agony is now that of the immigrant "out-of-place." To indulge in this anguish, however, is beneath human dignity. Mamma, therefore, convinces her husband that they must concentrate on moving to Germantown. As they look over their new home and Mamma is making encouraging plans for the additional work she will find in this better neighborhood, Papa makes the significant comment that wisteria is a beautiful plant that the English brought to America. Mamma, however, maintains a level head and persists in the conversation, to conclude that they will also rent a room to Mr. Dooley, who loves Italians. These cross-currents of spirit and enterprise are later climaxed when Mamma, prodded by Mrs. Lacey, receives Holy Communion. The comic element does not lag behind too long, however, and the final picture shows Papa, who, having sacrificed his red wagon and old horse, is ready for the safari into Germantown by driving his new truck. The mechanical vehicle is a symbol of the achievement of his American Dream. The resolution, therefore, is a testament of Mrs. Benasutti's treatment of the Italian-American family as a unit of human beings who function by action, whose use of the rhetoric of popular causes betrays their need for personal encouragement.

Mrs. Benasutti uses the various characters to personify the levels of her theme: Papa's love of music is equal to his love of functional objects. Since he had studied for the priesthood in his youth, he is not so adept at shoveling coal as he is at painting. With the practiced logic of a theoretician, he argues with Mr. Leopoldi over ideologies and politics. His creature love, however, endears him to animals and little children, who sense his indomitable faith. When he falls from a scaffold and is hurt, the daughters realize there is more to love than feeling. It is through Papa that Mrs. Benasutti personifies her theme that hardship is the catalyst of the good and graceful in life, and that an inherent part of one's hardship is one's self. The erstwhile seminarian infuses this belief in those around him. Rosemary, the narrator, for example, studies diligently, collects bills for her father, goes to secretarial school, works as a paid companion to old Mrs. Pierce, reads voraciously, writes constantly, and eventually competes with her "American" (non-Italian) friends. Encouraged by a literary prize and infected by her mother's dedication to hard work, she accepts as a privilege the opportunity to work in the knitting mills. Eventually, she is thankful, when she goes to business college, that the administrator is a strict disciplinarian, so that working in an office is both a pleasure and a fulfillment.

Mamma, as the constructive complement to Papa's nature, is the embodiment of the Italian-American attitude of optimism. Her realism curbs her husband's idealism and directs his energies into useful channels. Her simple objectives of "a steady job for Papa and a nice house" motivate the progressive action of the novel to a desirable conclusion. Because she is externally a functioning person, she surprises everyone with her instinctive insight into current events. She comments, for example, that Mr. Wilson should go back to New Jersey, because one man alone cannot save the world. There is a lucid Italian rationalism in the way she convinces Papa that he should fulfill his immediate duties.

Mrs. Benasutti extends this clarity to all the other Italian-American concepts she uses, but she introduces the reader to a distinctive flavor in that this family is "from the North" of Italy, close to the Austrian border. These Italians have physical differences, lighter complexions, smaller features, and a unique lilt to their voices. Referring to her own origins, Mrs. Benasutti tells how her father and mother were married at the Church of Santa Croce, which had once been a pagan temple. Mamma talks about her voyage to America, constricted in the ship's steerage in frightening contact with thieves and animals. The reader sympathizes with Nonna, who dreams of returning to her old mountain home. As for the family's lapsed Catholicism, the author explains this deterioration as typical of many immigrants who came to small mining and lumber communities where there were no Roman Catholic churches. Mrs. Benasutti is most convincing, however, when she details how she felt when she first heard the word "wop," an obscenity that keeps "howling" in her ears and fills her with shame. Like John Fante, she typifies all victims of derogatory racial nomenclatures. She writes that "All at once I was full of hate, of my mother and father, of the place I lived in, which had heretofore been as all other places, only more fun and was now, by a single word made dirty, unclean" (p. 85). She stores this sound in Rosemary's memory, and rewards her with the adventure of enjoying a neighborhood with open spaces and touchable flora.

Mrs. Benasutti's book is pleasant in tone, gentle in pace, and conversational in rhetorical presentation. There are no tense and tangled complexities in construction, and sometimes her style is identified with the colloquialisms of her characters. Italian words and idioms give her phrases authenticity and color. She creates images with an evocative nostalgia that sometimes blurs into romantic sentimentality, as in her recalling the words of a prayer, which "fell upon me like celestial rain, making me clean as the driven snow." Her dialogue generally catches the essence of her settings and the nuances of her characters' thoughts, especially of Rosemary's. As a novelist, Mrs. Benasutti has a sure grasp of place, which allows her to present strikingly visible contrasts when she describes Italian-Americans living in juxtaposition with their Anglo-Saxon neighbors. Back Street is as vivid as it is because the Tennis Courts are not too far; it is only the artifice of society that is impossible. Woven into the texture of the story, the Church year is reverently marked with references to the liturgy of the Roman Catholic Missal. Marking this time, the human world of dreams battles with stark reality in the mind of the immigrant Don Quixote, whose court of justice has convened in the bawdy steerage of the crossing. Like other Italian-Americans, however, Mrs. Benasutti has a lucid yardstick of calculated dedication, the very substance of Mamma in the novel. Her rational determination underlies the writing of this book, even though the material barely touches the violence, eroticism, and pychological probings that are the familiar scaffolds of many contemporary novels. Mrs. Benasutti's dramatic irony may be slight, but it is refreshingly palatable, as in her family's respect for their hero, Columbus, in whose honor Mamma makes a torte which, she says, is better than "the gem of the ocean."

RALPH CORSEL (1920–)

Ralph Corsel's first book, *Up There the Stars*,[2] is socially important, because in it the sounds of place and time are true. With cinematic and oral recall, Corsel tells an honest story of crime-breeding factors that are intrinsic to a fragmented section of the economically limited group within the American population. The ideas that Corsel develops are triggered by his ability to strike a familiar chord in the childhood recollections of the majority of those Italian-Americans who are now older than fifty. Without polemics, he dramatizes typical situations

2. Ralph Corsel, *Up There the Stars* (New York: The Citadel Press, 1968).

that have long fostered resentment, situations that have been either patiently endured or grimly overcome. His characters in motion rise above idea-types. These are people trapped in incidents that were common to a specific group. If they are type-cast at all, they embody a formula for the normal individual bound by ethnically strictured conditions. As a result, Corsel's account is symbolical of the Italian-American dream envisioned through a broken sleep jolted by nightmares of twisted arms, criminal seductions, and imminent destruction, all of which are eventually phased out with a projected optimism.

The point of *Up There the Stars* is that, in a harsh neighborhood where survival is achieved through ego-scarring hustling and rationalized hoodlumism, a growing boy must make the effort to look away from his sordid surroundings to view some light above the darkness. Romantic as Corsel may sound, his "look to the stars" remains the only hope for immigrant children shipwrecked on the rocks of the Depression. Furthermore, the oppression of a tyrannical father adds impetus to an ambitious boy's worshipful regard for the visible power of gangsters, who represent the zenith of success.

Frankie Andrini grows up in the streets and along the subways of New York, hustling for a few dollars, and, late at night, returning only to sleep at the home of his parents on Morris Avenue. Whereas Enrico and Maria Andrini had come to America with the usual intention of saving enough money to buy and own a small piece of land, Frankie dreams of becoming a gangster. He does not deceive us, however, because the reader suspects that the boy's violent nightmares are a repressed rebellion against his father's tyranny.

The struggle against oppression begins at the schoolyard, where Frankie beats Tony Esposito, the biggest bully in the class. Mrs. Gorcey, the school principal, reports to Maria Andrini that "Francis is a disturbed boy with lots of problems," but he is fundamentally an intelligent human being without the proper motivation to concentrate on his work. His ensuing misbehavior propels him to the main office at least once a week. Defensively, Maria urges Francis to bring home all the money he earns, but the father, fatigued like a beast of burden, yells at the boy and whips him. Frankie, we agree, is basically sound and straining for approval; for example, he is proud and vigorous when his father permits him to help with the wine-making, a man's work.

Growing up for Frankie is touch-and-go walking on a tense, taut line. Although he searches the ground, looking for lost coins, he is tapped at one point by an old man who warns him to look up, for "that's where the stars are." This advice is only a fool's babbling to the already cynical boy who continues to steal tools and candy, which he sells to buy Christmas gifts for his family. The irony of his situation is compounded when he curses at his father for throwing out the "pagan" Christmas tree that Frankie has bought.

For a while, Frankie's "stars" are Vincent Coll and "Dutch"

Schultz, notorious figures of the criminal world, and he hopes by petty thievery to prove himself worthy of his chosen heroes. Around him, the Italian religious "festas" and holidays are dim settings from which he escapes in Walter Mitty style with the self-induced excitement of being an identified underworld leader. A born mechanic, he trains himself to break, enter, and steal. With persistent enterprise, he sells what he steals; but he adheres to a level of integrity in his "summer-hustling" by selling peanuts, newspapers, and magazines at the ball-games. People admire how he helps his neighbor, Luigi, on his junk-wagon; his peers respect him in the card games in the neighborhood backyards. His development proceeds in sex, also, at first as a voyeur and then with a sudden experience with one of the local prostitutes.

Frankie's petty delinquency increases to serious juvenile crimes that lead him to reform school. Corsel never reduces his protagonist to anti-heroism, however, but keeps hope alive for this American Orlando, a tarnished knight of stellar quality. When, for example, Frankie has spent an evening dining with Mr. Gannes, his "Big Brother," at the fashionable mansion in New Rochelle, the young delinquent leaves with "a lump in his throat, and his heart bursting with emotions" (p. 141).

His high school years, hectic for his teachers, eventually end, and serve as a prelude to the abrasions of the Depression. Enrico has an accident, loses his job, and awakens from his American dream. Like numerous Italian immigrants, he cringes and says, "I wanted more for my sons than empty dreams and lost hopes—But—*questo è la forza del destino* . . . I didn't want to be cruel. I know how hard it is for a poor boy to grow into an honest man. He must be strong, disciplined. He must be hard as nails. I tried to do this for you in my own poor way. I wanted you to go to school. To be all the things I never can be" (pp. 216–17). Frankie, absorbing this desire, wants "to be somebody," and, using the only means available to him, turns to robbery, getting into trouble with the law. Furthermore, he rationalizes his behavior as vengeance for injury as he nurses the memory of the taunts he endured at Boy's Village, where the disciplinarian, Hawley, struck him in the face with "Come on, you little wop bastard, throw a punch at me" (p. 198). Frankie has vowed that someday he will "blow his brains out."

When Frankie returns from Boy's Village, he is further affronted by his mother's need to take in sewing. Corsel is deft in delineating the maturing process of the boy as he analyzes his perspective against his changed surroundings. Now Frankie's senses, writes the author, "were keyed to the music of the loud neighborhood voices and the smells of the Italian-flavored street" (p. 221). As he watches his father reading the *Daily News*, he laughs at the change; and father and son then laugh together that Primo Carnera "he knock out Irish Jack Sharkey with punch under chin in six rounds" (p. 227).

As the Depression grinds on, problems oppress the Andrinis from all sides. Despite the hopelessness, Enrico shouts that they will starve before they beg for one penny. With this endemic pride, the family manages. Frankie also finds time to fall in love and to accept rejection. Eventually, while working as a machinist's apprentice, he is tempted by his friend Tony Esposito to rob card-game gamblers. Corsel dramatizes the constant presence of the warring gangs on the streets and the exciting response of the younger men, who seek to derive some benefit from the activity. The writer has researched his story carefully, and gives authentic details of how Vincent Coll merged his gang with that of Jack "Legs" Diamond and how they went together to hunt out Schultz and his men. Vincent Coll's mobsters were indicted for a notorious crime involving the death of a child, but were found not guilty for lack of evidence. Strategically, with deliberate confusion of street-warring and police affiliations, Corsel points out that the men held for the murder included Philip Esposito, Dominick Ordiano, and Frank di Giordano, a manipulation by which the Italians were made the scapegoats of the real killers.

As a symbol of this scapegoat, Corsel's Frankie has many dimensions. The reader responds to the person and the mind of the young protagonist. When Frankie learns about sex from Stella, he is more naturally human than accidentally erotic. On another level, his filial loyalty to his histrionic and emotional mother is admirable and plausible. Beyond all emotional projections, however, his driving desire to "be something" either through singing or, desperately, through crime, is his extension of his father's thwarted ambition. Corsel wins our sympathy for Frankie because, though not heroic, this ethnic Peck's Bad Boy is really sincere in trying to earn his own way. Slightly subdued by the brutal shooting of John Dillinger, he utilizes his amatory alliance with his friend Anita, to get work with her employer, "Dutch Schultz," by whose machine-gun-implemented progress Frankie is still impressed. The sobering process continues; he begins to have a feeling of not belonging to the tavern crowds. Gradually, too, he feels a strangeness with old companions, reflecting that it was chance, not preference, that made him a part of their world. Finally, when the supposedly big "heist" succeeds, the truth strikes home that he might have been sent to prison for five years for stealing twenty-nine dollars. The reader applauds the turn toward reform in this amateur criminal, who is increasingly concerned about the family's poverty. Things became so bad that Enrico and the boys had to stuff in cardboard to line their shoes, and he felt like a fused bomb waiting for a spark to ignite him.

In degradation, however, regeneration is not easy, as Corsel shows. A climax must test the validity of purpose. Anita gets Frankie the chance to work for Schultz; in Staten Island he tends the coal boilers for a hidden still where the "bootleg" alcohol is made. Ironically, it is Frankie's fatigue from his all-night lovemaking with Anita that puts him to sleep at his post so that he barely escapes with his life when the boilers burst. Then, as he runs for his life from the "pistol" men disguised as hunters, he learns the bitter lesson of the total tyranny of organized crime. Discovering the only means of escape through a cemetery, he is a symbol of the desperate human spirit fleeing death. His thoughts are a resurrection: "I shoveled coal, scrubbed down vats. I hauled sugar bags and alky tins till my back broke. . . . I been risking my life—and for what? A hundred bucks a week. Big money! Big laugh!" (p. 367). Corsel shows Frankie putting on his shoes, mud-stained in his flight, and then walking again, straight across the middle of the cemetery (which might have been his death), climbing over a high wire fence (the arrival at the high truth that no amount of money is worth gambling your one and only life for), and finding himself on a golf course, a well-kept fairway from which he can safely look at the sky and, out of this night, finally "look for the stars."

Later, as Frankie leaves Morris Avenue, he thinks: "Someday I'm going to be—not a hood, but somebody" (p. 376). He leaves a note with "I love you, Mom," and, for the reader, enacts the irrepressible Italian-American dream, optimistically remembering to wave dramatically at the sky while he dashes down into the subway.

Corsel has created a popular-music syncopation of the themes and counterthemes of Italian-American voices and spoken choruses. He has created characters that live and think. Frankie is a symbol of nearly poetic conception, but of the raw school fenced in by the strictures of necessity. Around him, Italian-American life teems with the harshness that the national social structure imposes upon a new, ethnic, immigrant group. From the abrasiveness surrounding them, the various characters hone out the fine steel of their inner integrity—the need, the will, and, eventually, the grace to live. Corsel draws his characters against a graphically detailed background, every stroke an exact representation of objective reality. The rhetoric is not consciously literary, but it is authentic and demonstrative. His development of the protagonist, furthermore, emphasizes the thesis of this discussion, showing that from the low ebb of their struggle, during the worst economic turbulence in the most depressed area of our most congested city, the Italian-Americans confront crime (hostility), overcome it, and renew their faith in the continuity of the ideals of what to them is more than an adopted country. As one of them, the writer is giving an account of his own nation.

JOSEPH R. VERGARA (1915–)

Love E Pasta,[3] by Joseph (Joe) R. Vergara, is an appealing and successful narration of the experiences of an Italian-American family. Written in a smoothly paced, low-keyed style, the tale progresses evenly,

3. Joseph R. Vergara, *Love E Pasta* (New York: Harper & Row Publishers, Inc., 1968).

hinged firmly on the episodes of the father's struggle to earn a living while aiming for perfection in his trade. As each chapter unfolds, Vergara adds color and line to the portrait of the protagonist, completing the aesthetic communication with mild dramatic impact. Pop, however, transcends the father role; he is the idealized American immigrant who cherishes the opportunity to work and to earn the compensations of his own labor. That we as readers are drawn into the identity of the protagonist as a living person attests to Vergara's creative competence; that we are sympathetically engaged in Pop's successes and failures is due to the writer's sure dramatic sense. Finally, the pointing and counterpointing of the ideas that motivate Pop's progress elevate the narration to universality: the particular ethnical treatment is fused into the general pursuit of the American dream. In narrating the details of the human conflicts in this quest, Vergara manages a salubrious comic touch in nearly every scene, often shaking the reader into laughter that relaxes into a satisfied smile.

Pop is a familiar figure. Armed with his ambition to become a great singer, he left his native Calabria to realize in America the fruits of his talents. When he must earn his living as a shoemaker, he finds it imperative to do so in the best style. Believing that everything in America is possible, he resolves that everything should be put to right use. For example, lawns should be used for growing edible things; grass, says Pop, is made up of an army of parasites sucking the earth's lifeblood, demanding attention and returning nothing. The production of food, he believes, is a sacred rite; and he mutters against the blindness of a land where everything is available but the food is tasteless. He can not forgive the Puritans for settling here first and establishing the notion that the function of food is "to keep the body and soul together." Vergara is contrasting values in popular terms.

At times the boys in the family chafe under the crushing coercion of Pop's "training course," but they take a fatalistic attitude and submit to his insistence that they work for him in their spare time. They respect his precepts and principles, which he enforces with his belt. Thematically, Vergara identifies the reaction of the sons to this type of parental authority with the general rebellion of contemporary youth against the tyranny of adults and the unfairness of fate. Despite their resentment, however, the boys admire other qualities in Pop, for example, his sales technique, which is based not on pressure, but on the products being of the best quality of available material and delivered with excellent service.

Quality, therefore, is a galvanizing factor of Vergara's basic theme. Pop's activities are classified according to a value system in the relationship of these activities to the family and their environment. The protagonist is that American ethnic who wants desperately to please people and to create an amiable atmosphere. To do so demands an unashamed celebration of life, balanced by security and a sense of honor. Pop says that not everyone is lucky enough to be an expert shoemaker. "They gotta be satisfie' be dottore, lawyer. . . . Maybe you even be priest" (p. 96). Excellence, therefore, is the criterion, regardless of the area of function. Vergara emphasizes the pursuit of perfection in the dramatic effect of his protagonist upon the other characters around him. When Mom insists upon having their Jewish friend, Leon, for an Italian-style Seder, her simple logic is based on the fact that the Holy Family and the disciples, all of them Jews, must have had Seders. Pop, convinced that civilized man had long ago arrived at the Sunday dinner of ravioli, chicken cacciatore, and salad, overcomes his reluctance when Leon agrees to use Pop's favorite wine. Vergara's hero, whose only persistent determination is to become a full-fledged American, shrugs off the difference between ravioli and cheese blintz. Somehow, however, when Mom plays "Hatikvah," it sounds, says the writer, like "O Sole Mio."

Vergara does not indulge in polemics. The characters live and breathe, sharing their humanity with one another and moving sprightly, with a minimum of exposition intruded by the author. Tensions vibrate, with scenes of anguish contrasting with those of joyous relief. The episodes are their own explanation. For example, when Pop reads the letter announcing his mother's death, his stoic silence is more eloquent than any sound. He moves to the back yard, where, furiously digging up the soil, he hopes "to drown the pain in physical exhaustion." The author then, with a few details, describes the quiet uneasiness in the friends who come to comfort Pop, whose loss is shared by all of them. It is a unique loss, for, as Vergara writes, each man has lost a bit of himself and "one more tie with the old country" has been broken.

These themes appear in the actions of the younger generation, who are observing and judging their elders. Although Vergara tells us that Pop had come to America "to make a pile of money and take it back to Italy with him," the son now comments, "I wonder if I'd have the guts to go live in a foreign country like you did" (p. 147). This comment has a further extension when Vergara writes, in the chapter "Gypsy Shoemaker," that Pop is bored with the success of his business, that he is a pioneer, not a settler. This process of becoming a settler is what the Italian-American parent has found most difficult. In the scene depicting Pop's discomfort at the school play, Vergara dramatizes an Eliot type of objective correlative. Pop sits meekly at the back of the hall, conscious of the dye and scars on his hands. He is afraid that his accent, his work-roughened hands, and his worn-out clothes will embarrass his children. When he realizes that his son is winning all the medals of achievement, Pop cannot contain his pride. The haltingly articulate shoemaker accepts with a simple grace the congratulations of the town fathers, none of whom even notices his accent. The graduation, writes Vergara, "had unexpectedly achieved what twenty years in this country had not. . . . They were . . . part of the non-Italian world around them. And what's more, they were enjoying it. They belonged" (p. 186).

When the family loses the home during the Depression, Pop survives—again Vergara's thematic symbol of constructive determination and rugged optimism. The family accepts gratefully the rambling old Victorian mansion that had been decaying with emptiness. Vergara depicts the abandoned house as a symbol of the passing of cultures. It is Pop, the sturdy immigrant, who will restore this dying structure to a strong and habitable state. The challenge tests his vigor, ingenuity, and tenacity. The boys find it difficult to understand their parents' enthusiasm for transferring this run-down house into a palazzo. They wonder at their father's persistence as he refuses to be defeated by a succession of reverses. Vergara writes that his protagonist is pitched against natural enemies—hunger, cold, and the threat to survival. "But the talent to survive," points out the author, "was part of the heritage he had brought over with him" (p. 209).

The theme of seeking one's identity through perfection does not rest, however, on the level of economics alone. Joseph Vergara's Pop, as a culture hero, is not an immobile statue. Rather, his dimensions fluctuate with the constant chiseling of the compromise forced by conflict. As he pays less attention to the garden and his Caruso records, he also loses his old interests like the noisy card games with his friends. Now, politics, especially Italian politics, become important; but Pop knows that politicans must be watched carefully. Eventually, he arrives at the point where he must make one of the most tragic decisions that face the immigrant: to give up his Italian citizenship, his identity with a dominant and prestigious culture, and to embrace, instead, membership in an alien environment. His assimilative progress has been slow, although it has been accelerated by the son's graduation from college and imminent military service. He finds it imperative to return to Calabria, and he proves to himself that he has really changed and that the process of migration is a societal constant. In the end, Vergara's protagonist knows where he belongs.

Architecturally, a son's observation of his father's becoming an American is a theme structured here in many settings by means of various episodes. The point of the book is to dramatize these events on a stage set in a pioneer land. Because readers' attitudes toward these early events have changed, there is both pathos and a sense of loss in the writer's account of the old diversions of religious festas, the spaghetti-eating contests, the protective measures against the Evil Eye, the therapeutic animation of the games of scopa and morra, the communicative sweep of the gestures. Vergara, however, has illuminated these events with working symbols. The protagonist, who has dreamed of singing in the capitals of Europe, is in reality like the "passerotti" (sparrows), barely managing a chirp while his family are "too busy to worry about it." Hands are metaphors of enterprise: they thrust in the "morra" (game) for competitive stakes; they lift the sign to combat evil; they move backward to strike for discipline; they sweep in gesture to punctuate assertion; they run the machine; they hoe the garden for survival; they create art and music for things that will endure. Emotional attitudes have their symbolic behavior, also. When Pop is constrained to repair shoes in a despised cut-rate shoe-repair shop, he stops singing his arias. His spirit is perpetuated by Mom, however, in her attitude toward the piano. To Mom, learning facts from books is barely essential for living; of more importance is the "culture," which she interprets strictly as the ability to play the piano. This single skill, she claims, helps anyone to appreciate beauty in simple arts and crafts, to see the joy, the humor, and the charm of the everyday world. Therefore, Mom becomes Vergara's companion symbol to that of the protagonist—the supporting ingredient of a curative balm for the corrosive wound of alienation.

Joseph Vergara's book has authenticity and appeal. The validity of *Love E Pasta* is in its effective poignancy of recall and in its realistic presentation of situations and episodes that many Italian-Americans have experienced. The author writes with a respectful attitude, relieving the seriousness of his themes with a palatable comic treatment. He transcends the cruelty of human behavior with the warmth of sincere personality, moving his characters into different frames to vary the approaches to his themes. Vergara depicts Pop as the ethnically cherished type of Italian-American father; he extends the familiar cultural attitudes into the roles he creates for Mom and her friends; he amalgamates these attitudes into the centralizing structure of the family as a social unit whose strength is galvanized by respect and discipline. The characters act with warm impulses and human sympathy. As a narrator, Vergara handles details with authority, conviction, and some emotive nostalgia. These qualities are demonstrated in the chapters on the wedding, the Seder, and the graduation, but especially in the titling of Pop's meatless dinner, a sacrificial tribute to his renewal of faith in God for granting him his American citizenship. Although he fears the future because his three sons are about to serve in the army, the grateful father grins and salutes his citizenship. It is a credit to Vergara that such a conclusion does not seem melodramatic; his writing is unpretentious and persuasive, making optimism a human responsibility.

LUCAS LONGO (1919–)

Lucas Longo has been writing since he was seventeen years old, his first book being a collection of poems entitled *Three Views on Snow.*

After writing four short stories during his undergraduate years at Brooklyn College, he decided to write a book. The result is his first novel, *The Family on Vendetta Street.*[4] Longo gathered much of his material from his experiences as a social worker for the New York City Welfare Department.

The Family on Vendetta Street is an evocative novel, recalling the neighborhood situations with which Italian-Americans are familiar, but more deeply anguished than Vergara's *Love E Pasta.* Longo's book is a sociological document, but it is a dramatic and compelling presentation of highly motivated episodes that heighten the characters, whom Longo draws sharply in three dimensions. The novel is an analysis of the emotional and economic pressures that dominate personal, familial, and societal areas and lead to the inevitable violence that erupts from unrelieved tension. Longo tells the intimate story of one family group, around whom the ethnic neighborhood maintains an inherited modicum of good behavior in such a manner that the individuals move contrary to contempoary standards of ethics. That a person has the unquestionable duty to vindicate an insult to his honor is the motivating force of the action. Whether this motivation has any real validity in improving human relations supplies the theme of Longo's story.

The story of *The Family on Vendetta Street* unfolds from the point of view of Marco, who, like Longo, is a social worker living some distance away from his original neighborhood. Starting *in medias res,* Marco says that when he was eight years old he saw his middle-aged father, in one of his many rages, kill his young mother with four shots from a revolver that had always been loaded for action. That moment marks the beginning of a vendetta that continues for forty years. Marco's Aunt Rose adopts him, nurturing in him daily a vehement hatred for his father, his paternal uncles, and anyone who she felt had contributed to the tragedy. Supporting her, the Italian-Americans in the Brooklyn neighborhood all feel involved in a collective racial and family loyalty. Marco tells of this involvement from the points of view of various characters: Uncle Tony (his mother's brother), Nonna (grandmother Antonia), Zia Maria (the matriarch of the neighborhood), the father, the mother, the uncles, Aunt Rose, and Marco himself. With his father, Giovanni, in Sing Sing, Marco grows up in a protected atmosphere of his Aunt Rose's making, but the protective wall is pitted with hints and rumors. Marco proceeds to college, to marriage, and to a career in social welfare before his father is released. The scene describing his refusal to forgive and accept his father is one of the most truly tragic and poignant in the book. Longo tightens his story so that the reader is moved to pity and remains engaged through-

4. Lucas Longo, *The Family on Vendetta Street* (Garden City, N. Y.: Doubleday & Company, Inc., 1968)

out. Rejecting any approaches for a reconciliation with his father, Marco, though agonized by the pain he causes, controls his natural love for his parent because he is paralyzed by the ritual of hate with which his Aunt Rose has conditioned his behavior. After his father's death, Marco learns from his Uncle Amadeo that the tragedy had been precipitated by Marco's grandmother because of her sexual relationship with his father. The neighborhood has absorbed, recorded, and judged these events like a tribal jury.

Lucas Longo points out that educated hate is a tragic crippling of healthy and constructive human relationship. A vendetta that is programmed mercilessly hinders all attempts at reconciliation, as the writer demonstrates when Amadeo, after praying before Mary's coffin, offers his friendship, which is remorselessly rejected. In the progress of the vindication, when Giovanni's friends try to contact Marco after the father's release from prison, the son will not cooperate, admitting that he knows he is a trained soldier in the vendetta. Father and son weep at the sight of each other, but there is no reconciliation: this is the ultimate irony of hate. To an intelligent person, this kind of trained fixation is confusing and abhorrent. Marco admits that he is crippled by his disciplined loyalty to Aunt Rose, that he, though hungry for parental love, responds only with the reflexes that prevent the desired rapport with his father. Longo shows this behavior as a social disease, especially when Marco, returning home, cries in the arms of his wife, who asks him why he hasn't brought his father home to see the children and spend the night with them. There is, however, an optimistic resolution when Marco, questioned about receiving his father's inheritance, is badgered by his Aunt Rose, who insists on his taking the money that is rightfully his and not let it go to the uncles whom she hates. Resisting her, Marco goes to explain to his wife that he feels sorry for his Aunt Rose, who is living only for hate and her vendetta. In this way, he objectifies the engendering cause of his own hate and is at the beginning of his own salvation. The reader here is impressed by this instance of the universal need to obliterate hate through the liberating exercise of love. Longo emphasizes the point of the story when, in the end, he has Amadeo's wife recall that Nonna, like Aunt Rose, had always done everything out of all proportion, even love. The reader concludes that the root of hate is over-possessiveness.

The themes are dramatized by the interaction of the characters, especially Giovanni, the father, in his confrontation with Aunt Rose over the relationship with Nonna. The dilemma is compounded by the problems of the struggling Maria and the growing Marco. Giovanni is an introspective man who does not like people. Longo does not inform the reader why the husband and father is the perpetually angry man he is; impressions about him come through the hateful distortions of Mary's sister, Aunt Rose. Resenting her mother, and on the defensive against her sister, Rose is an obese, self-indulgent harpy of vengeance. She tells everyone that Giovanni is an animal; and, because Giovanni is so inflexibly one-dimensional, the reader believes the worst of this blasphemous and solitary tyrant. Although Marco declares repeatedly that he loves his strange father, we neither sense any warmth in Marco's words nor do we share any emotion they might insist upon. The nearest we come to sympathy for Giovanni is when he hears that his mother has died and he attempts to go to the rectory, fails to do so, and returns to cry out his grief. Generally, the author gives no motivation for this man's abusive language, which he uses so vituperously, for example, to stop Marco's baptism. It does not appear plausible that, in this neighborhood, Giovanni should refuse to have a godfather for the infant because he will not allow his young wife to talk to other men. As a member of an inner-directed world, he will be host to the other men in his store, but it is admittedly a world of hard laborers who use foul language and lead a shoddy life. Applying a dual standard, Giovanni is master in his home, frequently striking his wife and posturing as a captain restraining his potential violence. Longo hints that there are abnormal facets of this father's relations with his family: he times everything his wife, Maria, does; he is jealous of her cat; he seldom takes his family out; in group activities he makes violent scenes, like punching a man for dancing with Maria. He is similarly cruel to his brothers, especially to the mild Amadeo, who does much of the menial work for him in order to relieve Maria. Longo convinces us that it is quite feasible that a jealous quarrel is incentive enough for Giovanni to shoot his long-suffering and innocent wife.

All the other characters in the book relate actively to the incident involving Giovanni, Maria, and Marco. Zia Bel, the midwife, is a source of strength to Maria and Aunt Rose. Zia Maria is the omniscient pacifier. Nonna, the grandmother, is the most complex and attractive of the women, and the cause of tragedy, hers and the family's. She is subtle and gentle, but is also a paradox of loyalty and deception. While she loves her daughter, she makes no attempt to curb her desire for her daughter's husband after she has forced Maria into a marriage with a much older man. Uncle Tony, Maria's brother, ties the family together, solves their problems through his business connections with large syndicates, and keeps the family secrets during his lifetime. He counterpoints Giovanni in that, coming from the same background, he, with his diplomacy and intelligence, has become successful in contrast to Giovanni's self-inflicted defeats. Amadeo is Giovanni's whipping-boy, the meek one who perpetuates the family and extends it to Marco. Eventually, Marco, the assimilated son, educated and pursuing a profession, marries a Jewish girl and transcends the tragic frustrations of his origins to become an average American with contemporary problems.

Lucas Longo has written a good novel with a well-paced story, whose climax comes into focus after the reader has met the various characters affected by the murder with which the book begins. The portrayals of these characters are quickly sketched vignettes. The tense progress in the probings for the secrets in the neighborhood gives the novel its motion and tight structure. Aunt Rose motivates much of the action by her determination to brew hatred for the pursuit of vengeance. Marco is swept forward into this vindictiveness and he loses his father. Although this loss may appear as poetic justice, dealt against the father's own brutality, Marco emerges as the wounded hero. When the symbol of simple and unconditioned love, Amadeo, offers him solace for the future, Marco concludes that self-destructive hate can be overcome only by planned improvement in human relationships. Although Longo is sentimental at times ("What memories I have of that porch!") and melodramatic at others ("Dolls may break, but they never betray"), he tells a horror story in easy, fluent style. Although some incidents read like a sociological report, for example, the various developments of "Innocents" in chapter 17, the story has verisimilitude and excitement. The reader's imagination recaptures the community of Italian immigrants.

As we may deduce at this point, these immigrants are exceedingly varied. Longo creates no stereotypes, and many of his characters are recognizable and solid. There is Doctor Bentolinardo, who earns his father's disdain when he changes his name to Bentley. There is the judicious Zia Maria, a familiar figure in Italian-American neighborhoods, a member of an older generation who appoints herself the conscience of the community. Longo portrays Maria as another usual Italian-American type—the innocent girl who is easily deceived and is called a "cucumber" by her family. Collectively, the characters move according to protocol, as they do when Maria is sent to the hospital, and according to the laws of "respect" as when Lena welcomes the visitors under the charge of Zia Maria. Conventions prescribe every step of the funeral; at another time, a wedding is programmed with similar adherence to protocol. In the end, Marco rebels at the bitterness that Aunt Rose nurses as tribute to tribal vengeance. He discovers that he blames everyone for his unhappiness, even cursing his own "race."

To rebel against this rigidity is what Lucas Longo is prescribing. *The Family on Vendetta Street* is a tract on human emotions and the extremes of love that, when out of balance, lead to the extremes of hate. Longo foresees a happier future with control of these extremes. He also forecasts that the Italian-American's zest for life will increase, not when it is choked with vindictiveness but when it includes others. As Marco buries his vendetta, he fondles Amadeo's gifts of love and wisdom; but, as he speeds into the snowy night, like Robert Frost he must face the future to keep his promises.

9

RECENT ITALIAN IMMIGRANT WRITERS

Recent immigrants continue to supply fresh cultural attitudes to the American literary scene. These writers are generally notable not for purely ethnic documentation, or regional American treatment, but for their distinctive aesthetic concepts. Preserving their European frame of reference, their work presents an expertly crafted art that insists on organic control, undisguised good taste, disciplined aesthetics, and an unashamed propriety that often borders on elegance. Often their fiction transcends the excessive contemporary eroticism and introspection. Among these writers are three who have earned popular and critical attention: Arturo Vivante, Niccolò Tucci, and P. M. Pasinetti.

ARTURO VIVANTE (1923–)

Arturo Vivante is an Italian-born physician who now lives on Cape Cod with his wife and children. The social concepts and poetic quality of his writings were inherited from his family background. He grew up in Siena at Villa Solaia, the home of his parents, Lello and Elena Vivante. His uncle was the anti-Fascist poet, Lauro de Bosis, and his grandfather was the poet Adolfo de Bosis, who was recognized in Italy as the authoritative translator of Shelley. Vivante's fiction includes a book of short stories, *The French Girls of Killini* (1967), and two novels, *A Goodly Babe* (1966) and *Doctor Giovanni* (1969).

At the core of Arturo Vivante's writing is a witty and mundane affirmation. Because he has traveled extensively and has accumulated a storehouse of personal experiences, his writing reflects a kaleidoscope of adventures. Economic with words, he structures his stories with clear proportions and even balance. His prose is lucid, direct, and simple, honed to intensive narration and instant communication. With the easy understatement of the expert and the sure touch of the experienced director, he reduces the complications of human relationships to distilled moments of life. In so doing, he portrays a life worth living.

The French Girls of Killini

The French Girls of Killini[1] is a collection of twenty-one of Vivante's numerous short stories that have appeared in the *New Yorker* and other magazines. Since the present study is primarily of novels, I shall limit the discussion of these stories to a general evaluation of their importance as a pleasant and valid introduction to the quality of Mr. Vivante's fiction. The stories record the narrator's emotional experiences during a pilgrimage, first as a young man in Canada, then as a physician in Italy, and, finally, his marriage and settlement in America. Mr. Vivante's evocative ability strikes the reader immediately. For example, in the first story, "The Stream," the narrator subtly treats the development of his attachment to his cousin, Jane. His style demonstrates his attitude: "She didn't answer; there was no need. It was as if the enchantment would suffer from any word spoken, any move made, in that stillness" (p. 10).

A Goodly Babe

Arturo Vivante apparently can temper idealism without becoming cynical. His feeling that life should not be betrayed and that it should be lived with candor and integrity pervades his first novel, *A Goodly Babe.*[2] In this book he writes about Cosimo Lami, a young Roman physician, who, because he would rather write, is more interested in his patients as people than as medical problems. Cosimo speaks English fluently, and his office is close to the Piazza di Spagna. Because of this proximity, the American Embassy sends him tourists who need medical attention. One of these, Jessie, a student in Italy, comes to him and shortly thereafter he proposes to her. Not accepting him at first, Jessie flies back to Boston, but returns to Rome in the spring with the express purpose of working in Bologna. Eventually, Jessie and Cosimo marry, and, in due time, Jessie endures the still-birth of a deformed infant. Following this tragedy, Cosimo abandons medicine to devote himself entirely to literature. He and Jessie move to Cape Cod, where they eventually have a second child, a "goodly babe,"—a reference to *The Winter's Tale*, "A daughter; and a goodly babe, lusty and like to live."

1. Arthur Vivante, *The French Girls of Killini* (Boston: Little, Brown and Company, 1967).
2. Arturo Vivante, *A Goodly Babe* (Boston: Little Brown and Company, 1966).

As the story ends, Cosimo is looking forward to artistic fulfillment, and his optimism is the thematic projection of the basic idea of the book. Vivante is saying that our human love overcomes obstacles; it persists and becomes the ingredient of all other experiences in life. For example, when Cosimo hears of the suicide of Mrs. Lee, a former patient in Rome, he confesses remorse to Jessie, wondering if he had done enough to avert the tragedy. Perhaps, he thinks, he had been a doctor too limited in scope, one who cared for pain but disregarded sorrow. Vivante indicates thereby that one's scope should include the whole range of human relationship. This dimension of the theme is singularly dramatized when Cosimo, after the still-birth of his child, feels that the bond of pain they share is stronger than that of love between him and Jessie. Even their irritations with each other indicate their love. Vivante is showing that every finite thing is a part of the infinite. Cosimo recalls that for the caption for his college graduation picture he had chosen "A thing of beauty is a joy forever." When he finds a thing of beauty, perhaps a shell, he feels its link with the infinite. Vivante emphasizes that this joy may be momentary, but this moment is alive, meaningful, and very much worth having. Every experience is worthwhile, even the irritation and frustration that add to Cosimo's anticipation of their second child. When he takes Jessie to the hospital, he is reassured by the time-tested, time-honored routines, and is confident in the efficiency of "Good Old America." As he concludes his story, Vivante has Cosimo looking at his baby in his arms, a new beginning under his watchful eye, a member of a new generation to be molded with the utmost care that the old generation may give.

Arturo Vivante's theme has several specifically Italian interpretations. The problem of how the older Italians survived the struggle for assimilation is recalled in reverse in Cosimo's medical practice in Rome. His patients are predominantly old Italians who had once emigrated to America, served in the American Armed Forces during World War I, and later returned to Italy. Vivante portrays these men as a "helpless little group," who came regularly for Cosimo's signature. They had returned to their seductive little towns built high on mountains, the same towns Cosimo visits with Jessie, which will not be erased from his mind later. The permanence of the illuminating moment grips Cosimo as he goes to Rome with Jessie to board the intercontinental plane. They are lifted over the newly plowed fields, and he suddenly feels a strong attachment to the earth as he is uprooted from it. He finds the parting painful, and tells Jessie that he can no more go back than water can flow upward, but he has never "experienced such a stillness." Later, however, when he and Jessie go to Cape Cod for the first time, he confesses that he is glad he has come to America as an immigrant, "full of hope, instead of as a visitor or tourist" (p. 119). He has difficulty, however, with his addiction to certain "Italian ways," such as the manner in which his eye roves at the beach because of his basic need for companionship. Jessie, with her New England rectitude, cannot understand this gregarious instinct; nor can she perceive his need to visit his family in Italy while she is pregnant. This contempoary Italian-American is brought into focus by Vivante in the final chapter when, as Cosimo walks the streets of Boston alone, he gauges the wealth of the nation. Feeling uncomfortable as he watches a group of dancers in a café, he recalls his former life and concludes that he belongs nowhere—neither in Italy, nor in the United States. Because he cannot quite believe that "no plot of ground owns him," however, he suddenly feels that he will some day return to the fisherman's terrace near Porto Santo Stefano. With this instant insight, he identifies with the millions of immigrants in America whose cultural adjustment has been accompanied by the flashes of memory that have checked their self-destruction in their agony.

This novel, though light in texture, is woven with the basic pattern of universal human behavior. As Vivante weaves, he fortifies each thread by crossing it with another thread, that of the sharing of individual needs. Thereby he exposes both the frustrations and the satisfactions in the experiences of assimilation. To the reader's relief, Vivante is not intemperate with words, nor does he probe his characters' psychology. He disciplines his analysis, exposing a situation like a precisely cut organ at the end of a scalpel. People—Mrs. Lee, Jessie, the fisherman, every staff member of the hospital—are important as human beings as well as ideas or symbols. Vivante is incisive enough, also, to stir the reader's imagination to construct the environment of the characters in action. His descriptions of places recall the pleasure of familiar tours. With the art of apparent artlessness, the book is an ably crafted miniature that distills human truth.

Doctor Giovanni

With *Doctor Giovanni*,[3] Arturo Vivante goes back to 1948. His protagonist, Giovanni Arcetri, like Cosimo Lami, a member of the medical profession and speaking in the first person, takes a nostalgic bicycle tour in Italy. As Vivante evokes the familiar settings of Rome and its surroundings, he is more symbolic in this novel than he has been in his other narratives. This story is a frank celebration of life, with repeated references to the theme of regeneration. This idea retains its freshness through the zestful interpretations of the protagonist. Arcetri begins a romance, but is constantly deterred by circumstances. Vivante, alternating pity and humor, hereby supplies enough conflict to give the story substance. That he returns to Italy for his setting and uses specific objects and places as symbols emphasizes the pattern of those writers who return to original sources for the dynamic of regeneration.

3. Arturo Vivante, *Doctor Giovanni* (Boston: Little Brown & Company, 1969).

When Dr. Giovanni Arcetri decides to travel to "look for a girl," he optimistically leaves his parents, and pedals off to Rome. With a deft, light hand, Vivante takes his protagonist to the cafés and restaurants to join the company of other travelers. Giovanni attempts sexual adventures with various women. His inexperience makes him inept with the older Valeria, and his deference deters him with Daphne, who becomes ill and grieves for her dead pilot husband. Verging on mysticism, the solution at the end appears as a poetic turn of fate. The story becomes a symbol of the universal pilgrim, who, though saddened by the transitoriness of human experience, must continue to survive in the world.

The point of the book is that we should celebrate the very act of living life. To demonstrate this theme, Vivante uses the overall symbol of Italy for the idea of being alive. After the fall of Fascism, the Republic has a new air of freedom and "along with all the repairing there was a sense of regeneration, of healing" (p. 4). The author believes that this is the right atmosphere for art in any form to develop and thrive. On a personal level, hope is the catalyst of this zest; it is the contemporary form of prayer, as Giovanni Arcetri tells Sister Veronilde at the university hospital. This being in touch with God, Giovanni says, means acting spontaneously, doing something with complete dedication, unmindful of ultimate objectives. In this way, one makes the best of what this present life has to offer. On a universal level, Giovanni enlarges this theme by contesting a doctor's thesis that love creates the enzymes; on the contrary, says Giovanni, as water digs a stream, thought makes nerves and love makes the enzymes and the hormones; he says that love, therefore, is a spontaneous act. Away from the hospital, in the rural stretch between Suna and Grosseto, Giovanni absorbs the feeling of midsummer, of life full-grown. He reflects that this is what life is all about—the peak of beauty, the ripeness. He is grateful for the inheritance of the woods and the hills dotted here and there with groups of white crosses. He appreciates the sacrifice of the buried soldiers while he is absorbing the heart of his ancient land. The circling of the theme of celebration from nation to person and back again rests upon the transcendental notion that the celebration of life is better than life itself. In Rome, talking to Valeria, Giovanni, apologizing for not agreeing to spend the night with her, begs her not to make him her prisoner. He is not certain that she understands, but he means that reality is never what one imagines it to be. The imagination has the vision of art, while "what comes to be has the nakedness, the give and take, the uncompromising quality of life" (p. 99). He reflects that there is something about life that art is "glad" to be without, and he is not ready to put love out of the realm of art. Extending to further abstract levels, the joyous affirmation of life to Giovanni becomes intricately involved with the creative instinct. He tells the American tourist, Dorothy, who is studying painting, that when things are reflected, like sound on the surface of a river, they lose a certain crudity. Art, therefore, is a refinement, an intimate sort of reflection. Love, too, is a refinement of the person, making the person forget himself in regard for another. It is love that lifts everything above stark reality to celebrate the vision of life. Giovanni must rely on the comfort of this abstraction as he comes to the end of his frustrating experience with Daphne, although his reflections take a more concrete form when he remarks that distilled things like brandy and lines of poetry can help make the atmosphere serene. Cruel and crude aspects of nature, like death and disease, are constantly present to assert themselves, and one must constantly be on guard, but art, Giovanni concludes, the artificial and the human touch, is the only effective weapon, the sole salvation.

Giovanni Arcetri is the thematic instrument for Vivante's ideas. Giovanni admits his inordinate innocence. In specific terms, his idealization of life and love is extreme because, with medical school and the army behind him, good-night kisses are the extent of his sexual experience. He is almost childlike as he starts out on his trip, looking ahead and, as Vivante writes, "open-mouthed," drinking "the sunny air." In his freedom, he is able to pause to observe and go "off the track a little way." There is an evanescent quality in his professional attitude, which extends to his preferred vocation of writing poetry. He writes verses on the blank first and last pages of his medical books, on paper napkins, on the inside of match covers, on registration cards, his passports, in his check book, address books, and on any piece of available paper. He feels a physical exhilaration when he writes down his ideas; the writing makes him feel fertile and gives him "a teeming, warm, germinating, fermenting, bubbling sensation" (p. 76). Giovanni feels a personal joyousness in the celebration of life in art. His subsequent self-denial in abstaining from carnal indulgence and eroticism serves to intensify this ecstasy.

To the Italian-American writer, reaffirmation is an essential fortifier of morale. Arturo Vivante dramatizes the fixed reference the writer has in Rome, the Eternal City. Giovanni soothes the crying Daphne, who is telling him of her husband's death in 1944, and holds her while they look at the waters of the Tiber, "flowing as it had always flowed—in 1944, and in 44 B.C" (p. 147). Here Vivante is emphasizing the timelessness of the Tiber, of Rome, and of Italianism. The tower where they stay is also a monument to this permanence. Vivante effectively describes it as it "mirrored itself in the water, trembled, broke up, vanished, resurrected, intact, perfect a moment. There was a stillness around that approached eternity" (p. 173).

The novel is blithe and buoyant, and is also optimistically provocative. The reader may wish at times for some psychological motivation, but the unpretentious rejoicing of Vivante's treatment excludes such weight. With the touch of the romantic lyric poet, he has succeeded in giving the reader a flash of visionary renewal without nihilistic metaphysics.

NICCOLÒ TUCCI (n.d.)

Niccolò Tucci is the author of *Before My Time* and *Unfinished Funeral.* In both, he uses European settings for stories with continental themes. *Before My Time* has been categorized as a novel-memoir, and it is the imaginative portrayal of the members of Tucci's family. Witty and brilliant, it serves as an engaging introduction to his classically panoramic style. He portrays his characters through moment-by-moment shifts of emotion and thought that generate responsive actions in other characters. Rewarding to the reader as this absorbing novel is, its main relationship to the Italian-American writer is in its recall of the nineteenth-century cultural tradition, which gives both historic and imaginative support to his contemporary themes.

In *Unfinished Funeral,* Tucci moves his setting to twentieth-century Spain. The book's chief relationship to American culture is in the highly charged actions of his characters, like those of many of the protagonists of American fiction. There is, however, the added dimension of critical evaluation of the characters, which may well be the result of Tucci's Americanization.

Since Niccolò Tucci's materials are predominantly autobiographical, they can be understood best from the vantage point of the writer's life. Born in Switzerland of a Russian mother and an Italian father, he grew up in Tuscany. He came to America in the early thirties as an exchange student from Italy to Amherst College, with a reputation for brilliance, originality, and a Byronic flair. In this country he came under the influence of anti-Fascist historian Gaetano Salvemini and novelist G. A. Borghese. The association of these writers effected Tucci's change from his post in the Foreign Office of Italy's Fascist government to political exile. The association also influenced his attitude against authoritarianism, supplying the basic theme of his writing.

Tucci's first novel, *Before My Time,*[4] is an imaginative portrayal of the author's family and his pre-history. Framed by philosophical and psychological observations of Europe at the turn of the century, it is a Hogarthian, panoramic presentation of family figures surrounding an autocratic, wealthy widow, the Russian grandmother, the Grossmutter. With a kind of Proustian involution, the author describes a chain of recollected episodes set off by a childhood recollection. The story follows Mamachen from city to city, protected by an elaborate entourage, until she settles in Lugano, where her submissive daughter and traveling companion, Mary, marries an Italian physician of poor and obscure origins. The story involves numerous family anecdotes, ending with Mamachen's death and the assembling of all the relatives to divide her possessions. At this point, Tucci's bitter humor summarizes his acerbic treatment, which has paradoxically contrasted and integrated his analytical, lucid Italian mind with his emotionally gen-

4. Niccolò Tucci, *Before My Time* (New York: Simon and Schuster, 1962).

erous Russian nature. The book is a big canvas of wide scope and brilliant color, and its language is correspondingly detailed and prolix.

Unfinished Funeral

Tucci's second novel, *Unfinished Funeral*,[5] is set in twentieth-century Spain. In what has become almost an American tradition, he analyzes the behavior of a despotic woman, a psychically cannibalistic monster who destroys everyone around her. Tucci tells the story with some fantastic details that give the book the quality of a fable.

Ermalinda, the Duchess of Cambon de Triton, makes a ritual of maiming herself, imposing her suffering on her family and household and exercising "brinkmanship" with her seemingly imminent death. Preparations are always in order for her funeral: Arturo, the coachman; the gilded hearse, the black Arab horses harnessed and clad in deeper black; all the servants standing and the family waiting. She plays her part, and finally leaves the stage. Meanwhile her husband has committed suicide; her niece Beatrice is corrupted; and her son, Bernandasse, and daughter, Elise, destroyed. Even her lover, Tinti, a philanderer of magnificent proportions, is reduced to a moral pulp. All these people are cemented in their relationships by the basic deceit of the Duchess, which has spawned a network of lies.

The reader may conclude that Ermalinda is the personification of the vanishing aristocratic European culture, particularly in the power it exercised in royalist Spain. From the vantage of an American view, Tucci sees that culture as a monstrous destroyer of individuals. All the trappings are falsifications that live by intimidation and by exploiting death. There is a warning in Tucci's treatment that may easily apply to the dual morality of much of contemporary America, a theme that dominates the novels of Francis Pollini. For example, in *Unfinished Funeral*, old Tinti, on paying his final visit to the Duchess, comments that his lies have been temporary and changeable and that the eternal lies are those that devout people tell themselves. "Everyday" lies are less harmful, he contends, than those lies which deal with eternity.

This novel is not restricted to exclusively Italian-American cultural themes, but it has symbolic references for such themes. Artfully written with dramatic momentum, progressive dialogue, and poetic compression, it leaves a piercing impact of a perfectly aimed instrument. When the Duchess is informed that the hearse has been destroyed and that the horses and Arturo have been killed by a train, she digresses momentarily to comment "poor Arturo!" and prepares her act of having another heart attack. Europe, this Italian-American writer is saying, will probably always be this way, and we should look to our own truth. This truth includes the fact that the Italian who has come to

5. Niccolò Tucci, *Unfinished Funeral* (New York: Simon & Schuster, 1964).

America must now concern himself with the process of liberation from oppression that has become lethal.

P. M. PASINETTI (1913–)

Pier Maria Pasinetti, who usually signs himself P. M. Pasinetti, was born in Venice on June 24, 1913, and was reared in a stimulating climate of politics and letters. After earning a *Dottore in Lettere* from the University of Padua in 1935, he came to the United States to study from 1935 to 1937. During this time he published his first work of fiction in *The Southern Review.* Since then, he has contributed to other magazines both in this country and in Italy. He has also written feature articles for newspapers, and has successfully worked on screenplays. Mondadori published his first book, *L'Ira di Dio,* and three novelettes in 1942. Leaving Italy, he went to lecture at Göttingen and Stockholm, where he spent the war years, and then came to the United States in 1946 to teach at Bennington College while he earned his doctorate at Yale (1949). Pasinetti was naturalized in 1952 and has been a professor at U.C.L.A., where he was appointed to the University's Institute for Creative Arts for 1964–65. In 1965 he received an award from the National Institute of Arts and Letters with a citation for fiction written in "the grand style of tradition but with a probing imagination." His two novels, *Venetian Red* (1960) and *The Smile on the Face of the Lion* (1965), are set in Venice and are generic source-settings of *From the Academy Bridge,*[6] whose view extends from Europe to Southern California.

From the Academy Bridge

From the Academy Bridge is the story of an institute in California, which is set up with electronic computers to make an elaborate analysis of political history in terms of the rhetorical artifices and language patterns used by leaders in the past to exploit the minds and emotions of the populace. The objective of this institute is to expose the trickery, and thereby warn society, of the power of controlled communication to distort facts and to create international situations that promote wars.

The story involves the conflict between two groups at the institute, one comprised of those who wish to adhere to the original humanistic purpose of the computers to seek the knowledge *per se* of how the verbal ploys were used, the other consisting of those who want to use the computers and the new knowledge now as a political instrument. With ethical equivocation, the machines can be subverted to imple-

6. P. M. Pasinetti, *From the Academy Bridge* (New York: Random House, 1970).

ment precisely those results that the founders of the institute had undertaken to expose. Young Ruggero Tava, a Venetian, is invited to a symposium at the institute, where he can learn the details of its operation. The institute already has two Italian members, the director, Alphonse Rossi, and, coincidentally, a member who has the same surname, Gilberto Rossi, who was a friend of Tava's father, who had been killed at the beginning of World War I, before Ruggero was born. Gilberto Rossi, still suffering from the trauma of his friend's death, finds young Tava's calm equanimity offensive, while Ruggero, who has been inquiring everywhere in Europe about Rossi, looks to the older man as a father-figure. Rossi's educated humanism clashes with Tava's objective activism, and the progress of this relationship carries the momentum of the narration.

There are infinite nuances and levels of Pasinetti's larger theme. From the point of view of the people who muse over the Grand Canal in Venice, the idea of mechanized articulation is absurd. Venice is the mother city of outward direction. From this matrix to California, to the position of director of the Institute held by Alphonse Rossi, the author introduces his themes in a simple orchestration. Pasinetti says, "Meetings with him are like symphonies; themes emerge at the right moment" (p. 27). The machines at the institute, the newcomers say, can always emerge with right moments; they do not have the qualms of those who feel that machines might mean the intrusion of the robot into cultural life. The machine is the antithesis of the "Partibon spirit," or Pasinetti's Venetian background, of "complete detachment from life and at the same time total immersion in it" (p. 78).

Reflecting the responses of the individual, a Partibon says, at another point, that in every possible situation, public or private, all of us are given a chance to choose between different forms of shame. There is pontification in Rossi's concluding that the staid Fassolas of Venice are ephemeral vaudeville characters, while the Partibons are the men of tomorrow who will endure. Pasinetti's exposé of the semantics of militarism reveals his own bias as he describes the aunt who in 1920 and 1925 subscribed to newspapers that were seriously cultural and, as such, were vigorously opposed to the Regime that actually, later on, prohibited them. The political view is closely interwoven with the semantic. At the institute, Rossi makes "accurate little studies" of words like *freedom*, *enemy*, *heart*, and *blood*, alone and in connection with the "condiments" with which they are dressed by leaders in their oratorical sense. His co-worker, Blatt, says,

> "Wars have never been studied from the point of view of language, of lexicons; international treaties, press campaigns, speeches by politicans and agitators . . . examined from an L. & C. (Language & Communication) point of view. It's Columbus' egg; yet I believe we are the first to devote ourselves systematically to this kind of research." (p. 123)

He goes on to say that men go to war to get themselves killed because they are inspired by speeches from politicians and war poets, speeches that are actually linguistically incomprehensible to them. The institute also receives money to study how words have influenced history. This study includes the analysis, examination, discussion, and lexical cataloguing of the largest available number of "relevant" texts. Rossi sees, however, two levels of development: one on the vast resources of the Institute, well-ordered, catalogued, dehydrated, and electrified; the other, with the memory of his uncle's sinking his boots in rotting matter, saying goodbye to his soldiers as he goes to join his blond princess of *belle lettere*, a complicated, unclassifiable production. Pasinetti shows, however, that though there is this two-party, macrocosmic-microcosmic pattern at the institute, it is actually a sensitive model of a political structure in miniature, with real possibilities and subtleties that would eventually get lost in a macroorganization. Actually, too, he says, the whole structure is ready to organize a counter-brainwashing.

There are characters in the book who resist these themes. The Bickfords, for example, may be fascinated by politico-electronic power and by their claim to be individualists; but, as Blatt observes, if some political "big fish" were to arrive from the capital and stroke them with his fins, they would start purring immeditely. These characters intensify the purpose of the Symposium, which will review what in the lexicons of some European government classes is referred to as "verification." On the most personal level in the story, Ruggero Tava's constant pursuit of Gilberto Rossi's image runs parallel to the book's overall theme of search for exactitude in the computerizing of words. On a more abstract level, the metaphor of the Academy Bridge serves as a point of view, like Hamilton Basso's Pompey's Head. From this plane of meditation, through academic eyes, time and history flow by in which protagonists live and munipulate others, who with their planned politics of self-staging and self-mythifying, have fused something like the last intense "flare of an electric bulb before it goes kaput forever" (p. 189).

These themes are intensified in the two main characters, whose stories have Old British Empire backgrounds. When Gilberto Rossi thinks of Tava, he feels like a fictional character. After a conversation in which Tava asks Rossi about his flying experience, Rossi deflates the young man with, "I flew over Vienna . . . in 1917." Rossi is increasingly contrasted with the young man, however, whom he sees as belonging to the neo-human era. He senses that behind the polished good manners and the completely organized intellectualism of Tava, the young man has never worried over the problem of whether the mechanization of our world is a nightmare or a salvation. Ruggero has no career jitters; he is efficient and courteous, and adamant about leisure time. He knows exactly what he wants and is, as Blatt says, vertiginously well-balanced.

The conflict of these personalities symbolizes the search by the machine for the humanity of the past. On a restricted technological level, this is an externalization of the son-in-pursuit-of-the-father theme. Blatt remarks to Ruggero, "You are avoiding each other because you are seeking each other. Deep, deep down, your coming here has been a voyage in search of your father" (p. 219). Something must be a point of communication; herein is the main purpose of the Institute. It must do something so that human discourse may be less like a series of dialogues "between the deaf" than it is now. Many principal words of internal exchange have been so abused that they are no longer communicable. A verbal clinical record is necessary for persons responsible for the destiny of others. When Gilberto Rossi makes his speech on the value of pronouns, he does so with optimism. Sensing the hope in Ruggero,who is marrying and going to China, Rossi believes, as he states, that "these young people might prove capable of thwarting the eventual macabre leader, of catching him in the act as he abusively says 'we,' of balking his speech" (p. 261).

Thinking of Ruggero's plans for China, Rossi senses the repetition of history: China, Marco Polo, a Venetian, China. Behind all this, in this story Pasinetti shows that everything is made possible by American enterprise. The Italian in America, therefore, is the humanistic, unifying principle of the Symposium.

Hope emanates everywhere, and Pasinetti says that everything, including pain, has its charge of vitality. The vitality, however, is the catalyst of unity for the world, a unity on a worldwide scale, a network of relations among real people, individualized and not bound by any official ties. He says that such a unity would eliminate the troublemakers, the self-styled Men of Destiny. Ruggero is the new type of protagonist, a man who can pass unobserved and who is not the least interested in becoming either a star or a leader.

Pasinetti's Gilberto Rossi is a new type of Italian-American; for, he says, "the immigrant looking for America-America has long ceased to exist, and anyway, the Institute certainly wouldn't be the most brilliant of goals for such a person" (p. 334). Pasinetti shows, furthermore, that the Italian who comes to America today is a cosmic person arriving in a cosmic situation. The immigrant's ship is gone forever. The future of assimilation is like that of the Institute (p. 335).

Like his previous books, P. M. Pasinetti's *From the Academy Bridge* is serious and engrossing. With the form and treatment of a well-made nineteenth-century novel, Pasinetti presents ideas in human forms that live and change with their differences and their mobility. He explores the progressive growth in human relationships brought on by personal maturation (Ruggero), the conflict of ages (Ruggero and Gilberto Rossi), the memories of young loves (in prewar Venice), and the persistent veneration of tested standards (the Partibons). Pasinetti brings all these factors to bear on the threatening danger of technological criteria that attempt to objectify past experience. Despite the explosive fears, he maintains a ruminative tone that disciplines the electronically charged situation which, he says, is only a phase in the evolution of the cosmos. The fuse is in the hands of the word-manipulators. It is to Pasinetti's credit that he resists the temptation of sensationalizing his theme by using print-outs or mechanical illustrations. His own judicious use of language bears out his thesis, which gives permanence to understanding among people and durability to their use of words.

10

ADVANCED ASSIMILATION

Neither withdrawal into reminiscences nor default in confrontation is the most effective channel into the literary mainstream. Although the works under these two categories are, with the exception of the more universal and more widely acclaimed books by George Cuomo, important enough only to be stored as social artifacts, they are, because of their restricted treatment, of interest generally to the specialized reader. When the writings include familiar social and historical treatments, the novelist communicates instantly and effectively with a reading audience that can identify its own traditions with the materials. Therefore, with their increased social and economic solidity, writers of Italian ancestry have to a greater degree integrated their endemic concepts with those of the culture now native to them. Correspondingly, an increasingly larger reading audience has accepted them. The point I am making is, however, that these writers, although advanced in assimilation, have retained certain basic attitudes toward human relations, social structures, and individual resolutions. On the whole, the Italian-American novelist demonstrates active, extroverted sympathy, functioning communal respect, and dignified personal survival. Representative of a burgeoning group of those who are thus affirmatively assimilated are Ben Piazza, Eugene Mirabelli, Robert Canzoneri, and Frank Miceli. One notable exception is Mario Andrew Pei, who, acclaimed generally as an eminent linguist and distinguished scholar, has written some engaging and superbly literate fiction, in which he celebrates the function and adventure of the affirming human spirit. Other writers assert dominant themes that are used here as criteria for classification, primarily for convenience. As for Francis Pollini and Mario Puzo, it may be generally conceded that their works require separate chapters.

BEN PIAZZA (n.d.)

The Exact and Very Strange Truth

Starting to write while he was an undergraduate at Princeton, Ben Piazza was first published in the *Nassau Literary Magazine.* After earning his degree in 1955, he pursued a career of acting and writing. Piazza's novel, *The Exact and Very Strange Truth,*[1] though chronologically written before the maturation of assimilation, is, as a first novel, prophetic of a trend that is becoming normal. A youthful story in which the author recollects his childhood in the South, the presentation reminds the reader of James Agee's *A Death in the Family* in its evocative tone and reconstruction of a boy's reaction to the instability of the human situation. Piazza exercises both power and art in the framework of the book, which he builds on the scaffold of a journey that Mrs. Gallanti, the widow of a Sicilian-American shoemaker, takes with her three young children, which leads them from Little Rock to Savannah. Piazza tells his story from the point of view of Alexander, the twelve-year-old who, as he accompanies his mother, recalls his life prior to the trip. As he takes the reader through the parallel journeys of the present and the remembered one, Piazza reconstructs the episodes that dramatize the fact that everything is constantly changing. Elaborating the idea of fluctuation as it is demonstrated in the lives of all the other characters in the book, the writer universalizes his theme. Everyone is helpless before the impermanence of life. Some of the characters are convenient symbols of social themes related to the South, but the writer develops them sufficiently for the reader to recognize familiar human traits. Moreover, Piazza gives plausible enough motivation for his protagonist to resolve that the mutability of life is often for the better.

This is a convincing story about race relations in the South, stressing that the attitudes toward these relations are changing. Through Alexander we learn of the tumultuous courtship of the passionate thirty-eight-year-old Sicilian immigrant, Carlo Gallanti, and the beautiful eighteen-year-old Veronica Dillman from Paragould, Arkansas. The bride's family, humiliated Baptists, disown her for marrying a Roman Catholic, a foreigner. Subsequently the Gallantis have a large family, all of whom are supported by Carlo's shoemaking. To prove himself a respectable individual, Carlo builds his family the "Rock House" and disciplines his children with impeccable manners, strict morals, and undivided attention to their studies. An inevitable clash ensues between his Sicilian standards and the mores of the community in which the children are growing. Carlo gives his daughter Rosalie

1. Ben Piazza, *The Exact and Very Strange Truth* (New York: Farrar, Straus and Company, 1964)

a violent beating for trying to run away; young Carlo succeeds in leaving home; and Alexander feels the strap for using his father's razor. These traumatic experiences leave lasting marks on all the family, but some incidents bring them together happily. They decorate Christmas trees together; Quentin compulsively collects comic books with the help of the others; Veronica and Alexander shop together for gifts for the family; they go to the freak show; they share intimate experiences with Negroes, especially with Mary, the cleaning woman. As Piazza narrates these events, he probes the mind of the lonely Alexander, who tells much of the story from memory. The boy weaves a world of fantasy for himself, trying to people his isolated world. He tries to identify himself as the triplet of the Duke twins, whom he admires; he refashions the world of the freaks with himself as part of it; he searches constantly for a toy that "will last forever"; he makes a blundering attempt to share the marital intimacies of a man and woman whom he watches from a window on his paper route; he imagines himself as the savior who will make his mother well and happy. After his father dies and his mother is paralyzed, he takes matters in hand and brings out the concluding episode, which stirs the reader to anguished pity. We know, however, that the determined Alexander will find both restoration and regeneration in the world.

The point of *The Exact and Very Strange Truth* is that "it is peculiar how things can change so sudden. Things can be one way today and tomorrow be the very opposite" (p. 14). The feelings of people may not change, but the situations will. For example, people may threaten to burn Carlo Gallanti's shop because he is "a wop," but when he meets them with a shotgun, they do not bother him, not because they accept him, but because it is safer to avoid him. Piazza extends this theme. Gan-Gan, the maternal grandmother, reads to the children from the Bible that man gains nothing from his toil; a generation goes; a generation comes; the earth, only, remains forever. As a result, Alexander is obsessed with the impermanence of things. At the freak show he hears that the "Queen of Freaks" is the daughter of the King of China. He hears, also, the voice of the "wood lady" say that only love endures; and, then, when he asks the gypsy for the everlasting toy, she tells him that it is in the vision of the future, which she already sees in his eyes. He cannot understand, and confesses to Veronica that he wonders why things are so "funny." Once, all he wanted was a tricycle; now he is no longer interested. He thinks about death; if love lasts, then love means you do not want someone to die. At one point, later, at Christmas time, he concludes that if we were in a fairy tale, we would live happily ever after. With this gossamer thought, Piazza emphasizes the theme of impermanence.

The theme is crystallized when continuity is symbolized by things. For example, when Alexander picks up his father's razor, he reflects that this is an object that once belonged to his father's father, and, before that, to another father. This thinking intensifies the paradox that the razor is the catalyst of Alexander's traumatic disillusionment in his father's love. His mother fails to assuage his feeling of being lost. At school he agonizes with the need for recognition, trying to imagine himself as part of the "personality book" that he steals from Patricia Harper. He reaches the climax of his isolation at the Thanksgiving Party, when he discovers that his mother has not come to see him as a Pilgrim, although he learns the reason later. In the end, Piazza's extension of the theme of impermanence arrives at an optimistic solution. Gallanti's Shoe Shop is perpetuated in Rudolph's store in Savannah. A symbol of Rudolph's will for survival is reflected, also, in the action of his wife, Miriam, who takes the children to the shore to build a sand castle, "The Secret Place of All of Us," and leaves before the tide comes in. Alexander believes that there is a secret and lasting place where they can all live together and be happy. This plaintive child's hope dramatizes the final scene, when again things change abruptly. Piazza reassures the reader with the feeling that, once Alexander convinces himself that all things change, there is a permanence in the knowledge of the truth.

Other characters in the novel reflect this theme. Carlo Gallanti must adjust to the Bible-reading strictness of a Southern village. In his frequent quarrels with his wife, in his repeated denying of independence to his children, he must surrender. When he enforces his discipline through violence, he loses his identity with the children. The tenacity of his integrity, which by its strength helps him to build a better house than that of any of his neighbors, is the remorseless inflexibility that refuses to bend; he, therefore, breaks before his time. As a result, Mrs. Gallanti loses the fragile externals of her society; she is ostracized. Her physical beauty deteriorates to a grotesque mask in a paralysis that has the appearance of drunkenness; she dies, symbolically, with her small children around her, sitting in a theater while watching the cinematized drama of her own life, the end of the Southern myth eulogized, in "Gone With the Wind." Her parents are barely discernible to us, since Ben Piazza has made them vague afterthoughts of an exhausted glory. With her passing, regeneration animates her children in an amalgamated culture: Rosalie asserts her independence; young Carlo greets the world through his army experience; Veronica solves her problems with newly discovered practical resources (braiding her hair, for example, if there is no time to curl it); and Quentin makes songs out of fragments of conversation. The scene portraying the children's strange parade is symbolic of their thrust into a more complex society.

Piazza emphasizes the cultural tradition of the Italian-American by juxtaposing it to the unidentifiable morass that the Negroes were once forced to inhabit in the traditional South. When Mary's baby is bleeding to death, the hospital for whites does not "want" to take the black child, but Carlo Gallanti forces the doctors to do so. No Anglo-Saxon Southerner would have so broken the silent laws of "place." Piazza, therefore, uses "differences" to advantage. On another level, the boy Alexander wishes, for example, that he could speak Italian so that the other children would notice that he has strange things about him: he could seem like a foreign prince and his father be a king from an unknown place. He knows a special ritual; he is perhaps the only boy in the neighborhood who goes to the basement in the evening to draw a pitcher of *vino* which only his Daddy drinks, sitting at the head of the table. Piazza portrays other differences. He makes a satirical comparison of the family group pictures: the Baptist Church Choir with which Momma is photographed are all dressed in their best, but half of them are barefoot; Mr. Gallanti is in a picture showing him as a young man in the front row of an Italian army group "with long swords and high boots." The author emphasizes this irony when he writes that the preachers in the local pulpits use Mr. Gallanti as an example of the evil in this world, instigating the group of churchmen to write on the window of the shoe shop: "Get out of town Wop or Next Sunday Your Store Will Burn" (p. 18). In the ensuing confrontation, Carlo Gallanti's shotgun is the implement of social equalization.

The novel presents a well-balanced development of the steady process of cultural interaction and Mr. and Mrs. Gallanti make a family and a life together, this "Italian man" who has a wildness in him, a love of wine, singing, cars, and pleasures (perhaps forbidden); and this Baptist woman, the descendant of preachers who believed in Hell and Damnation, who never even associated with people who smoked, drank, or used profanity. This woman accepts her mother-in-law, who cannot speak a word of English, and her sister-in-law, Maria, who marries an Italian whom the family in Italy chooses for her. Carlo's wife willingly submits to his strong will, respecting his ideas that, for example, children should stay in their own homes because he believes that a family should stay close together in their own house. Next to his children, Carlo's pleasure is in his flowers, because he likes to see things grow. When he quarrels with his wife over the religious training of the boys, he shouts that he should have married an Italian woman; and, Piazza writes, "Momma wants to die." She and the children, however, warm to his Sicilian exuberances; the younger ones always greet him with his special kiss, the *pizzicuneddu.* Later, when he quarrels over young Carlo's independence, reconciliation is possible only by the father's nostalgic retelling of his immigration to America. Carlo repeats his own father's advice, "If a job is worth doing it is worth doing well." He ends his tale by recalling that when they lived in the house on Cumberland Street in Little Rock, the Ku Klux Klan burned a cross on the front lawn, and the townspeople insisted on referring to him as the "dirty wop" having "dirty children." For this reason, he explains, he has built the "Rock House"; he owns his own business, and he has plans for his children to have businesses all over the state. He admits that now no one calls them "wop" any more, but Alexander wants to be called an Italian boy.

Later on, when his father dies, Alexander stays close to his Aunt Sophia, who speaks no English. At school, when he tries for the football team, he argues that he is big enough, but the coach comments that he never knew that "Eyetalians" were blond-headed and so little. It does not help him, of course, to insist that his father is one of the biggest men in the town. The lack of logic in this argument is a prime example of the ambiguity and duplicity of more serious moral situations in the adult world . Piazza emphasizes this Southern dual façade in the exclamation in the Baptist Church of the "saintly" social leader, Miss Crandall, that "poor Veronica Dillman, she has a terrible cross to bear, marrying a sinning wop Catholic" (p. 131). In the end, when Veronica survives her Carlo and is left with her loneliness and paralysis, her greatest anguish is his absence. The marriage has been a successful one, and the children are prepared for a changing America.

Ben Piazza's novel is written with competence, plausibility, and impact. He illuminates the childish experiences of his protagonist with a refreshing emphasis on idealism and wonderment. While there is a seductive compulsion in the narcotic smell of the wisteria that suddenly quickens Alexander to his sexual awareness, there is a mystical revival of the gallantry of Galahad in the boy's urge to protect his mother's happiness. Piazza portrays his small hero with truth, grace, and authenticity. While his rhetoric is simple, he writes with a clean power that needs no coarseness. His scenes are graphic, especially when he is portraying contrasts. His special talent, however, is in his swift, perceptive strokes as he etches with precision the ironic situations when people say things that belie what they are doing. The reader recognizes the characters as symbols of situations in the contemporary world. With sensitive and disciplined imagination, Piazza, with a circular design, has evoked a unique childhood recalled from an uncertain present. He has written a socially incisive and pertinent novel in which persecution, ostracism, and inequity are effectively portrayed as the inevitable sufferings in the wake of change from parochial dishonesty to cosmic justice. Alexander Gallanti is the minority's young America that has decided to find itself and not lose the world.

EUGENE MIRABELLI (1931–)

Eugene Mirabelli was born in 1931 in Arlington, Massachusetts, of American-born parents and of Calabrian and Sicilian grandparents. After attending public school, he studied for two years at the Massachusetts Institute of Technology, then completed his undergraduate studies for a B.A. at Harvard in 1952 with a major in English. When he earned an M.A. from Johns Hopkins in 1955, he continued as a Teaching Fellow at Harvard, where he took his Ph.D. in English in 1964. Since 1965 he has been a professor of English at the State University of New York in Albany. He has written two novels, *The Burning Air* and *The Way In*, and is working on a third, *No Resting Place.*

The Burning Air

In an era when adolescence was being nudged into self-consciousness by books with histrionic savior-projections like J. D. Salinger's *Catcher in the Rye*, many a sensitive, unpretentious George was groping to meet life on its own terms. Such a middling hero weekends through *The Burning Air*,[2] Eugene Mirabelli's first novel. Because this book is valid for its generation, it deserves the response and recommendation given it by literary critics and professors.

The Burning Air is a deceptively simple story of two young lovers caught in the romantic ideal that all of life's meaning is contained in their having each other. This theme is developed on two levels: that of the personal conflict that arises from the need of each to fulfill himself as well as the other, and that of the universal disillusionment that ensues when the romantics confront the real world with its established pressures.

The events of the story move through the brief weekend in summer when George visits Giulia and her family to ask Mr. and Mrs. Molla's approval of their intention to marry. Though the weather is oppressively warm, the Mollas perform all the rituals to make George comfortable. Despite their hospitality, George senses Mrs. Molla's reluctance to have them get married immediately upon graduation from college. He makes friendly overtures to the impish and often indifferent younger brother, Michael; he is traditionally courteous to the Italian-speaking grandmother; he helps the sympathetic but laconic Mr. Molla with the garden chores; he controls his jealous anger when Giulia, during a quarrel, mentions a former lover; he masks his fear when he meets the Niemans, friends Giulia had made during their period of estrangement; and he convinces Giulia that their being together is more important than her accepting a grant to study in Rome. An air of expectation of the news about the grant hovers like a menace over the entire weekend. George and Giulia go dancing on Friday night and take Michael with them on a picnic to the beach on Saturday afternoon. Whenever they are alone, their lovemaking deepens their attachment and their security within themselves. Giulia promises that she will not accept the grant, that having George is alone essential to her. During all this time, Mrs. Molla, who dominates the household,

2. Eugene Mirabelli, *The Burning Air* (Boston: Houghton Mifflin Company, 1959).

continues to preach the idea that in our society a person must "be somebody." A high-school teacher of French, married to a self-made lawyer with a small practice, Mrs. Molla extends her own ambitions by pushing her children to seek wealth and position. At every opportunity, she makes George feel that he is inadequate. After the uncomfortable scene when George and Giulia openly confront the family with their plans to marry, the grudging consent weighs George down with a sense of failure. When they are left alone, George persuades Giulia to elope with him quickly, but the realization of his failure overwhelms him as she refuses to get into the taxicab. Then, as he prepares to leave, he hears discussion over the grant that has arrived in the mail. George must prepare for the inevitable.

Eugene Mirabelli here demonstrates the conflict of the practicing idealist faced with the strategy of the hostile realist. The nub of this conflict is the system of values one holds with regard to success. To Mrs. Molla, success is measured by "being someone." Her judgment of a person's "being" is translated in simple terms. As George goes to bed on the first night at the Mollas, he wonders why Mrs. Molla is trying to give him "a hard time," even to the extent of sending him to sleep in Michael's bed, although Mirabelli gives an apt explanation for this later. Some of his suspicion comes into focus when he is discussing Claire Nieman with Giulia, who says that Claire wants to be *something* and that the important thing is just that—to be something. He remembers this as he sits on the beach with Giulia, and loneliness engulfs him as he reflects that before he knew Giulia he never worried about being a nobody or a somebody. He had discovered, however, that he felt that he was nothing when he was away from her. Mirabelli writes, "Now there was always the knowledge that I was someone only because I was the man to her and without her to love me I would be nothing" (p. 61). These words echo a universal experience. As he starts studying himself, George realizes what Mrs. Molla means when she praises the Niemans in his presence and fails to make any reference to him. He admits to himself that the Niemans are the type of people who would successfully combine marriage and studying in Europe. The Niemans represent a high level of quality for him, since, for example, they openly spurn Richard Harrison Williams, whom their friend Linda married only because of his wealth and profession. George's uneasiness is justified, however, when Giulia asks Claire what Mrs. Molla has said about George, and the answer is "I like George, but—." This resistance on Mrs. Molla's part is not shared by Mr. Molla, who appreciates that the young people know what they want and what is good for them. Furthermore, Giulia assures George that she has never wanted to marry "a big somebody," and that her problem is to make him feel that he is something in himself. George, however, feels the reservation of any judgment in his favor. In the end he allocates his illusion to the past and consoles himself with the constructive thought that "Maybe the anguish of having lost something is more easily borne than the slow despair from never having had it at all" (p. 148).

The Italian-American quality in *The Burning Air* is easily and naturally reflected in the character of the grandmother, who always speaks in Italian and for the inherited tradition. Both Giulia and George, functioning within this tradition, have studied Italian in college. They had met, in fact, on a Saturday, after their class in Italian. The grandmother revives old memories for George. She has an old-fashioned espresso-maker, for example, which is just like the one his own grandmother used to have. As she talks, she reminds George of his old "Nonna," and he understands her in the same way he had understood Nonna—from her sounds, rather than from her words. The grandmother checks Giulia with gentle discipline, calling her a "faccia tosta" (a bold-faced one) when she contradicts her parents. Watchfully, the grandmother is always in the background. At times, her presence brings harmony to the scene, as when she gives tomatoes to Bernie and Claire on their departure. She is also the placating diplomat as she admonishes Giulia to be quiet and listen to her mother during the discussion of the marriage plans. Mirabelli brings this Italianate background into clear focus especially when he describes the Sunday dinner, giving details of the food, and expanding the discussion to include the family history of the Mollas, with all the details of the often-repeated stories. Giulia's father, as he enjoys his cigar, recalls for them all the past family dinners at home, on the one communion table of the Italian in America. The next day, as George looks out of the train window, he sees Giulia with her mother and grandmother "standing in back of her," like the old culture framing the scene of its progeny.

The strength of Mirabelli's novel lies in its sense of discovery. With great simplicity, he has created an Italian-American family that is a typical American unit. The protagonist, George, has no self-consciousness as an ethnic; his problem is that of growing out of childhood wonder into maturity, an experience that the reader shares. The universal truth of this experience is so fundamental that Mirabelli has avoided empty rhetoric, keeping his story line lean, straight, and taut. The entire treatment expands this sensitive touch, and the author resolves his story with the gentle anguish of growing awareness. As the author relates each incident, the reader responds to the fresh communication of feelings, many of which are evocative of anyone's first love, with the melancholy nostalgia of virginal perceptions that can not return. Avoiding obscenities, vulgarities, and self-indulgent extravagances, Mirabelli has witten in *The Burning Air* a novel that is simple and permanent, with a brilliant perception of the personal and social problems of the young in a structurally amorphous society. He has the talent to create a memorable story, and the art to tell it well.

The Way In

Mirabelli's second novel, *The Way In*,[3] enlarges his aesthetic technique with new dimensions of psychological introspection and structural control. Using the conventions of autobiography, he tells the story of a man's attempt to find himself, not by the wistful pursuit of parental places and elusive antecedents, but by the natural absorption of the minutiae of the whole range of experience of his daily life.

Frank Anthony Annunzio, efficient research analyst, starts his story with the cool detachment of one "who wanted to keep his own life in his own hands." He admits that, though he has always felt that he is different from other people, he has always had a longing to be like everyone else. His childhood had been singularly fortunate, since he matured as one of many children in a Sicilian-American family in Boston, a family whose ancestors had both wealth and power in Europe. Mirabelli's Frank is an atypical ethnic American, one who is not concerned with upward mobility, as least as regards social status; his problem is that he must democratize his family's aristocratic concepts to adapt them to the New England ethos. In a reversal of pattern, Frank visits his affluent grandparents in Sicily, and returns with a secure and discriminating social attitude. After his student days at the Rhode Island School of Design, he tries to succeed as an artist, but "chops" up his paintings and loses himself in the detail of drudgery as a technical writer for a research company called, simply, "Research-/Research." During this interlude he has a series of love affairs, slipping almost inanimately from one to the next. In a series of flashbacks, Mirabelli recalls Frank Annunzio's past in such a way that present experiences are given meaning, so that they eventually organize into a complete aesthetic whole. Experiences in the protagonist's past—his reactions to his Confirmation Day, for example—give depth, later, to the religious externals of the ceremony with which he is married to Nancy White. Likewise, his early participation with his family in music, Renaissance literature, and traditional art fortifies him, so that he can see through the sometimes postured academic milieu of post-graduate Cambridge, Massachusetts. Because Mirabelli presents each episode in chronological order, his protagonist appears to be floating, but we are reminded that he is constantly working on a series of sensual paintings. After the eventual consummation with Beth, who must anticipate any sexual activity with a whole night of driving at full speed on the highways, he wearies of this freneticism and is ready to turn to Nancy White, whom he pursues, wins, and makes his wife. Mirabelli ends his story as Frank has learned control, and can apply his abilities positively, so that he can rear and guide his child wisely in an enigmatic world.

3. Eugene Mirabelli, *The Way In* (New York: The Viking Press, 1968).

Eugene Mirabelli here tells a story of a common phenomenon with a religious dimension. When Nancy worries over the premature Gabriella, and cries that she wants her baby, Mirabelli writes that the baby "grows her own way." He says that this is the way of life, despite the heat of love; when we join in perfect possession, our dearest loss begins. Frank Annunzio is familiar with the necessity for the individual's isolation. He learned it when he heard of his grandmother's death; that day he felt a rope cut through, "cast off like a mooring." This memory only intensifies what he has previously felt in being "left out" and lonely. Often, as he left the office, he felt as though he would "drop dead of loneliness." After an acquiescent night with Sophia, the insignificance of what should have been the "most sacred" human relationship left him only with the relief of walking home. Out of his fragmentation, however, has come the need to join, and he joins what seems both unlikely and least available—he loves and marries Nancy, the "Yankee," descendant of Peregrine White, the first child of the Pilgrims. Mirabelli is thematically incorporating the completely accepted Italian-American culture as it identifies with the social establishment. With the status thus categorized, his more specific task is to explore his protagonist to the depth of his individual creative instinct. He, like Frank, is taught by his parent to "draw a face in a circle." The next step is to draw the body, but the body is only the shape within which the person is concealed. Through Frank, Mirabelli says that when one paints a portrait one must know a great deal about a woman and have done a great deal of painting before he can show the person behind the face. Gradually, Frank perceives the inner world. When he makes his simple proposal of marriage to Nancy, her monosyllabic answers are echoed by the chimes of Saint Paul's campanile. Up to now, he has been only "treading water" near the New England shore; now he is enveloped by the town's most significant embankments. With his marriage and career settled, he works at his paintings, in which he tries to create something through which he can "hear silence." He wants on canvas the stillness that will intensify the exuberance of his now-pregnant wife. When the baby Gabriella is born, the doctor tells Frank that the child is strong and has a good chance for survival. As a symbol, Gabriella is an extension of Mirabelli's protagonist, the Italian-American of this generation. Misjudged prematurely by a settled society, he must wait a brief time for proper evaluation.

Frank Annunzio, as is usual with the protagonists of most autobiographical novels, personally dramatizes the author's theme. As Mirabelli probes into the depths beneath Frank's casual exterior, he explodes any one-dimensional, simplistic explanation of a man's place in life. Frank admits that once he believed that life was long, that love is easy, and that his talent was as "bright as an ax." He has been slow to learn. He has finally perceived that he has not invented the world, and that what he has mistaken for creation is his slow discovery of it.

Mirabelli emphasizes that the world is a gift and that we delight in what we create; but we must surrender it, keeping only the passion. While it was good for Frank to have lived and loved in Cambridge, it is better for him to move on. The author has led his protagonist to the conviction that everything changes, the world hurries on, and the urgency of the future dispels loneliness.

With this optimism, Eugene Mirabelli is consistent with the Italian-American writer's pervading attitude. At the very beginning, Mirabelli writes that the inner man is not only knocking at the heart, but struggling to take over. The author then launches happily into Frank's formative experiences—his flowing with the excited crowds at St. Anthony's feast in the Italian section of Boston; his recall of his father, a successful civil engineer who gradually comes to administer the Pontone Construction Company; and the memory of his little, old, wrinkled, aristocratic grandmother. His reaction to his grandmother's ritualistic kiss symbolizes the literary revulsion of the Italian-American writer who has rejected his restricted past. Frank's father's silence after Nonna dies causes the banishment in Frank's mind, not only of the grandmother, but of the house and "whatever uncles, aunts, or cousins" in it. But, despite this rejection, Frank is the beneficiary of his parents' social inheritance; the old culture is synonymous with family. He remembers that his mother has repeatedly said that a good family means a good life, and this memory becomes the key to unlock doors in his subconscious. His mother's breeding, her education at the Reale Educatorio Maria Adelaide, the summers she has spent visiting the museums and galleries of Naples, Rome, and Florence, are all part of the novel's frame of reference. Furthermore, his own dreams are enlivened by his mother's recollections of herself as a young woman, when she attended the Symphony and tea dances, and met young men in Boston. All in all, his past is a panorama of large houses in Washington, Boston, and Palermo. This breadth of background marking his growth does not prejudice his attitude, however, when he teaches at a small private school; he identifies sympathetically with the community that founded the school, a people who had lived in such an isolated fashion, so independently, that the townspeople had resented them. In a later chapter of recollection, Mirabelli describes with lucid but economic detail the entire process of Frank's artistic progress and how he approached his isolation, which withered into loneliness. Frank recalls that though he could draw better than anyone at school, no one cared. For a while, he even refused to play with the other boys, some of whom had called him a "wop and a guinea." He remembers how his mother had gone through the long list of Italian navigators, artists, singers, poets, and then, as a non sequitur, had advised him to call his tormentor an "Irish mick." As a result of the schoolyard castigations, Frank turned his interests to his home, listening to operatic records, poring over the Gustave Doré engravings of *La Divina Commedia*, and absorbing the legends about Michelangelo and the great painters. From this urgent need to withdraw into his family's ethnical culture came the inspiration to tap his own creative potential, and his future took shape. He moved as though destined into the intellectual ambience of Cambridge, and there he found himself—an Italian-American thoroughly absorbed into the cultural mainstream.

Eugene Mirabelli's novel is a solid performance. Like a portrait of a contemporary man whom the artist has posed in the foreground of a fragmented landscape of primary colors and clear outlines, the work has great impact. Mirabelli's method has a deliberate pattern, suggesting that which T. S. Eliot first introduced in *The Waste Land*. Interweaving three chronological narrations, Mirabelli gives a relaxed but clear impression of his childhood, his quest, and his joyous commitment to a future in which he will build a family and a career. Mirabelli enriches his story with a wide array of minor characters, who come instantly alive. He is brilliant and subtle in symbolizing his themes, as in the kite-flying incident, when the kites and their motions reflect the personalities of the fliers. One of his most persuasive and memorable portraits is that of the wedding, which dramatizes the hopeful type of third-generation Italian-American as he becomes part of the very fabric of the American environment.

ROBERT CANZONERI (1925–)

Robert Canzoneri analyzes the assimilation of the ethnic who is the product of a fixed American regionalism. Though his father is Sicilian, Robert's mother is a cousin of former Governor Ross Barnett. Canzoneri grew up in Clinton, Mississippi, and pursued his education through Mississippi College, The University of Mississippi, and Stanford University. After serving as a tail gunner in a Navy bomber during World War II, he became a professor of English at Ohio State University. In addition to separately published poems, short stories, and magazine articles, he has written four books: *I Do So Politely* (autobiography), 1965; *Watch Us Pass* (Poetry), 1968; *Men With Little Hammers,* (Novel), 1969; and *Barbed Wire* (Short Stories), 1970. For the purposes of this discussion an analysis of the autobiographical work and the novel is sufficient.

I Do So Politely: A Voice From the South

The organic material of his later novel appears in Robert Canzoneri's first book, *I Do So Politely: A Voice From the South*,[4] a work that

4. Robert Canzoneri, *I Do So Politely: A Voice From the South* (Boston: Houghton Mifflin Company, 1965).

veers from sociological reporting to sheer fiction. In this book all the incidents are true and the characters real, but Canzoneri's treatment so defines a beginning, climax, and resolution that the narration suggests a miniature Henry James novel. The story dramatizes the conflict between the writer's idealism and the mental climate of Mississippi. On another level, Canzoneri presents the inconsistency between what a white Mississippian says and what he means. In Mississippi, double talk has become the rhetoric of an ossified culture based on only apparent acceptance of the law. Canzoneri dissects Mississippi with its racial stratification. It is the visible shield of Southern gentlemanliness that protects a Governor Ross Barnett as he bars the door of the University of Mississippi to James Meredith with the words "I do so politely."

To dissent to the ways of one's environment is to grow apart from it. As Robert Canzoneri disagrees—and he does so quite politely—with the thinking of the people of Mississippi, he assumes the burden that was once that of ethnic aliens only.

With selected, accurate details, Canzoneri recalls the incidents and people he has known during his childhood in Mississippi. Although his narration is, in his own words, "a fragment of the time as I have overheard it from some distance," it is a melody that we hear everywhere. It may have been dramatically orchestrated in Mississippi, but its variations are a national battle song. Canzoneri separates his experiences into three periods of time: prior to World War II, from then until 1954, and after 1954. In the early period, episodes intensify characters like Old Bob, who, though he lived in the vicinity of the white neighborhood, never violated the code of separation that had been drilled into everyone "along with morals and memory verses." Old Bob, who had always been a friend of "Dad" Canzoneri's, moved to Kentucky. When Dad visits Bob, he says he is so happy he could hug him. Bob says, "Why don't you?" And as the two men hug each other, they cry. They dramatize an eloquent testament, the Sicilian and the Negro.

In the second period, the Negroes mock their own debasement. Some press their cause by insinuating double entendres in stories, to the point where they as actors dissolve into clever comics not unlike Shakespeare's fools. The barrier before 1954 intrudes only insignificantly, and white life goes along smoothly in ignorance of the Negro world around it. Canzoneri details the shocking account of a fire that burns a house of pitch-pine in which a man is running from room to room in panic. The fire consumes everything because the hose of the fire engine cannot reach the nearest fire hydrant. Canzoneri sees tragedies like this also among the white people, since they, too, are tenant farmers. The social tie between the races is a kind of paternalism, a transition from the system of slavery. The author writes that he was never aware of a lynching, nor ever saw a Negro abused verbally or physically until he went to college. He is brought up "separate, but as a fact, not as a creed." When he returns to Mississippi as a teacher, he is a vehicle for the concepts of his father, who had been an evangelist, and of his maternal great-grandfather who had been in the Civil War. His teaching career takes him to Louisiana, to the North, and to the West. As time goes on, he develops greater understanding and more compassion toward Mississippi, which so many think of as being foreign. A young man tells him that Mississippi is where the "American disease has come to a head, so that we can see it. But the poison is in us all, and we must fight it in ourselves and in our communities" (p. 102). As a liberal, the author finds himself in a dilemma. His sister, Antonina, compounds his image when she becomes a missionary to Nigeria sent by the Southern Baptist Foreign Mission Board. Ironically, the Negroes in Mississippi do not attend the white Baptist church. Finally, with the Oxford riot in 1962, Canzoneri "viscerally" believes in the Civil War. After the riots are over, he agrees with a friend that Mississippi has changed; and that Southerners can not go back because of the very morals they were taught when they were growing up. As a Southerner, Canzoneri finds himself, in the end, still in the heart of the dilemma, without a solution. He admits, however, that what he cherishes in our past is the "line of intelligence and responsibility and courage and love that has come down through all our great men at their best, and through their critics and opponents at their best, and through the Puritans and the plantation owners at their respective best" (p. 181).

With this final testament, Robert Canzoneri affirms the theme of his book, that the best in our past has added up to a great deal, and that the present has immense possibilities. The theme is dramatized in the conflicting situations of the author-protagonist dissenting with the Southern character. The fine air of polite removal from reality is the thematic personification of the author's exemplary antagonist, Ross Barnett, who has the politically impressive way of not quite making contact. With mere politeness, Ross does not quite come to grips with the facts. In this way, he embodies the equivocation that defies clarification, and the status quo remains: the Negro people keep to their own separate society. Canzoneri makes the reader aware that this equivocation restricts the mobility of any minority that is "politely" accepted "in its place." Social paternalism is a small step toward assimilation, but the growth of responsibility parallels economic success, which eventually demands respect. Canzoneri consistently carries his theme in word-terms: human relationships, he says, must transcend name references like Negro, nigger, colored person, and darky. The reader knows that the author is thinking of corresponding terms that are used for Jews, Italians, Poles, and other ethnics. Canzoneri gets literary support for his idea of the primitiveness of racism from Shelby Foote, who, speaking on William Faulkner, remarks that Ross Barnett was not the first Snopes to live in the governor's mansion. In broader terms, the author writes that some Southerners are "terribly uncomfortable" in the North because of the "lack of politeness," the simple bluntness of the city folk. The outward courteous manner is taken for inner love, as a man's Christianity is judged by the amount of money he puts into his church collection. What Canzoneri paints for us is the blurred grayness of the fund attitude, demonstrated when the college dean says, "The state legislature has always granted us complete academic freedom here, and if we don't do what they want us to, they're going to take it away from us!" (p. 112). This duplicity is the very sustenance of the conspiracy of polite silence for the sake of racial segregation and white supremacy, and the fraudulence extends to nonracial matters. The result is the inability of anyone to focus on any problem directly, with consequent gross injustice or simple force. Mississippi's liquor laws, for example, are a caricature. Furthermore, the false façade of education for ignorance, honesty for lies, and democracy for autocracy breaks before dissent. Canzoneri is a dissenter, and he presents the problems involved in changing the mind of one who wants forgiveness but never correction. This mind fantasies a golden past, now destroyed by socialists, integrationists, Communists, and the federal government. It finds what Canzoneri calls "religious dodges," and defends itself with the manners of a lost aristocracy. And yet, Canzoneri concludes, there is much that is good in this; he is optimistic about the "immense possibilities"; and his own identification with this belief attests to the probable endurance of good manners in him and humanity.

Robert Canzoneri has written a socially valuable book that focuses dissension personally conceived; he is the protagonist of a defensive narration. Relying on his own experiences, he has done more than explore a hypothesis; he has structured his theses with setting, development, and conflict. Personifying his themes in commonplace personalities gives power to the argument. He makes a plausible defense for the minority as it confronts implacable, self-seeking supremacy.

Men With Little Hammers

With reference to Chekhov's statement that "behind the door of every contented, happy man there ought to be someone standing with a little hammer," Robert Canzoneri has written a novel about a man's conflict with hostile, intangible forces that seem to pursue him with indifferent remorselessness and comic repetition. *Men With Little Hammers,*[5] for all its presentation of frustration, is a sportive story with a pleasant comment on human relations, which here end satisfactorily. Canzoneri has an easy style that makes skillful use of cosmic irony. On a personal level he presents a situation that may apply to any group of people pitted against the pressures of a controlling environment.

5. Robert Canzoneri, *Men With Little Hammers* (New York: The Dial Press, Inc., 1969).

With low-keyed satire, he symbolizes his theme by placing his protagonist in a paradoxical situation that is paralleled by the activities of his youthful counterpart. Canzoneri's characters are victims of the intrigue and machinations of a less-than-average college faculty whose life and activities are restricted by the institution. He stages for us a small frontier version of C. P. Snow's sinister academe.

Ted Spengler, professor of English at Farber College, a small denominational institution in Indiana, is a liberal teacher and an inhibited man. The chairman of his department and the Dean of the college, Canzoneri infers, are the live factors of the "controlling" system, which is working to apprehend Spengler. Their purpose is set in motion when they assign Spengler to chaperone a trio of student writers at the final competitions of the regional collegiate writer's conference in New Orleans. The three students include Vito Angellis, a zestful "Greek" or Mediterranean-American; Ella Taine, a voluptuously developed but spiritually evangelical virgin; and Bob Homer, the stereotyped classroom "ideal," obsequious and precious. Although Ted Spengler takes seriously his responsibility to watch over his charges, he cannot control everything. One morning, at the hotel in New Orleans, as he approaches Ella Taine's door, he sees Vito leaving the room, an incident that starts a chain of comic misunderstandings that structure the remaining action of the novel. Among the participants at the conference are a poet, a dramatist, and the Dean of another college, all of whom share convivialities with Spengler, who later invites them to Farber. Although Spengler's chairman, Dr. Pullman, has personally sponsored Bob Homer, Vito Angellis wins the first prize for his short story. On the trip back, an alcoholic woman, Harriet Fleban, attaches herself to Spengler and embarrasses him when they all arrive at the railroad station. The welcoming committee and all of the college administrators watch Spengler and Vito unload the inebriated Bob Homer. The hapless Spengler is further embroiled in circumstances when he gets home and his wife accuses him of infidelity. As the year progresses, Ella Taine gets obviously pregnant; Mrs. Fleban haunts Spengler's classes; Vito increases his debaucheries; and the evidence mounts against Spengler's suitability for his profession. Dr. Pullman and Mr. Fleban watch Spengler closely, which activity comes to a ludicrous climax followed by Spengler's vindication. Then, at the end of the year, he must return to the ceremonies for the writer's contest. This time everything actually happens as it had been misunderstood to have happened before; but Ted Spengler is now judged exemplary, and he looks forward to a contented life.

In this novel, Robert Canzoneri is once more pitting the mind of the liberal humanist against cultural duplicity. The atmosphere in such a world is one of uneasiness. A person may be dedicated to and absorbed in his work, but someone is "always watching him," holding the little hammer of judgment over him, writes Canzoneri. Eventually, even the best men must become part of the official façade. Spengler sends a telegram to Pullman, making insinuations about Vito. The defensive professor has reason to expect trouble because he is protecting himself by plotting against the student. In line with his pose, he insists on remaining an observer only. He is enough of a hammer, he feels, when he assures Ella Taine that she is really on the way to being a poet. What he must put into action are his defenses against his chairman, who, as he senses, is badgering him. Furthermore, in making Vito suspect, Spengler reasons that it is the only thing he is doing wrong, and the only thing that will work out right. When the overtly respectful Dr. Pullman cannot believe that the "big greasy Greek" has actually won the contest, Canzoneri touches another level of irony—the inherent racism that will not admit excellence in a minority member. Dr. Pullman then becomes the "Rube Goldberg invention" that puts Spengler in position for the coup de grâce. Canzoneri emphasizes this with one of his few introspective lines, Spengler's reflection "We're glad to have you right where you are." This line repeats itself like a refrain. Spengler knows that Pullman is watching him during the months of his wife's absence, waiting for something to happen that will justify firing him. Since Vito is Spengler's disciple, he too comes under surveillance, and the attempt to trap him in the graveyard is an example of the ludicrous degree to which intrigue can go. Power adds to the evil of intrigue too, for Dr. Pullman, with tight control over his department, deliberately withholds from Spengler the letter from Dean Cracy offering him another job. The same power uses the hammer when the Dean presses upon Spengler the urgency of Ella Taine's going to a doctor, making it clear that he is holding Spengler responsible for Ella's "condition." Spengler does not know which way to turn. Canzoneri stations him at the center of his theme: "He just stands there, as in a wind, and life is blown up all around him" (p. 281). He can, however, move out of the wind, the writer shows. It is Vito, the "foreign" element in this structure of vice veneered by virtue, who deflects the course of destruction. Because Ella has, in fact, been virtuous, and because Vito will gather the ripe fruit of adventure, the future is theirs. Vito is the catalyst that generates a better world, a democratic America where no one is so "greasy" as to be without a hammer.

Spengler is, according to Canzoneri, the good man in established America, the vein of real culture that is the spine of our South. As the author writes, "Few people paddled more energetically than he to stay actively in midstream, remote from the stagnant backwater and the capsizing eddies of the fringe" (p. 3). He is also a dreamer, posing like a minuscule Oxford Don in his dark office, the white page of his book catching the smoke hanging underneath the lamp. On the rare occasions when Cazoneri probes the mind of the protagonist, the reader is moved by Spengler's frustration, epitomized by his thwarted desire for children his prim wife refuses to bear. He cries out repeatedly that he is lonely and that no one loves him. He is the rejected ideal of an old Puritan ethic. The extent of his aggression can be measured by the flippancy with which he plays on Dr. Pullman's name. Basically, he is loyal to humanity. When his wife is away, he maneuvers away from any infidelity, rejecting Harriet Fleben's advances. In his loneliness he accepts only the superficial friendliness of the Statons, a faculty couple. Significantly, as he sits alone in his office, he sees Vito running, just as alone, across the campus, and when Vito comes in, bursting with plans for a Florida trip, Spengler's loneliness is compounded. He does not succeed in reconciling with his wife; he spends New Year's Eve by himself, reflecting that all he now has is doubt and despair. He asks, where are the brilliant Ph.D.'s in the profession? After twelve years of marriage, where the offspring? Where the scholarly works? Like Job, he asks why he is so put upon by circumstance. Canzoneri then presents several dream sequences, from which Spengler concludes that the Vitos rush in where angels fear to tread. Ironically, later, it is because Spengler is not accustomed to strong drink, that he is able to maneuver the tumultuous party from which he emerges victorious. Finally, when he succumbs to the most casual temptation, his goodness is rewarded.

Canzoneri's two other main characters are superficial drawings. Dr. Pullman is a caricature of the despised administrator; the reader will be cautious in accepting his authenticity, suspecting that the author protests too much. He is a stereotype of the official who substitutes connivance for administrative expertise, refusing to reveal facts, and resorting to subterfuge. He caricatures the image of the carping American Puritan, pedantically pitying the daffodils because Wordsworth made them too common. Canzoneri goes to great pains to elaborate on Pullman's self-immolation as an intellectual and literary scholar. Vito is animated more through contrast with such a character than through detail. We feel his bounce with relief, and Canzoneri writes that the boy does things with such energy and force that everything around him reverberates. We suspect that the "Greek" in him is Canzoneri's Italian ancestry, and we understand the melodramatic description of him as a "vast land of abundance," flowing milk and honey and olive oil, whole vineyards whose fruit was once crushed into wine and now comes bubbling out as laughter. He has the casual vulgarity of healthy youth, but it is not so offensive as Will Pope's pornographic blurtings. We learn that he has a genius for compromise, inherited from his father, whose name was really Vito Spuminello. He provides the warmth, the vitality, the zest, and the good-natured integrity that galvanize Spengler's isolated idealism as it is pitted against the inimical system.

This novel presents a cinematic array of types in evenly paced comic episodes, but the author plays some obvious word-games that come close to cant, and his style is uneven. This lowering of standards is demonstrated in a verse in the final chapter: "I am the Captain of my fate/ I am the filet of my sole." He dramatizes episodes too often as convenient symbols; for example, the repetitive sounds of the telephone calls he receives from Mrs. Starnes, who watches everyone who goes in and out of his house, are "little hammers" behind his door. But there are also satisfying literary and art symbols, like the imaginative halo representing Pullman, as contrasted to Vermeer or Rembrandt. When the author becomes melodramatic, he is sensually poetic, as in his description of Vito's feeling the air with his hands, "tasting it as if it were the mouth of a young girl." For the reader who resists the progressive momentum, there still remains the satisfaction of the reversal of situations that activates Canzoneri's dramatic irony. His main power lies, however, in his metaphors. Farber College, a miniature America, now contains a successful "Greek." The institution that rejuvenates itself with a Mediterranean winner had formerly been known as "The Tennis Court" because it pounded life back and forth across a net within bounds, till most of the bounce had gone out of it, "and behind it all was one racket or another."

FRANK MICELI (n.d.)

The Seventh Month

In *The Seventh Month*,[6] Frank Miceli writes about a Vietnam War veteran's struggle to adjust to civilian life. Perhaps because his interpretations are not crystallized, the structure and rhetoric of the novel are uneven. There is an unfinished texture to the style, which may demonstrate a deliberate method on the part of the author to offer an organic metaphor for his theme that people who appear bright and wholesome on the surface are really cripples or abortions, as though they had been born forcibly in the seventh month. While, physically, persons may appear intact, actually they are psychically imperfect to the extent that they are constantly terrorized by their own emptiness, a loneliness that imprisons them everywhere. Miceli portrays several characters who personify their own preconceived ideas, and sets them in motion to illustrate the interaction of these ideas in our contemporary society. While Miceli is on one level demonstrating the behavioral patterns of a recognizable human being, he transcends this personality to analyze societal concepts that he organizes into cultural groups with ethnical references.

Frank Miceli and his wife live in Greenwich Village, New York City. A member of the faculty at New York University, he has also participated on a weekly television program, BLACK LETTERS, on

6. Frank Miceli, *The Seventh Month* (New York: Frederick Fell, Inc., 1969).

WCBS-TV. *The Seventh Month* is a winner of the Frederick Fell Prize Novel Award.

The Seventh Month is the story of Tony Niente, a veteran of Vietnam, who is floundering in the aftermath of battle experience. At home he feels oppressed by the presence of his broken father, a laborer who has been incurably crippled in an accident at work, and of his exhausted mother whose spirit has died with her husband's defeat. His younger brother, Rico, is one of the cynical young who escape into marijuana, a frustrated artist who paints grotesque abstractions on the walls of the cellar of the beauty parlor where he works. At the Big Neck High School where he teaches, Tony despairs about his profession because of the lack of communication between the instructors and their students. Disillusioned, he attempts to sublimate his drives by a furious pursuit of hollow love-making. In this manner, he anaesthetizes his emotions now, as he had with the unbridled experiences in Vietnam —murderous killings and sexual orgies—which Miceli describes with unstinting detail in the first part of the book. Tony cannot reach Anne, for example, with whom he relates in sexual activity but not with psychic rapport. She withdraws within her self-pity, blaming Tony for her abortion, attributing to him all the wounds she has suffered from her failures with all the other men in her past. Erica, on the other hand, with her confident beauty and open lust, is opulently protected by her husband, Jack, who is semi-impotent and establishment ridden. The author uses her as a symbol of the predatory woman of American society, playing amatory games, reciting heroic lines, and reaping the reward of measured passion. When she becomes pregnant with Tony's child, she refuses to break up her marriage, because a divorce from her husband would threaten her security. In time, when Tony's mother dies, he feels abandoned by two generations of women, and that his life amounts to nothing, a state symbolized by his name. As Miceli writes the last line, describing the worm coming out of the earth for "his turn on the cross," he forecasts some purpose to Tony Niente's future, for, as the earthworm's function aerates the soil, so a man's life regenerates the cosmos.

The point of *The Seventh Month* is that man, crippled, aborted creature that he is, must work within his weaknesses, because perfection is unattainable. Frank Miceli says that all his people are elements caught in a maze of changing conditions they do not understand, heading at different speeds toward destruction. In this way he accepts the Vietnamese boy who sells his sister for four dollars as he accepts the death of his companions around him. At home, he wonders about his old ambitions, and Miceli communicates to the reader the constructive-future theme as Tony asks if it is possible for an individual to live life in perpetual research so that the search itself is the fulfillment. The reason he feels out of focus is that he has not defined his goals. Perhaps only the *becoming* is significant—the forever changing, the forever growing. In more transcendental terms, Miceli writes that this "growing" causes the alienation from what we have known; that in knowing something new, we alienate ourselves from what we have been. Like Canzoneri, Miceli likens environmental incidents to hammer blows to the head, and suggests that what the protagonist must do is examine the hammer. The environment may be a physical structure like Rico's beauty parlor, which has replaced the tranquilizing effect of a church. Thematically, the search for meaning in environment may find creative expression, like Rico's paintings, which are illusions of life, phenomenological objectifications of what he carries around in his head. On the other hand, Rico, isolated like all human beings, cannot understand why Tony should want to go to Europe to write. Nor can Mr. Niente understand Tony's desire to go back to Italy, the country that all his people have left. He cannot understand why Tony, who has worked so hard to become a teacher, should want to end that career and "go back." Tony, member of the ethnically curious current generation, cannot even explain to his father that he has determined "to make his own work a labor of reparation to undo in others what had been done to him" (p.127).

Author Miceli proceeds to expand the personal theme to cosmic dimensions when he writes that Tony feels that in himself is an unknown province where there could be the entire panorama of his own identity, like a mirage on the horizon and in an enduring classical Greek ruin. He begins to realize that life cannot be lived without pressures, that his writing may be a failure because he has had no direction. He is convinced that he must "return again, to begin over," and with this conclusion, Frank Miceli delineates the contemporary Italian-American writer. Now Tony is weary of existing apart from things, of only talking about life. Humiliated and horrified by Anne's desperation over the abortion, he spends his nights in a bar. Gradually, he resolves that his recurring mistakes come from his abandoning his early childhood faith and innocence. Finally, he arrives at some positive thinking: he has failed; the world has not. It is he "who was born in the seventh month, prematurely, some part of him not fully developed, not fully grown . . . out of the Sicilian slavery of his past and into the servility of his youth his die was cast" (p.189). His feeling of inadequacy is intensified later as he visits with Jack and Erica, the established Americans. In his contrast of persons, Miceli is dramatizing his theme that some people, the newer immigrants, have not yet matured to American ways, while the earlier settlers are socially senile. Jack identifies his fear of death with his fear of having women touch him; Erica believes in the democratic way of life in a textbook way, while Jack doesn't believe in it at all. A product of nineteenth-century American thinking, Jack believes in two classes of people—those with money and those without it. To him Tony does not count as a person at all; Tony, on the other hand, feels that he is in the middle of some unarticulated violence between this man and wife. As he walks away from the luxury of their home, Tony feels that the mood of America is one of revolt because everyone "wanted to live like this," and that this mood is the tenseness of that contained violence. Later, when he makes love to Erica, he feels as though he is an insensate instrument of biology, because he had been in Vietnam, where there had been no personal touch to anything. This impersonalism, implies Miceli, is the other side of violence. As Tony walks the streets, he thinks back to the weary days out of which only loneliness has survived. Thinking of his father and his family, he resolves that he will never let life "rape him as it has his family, turning them into knotted, dried-up prunes, withering on the vine of the system" (p.283). Miceli then offers through his protagonist a unique instrument of constructiveness—anger. At one point Anne calls him the noble rebel who can not act. He, however, points out to her that she would like to keep all rights to herself and give him all the responsibilities. Miceli is again representing the crippled sense of ethics in established America. Tony, the new ingredient, is made numb by this moral abortion. For example, he is as void of sensation at his mother's funeral as he had been in Vietnam, and the cycle of things has become a circle of abstraction. In the end, Miceli resolves his theme constructively; the abstraction is as significant as Tony is willing to make it. It becomes a fact that lends to every moment of the present and the past a quality of inexhaustible depth. Later, thinking over the details of his mother's death, Tony consoles himself with the thought that the great compendium of trivia is organizing in his mind "like a piece of inexplicable poetry, sign and symbols fusing into sense" (p.361).

Tony Niente, though nominally a "nothing" in America's social complex, is like a neglected stick of dynamite in the nation's boxed-up unexpressed violence. His nightly recurring dreams of his experiences in Vietnam are the muffled explosions that might ignite the fire of power in him. Trapped by his room and his job, he dreams of saving money to go to Europe where he might investigate his origins and then decide where he is going. To rise at six o'clock for the train ride to Long Island to teach English in a high school has become a stultifying routine. Furthermore, he cannot rest, because the confusion in the country is destroying him. His mother wonders at the deepening look of pain in his eyes. His brother Rico's drugged life horrifies him. He seeks solace at the hamburger stand that reflects the Cro-Magnon side of America, and then takes a long way around to come home, to escape those with whom he has grown up, men who had married, had families, and had, "in very personal ways," remained faithful "to their origins." His own sheltered childhood had not protected him from the reputation of being violent, because he could win in any fight with anyone. But now he knows that his real enemy is himself. He feels that he is a misfit even in teaching, a profession that, he says, is "filled with crazy people doing crazy things" involved with organizational politics and intrigue. Absorbing some of the current revolutionary spirit, he feels that schools have a streak of cancer engendered by the administrator's basic dislike of people. His confusion is intensified when he forms his triangular relationship with Jack and Erica, whom he secretly envies. However, in their apartment he senses the emptiness which they, themselves, do not perceive, in their hodge-podge of furniture lost in anonymity among their abstract paintings. Although he wants Erica, he is not certain that he wants the trouble that comes with her; it would be like making love to her history, for she is the embodiment of a cultural idea that paradoxically preempts and post-dates his own. Her cool attitude warns him to use strategy. But his emotions are not for subtle use; the kinds he feels are hatred and despair, in which he indulges when he goes walking in his old neighborhood. This hatred does not stem from anything in particular; it is a whole disposition he projects to everything, a hatred of the seemingly infinite levels and cavernous growth within him that cause fear, loneliness, ignorance, suspicion, and doubt. This is the hatred that will ultimately breed the anger he needs, the hatred that is triggered when his chairman advises him how "to get ahead in this school," especially if he is to become a permanent part of the faculty. By crawling from bed to bed, he attempts to exhaust the corruption of his spirit. Eventually, he feels the regeneration of resolution in him, of good and proper intentions, such as wanting to talk with Rico, his father, and his mother. He knows he can return love, but it is locked untapped within him. He hopes to find himself by persuading Erica to leave her husband and marry him. She will not make such a decision, and he wonders if what is happening now is a peculiar payment for things he had done at some previous time, perhaps in Vietnam. In self-defense, he starts to dismiss Erica from his mind, recalling how cruelly she has hurt him, and concluding that legally he has a tremendous case against her. He rationalizes that it is because he has not been properly conditioned to harness his basic nature that he feels the need for murder in his heart, not in the illegal sense but something quite within the law and properly executed; something about the time he had spent in Vietnam was natural to him. As an embodiment of this feeling, he is the Italian-American who has compromised his nature to the nation's need and now demands active compensation for this compromise. This awareness overwhelms Tony Niente on the night before his mother's funeral. As he walks the streets, he "smells Vietnam," but the next day he will help with the details of the burial. When it is over, Tony, saddened by the inevitability of death, is challenged by the sound of Rico's breathing. The brother, the drug addict, has a loud and erratic breathing that sounds to Tony like something struggling to find coordination. To him, this is the crippling sound of war, sex, escape, and confusion.

Miceli has extended his themes into other characters. The father is the common Italian immigrant who has worked with handfuls of cement and mortar, but whose body is still powerful despite deterioration, a member of a passing generation. The accident that crushed the body under tons of debris for thirty hours so that now it only squirms in a hard chair is a symbol of the years of oppressed Italian effort, which now, like the sacrificed Sacco and Vanzetti, is breathing its last in the arenas of labor. Like his peers, Mr. Niente bewails the fact that he does not know what is going on in his house, that no one respects the head of the home, that there is no law and order anywhere, that "everybody wants it all for himself with no respect for the other guy." Nothing, however, dampens his optimism that his sons have their lives to live and that things will get better. That he fell on his job, and that the grandfather was killed that day, were each "just one of those things." In his dreams, however, he relives the accident every night, the nightmare of the Italian immigrant's broken American Dream. Awake, he believes that his broken body is an offering to all the bad days of his life in America. He is baffled by thoughts of the young people who are unable to work at the hard jobs he had worked on all the days of his life in America. When his wife dies, Mr. Niente learns that not everything is a question of labor, that man solves some problems with thought. He is made aware of what lies behind Rico's dreams. Miceli has made Rico the dark negative of his father's light. Rico buries his person and his love "under a scar," and works out his creative instinct tangibly in the basement room. Since he cannot afford to buy canvas, Rico paints the walls of the basement, which become a depiction of the wreckage of his mind, a symbol of the Italian-American's loss of fixed values. Rico, however, is sympathetic to the innocuous Anne. But Anne cannot survive in a society where Erica dominates, Erica the secure, selfish, self-indulgent, and predatory American woman who is often the symbol of America's soul. She most possess all men and the protection they supply, her cushioned security, while her conscience is assuaged by her psychiatrist.

The interaction of Italian and American concepts of culture binds the various characters together. In the fields of violence, Italian-American obscenity is translated into Anglo-Saxon terms: the battlefield is a common denominator for warring men. At home, Tony's relation to Vietnam assumes a dream-like quality, while his life in the old neighborhood requires a new dimension of rationalization. As he walks down the streets, he knows that the old people are looking at him: he hopes they will not talk to him, and he cannot tell his father what the trouble is. He has to fight with himself to devise plans to avoid his neighbors, and all he feels is a madness and an anger, something that must mean he has had a "great change in his genes." His father, broken in body, lies before him, still dreaming that in America all things come to a good end. Mr. Niente never admits that things will not get better, and he has tried to avoid a subversive malaise by teaching his sons to be "tough." When the grandfather died in the accident, he left Mr. Niente the house that he had bought and paid for when he first came to America. This house has sheltered a whole generation and their sons; Mr. Niente keeps repairing, repainting, and rebuilding. This is a symbol of what is real and visible in Tony's life. As for Mrs. Niente, it never occurs to her that the American way of life has betrayed her. Her kitchen routines quench her pain, while her sons and daughters and husband thrive in the Italian neighborhood. Although Tony understands all this, he cannot believe in the future, because the ratio of knowledge to awareness never seems proportional. He feels that the world is falling apart, the "far left" getting as crazy as the "far right," the Italian not quite in focus in the American Dream. Therefore, he thinks he can escape his dilemma by going to Europe. Rico, on the other hand, takes a hard look around him and points out that the Italian flag is a long line of wash hanging between two buildings, drying in the sun. The abstract dream must come to visible, concrete terms. Rejecting Rico's solution, Tony fluctuates between the past and the present. After making love to Anne, he feels debased, remembering that debasement once thrilled him as a scholastic virtue with which to cope with "all those Anglo-Saxon teachers." He now realizes that self-debasement is only a tired excuse for failure, for his inability "to accept his roots, his nationality, his language and lack of it, his father and mother who were to him total strangers" (p.139). As for Anne, following her abortion she recalls her previous life with her husband in the South. She remembers her former life with her parents, and all she hears now is Tony's footstep in the next room; she is the establishment, crippled in a hidden chamber of society. Tony's position, however, is not secure. At one point, Erica tells Jack that she cannot understand what Anne wants with Tony, since he is like a perpetual adolescent. She is, of course, debauched in her own behavior with Jack, who doesn't recognize Tony at all. Tony, therefore, stands nowhere. When his mother tells him she is worried about his not being married, he tells her that the Tony "from long ago is dead." When he walks into the living room where his mother is sitting, their eyes meet and they understand. Miceli explains their communication as the silent language of centuries. When Tony thinks of calling Anne, he cannot communicate with her in this way; he cannot say anything to her, because his feelings are too deep to make sense, and he is left with his despair. Later, with Erica, he feels his relationship to her dispassionately, and sees that for her he has made of himself just another toy. Was that his relationship? Is this the relationship of the Italian immigrant in the American complex, a child to be nurtured in the womb for a little while but not to be carried full term? Frank Miceli uses his protagonist in relation with the other characters to dramatize this question, a question that implies the abortion of everyone's American Dream.

This novel is profound in its probing of men and women to arrive at the truth of what causes the hollowness of people in a multiple society that has become confused. Behind the brilliant façade of personalities, Miceli illuminates the experiences of individuals who are framed in separate cultures. The old immigrants' dream of attaining work and freedom in America is aborted and they cannot transmit to their children the prerequisite for happy assimilation—a complete gestation period in the body of the nation. Frank Miceli has a powerful literary talent and creates settings for serious philosophical concerns, which he dramatizes through composite characters who succeed in stirring the reader's revulsion or compassion. Tony Niente, the protagonist, is "nothing" only as we see him as our own hollowness, for Miceli has the creative talent for drawing us into the empty shells of our own inner weaknesses. Tony's future, therefore, is ours; and the search for the direction of his life is our own search. The author explores, also, the meaning of the day-after-day existence of men like Rico in whom he discovers all the fear and terror common to people who are diseased, yet who must survive. Miceli has his finger directly on the pulse of the fevered person who feels insecure. He says that within the established status the emerging minority is still a premature infant who must be changed. He illuminates this idea with appropriate symbols; the very name *Erica* is America abbreviated, a metaphor for the aborted, traditional, national society. A sure craftsman, Miceli probes the minds of his characters, and, with them, argues out loud. He is good enough that he forces his reader to think, also. The glandular language demands attention; it is strong, unashamed, and sometimes poetic. With his overall metaphor, he convinces us that the chaos and confusion of one person's life gives a microscopic view of a national problem; we must see that Tony is much more than nothing.

MARIO ANDREW PEI (1901–)

The ultimate degree of assimilation demonstrated in the writing of an Italian-American is achieved with the balanced combination of creative artistry, social disposition, and intellectual comprehension. We find this combination in the fiction of Mario Andrew Pei.

Connoisseur of linguistics and eminent scholar in many different areas, Mario Andrew Pei was born in Rome, Italy, on February 16, 1901. His parents, Francesco and Louise (Ferri) Pei, brought him to the United States in 1908, where he earned his A.B. (magna cum laude) at the City College of New York in 1925 and his Ph.D. from Columbia University in 1932. After a variety of teaching experiences, he became Professor of Romance Philology at Columbia University, with which he was associated until his retirement in 1970. In addition to his intensive academic work, Professor Pei was Consultant to the Office of Strategic Services and the Office of War Information on the linguistic projects for World War II. He was also Consultant to the United States Army Language School in Monterey, California, and prepared for the Coordinator of Inter-American Affairs a series of radio lessons for the study of English to be used in South America that were eventually adapted by other government agencies for use in Europe, Asia, and Africa. In 1961 he was the North Atlantic Treaty Organization lecturer at the Universities of Lisbon and Coimbra. Professor Pei lectured also for Voice of America, Radio Free Europe, and before numerous professional groups associated with the science of language. A Phi Beta Kappa scholar, he is an active member of many professional organizations and has been awarded the George Washington Honor Medal (Freedoms Foundation), the Cavaliere Ufficiale of Order of Merit of the Italian Republic, and the Author's Award of the New Jersey English Teachers' Association in 1965 and again in 1966.

Pei inaugurated Columbia University's thirty-odd languages course, now known as the World's Chief Languages, designed to acquaint students with the world's dominant tongues. While he has been the associate editor of the *Modern Language Journal*, *Symposium*, and *Romantic Review*, he has contributed articles to the *Saturday Review*, *The New York Times Magazine*, *This Week*, and numerous other outstanding periodicals. Among his forty-five publications to date, the most notable are: *The World Language Series*, the *Holiday Magazine Language Series*, *One Language For the World*, *Consumer's Manifesto*, *Invitation to Linguistics*, *The Story of Language*, *Our National Heritage*, *The Story of the English Language*, *The Many Hues of English*, *The America We Lost*, and *Words in Sheep's Clothing*. His works of fiction include *Swords of Anjou*, *The Sparrows of Paris*, and *Tales of the Natural and Supernatural*. Pei's books demonstrate his catholicity of interests, which encompass languages, history, politics, economics, gastronomy, and fiction. His publishers note that George Bernard Shaw said of his writing, "Professor Pei's prodigious memory and knowledge remind me of Isaac Newton."

Swords of Anjou

Mario Andrew Pei's first novel, *Swords of Anjou*,[7] is a story whose setting makes good use of the author's medieval scholarship. In this book, a challenging exception to contemporary historical novels, the writer uses the *Chanson de Roland*, with all its embroidered legends, as the prototype for "largely fictional history outlined by the imaginative writers of the *chansons de geste*" (p.307). Pei has recaptured the spirit of the Middle Ages in themes, incidents, and rhetoric; and with vigorous narrative style and authentic detail, he demonstrates the spiritual and psychological causes of Charlemagne's retreat from Spain, the treason of his brother-in-law Ganelon, and the annihilation of his nephew

7. Mario A. Pei, *Swords of Anjou* (New York: The John Day Company, 1953).

Roland's rear guard in the pass of Roncevaux. Beneath the military details and romantic progression, however, lies the original author's legacy of something more than "an entrancing pulse-quickening tale." Pei has redefined for the modern reader the objective of Turoldus, the Norman abbott, of bequeathing to posterity a set of standards, values, and rules of conduct. This story, like its prototype, may be taken as a "lesson in loyalty and steadfastness and adherence to one's code of honor and ideals, no matter what the odds."[8]

Pei colors history with the pulse and adventure of love and glory. At the center of the story are two brothers, Thierry and Huon, young knights who survive innumerable dangers to win their loves and to stay loyal to their chief. The plot involves the historical event of the Emperor Charlemagne's being recalled in 778 from a floundering campaign in northern Spain to quell the revolt of heathen Saxons on the bank of the Rhine. The Emperor left his rear guard under the command of Hrodland, the Prefect of the Breton March. The guard and their leader were totally destroyed by Christian Basque mountaineers in the Pyrenees. Hrodland, or Roland, is the focus of the events surrounding the fighting in the pass, which are climaxed by the legendary hero's sounding of his famous horn. Egginhard, historian contemporary with Charlemagne, mentioned "Count Roland" as an important leader, but not related to the Emperor. Pei, however, creates his story from the version of Turoldus, including Blancandrin's false mission, Ganelon's treachery, the death of Roland and Oliver, Charlemagne's victorious return to Zaragoza, and the feudal council that pronounces the terrible punishment on the traitor. Pei develops Ganelon's treachery chronologically. Jealous of Roland's power in Charlemagne's army, the ambitious Ganelon betrays the Franks to the Saracen Marsile of Zaragoza. The loyal knights of Anjou, Thierry and Huon, who have accompanied Ganelon, are incarcerated by the Saracens, but are set free by the Emir's daughter, Esclarmonde, who has fallen in love with Huon, and by Doña Elvira, sister of Bernaldo del Carpio, the Spanish Visigoth who is hostile to the Franks. The patriotic ideals of the men at combat are tested as Franks, Saracens, Christian Spanish, and Basques rally around their leaders. Though there is no surviving the Moslem onslaught, Roland, Oliver, and all the doomed men offer neither surrender nor armistice. After the battle, the traitor Ganelon is exposed, and Thierry, as the fallen Roland's sponsor, defeats Pinabel, Ganelon's sponsor, in the trial by combat. Thierry's reward includes the hand of Elvira, a romantic conclusion that is neatly balanced by Huon's marriage to Esclarmonde.

Mario Pei has written that the *Chanson de Roland* is an account of the loyalty and devotion that a person owes his God, his sovereign, his

8. Mario A. Pei, *The America We Lost* (New York: New American Library, Incorporated, Signet edition, 1968), p. 188.

country, his family, his superiors, and his followers. The theme of *Swords of Anjou* is that the spirit of Roland neither appeases nor compromises with evil. In the exercising of this spirit, heroism is pitched against treason, for the purpose of the contest is the pursuit of justice, an effort that demands sacrifice. The eighth-century archetype of the modern war-hero valued his life as incidental to the victory of ideals. His involvement, however, was not always single-handed. The roaming knight often came upon whole villages gutted by war and left with "men, women, children, and a few renegades in Christian armor," a potent demonstration of the general brutality of a relentless enemy. This is the type of horror to which Elvira refers as she responds to the hypocritical words of the deceitful Ganelon: ". . . I saw what you had done to the Christian inhabitants—the men slaughtered, the women violated, the children hung up on trees to serve as targets for your archers, the priest suspended by his thumbs and tortured to death."[9]

Treachery, therefore, is the most subtle and intense force of warfare. Pei portrays Ganelon as the personification of the increasing seduction of factional and international treason. The traitor says to Thierry, "Think you there is room in France for both the houses of Ganelon and Roland? Men like you, who know every ell of Roland's country, every trick of Roland's fighting, every man of Roland's following, would be priceless in my camp" (p.60). Ganelon is confident that, with Roland out of the way, Marsile will award him treasure enough to buy fiefs and lands to become the richest baron in France. Eventually, as he swears to Marsile the death of Roland and all his band, he, with all the sincerity of a self-driven, injured hero, demonstrates the universal tactics that have been perpetuated to the creation of modern organizational Quislings.

The theme of treachery is orchestrated by varying instruments. Elvira, in counterpoint, keeps alive the refrain of the brutal dirge with which she relates how she and Bernaldo had been tricked by King Alfonso into believing that her father was being returned as a knight on a horse, only to discover that the mounted figure was a corpse. The father, Conde Sancho Diaz of Saldaña, had expired in prison while Elvira and Bernaldo were in the act of begging for his freedom. The king, a monster of cruelty, returned the minor lordling to his family in this macabre fashion.

Counteracting the incidents of treachery are the persisting and balancing feats of heroism. For example, after Ganelon has lied about having seen Thierry and Huon die, the momentum increases with spectacular deeds among Roland's knights. In response to Oliver's warning of the impossible odds against them as the result of Ganelon's plot with Marsile, Roland presses with the feudal oath, "For one's liege lord must one endure both bitter cold and burning heat, and offer up

9. *Swords of Anjou*, p. 75.

at need his hair and skin, his flesh and blood" (p. 170). Then, when Oliver urges his friend to sound the horn, Roland, with pity and contempt, insists, "We will fight friends! I'll lay about me with Durendal, till its blade is drowned in blood to the hilt." As Oliver persists, Roland assures him that the Emperor has left them to guard the pass with twenty thousand men "because he knew there is not a coward among them." This spirit infects the entire band. Later, when the inevitable destruction is over, Charlemagne's victorious army sets out from the fateful pass of Cize, and his men pay tribute to this spirit. Pei writes, "Few of the Franks there were who could restrain their tears. . . . where their comrades of Roland's command slept their last long sleep, guarded by the cross of Christ" (p. 253). The author has indicated that this is the "spirit of the Battle of the Bulge, not that of Korea."[10]

This codified loftiness of theme extends to the personal level. Baligant strikes Charlemagne and with his scimitar breaks his helm and wounds the Emperor, and the spirit of the Franks sinks as they see their leader totter and nearly fall. Duke Naimon then appeals to Charlemagne's sense of responsibility, asking him if this is how he upholds France and Christendom. Roused by the words, the Emperor triumphs over the enemy. As the Saracens repeat "The Commander of the Faithful is slain," they waver to defeat. The battle cry, therefore, embodies the man's name. It is "Charlemagne and Monjoie!" or "Vengeance for Roland!" The epic proportion of heroism is measured by the expansion of a man's legend. Hence, Thierry may breathe to his brother that Roland has never died and that he lives in the soul of France.

Thierry discovers further that cessation of war may also be based on personal considerations. Because he is in pain as he lies in his great pavilion, the Emperor is quick to agree to the scheme that saves the countless Frankish lives and ends the fighting. Later, after the triumphal journey to Aix, the knights and ladies renew their homage to the Emperor. As he strolls into the hall of his palace, Charlemagne feels that this is his own hour of victory, that he has kept his vow to free Spain from the Saracens. As Pei writes, "Forgotten in this hour were the seven long years of savage warfare, the wreckage of Saracen cities, the crash of embattled hosts, the cries of the dying. Forgotten, too, were the men who slept in the flower-covered field of Rencesvals, the heroes who lay in their sepulcher in the Cathedral of Blaye. The Emperor was back, with victory in his grasp!"[11] Only when Aude, sister of Oliver and the betrothed of Roland, rejects Charlemagne's proposal that she marry his son Louis and crumples to her death before him does Charlemagne's mind leap back to the reality of the power of personal human relationships.

10. *The America We Lost*, p. 188.
11. *Swords of Anjou*, p. 255.

Thierry also reduces the whole feudal code to personal behavior. When Elvira suggests to him that he may be released from his oath to Charlemagne, the knight affirms to her that he was brought up "in the school of Roland, my own." This training has conditioned him to "know" that one does not renounce an oath and that the knight owes to his Emperor his fiefs, his possessions, his service, his sword, and his life. Government in the entire feudal structure rests on the loyalty of each single knight, who, as Thierry puts it, says, "There is no turning one's back on one's duty" (p. 264).

This personal loyalty marks not only the knight's homage to his leader, but also his singular dedication of his love. As Thierry addresses Elvira with her royal title, he reminds her that when all Christian Spain is at her feet, revering her, she will have to remember always that there is one who would, if he could, do her greater homage, one who would kiss not merely her foot or hand, but would crush her to his breast and make her completely and forever his own. Pei emphasizes that this spoken promise of enduring love is firm and masculine, without fears, recrimination, or regret.

Unquestioned loyalty to a leader or to a woman extends its code to group relationships. When Ganelon tries to buy the services of the jailor, Basbrun, he does not realize that the incorruptible provost creeps to the adjoining cell, from which he can see and hear everything. Meanwhile, Ganelon is assured by his visiting uncle, Guinemer, that family loyalty is unimpeachable. His uncle promises him that everything humanly possible will be done to save him. "To do this we will leave no stone unturned, no path untrod. Your disgrace is our disgrace, your sufferings are our sufferings, your death would be the death of us all" (p. 27). Then, when Ganleon reminds his cousin, Pinabel, that the family clan's lives and fiefs are forfeited in case of defeat, the ready answer is: "We stand or fall with you, for the honor of the House of Mayence."

This cohesion within and adherence to a family code of honor underlie the force of factional unity, a force that centuries later, in maturing democratic societies, is still powerful as the economic and social integrating factor in the progress of ethnic minorities. The absolutism of personal duty to leader, woman, and immediate group is the all-pervading theme of current "inner-confederacy" novels like Mario Puzo's *The Godfather.* Dramatizing this strength of clustered unity in the retelling of the greatest of romantic epics, Mario Pei makes his novel bristle with the relevance of his characters to twentieth-century Americans.

Swords of Anjou, therefore, is a story of high adventure whose epic heroism is pertinent to current themes. Legendary stature larger than life magnifies the protagonists, be they friend or foe. But the author does indicate that the pursuit of the ideal should be the goal of human endeavor. As Elvira says, "Frank or Visigoth, what does it matter, so long as our Faith triumphs?" Furthermore, with the defense of the ideal as the major theme, all the corollary ideas concerned with human relationships are cemented. As Saint Gabriel forewarns Charlemagne with symbols of the approaching battle, so the fears of men and women caution them against impending dangers. Mario Pei often stages these human dramas with panoramic settings, ranging from the splendors of the court to the brutalities of man-to-man combat. With the expertise of the word master, the author turns medieval language into vibrant phraseology. To the bombastic promises of the envoy of Marsile, Charlemagne replies, "Mayhap your King may still save his soul!" Pei writes that then, as if awaking from a dream, the Emperor speaks with his customary decision. The style thus employs the stilted phrase of the medieval epic, while simultaneously interpreting the action in lucid, modern terms. The reader is also rewarded by the writer's etymological scholarship, for example, in the action surrounding the word *gab,* which becomes a dramatic device to develop the progress of the plot involving Thierry. The exotic appeal of the *Arabian Nights* is recalled in Huon's description of the Saracen Princess Esclarmonde: "Cheeks like the wild rose, lips like the pomegranate, eyes like stars in the blue-black night" (p. 90). That the author's rhetoric becomes poetic is particularly evident in his use of symbols. When Huon first attempts to make love to Esclarmonde, we are told that it was the old story of the brutal directness of the Frank pitted against the clever cunning of the Saracen—the great, heavy, straight sword against the curved, slender, keen-cutting scimitar. This metaphorical language intensifies tragic moments, also, as in the description of Roland's final action before he dies: "with the last remnant of his strength, he plucked from his belt his right-hand glove, and held it out to his Maker, in the last, supreme gesture of feudal homage" (p. 202).

Mario Pei elevates the mere account of a historical battle to humanistic terms. As an Italian-American writer, he interpets the great epic of Roland as a lesson in loyalty and steadfastness and adherence to one's code of honor and ideals, a lesson for every human being. Although he claims that the characters in his novel are eleventh-century Europeans, Pei, through his art, has demonstrated experiences that are universal today. Particularly, many of the assertions about fealty and duty reflect the attitudes of family-oreinted Italian-Americans. In another dimension, the author presents the preponderant characteristic of Italian-Americans as being conservative guardsmen of home and country. *Swords of Anjou* is meritorious for the enjoyment it gives the reader in swiftness of action and movement of plot; it is also thought-provoking for its challenging spirit that transcends the engaging episodes of violence and bloodshed, the unbridled passions, and the inflexible discipline of the code of the Middle Ages. In Pei's own words, like the *Chanson de Roland,* this book is recommended reading "for all those who think you can peacefully coexist with a treacherous foe who is determined to bury you, and who has proved time and again that he is not to be trusted."[12]

The Sparrows of Paris

A short novel, *The Sparrows of Paris*[13] is included in Mario A. Pei's collection, *Tales of the Natural and Supernatural.* With a scholarly museum curator who is an amateur detective as protagonist, this story demonstrates a connection between medieval demonology and the contemporary traffic in narcotics. Pei develops a rapidly paced plot, interweaving crime, addiction, and seduction with terrifying evidence of mysterious occult practices that are operating today. Pitting law-enforcement officers against the movements of an international ring of smugglers, the author warns the reader that the younger generation in America is menaced by organized foreign tactics. Events rush to a tense climax, engaging the reader completely and convincing him that the supernatural is plausible.

The plot is set in motion immediately. Heywood, the museum curator, is interrupted in his work of classifying Egyptian papyri when his friend Gesualdo Santini, the Deputy Chief Inspector from the Narcotics Squad, asks him to translate some medieval documents. The curator discovers that the papers contain several secrets that the Middle Ages had concealed, one of which concerned a Black Mass and accompanying orgies during which the participants ate and, by diabolical powers, were changed into strange animals. What Santini must prove is that the documents have supplied a method of operation to the brilliant and beautiful Ginette Desclos, a paleographer, ex-collaborationist with the Nazis, and current mastermind of a large narcotics smuggling ring with branches all over Europe, Asia, and North Africa. The New York police have evidence that the group has begun operations in America and is breaking the stranglehold of the Cannizzi-Keoghan combine on the local market. Price wars and gang killings are rampant; Santini is informed that the Russians are helping the Paris syndicate by supplying them with all the narcotics of the Balkan countries. As event quickly follows on event, Santini's daughter, Sylvia, is enmeshed by a member of the gang, the suave Señor Cienfuegos, who, having made a drug addict of her, holds her in his power as a pawn. The story hurtles forward in a rush of action on ships, on the streets, behind the doors of quiet office rooms where documents are stolen, within the iciness of chilling morgues, back to the benumbing luxury of sumptuous living rooms, and finally to the closing-in of the police net on its quarry on a side street not far from the Criminal Courts Building. In the swift press of the hunt, Santini tingles with fear, lest what he has

12. *The America We Lost*, p. 187.
13. Mario A. Pei, *The Sparrows of Paris* (New York: Philosophical Library, 1958).

read about werewolves, vampire bats, witches, and devil-worship can happen and is happening. Victory is his only with the help of the Boy-Scoutish Bill Freeman, Sylvia's temporarily rejected fiancé, and through his own determination that every member of the enemy gang be eliminated. The action is conventionally dramatized. The antagonists have a "tragic" flaw: they are so sure of themselves and their hideout that they have not bothered to keep a real watch.

The intensely charged plot is an allegory for Mario Pei's theme that, as once the entire population of Arles in 1289 went mad, turned to eating grass in the fields, and then to eating one another, and as the narcotics habit is spreading today among the young generation, so in a short time this country will be "a pushover for Communist aggression." The insignia of a small bird for *Les Moineaux de Paris* is in ironic contrast to that of the more rapacious tiger or bear. Furthermore, ideological factions flagged by these symbols appear dangerously remote to an indifferent populace that hardly reacts when it reads about gang warfare in the morning newspapers. Again, Pei points out that the urgency of a national situation is realized only when it becomes personal. As the uninvolved curator reflects, "To be mixed up. . . . It is indicative of the highly vicarious nature of our civilization, it occurred to me, that we can take all these things in our stride without batting an eyelash when they don't concern us personally. But let there be a note of direct involvement, and we somehow revert to the fears and tremblings of our medieval ancestors menaced by the bravos of robber barons" (p. 224). By using the device of paleographic research—the method of collecting facts and then formulating a theory—rather than starting with a ready-made hypothesis and then trying to find facts to fit it, Pei is suggesting how we should analyze the danger of political enemies. He shows that when the hypothesis emerges into fact, the reality is what we see. Santini concludes, "All I know is what I see! It had to hit me in person! I don't know what the hell it's all about, or if there is any truth in your medieval nonsense, Heywood! But I know it's a big peril, and I've got to fight it" (p. 284). In the end, the detective is satisfied with the knowledge that he has helped to destroy a menace and a threat. Shooting to kill is the only tactic, he believes, with which he can overcome the gang. One must not think of a Grand Jury, he says, when playing with rattlesnakes. The ideological implication of his assignment is evident in his report that the police used the gang itself to help wipe out the poison, and thereby "removed from America one of the most awful plagues this country has ever faced!"

The theme is particularized to Italian-Americans in the dramatization of several characters. The commitment to hard work, which is pervasively evident in this ethnic group, is personified in Lucy, Santini's wife, of whom Pei informs us, "Hard work seemed to be her beauty secret." With a willing sense of duty, she has kept a spotless house, has cooked incomparable meals, and has raised her three children in "the finest traditions of both countries." This is the frame of reference for Pei's presentation of the ethnic youth of America. He describes this family unit as a true American success story, combining the elements of solid, sturdy, God-fearing immigrant stock with the typical American virtue of sticking to what you want till you get it and giving full value for everything you get (p. 197). The author details further that Santini has an "honest southern Italian face" and that Sylvia is a "refined, handsome specimen of young American womanhood." He has also informed the reader that the uncle of this family was one of the pioneer Italian immigrants to this country, who had been living in California since 1890, and who left his estate to Gesualdo. Now, though the family live comfortably and are helped by servants, Lucy, typical of Italian-American women, insists on performing the more personal family functions, like cooking, for example. This strong family orientation is further supported when Santini tells about his sister, Julia, who had married the husband her family chose for her instead of the unapproved man she really loved, who subsequently died of melancholia. Now that his own daughter has become involved dangerously through seduction, Santini explains the need to apply his twofold method of defense. As a police officer (citizen) he must "get to the bottom of this thing, and wipe out the gang." As a father (family member) he must use the only means he has of redeeming his daughter. This Italian-American defender of the law is the symbol, therefore, of any American faced by a collectively organized political ideology that has become a personal threat. Will and determination and the belief in the success of swift action constitute the solution.

For all the weight of its message, *The Sparrows of Paris* is an exciting and thought-challenging book. It is first and foremost a superb story. The intellectual protagonist and the emotionally involved group in contest with the brilliant antagonists create a tense plot of menace and intrigue, which mounts to a level far superior to that of the popular detective story. There is an authentic academic aura in the telling that commands both literary and philosophical respect. As Heywood says, whatever the present-day import of the photostats may be, they hold a very definite professional interest. Exercising his linguistic knowledge, the author chooses not to detail brutalities and obscenities, thereby giving the reader a refreshing experience of disciplined artistry. As a result, the terror of the tale is correspondingly the more powerful and menacing. Although some dramatic incidents are told instead of enacted, as when Bill relates how he has been trying to see Sylvia, suggestions of the scenes work like poetic understatement. Furthermore, facts are enlarged symbolically, as in the case of the exposure of the strategic enemy positions in Elderberry Lane, emphasizing that danger lies on the street where we live. In the development of these incidents, emotions are used as dramatic devices. Mounting fear is deliberately intensified by the author with the revelations of strange and uncanny powers out of the Middle Ages—medieval superstitions that appear somehow true and relevant to the twentieth century. The reader's mind begins to personify objects that surround him. With Heywood, we see unearthly things: "Chrysler and Empire State were long, tapering, ghostly fingers, beckoning to mere mortals as they mocked them, reminding them of all the things in heaven and earth undreamed of by their philosophy. Were these spectral fingers bending over, reaching for me, I wondered?" (p. 300). The spectral fingers of a foreign ideology may similarly be reaching for us.

Tales of the Natural and Supernatural (Short stories)

While this discussion is concerned with novels, it is appropriate, because of thematic relevance, to mention here Mario A. Pei's latest collection of fiction, *Tales of the Natural and Supernatural.*[14] In addition to twelve short stories, this volume includes a reprint of *The Sparrows of Paris.* The range of these stories varies from ancient mythology, medieval legend and history, and incidents of World War II to contemporary problems of traffic and television. The tales, however, are consistent with the themes that Pei has enlarged in his longer works.

In "The Huntsmen's Banquet," for example, Pei demonstrates the transcendental ideal of personal sacrifice in destroying a despot in order to preserve the freedom of the populace. The author dramatizes the historical incident in Florence at Aldobrando Donati's banquet, to which the nephew is invited and through whom the story is filtered. At the end of the festivities, Aldobrando's mother, Monna Francesca, insists that he exchange toasts by drinking the wine that she has brought. In this way, by sharing his death, the old woman symbolizes the old standards of the integrity and freedom of Florence, which must be perpetuated at any price.

The frustration that the author shows at other aspects of the human condition is evident in "The Devil's Christmas." While he refuses the usual Faustian temptations, the scholar asks for a cure for cancer, literary and historical enlightenment for all people, and brotherly love all over the world. Although Satan consents to the first two, warning that intellectual progress is far from being a sure guarantee of moral betterment, he cannot do anything about brotherly love, even though the scholar would have exchanged his soul for it. What might have been grimly moralistic, Pei lightens with irony and wit.

The confrontation with the demon is further explored in "The Ritual of Ptah-Mes," in which the protagonist, Durante de' Medici, of

14. Mario A. Pei, *Tales of the Natural and Supernatural* (Old Greenwich, Conn.: Devin-Adair Company, 1971).

the fifteenth century, becomes involved through Black Masses with metempsychosis and reincarnation. Tempted to be God, Durante resurrects Ptah-Mes to enjoin him to reveal the ritual of Osiris. The reader is totally engaged in this Poe-like tale, but the fantasy here has a more authentic reality than is found in the nineteenth-century American's suspension from belief. There is an avenging through faith in Durante's psychological defeat by the dead man, and the reader feels vindicated that this foremost enchanter of his age has succumbed to an unconquerable force.

While the exotic lore of the *Arabian Nights* is recalled in "From the Further Adventures of Sinbad" to satirize the contemporary impossibility of parking one's car in the city, "My Brother's Keeper" realistically emphasizes that a man's common sense is his best friend in advising him that obedience to the rules makes for safe driving. Continuing in this mood for the current scene, the author reveals another popular theme, the humor in our insisting that we are victims of "bad luck." With Pei's characteristic ironic wit, he has the Professor end up in the hospital, with his attractive nurse leaving him in the care of a "battle-axe". "Kandyce Is The Winner" reveals Pei in an amusing, entertaining, and totally human treatment. In "The Roomette," however, he introduces the fabled device of a confrontation with a ghost at the place where a person has died in an accident. While Pei's story is located in a train, the reader recalls the legend of the hitch-hiker whom truck drivers see at the point on the highway where a young woman was killed in an automobile accident.

Pei is at his best in those stories where he reverts to the Middle Ages. In "The Bones of Charlemagne" are concentrated the themes the author has explored in *Swords of Anjou*. Here, however, he identifies the modern, inquiring mind with the objects it analyzes. There is a twilight zone of atmosphere with which the writer seduces the present-day character to bi-locate and thereby act and speak in the period of Charlemagne. The author becomes Sir Marius Peius, who consciously compares the Emperor's throne-room with the Rotunda of Columbia Law Memorial Library, the Sistine Chapel, and the lobby of Radio City Music Hall. With this timelessness of time, Pei demonstrates that the true scholar defies all peril when knowledge in his chosen field is to be gained, even if he must submerge his own personality. He therefore accepts Griselda's comment that he is a Roman and an American, born in a country where all men are lovers and raised in one where all men are exploiters (p.105). The reader suspends his belief to accept the writer's reversal of time when the scholar says that he has dislocated this time to come back a thousand years from a country whose existence is unsuspected, and to which he must report about the status of the Western tongue. Pei has succeeded by sheer story-telling in communicating that intermingling of centuries which is the real world of the scholar. This subjectivity is next diametrically opposed to the objectivity of external action in *The Lady Violante*, in which the code of love and chivalry forces Violante to reject Count Ruggieri so that she may remain faithful to her dead Emir. In so treating medieval materials, Pei can be as interior or exterior in method as he chooses, and the reader is engaged and informed either way.

Mario Pei, in pursuing and attaining high levels of achievement in his chosen work, has more recently applied himself to social studies on a large scale. In *The Flight That Failed* he reveals the strategy that Mussolini used to obliterate Italo Balbo, who, according to Il Duce, had become too popular with the people and thus posed a threat to the premier's power. As Balbo says in this story, "You know you can't touch me without plunging the country into civil war. I have my following" (p.62). Pei writes that the Air Marshall hated the "unnatural Nazi alliance with all his good, healthy Latin heart and soul." However, since it was Mussolini's belief that history always sanctions what the winner does, and he believed that Hitler was going to win, it was imperative for him to remove the controversial Air Marshall. In telling this incident of the planned bombing of Balbo's Caproni, Pei creates a superb, mounting tension out of the rapid progression of events, and heightens it for a dramatic climax.

Finally, with prophetic astuteness, in *1976* Mario Pei condenses succinctly his warnings for the future. He says that it is one thing to prophesy something in a book, and another to see your prophecy come true, for with shocking realism he here depicts the inevitable destruction of America as the result of the direction of our present policies. Reminding us that back in the sixties "some crackpots used to say that was just the way the next war would start"—without warning and with a rain of rockets with atomic warheads—the author paints a terrorizing scene of a man's awakening one morning to the knowledge of the real disaster. The announcement is made by "the authority of the Federal People's Republic of Caribia and its illustrious President-leader, Fernando Obispo" that all major cities, plants, military, naval, and air bases are in ashes and the "Caribian forces" are in command. The protagonist of the story learns that the United States of America no longer exists as a nation. When he asks what quarrel the Caribians had with the United States, he is informed that there is none "save that the United States barred their way to the dominion of the Western Hemisphere, a dominion which President Obispo had promised a selected portion of his people, including the Army officers" (p.133). The professor-protagonist, who is being used as a translator, learns that the major cities of Europe and Japan lie in rubble, that Soviet troops occupy the key centers of Western Europe, that Chinese troops occupy those of the Far East, and that the Caribians control the Americas. Radar-neutralizing devices have made it possible to direct undetected missiles from any part of the globe to any other part with absolute, unerring accuracy, no warning, and no possibility of retaliation. While no American installations exist, the victors "have an unlimited supply of atomic missiles, and the iron will to use them whenever and wherever the faintest measure of resistance appears" (p.136).

But, consistent with the theme of Italian-American determinism, Mario Pei's story has an optimistic solution. Wendell Koenig, a science editor, has told the Professor that there are several atomic scientists who have anticipated such an attack, and they have private laboratories all over the country. These men are well financed, well equipped, and constantly working on atomic offense and defense. The rallying-points of American scientists are the rallying-points of American resistance. Pei writes that the future is secure with "not the blind, futile resistance of desperate men armed with sub-machine guns and rifles in the face of atomic missiles, but the intelligent, deadly resistance of the world's finest scientific brains, outfitted with science's latest findings and most death-dealing implements" (p.142). Mario Pei deals a mortal blow to pointless formlessness in fiction by giving it a firm, organic structure disciplined by the habits of scholarship.

11

NOVELS "OUT-OF-PLACE"

In the attempt to be one in two worlds, each of a number of Italian-American novelists has returned to Italy for varying reasons. Some, like Jerre Mangione, have been able to intensify both worlds in themselves by discovering that, after a thorough search, their identity "belongs" in either place. Others, like Charles Calitri, have sought to explore the genesis abroad of an elusive ingredient in their Americanism that has made them different from their compatriots. Still others, like Joseph Papaleo, have engaged their entire emotional capacity to experience the concepts of the mother country in order to purge themselves of an undefined dissatisfaction with their "place" in America. On the other hand, some writers exorcise the struggle with being "out-of-place" by objectifying it as the problem of a deviant from the establishment, as Robert Cenedella does. Finally, all these motives seem to converge in the type of Italian-American writer like Joseph Arleo, who, grown, educated, and furious with the whole matter of real and psychic segregation, returns to Italy to demand an accounting with his father, who, having left America because of tragic political events, never came back to it even to see his son.

Being "out-of-place," therefore, has persisted as a result of a subconscious, intellectual attitude toward a minority, which has in real terms overcome the previous economic, educational, religious, social, political, and cultural differences. But there still was no final conceptual acceptance of the Italian-American novelist; he has had to expiate his being "out-of-place" by submitting to a baptism of self-abasement. In this way, by salvaging himself, he qualifies as a full-fledged, confirmed American.

ROBERT CENEDELLA (n.d.)

With dramatic reversal, Robert Cenedella creates a story in *A Little to the East,*[1] to present the conflict between the man who wants an assured identity with life and an antagonist who is obsessed with self-destruction. Precipitating the conflict are the environmental causes of which all human beings are victims. Cenedella demonstrates, however, that individuals are able to transcend the restrictions of inevitable events and that the spirit that engenders a man's behavior will ultimately designate his place in a given society.

Robert Cenedella was born in Milford, Massachusetts, where he grew up and attended the local schools. After college, he returned to Milford, a town very much like the Wickfield of *A Little to the East,* where he taught and became the principal of the junior high school. Eventually, he went to New York to work as a radio scriptwriter for various shows, including *The Helen Hayes Theatre, Theatre Guild of the Air, Studio One,* and *Cavalcade of America.* For television he wrote for *The Robert Montgomery Theatre, Lux Video Theatre,* and *The Alcoa-Goodyear Hour.* He become a full-time writing-staff member at National Broadcasting Company from 1953 to 1960. A number of his stories have appeared in *Good Housekeeping, Redbook, Playboy,* and *Woman's Day,* and he has written two plays that have been produced. *A Little to the East* is his first novel.

Cenedella writes this story to probe the internal struggle of a sanguine man's confrontation with the terror of the knowledge of impending death. Structurally, Cenedella uses the Jamesian method of narration from the psychological point of view of the protagonist, Joe Monti, a lawyer who is determined to save the life of Martin McQuaid, a murderer. As James often does, Cenedella reverses the roles of the two men. Joe Monti, who must die, is very much in love with life; he exerts a prodigious effort to save the life of McQuaid, who wants to die. Coming to a climax with varied dramatic tensions at the trial scene, the action is complemented by a constant, sensitive probing that uncovers the cause of the tragedy. With well-paced style, stark clarity of plot structure, and dramatic immediacy, the author engages the reader as a participant in this model of humanity on trial. Joe Monti's story is an internal pilgrimage to teach Martin the value of life. To succeed in his objective, Joe digs deeply into Martin's past, in which process Cenedella contrasts Joe's own past with pertinent symbols of music. The "perfumed music" that Joe plays induces him to recall his past happy life with his wife, Virginia, whom he loved but lost to cancer. Martin, on the other hand, has measured his life to the ritualistic sound of nasalized hymns and marching rhythms of strict conformity, which have been imposed upon him by both his mother and his

1. Robert Cenedella, *A Little to the East* (New York: G. P. Putnam's Sons, 1963).

wife. His burst of violence in brutally murdering his wife is a clashing of cymbals against a bitter repression under the nagging monotony of a primitive sound. As the lawyer pries open the resisting lid of Martin's contained cynicism and doubts, he forces the explosion and overflow of love and hate that take place at the trial. Robert Cenedella's protagonist is the symbol of justice operating with dramatic irony.

The theme of *A Little to the East* is that ethical conflict in human conditions may be solved by compromise with the letter of the law, just as the town has a right-of-way to the cemetery "a little to the east of the one claimed but for all practical purposes just as good."[2] In deciding who is guilty of transgression, the judiciary must theorize about the action of the defendent, exploring the causes of misconduct attributed to a person who is a substitute for the real object of the action. In other circumstances we often similarly vent our hostility in a direction away from the intended victim.

Joe Monti is more than a trial lawyer in an American court. His story is the perennial American success legend, a little out of focus. In his fifties, he has already matured to a vintage sorrow in being a bereft widower whose loneliness is intensified by the relentless demands of incurable leukemia. Despite this, he has a zest and pride in having achieved a firm status in his community, especially since he is the son of Italian immigrants. As with most segregated communities, the ethnic colony in which Joe Monti has grown up is a little east and a little south of the main street. Cenedella's protagonist is the embodiment of the warmth and humanity of the educated man who has been nurtured and supported in the self-sufficient Italian-American group. It is this engulfing humanity that helps Joe retain his happy memories of the dead Virginia and his tenacious will to absorb life in defiance of his consuming disease. Above all, he is determined to give external shape to his belief in the permanence of human love by salvaging Martin McQuaid.

Joe Monti became a lawyer because his "mama" wanted to be proud of him. In a series of stream-of-consciousness flashbacks, the author informs the reader that when Monti acquired his briefcase and secretary, he did not own a piano; he went home to a plate of gnocchi, to his mother's delight. Now, at the piano, his thoughts are of how he won Virginia Antolini from her family with the accepted Italian-American code of respect before he acknowledged his love. And, now, with Virginia dead for three years, he still smiles at her presence. He identifies Virginia with his daughter, and this identification includes his mother. As he probes into Martin's mind, exposing the obsessions lurking there, Joe is elated at his own method of catching the attention of others by seeming to ramble from the point. This characterization

2. *Ibid.* Reference to the Report of the Town Solicitor to the Honorable Board of Selectmen of Milford, Massachusetts, 1913.

of Joe Monti gives another level to Cenedella's theme, because Joe becomes the incarnation of Italianism in America—an intellectual trick before the nation's judgment—as with his talk and posture and shuffling gait before a jury that is persuaded to believe that what Joe "seemed not quite to be arguing for was just."

As Cenedella dramatizes Joe Monti, he activates his theme, because character and theme in this novel are one, which gives the novel a taut, single focus. Aesthetically, the structure is superb and compelling. Ideas are unfolded as personality traits. As the narration races on in the course of the meetings of Joe and Martin, the "red corpuscles had been eating the white." He weeps for the dead Gladys, Martin's murdered wife, after he has interviewed the socially pretentious Mrs. Wendell. Then, when he tells his daughter that he keeps reading *I Promessi Sposi* to keep his Italian franchise, Carlotta answers that she wishes he would act like "an American," and he almost hears "mama" in her voice. Cenedella writes that Carlotta returns repeatedly to this theme of Joe's Americanism, since he insists on Italian words of praise of her, despite her prim, catechizing manners, which have become emphasized since her marriage to Alvin, the New England "Yankee." Joe Monti has acquiesced to the folklore of both the Wickfield Exchange Club and the Sons of Italy, and still he would have liked five girls, "five chips off his graceful Virginia." It is Joe's Italianism, Cenedella shows, that makes him so personally involved with his client. Cenedella writes, "Martin became Joe, who stood glaring at Gladys, who turned into Virginia" (p.195). The dramatic tension of the personal theme results from the differences between the two women: Virginia, the "Italian girl with whom you could have a good satisfying arm-waving fight," and Gladys with all the "sweetness of a man-denying calm sensible American tease," which had led Martin to violence. Cenedella transforms Joe from person to symbol in making him a plausible composite of all the professional Italian-American men of a typical New England community. The figure that evolves, however, is surrounded by all the physical and mental weaknesses in the hysterical paralysis of universal contemporary society. Because Joe Monti breathes intensely the heady air of impending death, he becomes almost a Christ-figure; no sickness gets in his way. He knows he cannot save Martin McQuaid with facts and law; neither can the Italian-American come alive in the American complex with all its petrified fences of priorities. In the end, the Italian-American, any Joe Monti, is locked out only by the "amber ice" that is freezing out the life of his own blood. Joe Monti is the symbol of a generation that sacrifices itself for its own renewal in its children. As Cenedella writes, "he knew all his want to live all the time was a fear what he really had was the want to die like Martin and so he worked to make Martin save him . . ." (p.383).

Symbolized in the protagonist, the main point of the book is that the

Italian-American today is a lonely bicultural person, threatened with mortal severance from a pregnant tradition which, though dying in his bloodstream, is renewed by changing the genetic structures of future generations in America. The "facts and laws" are forced to compromise with the thrust to permanence that every human being inherits at birth. Life must go on.

This is a truth that is extended to other characters in the book. Martin McQuaid is not a criminal, but a psychological rebel against a strident, coercive mother who had bent his will with the language of piety. No court in the land would consider either neglected or deprived a child whose mother felt as Martin's mother did; but Martin has had to live with his mother's prodding against everything he did as a "sin." She has warned him that "if I hear you take His Holy Name in vain again, I'll break every bone in your body." Cenedella makes it plausible that Gladys should call Martin a "nothing," and her own alcoholism is only a bid for attention. Gladys has had a life of repression, vying with her mother for a superior moral position. Mrs. Wendell's characteristic pose was that of a poor, long-suffering, little-appreciated, well-respected-in-Trenton woman, a pose that Joe Monti would not dignify with any question. Joe's projection into Martin is necessary, because Martin is a robot, a fact that is dramatically highlighted when Cenedella differentiates between the two men's definitions of family (the model of American Society). Joe Monti's family, his world, are Carlotta and the memory of mama, papa, and Virginia; but Martin has no family except his brothers who are members of clubs, brothers who will not lift a finger to save him.

The novel is profound and aesthetic. In the structure of the story, life is in perilous balance with death. Robert Cenedella has Joe woo death with saccharine music and conservative suits, generalizing that life itself is a long suicide. This seriousness is made bearable through symbols, and everybody has a piano or a briefcase. Cenedella says that, as people "destroy a populace, play a song, make a motion . . . it's a positive iron-clad guarantee that if death is in the room, you won't realize it" (p.114). Cenedella depicts his philosophy by Joe Monti's plight, which on another level is the plight of any Italian-American raging for life in a social reversal that is diseased. Cenedella gains our sympathy because Joe Monti is humanity insisting upon spiritual immortality in the face of mortality that he must make transcendental. The author sets his scenes with authority and intense perception. The trial scene is high drama climaxing the psychological action. The explosive eruption of the moment of truth comes with the clashing of contrasted societies embodied in the two men who lay bare their lives before each other. Joe Monti's endemic Italianism wins with its method of moving east of the claimed right-of-way, but he succumbs so that he cannot be counted, and the only thing he can move is his mind. *A Little to the East* is an incisive, persuasive, and thematically triumphant novel that never loses its focus in the creative engagement of the reader's imagination. The writer is aware of the profundities of human experiences, particularly as they illustrate his ideas as variations of themes through the characters he portrays. *A Little to the East* claws at the reader's conscience, demanding reparation for the bloodletting that legality metes as punishment. The author demonstrates that an act of violence may come from a desperation too long repressed. The power of the book is similar to that of a well-made tragic play whose tightened drama is unforgettably portrayed by superb acting. Robert Cenedella emphasizes the tragedy of the relentless necessity of self-sacrifice in order to restore harmony to the order that regulates place.

JOSEPH PAPALEO (1925–)

With Joseph Papaleo the theme of being "out-of-place" solidifies with lucid definitions. With no equivocation in either defenses or charges, Mr. Papaleo writes fiction about the Italian-American who, as a stranger who does not know he is a stranger, must find himself. Papaleo says that his stories are about the "current conflicts of Italians in America as to identity, mores, and their changing ways of life."

The son of Italian immigrants, Joseph and Rosa (San Martino), Joseph Papaleo was born in New York City on January 13, 1925. His education was interrupted by his service in the Army Air Force during World War II. After receiving a B.A. from Sarah Lawrence College, he spent a year at the University of Florence, where he earned a diploma *di Profitto.* Now a professor, he is the chairman of the writing department at Sarah Lawrence College. Since the late fifties he has published stories in *The New Yorker*, *Commentary*, *Swank*, *The Dial*, *The Montrealer*, *Harper's*, *New American Review*, and *Evergreen Review.* His poetry has appeared in publications like *Common Ground*, and much of it laments the loss of integrity on the part of American-born children who mock the speech of their immigrant parents. On the whole, however, in both his poetry and fiction, Papaleo is urging the Italian-American to perpetuate his parents' American Dream. In seeking to return to the original cultural thrusts of the immigrants, Papaleo's protagonists find themselves "out-of-place" in both his novels, *All the Comforts* (1967) and *Out of Place* (1970).

All the Comforts

In his first novel, *All the Comforts,*[3] Joseph Papaleo introduces his first book-length theme of the third-generation Italian-American who is

3. Joseph Papaleo, *All the Comforts* (Boston: Little, Brown and Company, Inc., 1967).

vying for a place closer to the center of the stage that frames the national character. In the course of the plot, Papaleo's protagonist cannot find a fixed point for focusing his identity as the instrument of ambition, either his own or that of others. Several related themes broaden the story to greater than exclusively ethnic proportions.

On a universal level, the young lover of a neglected wife demonstrates to the dedicated materialistic husband that for a successful marriage the exercise of connubial love should be at least equal to the efforts to aquire possessions. *All the Comforts* is not a novel of racial protest, nor is it a diatribe expressing social anger. The donnée of the book is the pursuit of success, with all its rewarding acclaim and fame. Furthermore, the power of affluence must be insured by all the luxuries a commercial America can produce so that the entrepreneur may have complete possession of any given place. The protagonist, Vito Filippo, meets with little conflict in this aggressively materialist world. His personal progress is psychologically motivated by the episodic development of his erotic experiences with a married woman. To Vito, Helen Steinman is the sexual symbol of the social level he craves. There is little to impede or complicate his progress, and few of the tensions in the plot are internally dramatized. The extramarital relationship with an accommodating married woman is not only an incentive for the protagonist to make his decisions; it is a convenient device on the part of the author to create a point of encounter between two ethnic groups.

As a symbolic portrayal of the progress a person makes in moving from one social level to another, *All the Comforts* is a successful, artistic, presentation of hope. Although it does not press with the heavy pauses or minutiae of a Pinter play, the story does engage the reader as a learning observer of levels of human behavior. The reader likes Vito Filippo at once, and is relieved to know that this is a youth with dreams, one who has returned from college in the South and has begun to think of himself as a person at the "mike." Since Vito's experience has made him sympathetic with the Blacks, he looks above him to those whites who have succeeded and he says, "Sure, man, I'm gonna make it."

All Vito's actions are controlled by place. He becomes a delivery man for a delicatessen; in this capacity, he comes to Helen Steinman's kitchen, and, eventually, to the intimacy of the rest of the house. Out of sincere admiration and generosity, Vito helps Helen plan a dinner for her husband's factory associates. Cy Steinman, a one-dimensional cog in the clothing-industry wheel, is obsessed with expanding his business. Overrating his selling capacity, he splurges with an overabundance of food and wine at Mama Leone's. Then, without forethought, he leaves Helen to go home alone. Conveniently, Papaleo has Vito meet Helen on her way home; he takes her for a drive to Westchester and their liaison is launched. The graphic details of the scenes of their sexual encounters occupy much of the author's narration, but Papaleo impresses us with Vito's naïveté in being charmed by the decorative seductiveness of both the woman and her home—by the expensive details of the décor, and the animation given the setting by the physical presence of the woman he possesses. Vito has not developed enough perception to realize that this home is a brittle showroom for new wealth; he endows it with his own fantasies of becoming a singer and having all the status that accompanies fame.

While Cy is away, expanding the company into a larger corporation, Helen visits with her mother-in-law and her friends, discovering how really limited her world is. She revels in the beauty of the "hardness" of Vito's young body, the strength of his sexuality. She is like the secretary in Eliot's *The Waste Land*, brushing her hair as she returns to her bed, forgetting that her lover is still in the room. Later, when Cy returns, she allows the unsuspecting husband to find her undressed in Vito's presence, deliberately forcing the admission of the liaison. The enraged Cy, recognizing Vito as the "boy" whom they went to hear sing, must assert his prerogative as a Jewish husband, and he exiles Helen from his home. Then, advised by his mother and mollified by his own pragmatism, after a few weeks he calls Helen back. Meanwhile, Vito is on the road to fame.

As his friend Arthur tells Helen, Vito is different—a real pusher, a powerhouse. In basketball, in semi-pro football, when others are ready to drop, Vito pushes on to win. Papaleo writes that Vito had plans and stood above himself, unaffected by the hate he had the right to have, the hate of the stultifying neighborhood of the upper Bronx, where nothing ever changed. The problem with Vito is that, though he has a contract in his pocket to go to the Coast "to get started," he is not sure that he should leave his family and the Bronx, making a change of place from what he knows. He therefore looks to Helen to help him make a decision. In a long monologue, in which Papaleo leads the reader to probe Vito's mind, Vito comes to reject his present environment, "these crusts of bread," the Bronx and White Plains Avenue. He has a brief moment of self-hate, then, thinking of Helen, makes up his mind to "do it"—singing—and decides to change his name to Vic Phillips. Later, he tells his mother that he can marry anybody, from any background, because he does not have what he calls the neighborhood marks—the dark complexion and the wrong voice. Furthermore, he has inherited his father's passion for hard work, and he knows that success means an absorption of the "system," which has worked for all his "paisans" and even for college ball-playing. His one feasible move is to leave the neighborhood.

Papaleo succeeds in telling a story of the search for identity. He even has a level of poetry in the ironic situation that Vito, an Italian-American, identifies success with a co-ethnic group, the Jewish-Americans, instead of with the established WASPS. As a result, Papaleo dramatizes the idea that the American Dream is basically a pursuit of economics. The theme of mobility of place, therefore, has more emphasis in the novel than any of the characters; confusion about their progress controls the story—a structural flaw. The erotic experiences of Helen and Vito are bricks in the walls that firm the structures of the "where" in which each finds himself. Papaleo emphasizes this idea in Cy's conclusion that, after all, this person (Helen), and these rooms are covered and protected by his own walls. He loves what he owns and he will go on bettering his earning power. The psychological basis of the novel is barely developed and ultimately destroyed. Aesthetically the novel suffers from apparent lack of control, unprogressive dialogue, overexternalized action, and the sacrifice of tensions to a sociological hypothesis. The hypothesis, however, convinces us that the story is valid. Furthermore, the author's honesty gains the reader's interest and respect.

Out of Place

In his second book, *Out of Place*,[4] Joseph Papaleo masters more of the conventions of the novel and develops further the hypothesis that the Italian-American, now well-established both economically and socially, is still a stranger in his environment. Another level of tension is added to this predicament in that the Italian-American does not know that he is out of place. The novel hovers between the theme of innocence and the pursuit of identity. Aesthetically, this work shows greater control in the development of plot, since Gene Santoro, the protagonist, remains the focal symbol of the author's theme.

The scope and range of the book are widened to both sides of the Atlantic. Gene is emblematic of the Italian-American who has reached beyond Vito Filippo and the Upper Bronx, and has firmly established himself in Westchester, where he is a successful attorney with a fairly large-sized mansion to house a pampered wife. His sons are in the Eastern establishment preparatory schools; he belongs to the proper clubs; his family leans upon him.

When Carlo Marinaro, a native Italian who is married to Gene's sister, becomes thoroughly disillusioned with American materialism, he snatches his children and flies back with them to Italy. Gene must accept the family's assignment of bringing the children back, and his ensuing experience in Italy awakens in him a dormant part of his personality. To this revelation Papaleo devotes the second section of the book. The third phase of the narrative dramatizes the resulting dilemma of Gene's position, that he is still gingerly balanced on a point between two cultures. The thoroughly developed American of Italian ancestry has only to contact his ancestral home and his well-structured

4. Joseph Papaleo, *Out Of Place* (Boston: Little, Brown and Company, 1970).

place in life is transfigured. Forgione's river has become an ocean, and the problems of the protagonist are now universal and international. The Italian Elena loves Gene completely, and she is willing to trick him about the paternity of her child. Gene knows the truth, however, and must return home with the elusive strains of a persistent melody in his mind. Dramatically, Papaleo has reversed the symbols of the victims of a dual society. When Gene returns the children to their mother, they become typical acquisitive Americans, readily accepting the material comforts of their surroundings. Gene, ironically, becomes the wandering child of the family, and must return once more to the old society. The novel has fully developed symbols with fairly developed allegorical characters, but Papaleo is sometimes weak in motivation and uneven in development. Yet the people of the novel are imbued with life.

The point of *Out Of Place* is that, without his realizing it, the American of Italian ancestry has had, in his success with the establishment, to give up more than he has received and that, as a result, he finds himself subconsciously dissatisfied. He seeks a solution to his dilemma in the return to old values, and he may be the model for a national syndrome. The original concept of the American Dream may have deteriorated to a pursuit of plastic comforts; we need to restore ourselves at the wellsprings of our humanity.

Gene Santoro is the Italian-American who has arrived, perhaps suitably categorized as one of the Late American Rich. His success, however, has been assured by his father, who had amassed a fortune in large button factories and is now retired with three bank accounts, his wife, securities, children, and grandchildren. Gene is the "most American" of the children, and in the Santoro home his authority is automatic because he is an assemblyman, a Knight of Columbus, a member of the Chamber of Commerce, a member of two top-echelon clubs, a creature of parts, a past president of his trade-organization. As the family representative, he must be its executive. In Amalfi, on the mission to rescue his sister's children, he becomes involved with a siren. Ostensibly the seducer is Elena, a servant; but the girl is an embodiment of Italy, the Italy that has always lurked at the watershed of Gene's subconscious life. He cannot understand what it is that he feels about her, and when he takes her, she acts as if nothing had been taken from her—an untouchable entirety. She intensifies his person: he wishes the two children were his own. When he returns, his wife Francine does not, as Papaleo writes, catch the exile's tone, "the loneliness of killed pride." When he starts his business day again, the day has lost its usual excitement; it is a beggar with its hand out, a reminder of the contrast between the destroyed and the successful, and that the reward for having money is to keep working.

Gene is the instrumental key to the theme of Papaleo's narrative. The writer puts the protagonist in a sacrificial fire of displacement because of the children, who are the symbols of the world of the future. Gene says to Francine that their fear for the children is really the fear they have for themselves. This fear makes him uncomfotable before his own sons; they patiently treat him as a guest at their school. Papaleo stirs the reader's pity for Gene, who feels the indifferent detachment from the sons who have become two names to remember in his charities. Gene's loss extends to all his relations. In his increasing alienation, he recalls how his mother has gradually regressed into loneliness in the big house, complaining that they have all lost lovingkindness, some kind of love he can not understand, something open and flowing. When he takes Annie's children for a ride to the old neighborhood on Arthur Avenue, their revulsion at the "slum" fills him with despair, a shock at their betrayal. When he takes them to the club, the children feel a self-satisfied excitement, even though he still has vestiges of discomfort as the wealthy and pale Bronxville women smile at him possessively. When he refuses to accept his share of the cash his father insists on distributing, Gene strengthens his detachment. He drives near the river, seeking the innocence that contemporary novelists all pursue—a pursuit of lies, he knows, because most of the books are inadequately written by men who are still boys. The lies, however, are everywhere. When he returns to Rome, he knows that what he has felt about Elena is fantasy, and that she has lied to him about her child. Then he accepts his brother-in-law's bigamous marriage to Carla. He walks alone on the Calabrian shore, and he finds the wandering a good washing for his mind. But, as he wanders, he realizes that he does not believe in this wish to be alone. Papaleo says that wishing is something to do if a man does not have something to go back to; and this conclusion is the crux of his theme. The Italian-American always has something to go back to. When Gene now returns to Westchester, he tells his sons that he will go back to Rome. He is on the out-of-place see-saw; but his sons insist on finishing their education in their proper school, these sons who move with American athleticism and speak the Eastern "prep dialect." Papaleo leaves his protagonist in Rome, alone, wondering how the city will hold him in its continuum.

Carlo Marinaro's flight generates the dramatic tensions of the novel. Rejecting the waste-land values of American life and morality, Carlo insists that his children must not acquire what he considers the snobbishness and bad manners of this nation. To the Santoros, who have tolerated him as a "dumb wop," he is a social monster who will make fools of them in public. He, however, claims to have a wisdom the Santoros no longer have. He says that Italy is inside his head in how one should live, act, travel, and get along with people. Having come to America in 1950, he symbolizes ethnic defeat. He is too much of a contrast to the Italy that the Santoros (symbolizing most Italian-Americans) have sealed in a compartment, a memory of old monarchic Italy locked in their heads and somehow mixed with their frozen foods. Carlo sees the Italian-Americans as a government contained within their house, with a foreign country next door. Papaleo agrees that, with these people, their children are their art, and success is their science. Back in Italy, Carlo rationalizes his position, claiming that there are no wives in America, only drivers of cars, and "handles for machines." However, after his histrionics about keeping his children, Carlo accepts Gene's money to finance a bakery, and systematically organizes himself for a married life with Carla. With Annie, he had been a discarded instrument in an American machine operated by people who called themselves Italian, but who, Papaleo writes, are neither of one nation nor or of another; they are merely laborers. His defection has a tragic repercussion on Annie, who is abandoned to the role of keeper of the family home in Westchester.

The father, whom Papaleo calls "Old Santoro," is the Italian-American King Lear. He is the family patriarch, autocratic and domineering, who has no faith in the institutionalized process of finance. He has bought a large mansion in upper Westchester, to which the Santoros refer as the "fort" or the "castle." In this retreat, the family carries on all its activities. Old Santoro insists on dividing his negotiable assets, and he is impressed by Angelo and Annie, who cajole him, but he is infuriated by the honesty of Gene, his favorite, and disowns him. The conniving son and daughter then plot, unsuccessfully, to have the father committed to a nursing home. Symbolically, Old Santoro is an archetype of Papaleo's embodied theme. In an internal monologue, the father laments for his Gene, the son who is most like him and is a great success. He knows that Gene is better than the others, but that he is a wanderer like himself. Secretly the father feels that the son should "have had a new country." In Santoro's introspection Papaleo poeticizes his theme with beauty and lyricism. Wandering mentally, the old man calls for Gene, while he builds himself a rude hut with a pile of stones on the back lawn. Like Wordsworth's Michael, his son will have a patrimonial monument, a visual tribute to continuity. When Gene comes home to his father's funeral, he loses his sense of time. The father's death disciplines the conversation of the brothers, who now feel uncomfortable in the old neighborhood which houses the funeral parlor. Angelo remarks that the men and women here are jungle animals, even "our own people." The more they have, the more they desecrate the environment.

Among the others, Francine is a one-dimensional character reduced to simple responses to her husband, Gene. She is a casualty of his dramatic involvement with the children. She symbolizes the aridity of the woman who is cut like a paper doll and placed in position on a stage to be moved like a piece of setting behind the action of the motivated characters. Papaleo limits her motions to signs, but he allows her, with her pretty face, to take the sourness of acceptance. In an interlude of structural clumsiness, with the device of a conversation with Gene,

Francine reveals her Sicilian background. In a melodramatic speech, Papaleo has Francine orate satirically on the weaknesses of the old Italians whose ways are all gone and from which she has always wanted to run away. Francine's outcry stings Gene to the answer that Papaleo uses as a thematic key. Gene insists that though things are not so attractive in Italy, everybody has life "inside" of him and people are always moving; everything moves there. The Italians think more about living than they do about working. Francine concludes that Gene has lived through something independently of her, and she is at a loss, sensing that he feels that she is a ruin. She therefore correlates objectively the out-of-place theme, whose arrangement in her is in terms of sexual intimacy.

The novel is poignant and serious, although the development of the theme is uneven. Papaleo interrupts his dialogues with philosophic comments on women, personifications of nature, the problems of Italian-Americans, the idea that Italians have of Italian-Americans, their theories of rearing children. Some of these ideas are brought into enough conflict for dramatic tension, and they illuminate the experiences of the characters. The Italian-American women are shadowy, while those in Italy have a bright vibrancy. Gene, the central character, is a Hamlet-like victim of circumstances, victimized by his own success. Papaleo utilizes his protagonist to incorporate obviously the theme of the ambiguity of the Italian-American's place. Gene admits that the Santoros, like the other Italian-Americans, have realized their dream, the objective correlative of the dream being the guarded, isolated house in Westchester. But, says Gene, he doesn't think "any of us ever liked it here, this dead place with empty streets" (p.259). Speaking for Papaleo, he says that America has to make a statue for the Italian-Americans, the uncomplaining drones, the donkeys, and the "wop" who works, who lets "them" call him anything. He tries to revivify Francine, who is his "floating" Ophelia, by telling her that in Italy the Italian-American feels pride and has feelings he has never before had. But Francine is also caught; she must decide to stay where her sons are. Joseph Papaleo has succeeded in persuading the reader of the tragedy of the sacrificial duties that force the individual to stay "out-of-place." He has also succeeded in communicating by dramatic tension that the salvaging of the children, while it disrupts the equanimity of the present Italian-Americans, is the necessary motivation of the future direction toward better harmony in a less divisive world. Papaleo, while using the rhetoric of familiar ethnic histrionics, is insisting that the ultimate amalgam of future generations requires the increasing mobility of restless persons like Gene Santoro who must use their superior capacities. The shifting of scenes emphasizes that geographical points are temporary stage settings for the dramas depicting the values that make humanity at home with humanity.

JOSEPH ARLEO (1933-   )

The Grand Street Collector

Occasionally, a writer appears who has the masterful artistry to tell his story with sure precision, trippingly on the tongue, sawing no air, and gathering unfettered momentum. He amalgamates the situations of a people, a time, and a concept with brief, Homeric action. The communal disturbances of a segregated world, the personal quest for identity, and the interweaving of events with local and international governmental structures, all converge vividly in Joseph Arleo's *The Grand Street Collector.*[5] Arleo's recall is an unveiling of progressive experience detail by detail, honed to the essence of stage dialogue and possessing the steady, inexorable approach to the fatal and tragic confrontation that ends a Greek drama.

The son of Dominick and Giovanna (Puca) Arleo, both of whom were born in Italy, Joseph was born on January 2, 1933, in Brooklyn, New York. After attending public school in Brooklyn, he studied at Columbia College, where he earned a degree in 1954 in English and Psychology. In 1956 he received an M.A. in Comparative Literature from Columbia University. Advancing progressively in the advertising world, Arleo is an officer and director of the William Esty Company. He and his wife, Starr Taber Arleo, have three children. *The Grand Street Collector* is his first book.

The subject of Arleo's book is Don Natale Sbagliato, who has the political assignment of assassinating Guido Sempione, radical editor in New York City who features articles condemning Mussolini and the Fascist party in Italy. The main incident of the story is based on the life of Carlo Tresca, the Italian newspaper editor who was assassinated in New York, but whose case has never been solved.

Natale Sbagliato is a collector for the unauthorized lottery that thrives in the Grand Street community. He is considered an honest man, a respected citizen, and a helpful agent in an accepted activity in his neighborhood. Since his wife has died, his sister lives with him and his six-year-old son, Pietro. His loyalty and integrity are the contributing factors to his being chosen as the man who will perform the patriotic execution as a service to his Italian fatherland. His reluctance and fear, furthermore, are precipitated by the threatening force of the men who are organized to insure the infliction of punishment. Caught in this web, "Don Natale" obeys orders and is taken to Italy. Henceforth he is separated from his son, who, left behind in America, grows up in a confused environment, a victim of a bullying Irish "gang of hoodlums" who have read about the murder in the newspapers. Natale's sympathizers have woven a network of protective lies about him

5. Joseph Arleo, *The Grand Street Collector* (New York: Walker and Company, 1970).

in order to give Pietro the opportunity to believe in his father. It is the unraveling of this screening blanket that takes the maturing Pietro on an odyssey of former haunts and old newspapers in order to learn the truth about his father. By means of criss-crossing events with flashbacks to the original incidents, Arleo shows the full action of what has happened and engages the reader in the pursuit of Natale in Italy to the story's relentless conclusion.

In this book, Joseph Arleo is dealing with the nature of guilt and the suspicion of guilt. The theme is dramatized in the story of both Natale Sbagliato, who has committed a violent political act, and his son Pietro, who has been carrying the "weight of a father's guilt like a ton of stone for twenty years" (p.17). Natale, who has been obligated to Rocco Gargatto for giving him his first job in America, behaves out of loyalty to this obligation. Whatever it is that Rocco wants, Natale will do it, not questioning the nature of Rocco's interests. In his simplicity, Natale prays to San Gennaro, promising to trust this friend Rocco, who has become "The American right hand of Mussolini." Therefore, when Rocco's emissaries inform Natale that he has been chosen to remove Sempione "from this life," they pressure him with the argument that "in this way Rocco rewards your true desire to be of service to your country and to elevate yourself in Fascist eyes. At the same time, Rocco understands your desire to return his kindness and consideration of years ago" (p.29). It is the strength of this reference to personal obligation that activates Natale more than the argument that Sempione has been troublesome to America's government, too, because he has been a labor agitator in the factories. Alfonso Tedesco, who speaks for the Fascists, attests that the American police and F.B.I. would consider the removal of Sempione as good riddance. With this double plea to patriotism, Natale is pressed further when he objects that he is "not a gun." Tedesco assures him that, "the very offer of this honor . . . involves you inextricably. Rejection would be interpreted in Rome as expression of disloyalty. . . . The next candidate, already selected and schooled, would have not one assignment, but two" (pp. 58–59). Natale is thus neatly trapped, since he fears, above all, any act of reprisal against Pietro.

Sempione moves with the same inevitability toward the main event, feeling not guilt, but a dedicated belief in his cause. He tells the police that they do not have a nightstick big enough to break the backs of men with nothing to lose, who have strength in their will. Admiring the unruffled Italian radical, Sean O'Neil, a news reporter, recalls Sempione's frontpage editorial, "Down With Monarchy," which had led the Italian Ambassador to complain about a certain newspaper in New York, an Italian language newspaper that was printing unflattering things about the Italian Imperial Government, and who expressed his desire to see prohibitions placed in the way of the persons responsible. As the desired objective is expedited, the political dimensions are explored, with their usual, divided attitudes. While some argue that Mussolini has brought dignity to the nation of their birth, others insist that there is a difference between Fascism and humanitarianism. One man says, "there are things Mussolini has done the value of which I do not question. The fact remains he is a dictator. See how he has reached across the sea and killed Sempione." Another man answers, "Further proof of his ability to get things done" (p.99). Later on, this dual attitude persists in Pietro's Aunt Emilia's explanation that there are mistaken steps into which the best of men stumble, in good faith. She says to him that his father's love for him was matched only by his love for the country of his birth, and his desire for his son someday to attain a position of respect was matched by his desire for Italy to attain a position of respect now, in his lifetime. Pietro's position of divided loyalty is emphasized as Emilia reminds him that America was not at war with Italy at the time of the Sempione affair. Pietro's being "out-of-place" is dramatically objectified by his aunt's reminding him, "But then the war began, and he found himself allied to both sides, though bound to Italy by his presence there. Remember that every Italian in America had relatives on the other side—brother, cousins, uncles, nephews—flesh and blood that became our enemy, just as we became theirs, through the will of a lunatic. But to leave the country would have been an act of treason" (p.135).

Weighed down with the trauma of an unhappy youth, Pietro is determined to investigate his father's guilt. Unknown to Zia Emilia, he reads the letters that Natale has sent to her, happy to discover that his father has continued to love him and to worry about him. When he reads the old newspaper article at the library, however, Pietro finds that Rocco Gargatto had been a racketeer and that Natale must have created a fabric of lies to protect him. He fears that his father must have worked for Rocco in some capacity against the law. Later, he learns that Natale had been an accessory to Rocco's stealing the payroll of a railroad company, a desperate act against the unreasonable pressure of the Irish foreman. Then, having no other resources for work, the men resorted to bootlegging. Like Pellegrini,[6] Arleo explains how the Italians felt about the morality of selling wine. As for Pietro, "The weight of all he had learned that night tired him and he wished he were asleep somewhere far from the responsibilities he felt forming about him, responsibilities that included the justification of his father's life and abdication of family, and the redemption of his own past years of ignorance" (p.152). His own association with his "justification of his father's life" is not relieved when he visits Sean O'Neil, who defends Sempione, saying, "The guy simply was fighting for the rights of labor at a time when God knows the working man needed organizing. It's going to happen someday in this country with the colored people, you

6. See Pellegrini, chapter 2, above.

watch" (p.179). Of the facts, Sean can tell him only that, because he had been identified, it was necessary for Natale to leave the country after the assassination. With the ammunition of these sparse facts, Pietro protests to his Uncle Georgio in Masinalto, Italy, that he is a murderer's son, and has been nurtured by deception. He says that he feels as though he had been born at the age of twenty, without parents and that he did not know where he was. His studies had no meaning for him, and he could not cultivate interest in anything or anyone because he felt nothing to draw from. This is the bottom of the despair of the immigrant's protected son. The son can not judge as guilty the firing hand of the "modest man [who] responded to the call of his Motherland." Nor can he glory in the inheritance that this Italian father now passes on to his descendents. The real horror of guilt is in the total involvement of all humanity in universal evil, which Pietro recognizes as he faces his father and realizes what has happened to him.

For the Italian-American, assimilation has contained a degree of the evil that has needed to be redeemed. Arleo writes, reflecting the thoughts of Colonello Alfonso Tedesco in the story, that the Italians in America have joined social clubs and have become pretentious. He points out, however, that they have previously accepted degraded employment—pressing clothes, shining shoes, serving food, digging ditches, sweeping streets, laying rail: "the slave-labor of their Anglo-Saxon masters. But now this collector was ready for redemption" (p.20). Full acceptance, therefore, must suffer violence. As Natale says, while he is waiting for the policeman who will take his "protection" money from him, American newspapers do not print anything of the dignity of Italy, but that they will get a shock one day. At another point, he reflects that though he has escaped a "death in life" by leaving Italy, he has accomplished very little in the new country; he is "nothing more than another greenhorn in Little Italy" (p.36). This lack of recognition is an abrasive frustration. Natale tells the child Pietro that he will learn of the railroad in his lessons one day, . . and that perhaps "they" will not say Italians built it. But these words are as little consolation to Pietro as are his father's assurance that the dead mother has "put away her dreams" in him. The boy cannot even understand Natale's disdain of the "Americans" who come down to Mulberry Street to watch the "festa," and why his father says, "How they love us . . . this time of year" (p.68). Later, as Michele Volpe makes a speech, the words penetrate the subconscious, despite the florid phrases: "I know the agony of words malpronounced and improperly used, the laughter and scorn of ignorants heaped upon you like shovels of earth on a living grave. I know the pain and demoralization of the second-rate citizenship imposed by the ruling classes . . ." (p.51). But, in his reply, Guido Sempione poses the challenge that racketeers make a business of politics, exploiting the immigrants, talking of Michelangelo as though salvation waited in the past, but stalling minimum wage legislation until the workers die at their machines. Sempione's words, however, have little force with the Italian attitude in America that there is no crime in lottery, for example; and Volpe is a living symbol of the people's resentment.

Ethnic problems are reduced to personalities motivated by brutal fundamentalism. Arleo writes of the usual, bullying gang that pits its force against a single, frail opponent: the Shamrocks versus Pietro. Many battle cries are reduced to the single line: "Y'hear that? The little wop doesn't know where his wop father is" (p.111). The vicious attack that follows is a dramatic picturing of what the Italian-American feels as his predicament in other levels. From the basest point to every conceivable height, his struggle becomes one of image. In this struggle everyone participates, even the poorest housewife, like Zia Emilia who constantly cleans the bare floor, so that no words can be said against her. To clothe the image, the women are never disheveled; the men are always clean-shaven. Furthermore, the second generation insists on speaking the best English they can master, especially in Brooklyn, writes Arleo, "for Brooklyn was America as Grand Street had never been" (p.115). In nurturing the image of dignity, immigrant parents have often been fetishistic about education. When Pietro goes to Italy, his uncle Giorgio assures him that he is proud of his nephew, that he is the son of his brother and that he has been to the university. Formal education is equated with social status. This status is not compromised, however, in the Italians' judgment when they discuss Natale's occupation. Even to Pietro, his father's having been a lottery collector has always been part of his unconscious recollection. Arleo writes, "But at that time, at that place, the occupation had not been a dishonorable one; to have been apprehended on that score in those days was little worse than getting a speeding ticket today, and there was something vaguely romantic about both those infractions of the law" (p.154).

According to Arleo, so occupied is the Italian in America with the cult of "respect" that even in politics his aggressions become a stumbling affair. When Pietro goes to Sean O'Neil for information about Sempione's assassination, he gets a lecture about the techniques of violence that contradicts the literature about Italian skill in organized crime. Sean says, "I've always loved and admired and respected the Italians. . . . But I still can't figure out why they don't stick to making love and racing sports cars instead of getting involved in things they're just no good at, like war and intrigue" (p.174). Then Sean informs Pietro of the clumsiness with which the assassination was executed, and that Natale was identified because of the flower in his button-hole. This lack of technique of the Italian in modern warfare is reiterated by Rocco, who derides Mussolini, who has been ecstatic over the Black Arrow division in Spain. Rocco says to Natale, when they meet in Italy, "The Germans' tanks blast their way through Republican lines and that one pushes in behind them the reluctant infantry of the Italian army. When the world is not laughing at us . . . it sees us with contempt. Ah, I shock you. I am a realist—economically, politically, morally, and militarily—and you and Il Duce are idealists" (p.264). In these words Arleo is demonstrating the equivocation that underlies the Italian-American's involvement with guilt. At dead center between idealism and realism, between integrity and necessity, the son can only look upon his father's mutilated face. As the recipient of the "benefits" of this primitively impressed violence, the ethnic American is forced to delve directly into the pattern of criminal activity before he can expunge his guilt and redeem himself.

The characters in *The Grand Street Collector* are all contributing factors to the main action by which the plot dramatizes the theme. Pietro is the Italian-American writer seeking to find his place, insisting on the facts of his inheritance as illumination for his interpretation of the pesent. Natale Sbagliato (Mistaken Christmas), Pietro's father, is the misunderstood immigrant, the victim of his native condition and of the societal structure of his adopted country. Guido Sempione is the catalyst, the antagonist to the bloated idealism of Fascism and to its counterpart in America, the sacrificial hero. Sean O'Neil is the contemporary observer, the link between the present minority and the economically established older groups. Assisting his role are the many minor characters like Zia Emilia, Mario, and Giorgio, like a Greek chorus commenting on events and persons. But, like Brutus, making much of honor while expediting his own enterprise, Rocco Gargatto is the "somebody" who directs the action from within the play while he clarifies its theme. When all the characters have helped Pietro gain the knowledge he has sought, Giorgio tells his nephew to go back to the country of his birth. With these words, the reader, too, is advised that the pervading protagonist is America and that the enigma of guilt is her particular problem.

Joseph Arleo's *The Grand Street Collector* is an aesthetic accomplishment and a compelling document. With artistic control, the author informs and impresses. With masterful dramatic progression, he dramatizes ethnic characteristics and personal distinctions. More than any other Italian-American writer, Arleo succeeds with the rhetoric of the Americanized Italian idiom. When he writes "The soul of God is a baby. . . ," he is translating the common Italian phrase, "*L'anima di Dio è un figliuolo,*" which is partially dialectal. At times, the translation is purely metaphorical, like the sentence, "Your speech is like a colander, thoughtfully formed but full of holes" (p.119). When he writes straight narration, Arleo has a firm grasp of the English language, which he charges with just a sufficient amount of vivid description and exposition. The well-made plot exemplifies the balanced completion of carefully mounted drama. As readers we are excited, informed, and challenged, and Joseph Arleo's Natale Sbagliato and

Pietro have become part of our social and literary history. We are convinced, also, that we have tampered with the definitions of guilt as they relate to the criminal activity in our history, in which we have engaged to achieve place.

12

CONFLICTS WITH THE LAW

Many works of fiction necessarily demonstrate the conflicts of traditional concepts with those of a new environment. Sometimes these struggles intensify to such a degree that they erupt into violence and criminal infraction of established law. An act that is classified as a crime, however, may have extenuating circumstances, such as innocence, as in the case of Frank Canizio's *A Man Against Fate*, or the inflexible restrictiveness of an inherited climate as in Vincent Siciliano's *Unless They Kill Me First*, or the stranglehold of a weakness like drug addiction in Alexander Trocchi's *Cain's Book*, or the variety of evils infecting society, as in the themes of George Cuomo's books.

Since criminal violence is a major problem in the contemporary scene, it is reasonable that current writers of fiction are using themes that reflect it. The Italian-American has had a unique burden in being made the scapegoat in the reporting of this violence by the mass media and story-tellers. Reliable studies, however, reveal that this ethnic group today is no more criminal than another. Writers of fiction, it seems, find a ready audience for these themes, especially when they use characters having an exotic aura because of their non-Anglo-Saxon names. Following this trend, even Italian-American writers have discovered that these themes and characters are more likely to insure a reading public. George Cuomo, for example, is the first Italian-American writer to have a novel chosen as a Literary Guild selection, his timely book *Among Thieves*. Of course, there are other writers who have used every conceivable plot in exaggeratedly popular and often vulgar terms. It suffices for this discussion, however, to select representative works of the more dominant themes. Separate chapters are devoted to Francis Pollini and Mario Puzo, whose themes are more extensive than their violent plots and whose treatments are more comprehensive of the American scene.

FRANK CANIZIO (1913–   )

A Man Against Fate

Frank Canizio's book, *A Man Against Fate,*[1] is a story related to Robert J. Markel, who in turn writes word for word all that Canizio tells him. An abbreviated version of the story first appeared in *The American Weekly,* but the book form includes many details omitted in the newspaper version. In this autobiographical novel, Canizio exposes his Sisyphean struggle with the police and the courts in his attempts to rectify an unjust judgment against him by which he is sentenced to a fifteen-to-thirty-year prison term for a crime he has not committed. The story emphasizes the frustration of the underprivileged who seek redemption from a hostile, systematized environment. Canizio here symbolizes the predicament of a whole segment of Italian-Americans who are victimized and exploited by powerful individuals of ruthless ambition.

Canizio describes the sordid background of his life on the streets of Brooklyn. He is only five years old when his mother dies and his father takes him to St. John's Catholic Orphanage. Not hearing from his family during a period of four years, Frank, frightened and resentful, compensates by becoming the most unmanageable boy at the orphanage. Then one day his father comes for him, but soon afterwards the older Canizio disappears with the woman who is supposed to take care of the children. Spurred by his hatred for his father, Frank takes to the streets. At fourteen, he writes, he doesn't know anything except being afraid. After he is placed in the New York Catholic Protectory, Frank's life starts a pattern of escape. When, with two friends, he finds he does not have the money to pay a taxicab driver for his fare, the policeman who comes by insists that Canizio is holding up the driver, even though the driver denies this charge. A chain of events is set in motion at the end of which Canizio is given the long prison term. For years he is a desperate escapee, but he is always caught and recommitted. Only when he gains confidence in himself through reading Emerson's *Essays* does he apply himself to study a legal plan to gain his freedom. Encouraged spiritually by a priest, and aided by skillful legal assistance, he carries his battle from the lower courts to the Supreme Court. By means of *coram nobis,* an effective writ, he is able to call attention to the flaw in the original sentence and gain his freedom.

The point of *A Man Against Fate* is that the individual, even though he may be blameless, may be both punished and overcome by circumstances if he does not rely upon his own resources to battle and vanquish hostile forces. Pitted against blind fate, we may be tempted to cry out and vaguely strike back at an unknown enemy by beating weak

1. Frank Canizio, *A Man Against Fate* (New York: Frederick Fell, Inc. 1958).

fists against an impenetrable wall. We must instead have faith in our own reason by studying the circumstances, and planning a strategy; must seek encouragement from spiritual soures, and pursue our course with the aid of professional expertise. We must not allow the ironies of immediate situations to paralyze our efforts to attain long-range objectives.

Frank Canizio keeps his own goal in mind for many years: to escape from an unjust punishment and become a free man. At the outset, he cannot quite believe what has happened to him. He has years of time, however, to shape his convictions, and he finds that he is constantly on "the outside, looking in at a group" where one man trusts only the one next to him. His frustrations compel him to curse and scream, because "nothing ever worked" for him. The theme of frustration extends into a pattern of action and reaction between the hunters and the hunted. Canizio does not allow the action to become a circle, however; he resolves to "get through." At one point of escape he almost gives up, when he contemplates that it has taken him "twenty-four lousy years to get here—right in the middle of nowhere." He starts to cry, softly at first, then louder, and then louder still, until he loses control and becomes frightened again. His fear provides the impetus for further action. When he succeeds in swimming across the Hudson River, he feels a heady moment of triumph and knows that he is "good at this game." It is not his own reliability that fails him, but that of humanity in the person of Goldie, who, for his own profit, reports Frank Canizio to the police. Something of the experience cannot be erased; while the police are looking for him, Canizio enjoys knowing that everyone is paying attention to him. This need to be noticed is even an inducement to crime. Yet, when he is caught and returned to prison, he finds it a relief to plead guilty to everything because he is so tired. Confusion overcomes him and he no longer knows what he wants. At Sing Sing he makes the significant discovery of *Emerson's Essays*, and in his battle against his fate, he now has the incentive to build his hope on the structure of self-reliance. Thematically, the story now becomes defined by the Emersonian philosophy that nothing can bring you peace but yourself, in the triumph of principle which transcends behavior. This insight clarifies for Canizio what has been an amorphous suspicion that something about his case has not been quite right. He now, with his new light, begins to see a direction; he must read more; he acts on Emerson's suggestion to go to Plato and Milton. He feels less lonely; his brain is "beginning to wake up." As his reading progresses, he feels that for the first time in his life he is applying himself to something constructive. In the prison yard he urges his friend Hop to eat because "we're going to make it." Hop is infected by his enthusiasm and gives Canizio his guitar. The instrument becomes a physical expression of the theme. Canizio plays it to amuse the others; he enjoys doing something for others, and this projection strengthens his self-reliance. The men like the music and they like Frank.

Being liked is a weapon against the old blind fate. He decides to augment this respect by studying law. When he is put into solitary without reason, he decides not to feel sorry for himself, and continues his studies. Hope breeds hope, and he learns that the real way to escape is to use the very law of the land that has imprisoned him. By the writ of *coram nobis*, he seeks the "triumph of principle" because he has never had a lawyer. Canizio's theme echoes that of numerous ethnics, in that he needs an iron will and in that once he starts it will be impossible to give up, no matter how dark things seem. He knows that he must set the wheels in motion for himself. He will not give up; he will go to the Supreme Court. His optimism feeds him. With optimism comes emphasis on the beauty of the law, "which is prosecuting you" but also "stands to protect you." He tells Father Hyland that his confidence is not only in his heart but in his head, too. When he temporarily loses his case because of a loophole, his frustrations renew his bitterness; but the human factor of intelligence saves him in the person of District Attorney Siegal. At this point he is like many Italian-Americans who have done everything possible to redeem their maligned integrity, but cannot succeed unless the disinterested instrument of the law cooperates to act. As the case proceeds again, Canizio, back in prison, feels that he really belongs in prison, the isolated place. But with his old perseverence, he sets about getting the State Supreme Court to grant a rehearing. He dreams of success. The only joy he seeks is that of working. He finally succeeds. At Christmas time, after Judge Marasco has finally granted Frank Canizio his freedom, the ex-prisoner finds the world a strange place. You cannot retreat, he reflects; you have to do something with yourself. In several scores, Canizio has repeated the same theme and he makes a reprise as he records that faith works both ways and that peace comes with the triumph of principles.

This is a discovery that two other characters have helped to expedite. Father Hyland, in giving Canizio an opportunity to extend his humanity by being of service to others, is the instrument of release from frustration and of solace for a lifetime of loneliness. The priest exposes for Canizio his latent spiritual resources that have already begun to stir in response to his reading. Then Canizio can find in Judge Marasco the sensible solution to legal equivocation. A symbol of the law of the country, Judge Marasco is to Frank Canizio a man of decency and courage. In the interaction of one character upon another, in the final court scene Canizio admits the value of Mr. Siegal's fight against him, for Siegal has exposed the truth, that the People were wrong and that Frank Canizio is innocent. Frank has grown another full dimension from Siegal's battle: he has learned to respect an antagonist who forces him to sharpen his own weapons. Respect, the ultimate mark of character, creates the new level on which he can now pursue his case.

As in the writings of a great many Italian-Americans, we find with Canizio that the achievement of respect for himself and his associates is the supreme performance. All other action leads up to this. In this novel, Frank Canizio has made the usual references to the denigrating epithets of *guinea* and *wop*. He gradually develops an immunity to this type of racial baiting, as he does with the prison guards who suspect his readings. Eventually this tolerance develops into security as, for example, he learns that his family has secured the help of an attorney whose name is John Oliva. In the end, Judge Marasca, the embodiment of his own integrity, is Frank Canizio's salvation.

The Phoenix-like evolution of this Italian-American in his confrontation with the law is effectively told in a candid and conversational style. (Canizio does not indulge in intricate paragraphs developed from outlined topic sentences.) The novel is a poignant document of human frustration bursting with anguished emotion. And Canizio has the literary talent to create valid symbols. For example, when, in the end, he reviews that he has been a prisoner for twenty-three years and now he is some kind of man, he reveals to the reader the parallel between his situation and that of his ethnic group, which for so long was held in a social prison by the larger society.

VINCENT SICILIANO (n.d.)

Unless They Kill Me First,[2] is an autobiographical document attesting that circumstances aggravated by corrupt authority may injure the underprivileged victim indefinitely, especially if this victim is already handicapped by ethnic limitations and dubious legal activities. Vincent Siciliano (The Cat) tells his story within the conventions of a well-made novel, arousing the reader's attention and sympathy. For most of his life Siciliano has seen crime as a routine happening. Because he has survived seven attempts made on his life, he has earned the alias "The Cat." His book exposes various operations of crime syndicates; he courageously gives the names of contemporary figures, especially of those who are still threatening him. This disclosure gives fascination and authenticity to a story of tense conflict between the protagonist and his competitors in a struggle for power within his particular organization. The author's hypothesis is that a man becomes a criminal as a result of an intense economic struggle, one that is controlled by the underworld hierarchy and spurred on by cooperation of the Establishment, of the men in law and government. Accord-

2. Vincent Siciliano, *Unless They Kill Me First* (New York: Hawthorn Books, Inc., 1970).

ing to Siciliano, his story is one of survival by "making a living in crime and then about working *with* the police, and to hear the way some people figure it, one's as bad as the other" (p.5).

Vincent Siciliano is an Italian-American who was born into the wealth and power of a crime syndicate. Growing up in a mansion in West End, New Jersey, he has been exposed to all the personnel and programs of the ruling hierarchy of the Eastern syndicates. His father was known as the "King of Ravenswood," but the children had an unorthodox education. Vincent, a troublesome boy at school, never completed his elementary education. He writes that "everything I learned from then on I learned by moonlight—in the streets and in the jails and police stations" (p.25). Siciliano's story is a rapid succession of criminal episodes that lead ultimately to the struggle for life itself. Beginning with the stealing of a bicycle, because the "bike was there," he nurtures the philosophy that everything in the world belongs to whoever has his hands on it. Gradually, Siciliano perfects his talents in gambling, robbery, loan-sharking, police protection, organizing brothers, and other activities, from which he graduated into the more powerful and competitive organized factions. By carrying the gun his mother used to kill his father's sweetheart, Vincent Siciliano, at the age of fourteen, has his first major confrontation with the law. After this, events follow rapidly. A crisis is reached when Vincent's father is killed, an act against "authority," as he calls it, which launches a war between him and society until he finds the murderer. In this campaign to vindicate his father, young Siciliano is defended by some of the powerful members of various syndicates, while he makes it his objective to concentrate upon the man whom he discovers to be his enemy, Bobbie Cervone. Ironically, Frank Siciliano has helped Cervone to start his career; but when Cervone becomes the most formidable power in the East, it is necessary for him, according to a given code, to liquidate Siciliano. The reader learns the ramifications of influence that a power like Cervone's exerts in labor unions, building interests, usury, and the protecting courts and political offices. He is engaged, too, in the intense progress of the deadly conflict between his power and the threat to that power in the person of Siciliano. Of the seven attempts made on Vincent Siciliano's life, one almost succeeds; the ensuing legal procedure is a mockery of our courts. Siciliano survives bullets and bombs by the most ironical coincidences, which would seem implausible if they were not based on historical fact.

The point of the book is in Siciliano's exposure of a phase of this country's dual morality. He, like individual members of most minorities, has heard all the legends of "rich people who stole in their way and the politicians." The right and the wrong of the criminal world, he believes, is the right and the wrong of the men who run the world. The police, for example, are not the enemy of the criminals; they "just had another racket." Furthermore, Siciliano writes, the motion pictures are fascinating only because they make crime appear different from other business. Actually, he says, the robber uses a gun, and the banker uses a pen. The distinction he finds between organized crime and other business is that "it" works twenty-four hours a day, and not with schedules and timetables. When he speaks of an outlaw, he defines him as a man with no law on his side; the "organization" has its own law in addition to the law it buys. Psychology contributes to the power of this law; for example, the officials of an organization sometimes decide to obliterate a member, who must be killed "for the good of the organization." Siciliano shows that the greatest dissipation of the law results from the inequities of the parole system, which inevitably cancel the power of law enforcement. Corruption is all-pervading in his description of the situation at Welfare Island, which is more bizarre than John Garfield's exposé in *Blackwell's Island.* The corruption extends to the prisons, where the convict confronts perverted sexual attacks and other crimes.

In the end, even this story of violence ends on a constructive note. Vincent Siciliano learns that Cervone, who has missed so often, has canceled his "contract" against the "Cat." Siciliano, however, is not finished. He wants to penetrate the body politic of Washington to have them learn where the source of crime lies. He believes that it is the "moral" people who make organized crime work, because it is they who support the activities that the syndicates supply. Siciliano wants to do something about the Cervones who rule with the very tactics for which others are convicted. He will keep working to make matters right.

Vincent Siciliano is the personal dramatization of the conflict between the individual and the corrupt organization of the law. As an Italian-American and heir to a way of life, he is on the scene by the accident of birth. The morality he absorbs from his environment and from the streets is a societal phenomenon. He says that he has gone to a practical school, listening to his father and his friends, instead of listening to schoolteachers about the way things "are supposed to be but never are" (p. 28). He claims that he gets into trouble with "the other side," where politicians and law-makers hold the little scraps of paper that computerize one as a criminal. Siciliano defends himself as a human being, a "very serious and very respectful" one who, like most successful organizational men, does not look for trouble. When his father is murdered, he does not panic; he declares a war. As a result, he must be prepared for the organization's strategy. Because he is a "loner," he decides not to obey all the rules. He really does not want to be a part of the organization. But, because he knows that he is already "somebody with some connection," his battle will be serious. There are other dimensions to him, his religious training, for example. He knows the Mass; while he is in prison he studies Latin because it seems a logical thing for a Catholic to do. To him religion is a part of his scenery, not a judicative mentor. He shouts to protect the Immaculate Conception, not because of the dogma, but to defend this part of his own person. This kind of irony is intensified when he admits that he has been a murderer and subsequently the Army rejects him. He must live with life's paradox; hate, for example, is the instrument with which he must save his life against Cervone's attempt on it. It is this hate which encourages him to work with the police against his enemy. It is this personal hate which, in the end, develops into a crusade for reforming the law.

In this novel, the isolation of being a criminal intensifies the fragmentation inherent in belonging to a racial minority. Vincent Siciliano's first connection with a gun arises from the combination of his father's occupation and his mother's inherited Italian code that she must avenge herself on her husband's mistress. Another dimension of Italianism is present in the father's maneuvering to free his wife of any guilt for the murder, because there is a difference in "being one of the wives and one of the girls." Vincent learns more of the strict sexual code of honor when he becomes involved with a young woman whom he must marry because honor demands that he make an "honest woman" of her. His Italianism puts him at a disadvantage with the police, however, who, he contends, are predominantly Irish and hate Italians because they have to "pick some group to hate because somebody probably hated" them before. In the organizations, ethnicity is a galvanizing factor, although the Italians are the most powerful group, he writes. Even without a plan or a leader, they stick together in an extremity. The cementing force of this ethnical organization comes from what Siciliano calls "layers and layers of people who just didn't care." The organization gets its strength from the dedication of the men who become executives after climbing the "hard way." Left to themselves as an isolated colony of society, these people desperately reach here and there for what they need; many of them are hurt; much is wasted. Furthermore, as Siciliano writes, the organization idea has convinced people that there would be enough for everyone if everyone would cooperate. That the organizations have each become a law unto itself has come about through the malfunction of the officially established law, according to Siciliano. In any event, the reader is convinced that equivocation in terms such as *crime* and *legitimate business* as applied popularly to Italian enterprise in America needs extensive exploration and an honest definition free from prejudice.

Unless They Kill Me First is a stimulating, informative, violent, and, paradoxically, encouraging book. Racing from episode to episode, Vincent Siciliano weights no detail with extra verbiage. Challenging the intestinal fortitude of the reader, he exposes the facts of a raw conflict between a man's basic need for survival and his integrity in satisfying it. The style is straight, simple, and colloquial. Sometimes the phrasing carries an ethnical tone, as in "it's-a nice to visit," which gives the story authenticity. Siciliano's most noteworthy achievement, however, is his use of irony, a structural definition of the paradox that imbues his theme. The reader is impressed by the information in the book, the momentum of the narration, and the resolution of future rehabilitation, both ethnical and ethical.

ALEXANDER TROCCHI (1925–)

There is a state in his fragmentation in which the isolated individual lies atrophied, insensible of surroundings and indifferent to direction. An entire group of racial or ethnic people within an established society may find itself in such a state of suspensed animation. A slave society may be bound by an economic system; an immigrant group may be paralyzed by inadequacy engendered by ignorance of local customs and laws; a family may be ostracized because of a suspected infraction; a person may feel forced by intolerable conditions either into hedonism or physical destruction. Today an increased number of maladjusted individuals are finding an escape in the use of drugs; in so doing, these addicts are at odds with both society and the law. They represent, in fact, the ultimate degree of alienation.

This alienation is the theme of Alexander Trocchi's *Cain's Book.*[3] Trocchi himself admits that he is aware that his book is reality and not literature, and that he has chosen his title to classify his subject as the profligate, the malcontent, and the licentious. What he writes is a "work in progress," a "kind of inventorizing."[4] In a climate of negativism, the book is valid to this discussion for its representation of the Italian-American writer's integration in a specific phase of the current scene. Trocchi's story, furthermore, deals with the effect of organized crime and its immorality, which will scarcely be amended by the simplistic solution of a prison sentence. *Cain's Book* is an unconventional novel, written like an autobiography, in which the author writes as from a drugged vision. Sharing but this flat apprehension of reality, the reader, by absorbing the formlessness of the story, absorbs the inner world of the addict's lack of focus.

The story follows the form of a journal. Joe Necchi has been writing his autobiography for an indefinite time, and has decided to create a book. The result, therefore, is a story within a story, supplying the device for narrating what has happened in the past. Joe is now a drug addict who works on a barge that plies the bays and rivers of New York. In his endless search "for another fix," he wanders in and out of the world of the other addicts around him. With his mind wander-

3. Alexander Trocchi, *Cain's Book* (New York: Grove Press, Inc., 1960; Evergreen Black Cat Edition, 1961).
4. *Ibid.* (Evergreen ed.), p. 232.

ing as freely as his barge, Joe recollects the Europe of his youth. From his inner world we learn about his family background and his friends in Glasgow, London, Paris, and Athens. The most important single fact we learn from this introspection concerns Joe's father, a misplaced Italian in Scotland, of whom the author writes, "My mother was proud and my father was an unemployed musician with the name of an Italian" (p. 85). Totally alien in the environment of Glasgow, the father lives an aimless life. Trocchi says, "He was chosen by an old selector system of tested rites. He gargled, watching his eyes in the mirror. He polished his shoes. He prepared his breakfast. He shaved. After that he staved off chaos until he had purchased the morning paper. Births, marriages, and deaths. He moved up and down the columns at the edge of himself . . . at the brink. There is no suspicion so terrible as the vague and damning awareness that one was free to choose from the beginning" (p. 87). It is this terrible suspicion that supplies the tension in the progress of the story, the comparison between what might have been and the endless floundering of the present situation. At one point Joe almost becomes involved with the fate of the artist George Falk, a relationship that encourages him at least to continue his story. He has been "on the scows" since he arrived from London and ended his affair with Moira. His situation does not change appreciably, however. He says that he was living on a moving object, with every few days a new destination, but always into the same situation. He has an abrasive contact with "the Swede," whose attitude is demonstrated in the words, "Yah! here in Amerika yo got de great mixture. All kom here. Too many wops maybe. An dere's de niggers. I'm not for to discriminate against any man'n here in Amerika dey's all equal, dass de law . . ." (p. 122). Any challenge, however, is short-lived. Even the trouble among the women touches him hazily; and he is cool in a police raid, regarding the policemen as though they were straight out of Kafka. He remembers that his father has told him that they are alike, father and son. After relating the several developments with fellow-drug users, Joe Necchi, in a circular motion, returns to the beginning of his story, whose writing is for him a tentative organization to a sea of ambiguous personal experience.

Woven into this structure is Trocchi's theme of the ambiguity of the world of escape. He asserts that the mind under heroin evades perception as it occurs ordinarily, that one is aware only of contents. He explains that things moved or they were subversive, and concludes that it was to escape from himself without going away, to retreat into abeyance, that he soon came to be on a river scow. The alternatives were prison, madhouse, or the morgue. Trocchi here demonstrates that there is no more systematic nihilism than that of the drug addict in America. The progress of the characters is subsequently an illustration of this theme. This exercise, however, demands a certain caution. The author writes, "A man will find out who he is, Cain, Abel. And then he will make the image of himself coherent in itself, but only in so far as it is prudent will he allow it to be contradictory to the external world. A man is contradicted by the external world when, for example, he is hanged" (p. 39). The protagonist of such a drama becomes a nameless man, a "Joe," who in the darkness may meet the warmth of another through "Belt, thighs, knees, chest, cheek." The author is concerned with this rejected nonentity, claiming that the citizens of America use the addict as the scapegoat for all their evils. The citizen can sit back feeling exonerated and watch evil get its deserts. In this way, everyone gets something out of the drug traffic except the user. At another point, he identifies the socially victimized "junkie" with the man who writes. He says that "the great urgency for literature was that it should for once and for all accomplish its dying, that it wasn't that writing shouldn't be written, but that a man should annihilate prescriptions of all past form in his own soul . . ." (p.53). In this way he explains the structured idea of his book. The formlessness is as he has lived, destroying his awareness. In this way the writer loses all social identity and has deliberately created what he calls "a terrible emotional smear." He has been living destructively toward the writer in him with "the critical justification in terms of the objective death of an historical tradition . . ." (p. 218). Despite this destructiveness, he is not entirely hopeless, for he has found the place that is not dead; it is "where a number of men and women for whatever reason tried to strike permanently against uncreative work" (p. 224). The man who is part of a permanent minority cannot have his differences removed by any "hymns to democracy." Trocchi writes, expanding his theme to cosmic dimensions, "All great art, and today all great artlessness, must appear extreme to the mass of men, as we know them today. It springs from the anguish of great souls. From the souls of men not formed, but deformed in factories whose inspiration is pelf" (p. 220). It is the artist's need to escape form that makes him walk alone in order to escape the "rigid structural 'soul' that threatened to crystallize in history, reducing man to historicity, the great mechanic monolith imposed by mass mind" (p. 246). The form, according to Trocchi, is anything established with the strictures of literature, law, politics, or society; and the relative alien is the artist, the fugitive, the dissenter, and the ethnic alien.

The son of an Italian, Joe Necchi recalls an Englishman who married a Negress. Trocchi writes, "For me she symbolized the vulgar triumph of all the tawdry goods, spiritual and material, which were foisted on the African in exchange for lands and freedom. *Ave Caesar! Nunc civicus romanus sum*" (p. 61). He dramatizes the parallel American exploitation of the immigrant. But America has had historic precedence in this behavior, especially in England, where Trocchi's protagonist "could feel nothing but outrage at a system in which, by virtue of my father's name and fortune, I found myself from the beginning so shockingly under-privileged" (p. 186). His father, however, has managed to retain his self-respect. For example, at the London shop, looking for hats, the older Necchi shows his worn Borsalino, unashamed of the discolored silk lining, but insisting, before his son, upon the quality of "the best." This adherence to quality is like Joe Necchi's writing according to the tenets of his own artistry. It is also a serene fragmentation into timelessness, the necessary plane for creative work. Necchi has inherited his father's aesthetics and not his mother's Scottish industry. He, therefore, like his father before him, must strike a pose and live by dissimulation. Trocchi writes that the fact of his Italian ancestry—the name of his great countryman, Macchiavelli, was used in Scotland almost solely as an opprobrious epithet—had made the mask inevitable. Now in America, Joe Necchi—like his Italian father, the unemployed musician who had fought a cold war of his own—must fight a war no less idiotic, "which has been going on since I was first informed men banded together in military groups" (p. 249). The war is not only in the military, however. In society the struggle is to obliterate the artificial boundaries of imposed forms. The drug addict is the extreme offender, but Trocchi presents him as the symbol of his own Italian-Americanism rejected from the statutes of a literary code of laws.

Cain's Book, this little voyage in the art of digression, differs from contemporary conventional novels as Joe Necchi differs from the accepted citizen. As if with jagged fragments of a broken looking-glass, Alexander Trocchi reflects a contemporary problem. The writing is the message; the formlessness is the document of the condition it records. With this deliberate external artlessness, Trocchi's prose is vigorous, sharp, and often poetic. Although the novel offers no central tension, since there is no conflict between characters or within the protagonist, it is like the blueprint of a person, in which escape is metaphorically portrayed in the appointments of drug addiction—the mats, the syringes, the needles, the powders, and the pills. The book is a valuable document, a minor, aesthetic, mobile house of art. Aesthetically formed to demonstrate its theme, the novel's spatial structure is not able to withstand the critical judgment prescribed by established standards. The artlessness of *Cain's Book* symbolizes the undefined theories of literature, writers, and cultural standards, and the interaction among all these categories.

GEORGE CUOMO (1929–)

In the tradition of Lawrence Sterne, George Cuomo writes comic novels which, under a surface of wit and calculated chaos, are serious and thoughtful comments on life, art, and human relationships. Writing often with on-the-scene reportorial authenticity, Cuomo has an accurate ear for character-revealing dialogue, often wandering into digression, and sometimes creating irony with absurd or grotesque and even tragic situations. His themes deal with the infections of society and the situations through which they influence the lives of all types of people, be they cooks, artists, athletes, or rogues.

George Cuomo, the son of John and Lillian (Vogt) Cuomo, is a third-generation American whose paternal grandparents came from Italy. He was born in the Bronx, New York City, on October 10, 1929, and attended the public schools in New York. After earning his B.A. (magna cum laude) in English from Tufts in 1952, he went on to Indiana University for an M.A. in English in 1954. He has worked as a clothing salesman, a factory hand, a newspaper man, and a university teacher. After teaching English consecutively at the Universities of Indiana, Arizona, Victoria, and Massachusetts, he became Professor of English at the California State College in Hayward, California. He and his wife (Sylvia Epstein) have three sons and two daughters. During all the time that he has been teaching he has written poems, stories, a textbook, *Becoming a Better Reader*, and four books of fiction: *Jack Be Nimble* (1963); *Bright Day, Dark Runner* (1964); *Among Thieves* (1968); and *Sing, Choirs of Angels* (Short Stories) (1969).

Jack Be Nimble; Sing, Choirs of Angels

George Cuomo's first book, *Jack Be Nimble*, is a short, humorous work about large-scale college football. The plot is well sustained with the suspense-filled momentum that distinguishes his longer novels. While the story abounds in hilarity, it is at the same a penetrating portrayal of some of the serious weaknesses in our social traditions. The pace is rapid, the dialogue incisive, and the reader reacts with solid pleasure and remembers its thoughtful message.

Sing, Choirs of Angels is a collection of thirteen short stories about American people in various situations. Each story is a compact drama, an episode that instantly brings the human being to life. The stories offer a variety of subjects, as indicated by some of the titles: "A Man's Crazy to Want to Go to Philadelphia," "The Deliverance of the Pure," "Sing, Choirs of Angels," "Sophisticated Lady," "Looking for a Job," "A Part of the Bargain," "And He Shall Have Music." With the same sharp irony that marks the short stories of John Cheever, Cuomo succeeds in dramatizing the tragicomic situations of the human condition in contemporary society. The sophistication and subtlety with which he handles the husband and wife relationship in "Oceans Apart," for example, demonstrate his craftsmanship and mastery of the rhetoric of fiction. The short stories provide distilled forms of the aesthetic structure Cuomo uses in his novels.

Bright Day, Dark Runner

Cuomo's second novel, *Bright Day, Dark Runner,*[5] is a large, fluctuating, picaresque tale of a wandering chef who confesses the loves, hatreds, conflicts, deprivations, and tragedies of his past. Mr. J. I. Le Blanche, the narrator, interweaves the account of his employment at a summer resort with memories of his unhappy childhood and tragic early manhood. Beneath the surface of comic events, Cuomo is expanding the normal definition and evaluation of art. That he chooses to portray his artist as a middle-aged cook demonstrates his idea that art may have unorthodox applications. He says that "cooking is the greatest of arts," and then goes on to define art as "muscular, supple, vigorous, tough."

Mr. LeBlanche, the protagonist, is at the center of a father-and-son story. As a cook at The Mariner, a resort hotel on Cape Cod, he is surrounded by classified personnel whom Cuomo develops into the people who recall and regenerate the incidents of the past, making these events bear upon the actions of the present. There are Mr. Wenn, the proprietor, who is emotionally unstable; Philip Gear Manchester, the ubiquitous Cerberus, who has a vengeful and misanthropic perception of what is evil, especially in the presence of a weekend guest, Schwartz, a music-composer; Geraldine Bonner, Le Blanche's companion of mature womanly comfort for this summer; and the seductively innocent Sandra Miller, whom everyone loves and who would concentrate on the muscularly flexible but spiritually ossified Lawrence Jenkins. There are many other people whose adventures touch Mr. Le Blanche's life enough to tie his narration of the present to the past. He tells of his deprived childhood with a tyrannical father whose anger stemmed from his implacable bitterness at having lost his wife at the birth of this son. When the boy frees himself to work as an apprentice to an artist, he awakens to a challenging and expanding world. Deciding to become a cook, he dedicates himself as an artist would to the most sublime vocation. In time, he marries the handicapped, lonely, but appealing Dolores, with whom he is happy and who bears him a son. Tragedy strikes with the reappearance of his father, who, broken and insane, engenders the violence that leaves Le Blanche bereft of father, wife, and son. Wandering from city to city, he spends his summers at resorts. At The Mariner, Philip, in blind pursuit of a hateful vengeance, sets in motion a tragicomedy of errors that culminates in several surprising revelations. In the end, the acute irony of Mr. J. I. LeBlanche's situation in his reversed relationship to the beleaguered Schwartz is a heightened dramatization of both the plot and theme.

5. George Cuomo, *Bright Day, Dark Runner* (Garden City, N.Y.: Doubleday & Company, Inc., 1964).

In this book, George Cuomo analyzes the meaning of life as interpreted by art, the form of art being not so important as its intensity. The aim, therefore, is that of perfecting one's capacity in any given area without paying formal respect to institutional standards and abstractions. A person's unconscious prejudice or his eating habits may be deterrents to his attainment of an aesthetic life. Such a personal interpretation allows Cuomo to have as many levels for his theme as he has characters and situations. On behalf of Mr. Le Blanche the author writes, "For in *my* kitchen any flaw was mine," and no trifles must interfere with the whole of euphoric intensity that attends when a man comes "upon whatever it is that, finite and concrete and objectified, represents not only the infinite longings of one's life, but that, in essence becomes the very manifestation of one's being" (p. 17). Mr. LeBlanche objectifies his being in his relationship with people, whom he classifies into four kinds worth saving: the rich, the poor, the brilliant, and the retarded. Cuomo's story elements include these four types. Since the poor are usually limited to their work, this work becomes the organic matter of their art form. Therefore the reader accepts Cuomo's statement that cooking is the greatest of the arts and that thus by all that is just, cooks should be equated with composers, poets, painters, musicians. Also, he contends that just as the artist's job is to hurt the world into awareness, to play the devil's advocate, so the world's role is to hurt him into art; "and if the rules are followed, neither one can beg favor" (p. 26).

Mr. Le Blanche learns more about these rules from Mr. Wafton, his first master in cooking, who teaches him that for the artist there is no peace in creation; there is only debilitation without it. This creative world conflicts, however, with the hostilities of the resentful antagonists like Phil, who tells Le Blanche that his pursuit of a victim is adventure. The adventure has specific rules, says Phil, for destroying the victim's concept of his own world: one allows him to keep his health, property, and wealth, and avoid personal revenge. The Phils, therefore, according to Cuomo, are the real perpetrators of that action which others interpret as accidental or fatalistic; for example, in his misanthropy he leads the group of older women on a bizarre tour in which he deposits them in the foyer of a bordello and then disappears. Le Blanche, however, stodgily maintains his standards, with his very disability, the malfunction of his feet, spurring his art. Cuomo's comic attitude leads to this pedestrian application of artistic discomfort, assuring the reader that "If an artist's work gets too pleasant, he degenerates into a hobbyist. It's got to hurt a bit" (p. 67). The simplistic and ironic twist is that Mr. Le Blanche injures one of Mr. Schwartz's feet, and the action destroys the peace the music composer needs for his work. From this base, however, Cuomo extends his theme of art to all levels. In the flashback to LeBlanche's childhood attempt to attend Mass against his father's wishes, the author demonstrates that the ritual of the Mass is an externalization, an art form of the spiritual dreams that the boy had previously envisioned from the pictures in his Missal. Ironically, the boy's father attends Mass for the opposite reason, because as a Catholic, he could not conceive of cursing God outside the church. His undefined hatred needed a context, an avenue of communication. That this counterplay of evil and good is essential to artists Cuomo exemplifies in the words of the masterful painter, Paladler, to whom Le Blanche is first apprenticed. He says, "I have to have evil in here somewhere; I have to have meanness and cruelty and spite" (p. 119). On the other hand, Paladler is determined to teach the boy; but this desire proves to be a vision beyond his powers of achievement. Eventually, Cuomo applies his theme to the art of writing, since Le Blanche is directly addressing the reader about the book he is writing. He concludes that it is generally difficult for any artist to show moderation in his work. Le Blanche both cooks and writes, therefore, with equal difficulty. In reference to this attitude, Cuomo mentions Hazlitt, who wrote in 1826 that Americans would probably lose their freedom because the energy necessary to acquire freedom, and the ease that follows the enjoyment of it, are almost incompatible. Phil maligns and calumniates Schwartz by spreading rumors that he is making love to Sandra Miller. Phil admits, however, that Schwartz has jarred him by being so secretive, and that something in Schwartz has the fascination of evil. Le Blanche must accept the validity of this reasoning, since it is a similar logic that convinces him that he must accept the terms of his hateful sister-in-law, Betty, who will adopt his son after Dolores is dead. He has learned that love has not been enough to save him, nor Dolores, or his father. What the boy needs is discipline, and with Betty he will be safe. Difficulty under Betty would give his son the same opportunity for fulfillment that difficulty gives the artist.

Later, Le Blanche can apply this theme in cosmic terms. He observes the hundreds of people who come to the restaurants; he studies them through the wall cutout from the kitchen, and concludes that realism and life are "the deadest thing in the world. Get enough of it and you're ready to start reading *Ivanhoe* again" (p. 330). Eventually, Cuomo writes, everything goes except "you," and that "with a little determination you can will yourself out of existence," so that "you're what you don't see, and don't think about: the guy with a dead wife, the fellow killing his father with a thick cane" (p. 354). The resolution of the logic is that the person does not matter so much as his art. Le Blanche's art may end in the "rumbling mechanics of physiology"; it may not be much, but he has perfected it, and he celebrates it. Finally, when he visits the Schwartzes at their home, Le Blanche, in an ironic reversal of the parental role, retains his identity and accepts Renee Schwartz's defense of her husband's independence in working without contracts, also that "people resent success. . . . They're fond of talking about luck and breaks. . . . That really infuriates me. . . . Why doesn't anyone ever admit that people become successes because they're willing to risk more and work harder than other people? Peter's worked hard all his life" (p. 394).

The theme of art achieved by dedicated labor Cuomo applies in many areas, specifically to ethnic locations. Sometimes his thesis is demonstrated in negative terms, as when he questions the mentality of persons who equate dishwashers with cooks. He writes, "We are, alas, the Jews and Negoes of the working class, lugging our little ghettos and yallertowns with us as we go" (p. 107). Frustration in creating an art of work may be inevitable, as it is to the butcher boy's German father who fears his son's going into the army to fight against Germany. The butcher, who has labored so fanatically all these years for his son, is torn by patriotic emotions that must remain unspoken. Cuomo, as an Italian-American, creates this "out-of-place" person as an extension of his own situation; furthermore, this concept of misplacement is embodied almost as a fetish in the character of the homosexual Phil Manchester, whom the writer finally draws with a comic face "perfectly deservedly ironically appropriate to the kind of miserable world he had without his consent been born into" (p. 276). The larger application of the ethnic's sacrifice, however, is in Le Blanche's resolution to give his son to Betty "to unload my burden upon her and lure her into carrying out the revenge for which I had neither heart nor patience" (p. 317). This is parallel to the sacrifice the ethnic parent makes in allowing his children to grow up in a hostile environment, which must also assume the responsibility toward those children. For the Italian-American, as Cuomo embodies him in the artificially named Le Blanche, growing up in this country, albeit under hostile conditions, is shown to have much to recommend it. After serving in the war, Le Blanche recalls, he felt patriotic; and it may be that that love of country is still there "under all those breadcrumb layers of professional malcontentism. Who knows, maybe when I'm about to die I'll ask for a flag-draped coffiin. Most of us in this country are more or less deathbed Americans" (p. 338).

Bright Day, Dark Runner is a big, excursive adventure story of a middle-aged workman-hero whose defections keep him on the low road of aesthetic lyricism. The comic treatment emphasizes its tragic base, both in the personal history of the protagonist and in the larger metaphor Mr. Cuomo creates of the person whose situation "out-of-place" forces him to embrace evil in the release of his higher powers. Crimes are attempted and committed, but these are undercurrents beneath the directions of the flowing of human events or the deprivations and frustrations of distorted love or blind hate. Cuomo explains everything in detail—the present, the past, and the amalgamation of both. No art and no person remains unexplained. The language, like Le Blanche, has imagination, verve, and vitality. Symbols are largely visual; the paradox of the necessity of evil in the attainment of good is seen in the protagonists's name: Judas Iscariot, the arch-concept of denial, juxtaposed to Le Blanche, the whiteness that summarizes all color, all good. The protagonist must ultimately sacrifice his identity, which encompasses an evil past, in order to face a future redeemed. Sometimes self-conscious, as when the author refers to his writing of the story, Cuomo retains a vigorous narrative pace. With the eighteenth-century novel obviously disciplining his structure, the author injects into the story his evaluations of art, prejudice, patriotism, eating habits, love, marriage, and the American way of life. Pleasant to read, the book remains in the reader's memory.

Among Thieves

In his third novel, *Among Thieves*,[6] George Cuomo presents the multiple facets of our present-day prison conditions, the prisoners, the guardians of the established law, and the pressures for reform. That Cuomo responds to a strong national pulse is supported by the fact that one issue of *The American Scholar* is devoted entirely to articles on crime and punishment.[7]

While Raskolnikov in Dostoevski's *Crime and Punishment* has rationalized his crimes with grandiose Napoleonic theories, concluding that punishment, instead of redeeming him, has been only a crushing process of senseless suffering, Mel Simmons in *Among Thieves* is, in contrast, a prisoner whose harmful acts are those of an irrational mind operating only for self-preservation. Between the poles of these two prisoners are many men enduring incarceration with various degrees of punishment for various kinds of crime. The question that society must pose for all these people is whether the treatment of crime today is either moral or effective.

Philip Paul Hallie of Wesleyan University writes that our great concern is understanding the relationships between crime and punishment, "these two evils." Summarizing the conclusions, Hallie says, "The unanimous answer of the writers in this volume is that Raskolnikov was right to raise the question and to face the destructiveness of incarceration"[8] Concluding that there is no apparent connection between penal suffering and resocialization, and referring to the reports of Glaser and Zeisel, the editor shows that the custodial function of the prisons works against making a man a creative individual in society. The study, however, is concerned also with the victims of rapists, pickpockets, muggers, and the more violent crimes, avoiding

6. George Cuomo, *Among Thieves* (Garden City, N. Y.: Doubleday & Company, Inc., 1968).

7. *The American Scholar* 40, no. 4 (Autumn, 1971).

8. Philip Paul Hallie, "Raskolnikov, the Scholar, and Fresh Air," *The American Scholar* 40, no. 4: 581.

concentration of interest on prisoners alone and the falling into what George Bernard Shaw called the "Devil's sentimentality," the smug insensitivity of those who insist on believing that *"tout comprendre, c'est tout pardonner."* As a result, this comprehensive study comes to the fair conclusion that "illegal harm (crime) is, after all, the main justification for legal harm (punishment), and that it is as dangerous to separate them forever as it is to lie to ourselves about their relationship with each other" (p.582). Violence, therefore, hurts all victims equally. Because we dare not assume that sheer suffering will free us all from harm, we must undertake prison reform. Already some of our states are responding to this need. A federal judge in Virginia has banned the cruel and inhumane treatment of inmates in the prison of that state; in Pennsylvania such treatment has been banned through promulgation of State Attorney General J. Shane Creamer's "Bill of Rights" for prisoners.

It was inevitable that Italian-American novelists should become largely concerned with crime and punishment as subjects for their themes and plots. This interest we have seen demonstrated as inherent in the social conditions forced upon ethnic groups in the process of American assimilation. As microbiologist René Dubois has pointed out, violence and conflict need not be analogous in all respects to the nurture-versus-nature controversy. Actually, he claims, there is no genetic coding that inevitably results in aggressiveness, but only a set of genetic attributes for self-defense that may express themselves as aggressiveness under particular sets of conditions. Therefore, certain men act as killers under certain conditions because the social environment distorts the instinctive responses essential for self-defense. Furthermore, people develop hostile attitudes toward strangers, since the unknown may be a threat. Dubois writes: "The concept of foreigner in human life—along with the undertones of mistrust and fear associated with the word in all languages—may well have its biological origin in the hostile reaction of animals to strangers of their own kind moving into their territory."[9]

George Cuomo writes at length in *Among Thieves* to include as many people and dramatic props as possible; the chief, the victimized family, the prostitute, the parole officer, the warden, the police, the guards, the newsmen, the politicians, the theoretican, the television commentator, the insurrectionist, the innocent bystander, the stolen cars, the adultery, the rifled cashbox, the murder, the guns, the cells, the hobby shops, and the detailed riot in the prison. Cuomo shows his prison story from the point of view of the prisoners, the institutionalists, and the observers. The story is activated by criminals, victims, police, and the public; the events are reportorially accurate, and their progress

9. René Dubois, "The Despairing Optimist," *The American Scholar* 40, no. 4: 565.

gives the reader a meaningful, unforgettable, and thought-provoking experience.

Cuomo introduces Mel Simmons as an appealing fumbler, sophomorically dreaming of some undefined adventure, lazily watching television dramas, cheerfully playing with his son, indifferently looking for something to eat, unenthusiastically responding to his duties as husband and father. Having learned how much easier it is to steal money than to earn it, he is a petty thief on parole, a congenial malcontent who is willing to be supported by a conscientious wife. In his late twenties, he has no notion of high ideals; he is willing to steal cars in order to exercise his sexual proclivities in the back seat with available females. When his wife, Peggy, gets him a laundry-sorting job, he likes neither the work nor the idea of working. Hoping to get a better car, he stays with his work, but spends most of what he earns on the available Reena and Dolin. Eventually he negotiates with a friend, Margolis, to carry out a robbery, a large warehouse raid.

Meanwhile, John Mancino, a local broadcaster bored with his noonday interview program and its light-chatter vein, seeks a larger and more serious audience. Tall, handsome, and attractive, Mancino is adulated by women; but he is realistic and intelligent, hoping to improve his professional image as a serious person. He therefore plans a three-way survey of crime, to present to the public the prisoner's comments, the warden's explanations, and the politicians' strategies. Mel speaks for the prisoners in an oddly mixed narration of fancy, fact, some detail, and some nonsense. "Flash" Fleishman, a former college professor who is now assistant warden for treatment, rehabilitation, and education at the state penitentiary, speaks for the program he is instituting for the prisoners. Mancino himself interviews the politicians, including Kale, who is hoping to become the District Attorney. The publicity that Mel garners from his television appearance makes him too vulnerable a risk for Margolis to use as partner. Resentful of his rejection, Mel decides to go on his own. He maneuvers his way into a gas station, robs the cash register, and, on his way back to his car, commits murder. A few hours later, the police stop him, arresting him for car theft. He is sentenced to two to five years to the prison where Chief Warden Griffing is an efficient, traditionally inflexible tyrant. Under him, Wardens Fleishman and Dowler are competing for his approval, confidence, and support for their respective ideas. All these events take place against the background of a political campaign for the office of State Attorney General. Everyone is brought together in the fearful and violent prison riot that dominates the second half of the book.

In portraying his characters in action, Cuomo points out that nearly everyone is misinformed about crime. He uses this book to inform the reader, showing that often the officials do not know how to do the right thing and that the criminals do not always do wrong. People like Kale, who is running for public office, make simplistic statements like "I'd like to see you work in something on this whole business of parole and rehabilitation."[10] But when Johnny Mancino approaches Mel in the attempt to do something, Mel answers, "There's a catch in here somewheres" (p. 65). Johnny, from his vantage point in broadcasting, understands both Kale and Mel, knowing that Kale will probably resent that Johnny is learning that "the whole system's rotten—I've been doing some research . . ." (p.69). When he broadcasts over K-SUN, Johnny reports that an increasingly large number of men and women from all economic and social levels, from all cultural and ethnic backgrounds are rejecting accepted values and are turning instead to crime and lawlessness. The ethnics, therefore, are using crime as a means of breaking down the established values. In the prison, where all levels of society seem to be brought toegether, the worst punishment is loss of individual freedom. But Mel tells Johnny that most men are in prison because of bad luck. Mel, who is not an "ethnic" defined as a minority, feels that he is motivated only by the need for money. When Johnny asks him why men commit crimes, Mel answers that he doesn't know. As an inmate he is bored by a letter, for example, from a woman who assures him that his being in prison is not his fault, but everybody else's. But Johnny persists in helping Mel, even though the police warn him that Frank Kale is not being helped by defending ex-convicts. When he interviews Fleishman, the posturing theoretician, he refers to the National Commission on Law Observation which has reported that the prisons have not succeeded in reeducating or reforming prisoners to rejoin the community with no desire to commit further crimes. Fleishman informs him that prisons deal with inmates who are dedicated failures to whom society offers the choice between "different kinds of unsuccess." The erstwhile professor speaks for the prisoners, saying, "We discipline them rigidly, yet hope to teach them self-reliance. We regiment them and depersonalize them, and yet hope to make them respected individuals. We suppress initiative and independence, yet must teach them initiative and independence . . ." (p.163). There is a relationship, Fleishman thinks, between this destructive method and the reasons for which the men are incarcerated. He believes that the surest way to produce a criminal is to expose him mercilessly to all the rewards our society can offer—cars, homes, clothes, prestige, power, leisure—and then deprive him of any legitimate means of attaining them. When this deprivation translates into criminal action, like the robbery Fleishman has witnessed at the drugstore, it is a paralyzing revelation, the realization that exposes the inadequacy of mere theory. Cuomo reveals through Fleishman the inadequacy of good intentions and even of research, if they are isolated from experience through participation.

10. George Cuomo, *Among Thieves*, p. 56.

Some of this experience has culminated in the formulation of the fifty-six rules listed in Cuomo's chapter 10, which must apply to all kinds of inmates and their possible behavior. To men like Mel, life in prison becomes preferable to life "outside," since he is protected by these rules. When he thinks of freedom outside, he is frightened. It is exactly this satisfaction with submission that Flash wants to battle. Cuomo writes, "He wanted to remove all custodial officers from the shops, to reduce as much as possible the atmosphere of repression, of imprisonment, from those areas that were essentially educational and rehabilitative in nature" (p.253). Flash reflects again and again, that in college radicalism is easy; but here just doing the job is a struggle. Flash then remembers DeVoto's line that we do not need Freud to tell us that our life is dream-bound, deathward and in the dark. He thinks about his being a Jew and that every Jew has a right to be a gentile because "a man has a right once in a while to be free of all that persecution, those long bloody centuries, to join the winning team for a change" (p.281). With these words and through the extreme example of the story of these prisoners, Cuomo is appealing to the reader to try to understand the member of a minority. Johnny Mancino, of the Italian-American minority, suddenly identifies with the prisoners, and he thinks he may never get out again. Cuomo writes, "the criminal in us all, the deep-seated conviction of guilt. They've found me out at last!" (p.339). It is Mancino, therefore, who becomes the author's spokesman, although the metaphysical abstractions are embodied in the airily contemptuous Flash, who thinks that it is not in the ranks of Security that you find sentimentalists, would-be poets, do-gooders, intellectuals, fragile souls or stutterers. You find that sort in treatment. He knows, however, that behind the insurrection is the racial hatred that the inmates have for the Negro Walker. He knows also that Kale does not want to hear any reference to this. Flash, for all his contempt, says nothing, since he has the economic burden of a wife and five children. He is not even so straightforward as the inmate Orninski, who is the leader of the insurrection. He studies the texts on prisons and prison reforms; he talks like a prophet; he desires acknowledgment, but often he does not know what is going on around him. It is Orninski, who, as a leader of a riot, embodies the savior complex, believing "the other cons they'll say that guy there that's dead now and all covered with his own blood, at least he died doing some good for guys just like him" (p.439). Only when the riot is over does Flash, having symbolically lost his glasses, feel that he is a blind man among thieves. As Bostick comments that the dead Dietz was a good man, Flash thinks: "Maybe someone will say the same of a certain blind man of the desert who fell among thieves on his way to Jerusalem. But who?" (p.461). With these words, George Cuomo lifts his theme to the plane of poetry. With the symbol of the blind man firmly in his grasp, the author intensifies it with the final ironic twist that the truth of the events in the riot will be distorted and given to Johnny Mancino to broadcast so that Kale may continue his civil rights crusade and Flash may get his minimum security unit. Every man has some evil, Cuomo is saying, and all walk together, white, black or whatever, as they do at the end of his story.

The themes of this book are stated in ethnic terms, but only minor details structure the Italian-American treatments in the stories; for example, Mel frequents Rigoletto's and no racial point is made about the place. The author portrays Mel's language in his own terms, delineating through his speech the limitations of the character, and contrasting him to what might have been a racial reference of another type. All racial hatred is exemplified by attitudes toward the Negro, since currently the Black revolution supersedes other causes. Mel says of himself, "When he was a kid somebody should've just done the job with a little black paint, once and for all" (p.50). Cuomo reverses old roles in this book. He has Flash describe his neighborhood, saying, "It's crawling with foreigners—niggers, kikes, wops, poles, chinks, the whole show, the rainbow, from *A* to Z. And it's great, Padre, it's the American way. I don't want my kids growing up prejudiced" (p.193). It is the more emphasized that the Italian-American's situation has been one of a repressed minority that has had to find some relief, that has been classified as, and sometimes proved to be criminal. *Among Thieves* gives a dramatized portrait of this condition in different terms. Pursuing his theme further, Cuomo has Johnny Mancino enter the hobby room where Mel and the psychosomatically ill Orninski are, and Orninski flicks the flashlight on Johnny's face. Cuomo writes for all Italian-Americans as he says "He didn't look scared—actually he was standing very calm, very steady, with his mouth closed tight and breathing very quiet—but the way his face looked you got the impression that he figures he could just as easy get shot dead right this minute as anything else he could think of" (p.337).

Among Thieves is a massive portrait of strong, dark colors. Against the dark background of mindless murder, Mel Simmons is a wavering blur of blues and greens, never quite clearly focused. Cuomo's masterful skill in narrating with the rhetoric of his character renders the style so real and immediate that scenes are both photographic and charged with soundwaves, and the reader participates. The plot is presented in every detail with great skill, Cuomo managing to shock the reader into the awareness that he believes is needed for prison reform. The book is evenly balanced, well sustained, and compelling. Cuomo tells an exciting story, and impresses on the reader that no one walks alone in crime unless he is blind.

13

FRANCIS POLLINI (1930-)

One of the most representative Italian-American writers to emerge during the past decade is Francis Pollini. An arch-experimenter with style and a literary artist, he creates sub-heroes who personify a dichotomy in involvement: every individual is a split personality, a hyphenated alien; and American society is an aggregate of imperfect fragments whose smoothness is only on the surface.

Forcing the language into harsh disharmonies, Pollini pulls at the very roots of rhetoric to expose the American conscience. He presents as his flawed tragic hero a double-focused image of disillusioned idealism. His electric-shock style intensifies both the language and the progression of episodes in his books, and it is becoming more acceptable than it was at first, for it reflects the same intensity that is now shaking all the other arts, visual and performing. In the need to underscore his message of truth, the artist seeks to overwhelm the senses. For him the Vietnam experience has crystallized a larger national situation, which he dramatizes progressively in each successive book.

Pollini takes a personal approach to his materials; the reader senses that many of the events are associated with the author's own experiences. Born in 1930 in the small coal-mining town of West Wyoming, Pennsylvania, Francis Pollini is the son of Sam and Assunta (Ciani) Pollini. After earning his B.A. in 1951 from Pennsylvania State University, he served in the United States Air Force from 1952 to 1957. Presently he is writing in London, where he lives with his wife (Gloria Ann Swann) and their two daughters. In addition to a volume of three plays, he has written five novels: *Night* (1961); *Glover* (1965); *Excursion* (1965) *The Crown* (1967); and *Pretty Maids All in a Row* (1968).

Pollini is realistic, and he believes that a writer should be a serious artist and dedicated worker; if a writer is not serious he should call himself, quite frankly, an entertainer. Pollini's work holds rampant sex and violence. When he makes use of aesthetic he does it to intensify the panic that mounts steadily in the development of his themes.

His quest is for reason. His novels explore the dilemma of the person who is seeking a beautiful world, but whose heart and anatomy have been atrophied by crime. Each of his protagonists, name him Marty, Glover, Stanley, or Tiger, is in turn an image of the country that has been ideal in its dream, but has become corrupted by war. In simple terms, Pollini's overall tragic hero is the American Dream.

It would be difficult to find a more fitting voice for our total anguish. Midway between racial types, a "white Southern European ethnic," a son of the working class, an immigrant's child educated to a high level, a soldier baptized in the fire of the nation's military effort, Francis Pollini is conditioned by place and training to probe our psychic problems. Although the characters he creates are strident symbols, he manages to illuminate even the stereotypes with the flash and crackle of his prose, which highlight the stygian relationship of people to one another. He occasionally reverts to melodrama as he writes such phrases as "her face was before him" and "he was falling into a dark tunnel," but these utterances heighten the dramatic tension. The reader often identifies himself in the action Pollini depicts, whether it be with the victim of brain-washing in Korea, of an exhausted aesthete, the ribald amorality of the American male abroad, the seemingly heroic façade that conceals a schizophrenic educator, or the homicidal instinct of a celebrated boxing champion.

Night

The first of Francis Pollini's novels, *Night*,[1] is a plunging initiation for the reader into a "style that does," which sets the pace for all his later works. The book ranks with Pietro DiDonato's *Christ in Concrete*, Rocco Fumento's *Tree of Dark Reflection*, Mario Puzo's *The Dark Arena*, and—outside the Italian-American category—Ernest Hemingway's *A Farewell to Arms*. As a major contribution to American fiction, *Night*, while reflecting an ethnic past, cuts through to the essence of the average American's dilemma. This book is Pollini's first outburst, and he seems almost to be screaming with the intensity of an indignation that is personal and visceral. In consequence, his prose is a mélange of poetics, dramatics, reflections, tense narrations, and dialogue that is as obscene as war itself.

This novel is about the brainwashing of American prisoners of war, exposing the conflict in Korea as *A Farewell to Arms* depicted World War I. The central event, Marty Landi's nightmarish resistance to his inquisitor, is a parallel to his recollection of his family's resistance to a hostile environment. Unlike Hemingway's Frederick Henry, who was one of those who retreated from Caporetto, symbolic of America's disillusionment in the objective of that other war, Marty, although he

1. Francis Pollini, *Night* (New York: G. P. Putnam's Sons, 1961).

holds out, must eventually make a supreme sacrifice in order to reconcile his place in the moral order. In making this effort, he accounts, by means of monologues in flashbacks, for his behavior as a response to his mother's and father's broken experiences. This fatalistic control by his conditioning defines him as a contemporary Greek hero.

The driving force of Marty's past is that he has been victimized by his childhood surroundings. Now, as Ching, the subtle inquisitor, probes into Marty's former life, he touches as though with an exquisite electrical instrument the traumatic wounds the boy has suffered for his mother. The patient and cunning Oriental exposes a view of the room in Trent Street where Marty's mother had felt enslaved and degraded, away from the better conditions she had left in Italy, the country and the village where she had known both love and respect. Ching's sing-song chanting is confused in Marty's mind with his mother's past moaning for her loved ones; Marty recalls his mother's mental collapse under her despair, an active condition that had kept him constantly and violently ill with uncontrollable spasms. In time, his mother's agony had transmitted its bitterness to him (as he recalls in a reverie induced in another session with Ching). He remembers that, when he was playing with his companions "in front of Blake's house," the irate old man had ordered him to "Get the hell up your end of the road, Dago." Now, under Ching's relentless pressure, Marty's thoughts ramble, "Great-great-great-grand-cousin emptied slop pails on the Mayflower. . . . Good old Ching. Damn good to me" (p.256). As his wary oppressor grinds on in another session later, Marty loses all sense of time, feeling "Ching here in hell with me," and his mind slips back to his childhood paroxysms of fear. He is screaming at the sight of his father in the coffin, the body having been smashed to a pulp in the mine. In the brain-controlled session, Marty yells, "Mamma! Babbo! No! Please! Not me!" And Ching lulls with him "they're all right . . . ," and then soothes him with "and you know who did it. . . ." Ching keeps pushing to the back of Marty's mind to the moment of the mother's death, and Marty seeks refuge in her plight. In his induced reverie he recalls that she had learned only a few English words and that her past "true" land had sustained her. The new country, the new life, had been a horrible nightmare, and her death had taken a vital part of him with her. Ching now takes him to that gulf of death into which he is falling, pointing out to Marty that being a soldier for America has not changed his role.

Acceptance, therefore, is the instrument of seduction that Ching uses to control the prisoner's subconscious reaction. The progress of this masterful probing is Francis Pollini's story, which he builds around the episode involving a group of American prisoners taken by the Chinese during the Korean War. Every minor incident develops the progress of subjugation of the prisoners to the brainwashing, to which a number of them capitulate. Those who succumb join the

"Progressives"; those who resist are classified as "Reactionaries" and are put into a separate compound where they are starved or frozen to death. Phillips, the leader of the "Reactionaires," carries out night raids on the huts of the "Progressives." At first he tries to talk to the "wized-up" men; then he makes physical attacks upon them. Finally, he strangles seven of them in a raid, an action that brings severe reprisals. Intermittently with these incidents are presented the interviews in which Ching attempts to break down Marty Landi, who resists both Phillips's violence and the seductive arguments of the Chinese interrogator. Pollini's hero is an intracultural ethnic, a self-respecting patriot who believes he can preserve both his honor and his life.

The point of *Night* is the demonstration of the testing of the American as the twentieth-century apex of success. Pollini creates the Italian-American, Marty Landi, in this role, because Marty as an individual has survived his test in an Anglo-Saxon society at home. In the Korean camp the situation is enlarged. As Marty is fed only enough food to sustain the amount of life needed to feel the torture that might force him to make a false confession, his mind drifts in a vast ocean as he recalls his father's keeping his mouth shut against his mother's tirades. The present assaults, therefore, are familiar, and he controls his vulnerability to all kinds of trickery, treachery, and seductions. When the assault is compounded by the nonresisting men in the outfit, his own fear of himself allows them to punch him to unconsciousness. The autocratic "lessons" of brainwashing win most of the men, who become "wized up" to America, its values, its capitalistic system, and its government. Marty finds it easy to despise the traitors, but his quiet struggle with Ching is a war of nerves. Pollini emphasizes the isolation of this loyalty, especially with scenes of men who are dying of the cold. The river, which might be a point of communication, is frozen. The men who have resisted their tormentors are freezing to death, while the "Progressives" are warm and well fed. When the "Reactionaries" submit to shock treatment, Pollini is ironically using America's technology in the Chinese attempt to "get through to them." The theme is intensified in the monologue in which Marty recites a litany about the NOW, a stream let loose by electrons. He remembers the "curse of the whole spinning" back to a source that had been still and unbearable. His internal tension is increased when Ching, offering Marty warm food, suggests that he may stay when "it is all over," to which suggestion Marty responds only with silence. But Pollini stretches this silence in Phillips's monologue with God, the dramatic point at which the theme transcends all the characters and becomes heighened in its tragedy. Phillips is the catalyst of the action, the inevitable struggle between the factions; and so he plans his raids.

The theme is expanded and personalized in Ching's explanation to Marty of what he thinks of America—an ignorant mass led by criminal leaders and educators under a cannibalistic economic system. As Ching expounds what he believes to be the "enlightened philosophy of China," Marty goes to sleep. Pollini achieves ironic levels in his portrayal of Willie Coughlin, the stereotyped, ignorant Mississippian who, while despising Negroes, has become a willing "Progressive," anxious to take the slain Slater's place as leader. Still another level of the theme is that of mysticism, in Brandon, who dreams that he is caught on a log that continues to spin until he is thrown into the water to drown. But it is the Negro Johnson who dramatizes the microscopic model of the worldwide conflict as he resolves to study the brainwashing "lessons" carefully under the instruction of the "wized-up" Coughlin, who knows that Johnson does not have the mentality to remember anything. Dramatically, in testing the power of a belief in America, Pollini climaxes his story with the completion of what Hemingway had developed only to the point of expectation—when Robert Jordan was waiting for the Fascists to decapitate him in *For Whom the Bell Tolls.* Finally, in contrast to Hemingway and Frederick Henry's resigned walk into the rain in *A Farewell to Arms,* Pollini deliberately sacrifices Marty Landi to the sin-cleansing ocean, where "there is a silence where no sound may be," an act of retribution purposely chosen, having made its peace with the mind that survived human brutality.

Pollini intensifies his themes poetically in the use of symbols. Sleep is a metaphor for isolation; it is also a cue to dream sequences with realistic interpretations. As Paulie awakens from a dream, he asks, "Where's the ice cream?" Pollini uses this question as a refrain, using the ice cream as a symbol of the American's constant pursuit of the luxurious, resenting that in the frozen hut the only reward is the cold. The freezing point is a symbol of the lack of human contact. It is also a symbol of the isolation of the men from the loyalty they once had for their causes. As the defecting men huddle around the stove, plotting against the loyal ones who wish to organize the raid, they dramatize the universal urge of people who fight to survival, above dying for an abstraction. A single character is sometimes more of a symbol than he is a man, as is Phillips, a composite of all the regulations that make up the effective officer and patriot who never loses sight of his objective. On the other hand, there is a recognizable Quisling, the natural enemy of the patriot. The cowardly Robert symbolizes the selfishness of all the men who have become "Progressives." But the overall symbol is what most pervades the novel—the dramatic struggle between Marty and Chiang, the confrontation of opposing ideologies.

The novel is factual and informative. Pollini has heightened the episodes with a style that echoes the action. He depicts Marty Landi's struggle from within Marty's mind; he creates some of the tension through the interrogator Ching, the human embodiment of a dissentient relationship. Pollini convinces us of the terror and threat of men like Ching, who is American-educated, intelligent, sensitive, and cogent, with the voice of Marxist criticism of American civilization. Ching is the ultimate refinement in the application of torture, since, as he constantly reiterates, the Chinese are not "the savages" that the Germans are. Other characters in the book demonstrate what the author calls the "spinelessness" of some Americans, especially under the stress of war and as they are crushingly oppressed by the superior cunning of the Chinese. As a novel, the book contains shocking material, but its purpose is important. The setting in Korea has authenticity and power, and the theatrics are sustained not only by the young idealistic Marty, but by the Bunyanesque Phillips. The writing is an aesthetic triumph in the contemporary style, which is closely related to the gaudy brush works of today's artists on canvas and to the abrasive clashings of today's composers of strident, cacophonous music. The interviews between Ching and Marty remind the reader of the "framed" scenes of a Pinter play. The book is disturbing and thought-provoking, and persuades the reader of the need to know the conditions that create dilemmas for the national conscience, local conditions that extend to the far-flung arenas of men in bloody conflicts. Pollini has recorded an agonizing challenge to the abuses of power; he has written a book that documents the process of the desecration of the mind, the desolate night of a world at war.

Glover

With his second novel, *Glover,*[2] Francis Pollini salvages the realities for which Marty Landi sacrificed himself and creates the prototype that develops through his ensuing stories. *Glover* is a long narration in the present tense, often in the present progressive tense, of what may be accepted as the official United States general issue of the military man, the "sackartist," made and in the making. It is a satirical novel in the category of the works of James Purdy, filtering through the guttural musings of a sub-rational mind, a biting attack on the smugness of those who disdain white, middle-class, ethnic America.

In this story Joe Glover, the son of a car-dealer, is an Airman Second Class, a former football star who is stationed as a military policeman at an American base near London. Mobilized primarily through lust, he is a one-man sexorama, a colossus of unsuspected eroticism in the biped brute. He services mechanically all submissive women, single or married, to whom he refers as "bloke stuff." Busy starring in an Air Force recruiting film, and busier with his nightly prowling, Glover falls asleep in the classes of anti-Communist indoctrination, and during the lectures on weapons, he dreams of women who carry enormous missiles. He crushes groups of Englishmen in taverns in scenes that

2. Francis Pollini, *Glover* (New York: G. P. Putnam's Sons, 1965).

alternate with nightlong sex relations with whomever is available. The nearest he comes to a really human relationship is with Pristine, the intellectual, whom Pollini ironically counterpoints to Glover in character. Glover tests his full capacity, however, with the married Judith, who works at the Service Club, and succeeds in getting her pregnant. Judith leaves her husband, a dull bus driver, and rents a room near the base, expecting to marry Glover. In his determination to abort her through sexual savagery, he hurts her and she bites his hand. Attempting to stifle her screams, he suffocates her. With no show of emotion, he goes on his way. Intermittently with his affair with Judith, Glover has been visiting the apartment of his adjutant, Lieutenant Patton, an effete, intellectual homosexual who entertains a literary coterie. One of this group is the attractive Pristine, a celebrated literary critic, who is fascinated by the physical primitiveness of the sexual Glover. She finds him an exciting oasis in the desert of her anemic life with her own husband, Tony.

When Glover is brought to trial for murdering Judith, all his friends and the members of his outfit attest to his exemplary character. Pollini performs a master stroke of irony in the comic exposure of the righteousness with which everyone defends the image of this ideal American airman who has been chosen as the representative star in an Air Force recruiting movie. Lieutenant Patton provides both an alibi and an expert advocate for Glover's defense. Between them, they fabricate a story that Glover was bitten by a lunatic prowling the front of Lieutenant Patton's apartment and claiming that he was a tiger. Pollini satirizes both English justice and the morality of the American Air Force Command, which defends Glover with fabrications. The colonel has food brought to Glover's cell; Chaplain Fink prays for him; Glover muses with his own navel in staccato "self-interrogation," the closest he can come to introspection. Pollini punctuates the pervading irony of the story in the end, with the triumph of Glover, who is a parody of the modern American ideal, a demon of savage impulses under the façade of banal heroics. Glover is our contemporary sanctimoniousness, a maniac of instincts, who gleefully spouts: "Ha, Ha. Oh, man. There he goes, *The Saint* Glover. Ha Ha. Yo. *Saint Glover.* Oh, man. Wo" (p.399).

In this book Pollini forges a warning and forecasts an apocalypse. He dramatizes several contemporary attitudes toward war, and the tensions created by the people who embody these attitudes. The Colonel states that who controls aerospace commands the world, and who commands the world controls all its nuclear weapons. In counterpoint to the imminent danger, Pollini places the base instincts of the oversexed Glover and the preciosity of the effete Lieutenant Patton. Pollini has given Glover a veiled Italian-American background in the portrayal of his family relationships as they are exposed in his letters from the adoring, scholarly sister, the adulating mother, the hard-working, loyal father, and the concerted effort of all of them to support him with blind belief. Although all this constructive support for him may succeed in protecting the image of the hero as the world around him sees him, one must be wary of Glover's future. All the characters in the book rally to Glover's side, but the fact remains that he is a murderer, and a savage one. For Glover's name, Pollini has chosen "Joe," the universal name for the American military man, and for surnames plays on "glove" for his sledgehammer fists and "lover" for his erotic impulses. In our national character we may appear exemplary and saintly, but in our warring role, we are revealed as self-interested, murderous, and diabolical. Containing this dichotomy, we, like Joe Glover, are headed for self-destruction.

Pollini expands his theme in various ways. In a revealing monologue, Lieutenant Patton analyzes the dramatics of his fellow-Americans, so "immaculately conceived," "so well-scrubbed, cleaned, polished." As human beings, we wallow in respectability. Pollini says that we exist in a brothel-culture, where the crass, inane masses are like sheep being led to slaughter. Patton muses that on the Base there is sufficient destructive power to efface Europe, and Glover is its guard. Glover as protagonist is clearly here, as Patton calls him, the "superb specimen," the archetype of the whole human species; Glover who would have been absolutely superb in a cave. In a subsequent monologue, while waiting in his office, Patton reflects that, considering our nature, it is amazing what we have accomplished. Our bank accounts swell for future survival, for which we engage in the dullest professions and the most meaningless vocations. People with artistic natures suffer, for they, too, have weaknesses that need money, for example, the desire for comfort and the passion for offspring. The artist's relation to Pollini's theme is further clarified by Pristine, who says that the "great thing" is for an artist to get lost in his art. Even Glover exemplifies this belief, because he is an artist in lust.

When Patton is alone, he thinks about Glover as the representation of mankind's division. All men are the same, he thinks, and in the two great blocs of the world, the two most grossly materialistic societies are poised, one masquerading behind the pious mask of democracy, freedom, and Christianity, the other doing a jig behind the façade of collective honesty, innocence, and humanity. Man, therefore, has reached a crisis by himself; and there is no answer to his questions. Since all of us are dismal, cruel, brutal, pretentious, loved, loving, hated, hating, deceived, deceiving, all of us are innocent; and so Glover is innocent. Conclusively, justice must be twisted to defend the transgressor, as Wykeham-Tiennes does so ably, since society is the greater brute.

With this moral frame, Pollini shows his master craftsmanship in the ironic portrayal of the criminal Glover as defendant at the trial as he is called "the normal, young American in uniform, dedicated and trustworthy, loyal to duty." However, after all this, Pollini does create a solution to the apparently inevitable horror. Pristine Hope-More offers the narrow path of salvation in her preference for literature with a "moral fiber." Obviously speaking for Pollini, she asserts that literature must have hope in it and should show "humanity in its finer hours," and must not abandon that humanity. Literature must see the good in man; it must not dwell only on corruption and despair, and it must be positive in tone. This constructive theme is finally dramatized as Glover and Lieutenant Patton stand before the giant ape's cage in Regents' Park Zoo. Patton, discussing an author's work, cries out that in the book there comes that moment of clarity, real life, when man becomes aware of his predicament, the brute existing along with blind beauty.

Pollini thus develops his themes in the growth of his characters. Glover's muddled mind is that of mankind. His detailed litanies of sex and the jingoism of his verbal refrains are like societies' platitudes. As he reveals himself in his letters home, he is the product of the successful middle-class America that believes its progeny should not suffer as the previous generation had. Glover's brutal attitude toward women as sex objects "on the hoof" is an extreme of irresponsibility as a human being. Pollini has made him bigger than life, even if it is a brute life. Glover cannot understand Harrington's excitement over sunsets. He is cruel to Forney; he has the instincts of a ram with a herd of females, keeping an inventory of their sexual rating (prototype of Tiger McDrew in *Pretty Maids in a Row).* His obsessions are purely physical and he stands for long periods of time before the mirror preening like a champion, gloating, "Who else around's handsome like you, Champ? The *physique,* boy" (prototype of Stanley in *The Crown).* The only reflections in his mind are of the football plays of the past, and the sound of crowds and cheerleaders. He thinks of servicing whole groups of women, one by one, and Pollini makes him the embodiment of brutal collective action versus the sensitive individual. He is crude to the point of violence, even when he tries to make a purchase at the bakery shop. Like the society he symbolizes, he has an exceedingly handsome face, but his speech is as blunt as fists. While others talk about books, he thinks of female bodies. Glover has no reaction at all when he hears that children have been killed in a bus accident. Likewise, he is indifferent to the letter he receives from the faithful Mary at home; he doesn't even finish reading it. Like a predatory animal, he has a voracious appetite; like a brute, he is insensitive to anyone's feelings. At a bar, an Englishman asks him, "Hasn't anyone ever taught you how to behave yourself?" When Judith tells him of her tragic marriage, he refuses to listen to her troubles. He will not use his mind at all. Even as he pulls along with the Bay Chief troops, Glover is cursing, stumbling, letting himself be bumped and carried along by the movement. Forney tells him that four men have died in a Volkswagen, and Glover sits in silence. When his mailbox gets stuck, he pounds with a fury that might break the whole post office. His negative mental attitude baits Fineline in Education, but his lack of articulation is interpreted only as his being quiet. He is derisive of Johnston from the USI office, and he is contemptuous of the education courses. His callous attitude reaches a high peak when he decides to kill Judith's unborn child. When he suffocates her, it is a mechanical, perfunctory act, monstrous in its detachment. That he practices boxing in his shower the next morning and plans for his next conquest is an appalling symbol of a nation absorbed with intermittent lust and violence. When he hears the footsteps of the police approaching, he reacts only physically in that he feels cold. The grotesque nature of his invulnerability is ironically reflected in Harrington's remark, after Judith's funeral, that "Some nut had done it." When he sits to face the jury, his thoughts are of preparation for his future. He will get himself in shape, and, sanctified by the false structure in his favor, dreams of himself as General Glover. In the end, he is the ultimate parody. As Lieutenant Patton had once brought him to a party, Glover might take an ape to the next one.

All the other characters in the book are related to the central position of Glover. They too are varied levels of the main theme. Londo and Fosco are noncommissioned officers who act as a chorus to Glover's principal lines in the drama. Fineline is a challenge to the atrophy of organization: education hopelessly frustrated within a lethal system. Harrington plays the role of innocence, highlighting Glover's lust. Forney creates the tension of antagonism that lies in the threatened recognition that there is evil within the protagonist. Lorna, who has chosen to love Harrington, knows Glover and rebuffs him; but Judith, the main victim of his criminality, is the embodiment of the pathos of passive humanity destroyed by its activists. Pristine, Pollini's oracle, is the goddess of the mind, the mentality that sharpens and feeds itself on the exploitation of the irrationality in mankind. Chaplain Fink personifies the corrupted morality of the Church; Etienne is the double-edged sword of English justice. Various characters whom Pollini vilifies are recognizable as writers for *The New Yorker*, current English authors, members of the United States Officer Corps, literary critics, and educators. Pollini cuts through the American auto-oriented culture, the atomic deterrent, family unity, and exploited womanhood. Of all the characters alongside Glover, the most impressive is Lieutenant Patton, his antithesis, who is a frustrated writer, a homosexual who at one time had desired to become either a ballet dancer or a monk. As Patton reflects metaphysically on the state of the world, Glover physically participates.

Aesthetically, Pollini has crafted his novel well, using large symbols. Glover, with six guns holstered, towering over the bleeding Forney, is a symbol of military might. The aggregate power of this militarism is apparent in the B-52 that Colonel Button watches as he comments on the structure behind the power, the organization of small compartments, so minute, so specialized, that even an idiot can handle them. Violence has various symbols, like the entry in Patton's notebook, where he has described the scene of girls attacking an unripe pear tree while yelling obscenities. He shudders at the paradox of the monstrosity beneath the sweet and pretty surface of little girls. The Air Force, too, has an ironic symbol; it is a process of movie-making, the related symbols being the Airmen as national types and their planes as the artifacts of a technological culture. Whatever brutish dreams Glover has, they are the fantasies of his conscience and of the universal conscience of humanity. Like a sword pricking this conscience is the symbol of the steeple upon which Patton repeatedly reflects as a superb structure, a strong, graceful thrust of inquiry that has no answer but death. At times Patton sees the steeple as a phallic symbol, entering into the continuum of life. Sometimes these symbols converge, as, for example, when Glover attacks the local police officers and embodies universal rebellion against authority. The most effective symbol, however, is in the juxtaposition of Glover and the gorilla at the zoo. As Glover grunts, he stares at the meditative brute. The last line of the novel punctuates the meaning of the book: as the old ticket collector (fate or death) stands at the pier, the boat moves off with its human passengers.

By reference and suggestion, Pollini shows that Italian-Americans are now an assimilated part of the national structure. The noncommissioned officers, Londo and Fosco, are not marked for their ethnicism, nor is the commentator in London, Jim Funero. Pollini, the reader suspects, feels no defensiveness in creating Major Battone as the Operations Officer. So well adjusted have the Italian-Americans become in this novel, that they can ridicule the former racial slurs by using them comically among themselves. For example, while relaxing with a group of other noncommissioned officers, Londo laughs with Cattriano, who asks him, "Guinea, how do ya like our spaghetti?" Pollini implies his disapproval of these terms, however, by not using them in any other kind of situation.

The novel *Glover* is a terrifying warning. The effectiveness of the protagonist as a culture-creature is largely the result of Pollini's sense of irony in employing fragments of dialogue for his "groundlings" in contrast to the long, inner monologues of the more intellectual characters. The author depicts Glover's brutishness with a tautness of style, an exclamatory argot that outdoes Tom Wolfe and rivals the obscenities of Henry Miller. His words are like machine-gun shots for the histrionics of a frustrated homosexual, the currently recognized isolated individual. Pollini appalls us as we realize that he is holding a mirror before us of our contemporary civilization. He sets his scenes with authority and assurance and creates a stark drama with plausible motivation of its many tensions. Glover is more than a particular brute; he is a force exposing us to our terrible inner evil and our need to grapple with it. The novel is persuasive and unforgettable, and Pollini has created a monstrous symbol of the corrosive faults of our humanity.

Excursion

With the novel *Excursion*,[3] Francis Pollini adds the dimension of motion to the function of words as instant dramatic communication. *Excursion* is an experience in which Janet Hunter, an American ex-prima ballerina, a little past her twenties, goes alone on a pilgrimage of adventure in Europe, searching for what she has lost of the dancing triumphs she had had in the cities of Western civilization. The excursion is an erotic performance of sexual saturation, interpreted in the art terms of the dance. Controlling her movements, Pollini leads the ballerina through a dreamlike maze of sensual trippings through cities, country scenes, exotic meals, strange rooms, and multitudinous encounters with sex. An unashamed narcissist, Janet saturates herself in sensuousness in order to forget the double-edged, near-fatal wound dealt her in the loss of her art and the death of her brother. Seeking only spontaneous delights of the moment, she loves, and is loved, to the sound of easy laughter. She and her former friends, whom she unearths from their various retirements, renew their "swimming in a circle in the warm waters, round and round slowly" while they jaunt from city to city. Her conversation is studded with the jargon of the ballet. In her mind, the stories of ballet assume reality that constantly revolves around her past with her brother Carl. Like some critics in an audience, the members of her family are grotesque misinterpreters of ballet movements; but, like a skilled dancing master, her wise friend, Signor Armandi, can evoke the truth from her. She is then able to dispel her false notions. Her journey is a brave attempt to assuage her grief over Carl's death, which had suffocated her art, and now she tries to transfer her love and hopes to young Fred. Finally, when she attempts to recreate her former beauty in order to win Fred, thereby to grasp the one reality that she feels might surpass the mystical aura of her art, she is forced to face the future by admitting the tragic truth.

This truth is what the book is about: that the artist who becomes disenchanted by his art and turns to reality is rewarded with heartbreak. In *Glover*, Lieutenant Patton was able to tolerate his place in humanity by his dreams of being a ballerina, a transfiguration of the creative process, a protection from the factual horrors of war. Now, in *Excursion*, Pollini explores his dream. He creates a dreamer who has exchanged the restrictions of frustrated homosexuality for those of a nymphomaniac.

3. Francis Pollini, *Excursion* (New York: G. P. Putnam's Sons, 1965).

Early in the story, in chapter 2, Pollini sounds his motif that everything happens because of the "Beast" within us, in each and all of us. Actually this theme is recognizable in all of his works. The Beast is the competitive animal in man who wars with the predatory establishment, as Hamilton Upwind, Janet's cousin, shows in his fears that Janet may come back from Europe with socialistic ideas that will destroy the country. Pollini extends the meaning of these fears when he explores the ethical musings of the Senator on the situation of a fundamentally moral society in our nation. We base our lives on moral principles, he says, but we have trouble in living up to them because the urge is so powerful to return to "our primal, animal state, which is always there, lurking, calling to us" (p. 61). The Senator is certain that this animal state has caused agents to be disguised as the "eggheads," tucked away in some corner of some university, or writing for some subversive paper or magazine, or acting, or painting. He is particularly suspicious of college professors. But at the base of all his suspicions is the universal absurdity in the universe, which underlies Pollini's theme. Late in the book he has the now jazz-inebriated Janet speak for him: "Man the Beast. Incarnate of every evil." The only truth, then, is the moment.

With his lethal timelessness, man, according to Pollini, pursues death, because matter, even live matter, is an absurd monstrosity. Thematically, therefore, Pollini identifies this absurdity with man's lack of history, and, in turn, with man's admission that he has no place in time; he has become a monster. Personifying this reasoning, Janet is willing to go with Miguel to all the clandestine haunts where revolutionaries meet, all those who hate the Church and the Government. These people function entirely on committees whose one objective is to obliterate "the whole thing from the bottom." Later, however, when Janet is chatting with her friends Marcello and Gino in Italy, Gino argues that what Italy needs is capital investment, industry, and economic expansion to eliminate the central problem of grinding poverty. Pollini is stressing the need, therefore, of universal cooperation for positive and constructive action. In words spoken by Janet, he asserts that Italy is "My Italy" and the great fear is that "they," the nihilists, might "blow it up." As she, in her mind, is dancing an adagio in a ballet, she remembers that the principal quality of adagio is control. When the conversation turns to literature, the Princess emphasizes to Gino that men like D. H. Lawrence started the process of moral corruption, the seductive beginnings that bred the current monsters. To regain her equanimity, Janet must go to Rome, the eternal reality, in order to "hold time." In reaffirmation she resumes her natural romanticism, accepts Signor Armandi's invitation to go to Capri, where, alone in the opulent library, she reflects again on the indifference of life, and the constant terror and fascination of death. The tension of life is dramatized by the fact that the human being must continue to grapple with his creative instinct. As Janet says to Armandi, she may have ended the steps and the movements, but she has not stopped the dancing. Pollini emphasizes that art is intricately involved with human experience, just as Janet's last role coincided with her brother's death, and, illustrative of this theme, Pollini's protagonist returns to America to resume her art. She must learn that her art has been her consuming demon. Yet Pollini insists that art is the positive spirit of mankind; it is time, "the metamorphosis of desolate violence into ravaged silence," that is killing us.

The basic themes have several levels demonstrated by the various characters. The attempt to get lost in one's art generates all of Janet Hunter's action, a precept much exaggerated in America, where parents motivate their children to the extreme, as did the Hunters, especially Janet's father, who had pressured her into her career from the beginning. This has turned Janet more and more within herself, so that as she dances, she watches herself. She is possessed by her own self-love, which devours her night after night. When she prepares to go out with her friends in London, she muses inwardly about how she loves herself in chiffon, and she recalls how Carl has loved her. The sensuality of incest seems so normal, another dimension of loving herself. Her desperate nomadism, hurtling her from Spain back to Paris, is a vortex drawing her down relentlessly. Others make the moves for her, and Pollini indicates that someone has hold of her; she seems to be whirling around with someone. In her hedonism, she remains barely conscious of where or with whom she is. After she receives a letter from Fred, she thinks again of Carl, who had loved her eyes; Pollini writes, "She adored her eyes. . . . She blew a kiss at her face." Finally, under the gentle guidance of Signor Armandi, she breaks out of her self-centered dreaming and wants to go out for walks. With his probing, she recalls her choreographer, Bernier, but her self-obsession blurs all objective details. Like a physician making a suture, Armandi makes the connection between Bernier and Carl. At that moment, Janet is able to break through her narcissism and admit that Carl is dead and the incestuous love is over. Her plan to return to Fred, then, is an attempt to reconcile herself to a positive morality.

The other characters are like supporting dancers around the prima ballerina. Judge John Carlton Hunter reveals the beast in himself in his elation at sentencing murderers to death, but he demonstrates another side when he thinks of his niece, Janet, "the one true bright spot of his life." His own children, involved with drugs, give him no pleasure, but Janet has been "his honey, his treasure, his pride and joy." He excites himself thinking of this theatrical favorite who transported her audience "in her moment, her glorious supreme moment!" He it is who urges the others in the family to look after her; he writes to her to bring herself back to start all over again. Lieutenant General Roscoe Hawthorn, the cousin in England, is annoyed at his responsibility for protecting Janet in Europe; ironically, he is too occupied with Security. Pressed by Washington to make a report to the Congressional Committee, he seeks physical comfort by rubbing himself with baby powder. He counterpoints Janet's narcissism, and is a reprise of the melodic dreamings of Lieutenant Patton in *Glover.* The human situation has become more tragicomic in him, however, since he has a wife who overwhelms him and can knock him unconscious with a true punch. Dr. Hamilton Upwind, ex-Harvard surgeon who has made serious mistakes like amputating a wrong arm, has alcoholic fantasies and erotic dreams, remembering his amorous experiences with the ballerina. But finally satiated with physical pleasure, he can no longer understand what the family sees in theater. His thoughts are disassociated, hopping from the problems of medicine to the "shrewd little outfits" the ballerinas wear that elude his finest high-powered hunting binoculars. For him the art of the dance turns into "a vile, adulterous affair."

It is for Signor Armandi to understand the artist-lover Janet, and that what is imprisoned in her must escape and reveal itself. His gestures are loving, reaching out in gratitude and affection. She is strangely affected by him, aware that the sun, the sea, and long life are in him. His depth inspires her awe; his stability in large part stems from the fact that his ancestors have always lived where he does. From the citadel of his steadfastness, he is able to help her and lead her to regeneration.

There are various symbols in the story. Janet Hunter is the active maturation of Lieutenant Patton's frustrated dreams of fulfilling the creative spirit. The dramatic tension is caused by the consumption of the creative spirit, violently associated with the death of incestuous, narcissistic love. Janet's odyssey in Europe is described in terms of the ballet, the whole trip being a performance ending with a heartbreaking curtain. At one point Janet is symbolized by a statue—staring, unseeing, unhearing. In this way Pollini uses objects dramatically to symbolize states of mind. Dr. Hamilton Upwind is very much disturbed by his younger brother "Ray, Ray," who is immature and seeks the comfort of a teddy-bear. We are reminded here that Evelyn Waugh used the same symbol in *Brideshead Revisited.* Places, also, take on symbolism; for example, Rome, "golden city," is the haven of everlasting culture. The act of going back to Rome is a return to stability. A larger dimension is manifested in the discussion of Europe as a second home. Europe is where Janet must find herself; Pollini is here dramatizing what other Italian-American writers have written, that the Italian-American (and it is the Italian-American in Janet that is constantly lurking behind her concepts and her behavior) must explore the place of his roots to understand himself. There are other uses of this kind of symbolism: when Janet visits the village and watches the children at their war game, Pollini is objectifying in little the world situation. A particular game may stand for a cosmic idea, as is shown in the action of the men who jump on the trampolines. Symbolizing current society, the men, including the Judge, flop, roll, and fall, and they cannot find their feet. Upwind springs higher and higher, and his zest is that of any man who engages competitively in life. On the whole, it is Janet Hunter's particular experience that is the symbol of the book's underlying theme. Europe has brought back her dead things, put them together, and made her alive again. Restored by Armandi, she now has a sense of direction. Experience and a place have given her a new stability. Italy has become her place, because she has found herself there. In the end, after smoothing her lovely dress, symbolically white-gray in color, she looks into her own eyes in the mirror and says, "Italia—."

The themes and symbols of *Excursion* are thus entwined with the meaning of Italianism. As she is planning her trip, Janet, thinking of light, conjures up a vision of Italian hills and a villa facing "southeast, [of] white stone, [and] pink-roofed." She wears a "light" frock as she approaches Genoa, and she is thinking of Italy, her favorite "treasure place." She is convinced that she should live there, and she envies the people who are born to the Italian language. At another point, sensually overcome by the beauty of the women around her, she thinks of them as "Wonderful Italian young ladies," somehow different from herself. To the exquisite Marna she confesses that she looks upon Italy as home, and that nothing compares with it. She must check herself not to seem maudlin. Later, she comments to her friends Silvia and Pietro that the essence of beauty is in Italian music, the irresistible rhythms of it, yet the sadness of it. Still later, with Armandi, she realizes that it is his Italianism that disciplines her American frivolity. Thematically, Pollini shows that the traditional positive outlook of Italianism is the respite of the Italo-American (since he is present in all these scenes), and is a constructive influence for the regeneration of contemporary America.

Aesthetically, *Excursion* is a futuristic masterpiece. Writing typically in the present progressive tense, Pollini communicates emotional experience with poetic frenzy. At times his verbal fragments are like staccato barks; one or two words may constitute a line. He uses syllables like measured sounds, as a dancer uses steps to form part of a movement, as when he writes,

> "Shall I bring two, Signore?"
> He turned to Janet.
> "Can we take two?"
> She smiled.
> "Let's try to take two."
> He turned to Maria.
> "Bring two."
> They were laughing. The three of them, now,
> in the warm, gentle night, laughing." (p. 155)

Like a ballet, each measure of rhythm is organized and controlled by the director, Pollini, in a prose that varies from formal and stately to staccato and urgent, and then to loose and languid. As with Eliot's *Waste Land*, the method is the poem, the performance of the words. When Pollini's characters have imbibed too much, his style becomes that of a garrulous drunkard. When Janet is lost in libidinous experience, her speech is incoherent and sensual. Then, when her musings wander into timelessness, Polini invites the reader into an experience of inner detachment. When the author pulls the episodes together, however, he directs the action sharply, with terse narration. The reader feels, on several occasions, that the writer could tighten the phrases and not be so profligate with the subcultural jargon of love and lust. Pollini's trademark as a word of address, which he uses in all his books, is the term *honey*. His characteristic words, however, are shocking jabs of colorful verbalization that suggests abstract painting.

The novel is pulsating, disturbing, and, ultimately, exceedingly serious. In this story, Pollini has reached far beyond the sociological "Little Italy." In *Excursion*, the protagonist, a composite American drawn with overtones of the author's attitude, returns to Italy in the manner of a James character sojourning in England and on the Continent. She is, however, her own ambassador. Dramatically regenerated by the original culture as embodied in Armandi, Janet Hunter analyzes herself and musters up the courage to resume her life. Rome, the touchstone of the creative discipline of America's inherited Western civilization, gives her what Pollini calls "direction." Out of the depression and the inevitable loneliness of his protagonist, Pollini resolves his story with the basic idea that personal abandonment is both essential and constructive in achieving transcendental integrity, be it in art or in the social order.

The Crown

Francis Pollini casts his increasingly typed protagonist on a platform of crisis in his fourth book, *The Crown*.[4] Like its predecessors, this novel is styled with blunt dialogue and an architectural design that is its theme. *The Crown* is ostensibly the story of a prizefighter, Dave Stanley; his manager, Farn; and his mistress, Sheila Benton, who attempts to separate him from both the manager and the ring. Through the actions of these characters, Pollini exercises in a circumscribed area his ideas about the abstract contentions and physical sparrings that are the lot of the underprivileged individual in an affluent society.

The action in this book is direct, progressing on a straight, simple line. Dave Stanley surfaces before the reader shadow-boxing with the director Farn and the erotic Sheila. Farn, a professional manager, has discovered David at Pennsylvania State College, and trains him to a

4. Francis Pollini, *The Crown* (New York: G. P. Putnam's Sons, 1967).

series of victories that culminate in the heavyweight championship. David's parents are both dead, but he especially remembers his father, who had been a coal-truck driver, a "jack-of-all trades." Such memories are all that sustain him the several years he serves with the Army in Korea. At the end of that service, he has been able to go to college under the G.I. Bill. At college David is quiet and scholarly, making little reference to his past as a combat soldier in Korea. The one thing about which he is assertive is that the college degree is essential to him. In due time he accomplishes all his objectives—the degree, the reading, the victories in boxing, the middleweight championship, wealth, and the heavyweight crown.While achieving all these goals, he allows himself to be seduced by Sheila, who, by forcing him to analyze himself, becomes the instrument of destruction.

The man of scholarly disposition who survives military training and combat has a crippled reflex to engagements in a competitive world of civil accommodation. Pollini elaborates this idea with a minimum of episodes, enough only to build emotions on shattered emotions to a point of intense drama. Even a conventional character like the pugilist's manager is not commonplace with this author. The reader participates in the character-boxing-match between Sheila and Farn, a psychic sparring that accompanies the actual fighting-rounds as they proceed to the winning of the crown.

Pollini is saying here that we as a nation have the obligation and the material power to be victors in violence, but that in exercising our physical superiority we defeat our conscience. Were we to penetrate this conscience, we would turn this violence upon ourselves.

This theme operates in *The Crown* primarily through Dave Stanley's attitude in the boxing ring. As he explains to Farn, he sees everything from the ring as a whole setup, the long story, the entire world. He goes into tirades of hatred against "them," meaning all those who conform to the social structure, those who take orders, ready to do anything with "their hands, a plane, a missile." He fumes about the lies of history, especially what has been taught between 1860 and 1910, the period that coincides with the Italian immigration years. Dave says that when he "connects," he does so with each and every one, with a power built on hatred. The opponent he fights is the stranglehold on life that "they," the establishment, have. One reason why we cannot break this stranglehold, Dave argues, is that our writers are part of our fraudulent culture. He extols Camus, insisting that such a writer has hold of real "chunks" of truth, while ours flatten out the truth, turning out pap by the bushelful for the money of the "great American Public," as Pollini calls it. As he raves, Sheila feels that his words really are implanted by the "malign" Farn, the director, in the same manner that men are trained by government agents. She imagines Farn as Cerberus and as a destroyer-god, while she thinks of Dave as a god of finely controlled and directed primal violence, a violence that she finds sensually beautiful.

However, when the challenge to change from a middleweight to a heavyweight presents itself to Dave, it is a challenge to rise above mediocrity, which requires "a whole new way of things." Farn knows that such a battle means learning everything all over again; this is the very essence of the method of any revolution. At this point, we sense that Pollini is speaking in cosmic terms. The rhetoric of relearning on another level is phrased in Dave Stanley's own words as he orates against the policy of making everybody equal. What the system cannot stand, says Dave, is the fact that people are not equal and that not everybody can be pulled up or down to one level. The only effective equalizer is the Bomb, the ultimate escape into history for a society that equivocates about equality. Violence, therefore, is the goal of all activity, and acts of violence are methods of equating all things, even sex. David tells Sheila that there are writers who identify sex and violence, writers like Nietzsche, Strindberg, Camus, and Pinter. The only way to improve the equation, he thinks, is "to move up a notch," and this kind of thinking is his only motivation toward a new way of things. However, as he plans to "move up," Sheila is contending to reach his inner soul. What she does not know is the substance of the confession that David makes to Farn that, despite everything, life is a "swindle," and that only death is a winner. With all her incisive penetration into his subconscious, Sheila cannot reach David's real depth. She is too obsessed with her sexual activity, believing that the "once-secret ritual" is universally public, and that her constant presence in the pool and in the home, for example, will win him completely and defeat Farn's power, which, after all, she believes, is based upon commerce. She uses an intellectual jargon to overwhelm David, embellishing their sexual activities with word phantasies. She is, therefore, staggered when she learns from Farn that David is going "to move up." When, however, she contemplates David's lessened chances of winning, she experiences a delightful surge of confidence that then she may penetrate the madness in him, bringing him back to relate to the "primal object," and making him a most magnificent partner for herself. She also starts to question David about Farn's practical investments in him, and she keeps up a steady stream of conversation on various sociophilosophical subjects like existentialism, urban renewal, American civilization, phenomenology, and her fear of guns. Her efforts do not swerve David from his precipitous advance to the great fight before the roaring crowd, the world he defies. When in the fourteenth round Farn says, "Kill him," he sees the release in David of the murder and white-hot fury that win the fight, while David, the winner, demonstrates no awareness of his victory. When, in the end, Farn smells the powder of the gunshots, he reveals that "it was Iwo, all over again"; all this action equates with the former involvement in war.

The novel is really about Dave Stanley's subconscious, which is the symbol of a subcultural group, a minority in the nation, and, summarily, of the nation itself. Dave is more than a pugilist; he is a powerful culture-figure articulating the popular philosophy of nihilism. Because he hates the world, he enters the boxing ring with the avowed express intention of killing a man. The memory of his deprived childhood feeds his vengeance, and he pummels his antagonist to please the bloodthirsty crowd which, to him, symbolizes the world he loathes. This is not the world he had wanted when he read so much in history and literature. He has more than a cursory knowledge of Camus, Strindberg, Pirandello, Nietzsche, and the contemporary writers. When the members of the Press interview him, he disdains some of them, especially those from *Time* and *Life*, against whom he feels a special grievance. During the weeks while he trains relentlessly, he gives lavish parties where others indulge, and he limits himself to talking. Like a monk, he regulates his life, avoiding women, and never swerving from his training. He confesses to Farn that if he were not allowed to fight, he would murder somebody, because he hates the fraudulence of the world and all the people in it. Yet, as Sheila observes while she dances with him, he has a powerful charge of life that almost suggests madness. She senses the alarming violence in him, but she finds it intoxicating and beautiful. When he talks to the party crowd, she listens and is stunned to hear him say that all courts, judges, lawyers, police, and prisons should be obliterated. He has an incantatory mode of delivery, with the theme, "Get rid of the works." His method is clear; he illustrates it when he uses Farn's gun, never missing the target. Farn says that David spars with a training partner in the same way, studying the man and then becoming the man in several weeks. Eventually we feel with Sheila that it is the fear of death that compels his brash attacks. In brief references to his past life, he admits that he has had to learn about the four dimensions of human personality—the genetic, topographic, dynamic, and economic; but we feel that he is obsessed by life's dynamics, the mechanisms of operation.

Farn and Sheila are sparring partners over the control of these mechanisms. Dedicated to his charge, really innocent of malice, Farn would like to protect David from Sheila's temptations. Farn is uncomplicated; he has little subtlety and less perception of intrigue. Beauty to him is in performance; and the man he is directing is a power-house of aesthetics, because he can channel his energies into victories. He appreciates Sheila's exquisite and contained beauty, but he is inarticulate and uneasy in her presence. Yet, with all his innocence, he has a premonition of the danger in her as a threat to David's equanimity. He knows that Dave is "ten times smarter" than he is, but he has "that scared feeling" biting him deeply about whether "Sailboat Charlie's wife [Sheila] can drag him [David] under." Laughing at him, Sheila perplexes him, and he admits he respects her, although his uneasiness about her never leaves him. When she tries to humor him and induces him to confide in her about himself, he gives a schoolboy's recitation of his dossier. He emphasizes the importance to him of his having been a Marine on Guadalcanal, and Iwo; and she stops laughing at him. He refuses, however, to tell her anything about Dave. As time passes, he watches her, observing that "they are all enjoying themselves," and reminding himself not to worry. But he cannot help himself, because he notices that something is "burning" in Dave, something extra, and Farn is confused because he is helpless to do anything about it. He has no way of knowing what Sheila is thinking of him, nor that she considers him dispensable. As for Dave, to the director, the champion in the ring is beauty in action; but Farn also sees that as Dave fights, his face becomes a mask of power and fury. In that face is the world, his fascination with murder pitted against it; and, as he wins the crown, Dave loses all his awareness. When the last bout is over and they are all back at Dave's house, the final terrifying incident is the champion's inevitable personal identification with a foregone conclusion. Dave is the functioning American conscience sentenced to death by its own moral judgments.

The protagonist of this novel of Pollini's, Dave Stanley, is also the functioning Italian-American. When Sheila, the obvious American society-cultist, spars with the legal structure symbolized in Farn, she would predatorily possess Dave's being. In her own words, however, the matter "non è facile" (p. 88). The fact that she thinks in Italian terms attests to the contemporary acceptance of Italian culture; a generation before might have disdained it out of ignorance. This easy fusion of culture is emphasized when Sheila, curbing her desire for wine at dinner, chides herself with the words, "Sweet little WASP you!" Later, after talking with Dave on the telephone, she reflects, "Terminata conversazione!" (p. 128). She uses the Italian term actually as a display of quality. When Dave, on more personal terms with her, is describing the Italian-American girls of his home town in Pennsylvania, he delights her that he compares her with them, whom he calls beauties, "marrying beauties." She feels that she is really probing into his inner self. After that, as she increases her possession of him, she absorbs and uses naturally Italian cultural characteristics as her own. When, sitting near the pool just before the final boxing match takes place, Farn talks to her, she casually shows him what she has been reading, the latest work of an Italian writer. No obvious point is made of her choice, an acceptance that symbolizes the assimilation of ethnicity. On another level, this unobtrusive acceptance applies to Pollini himself, the Italian-American writer as an unquestioned component of the mainstream of our national literature.

This novel is a masterful work of limited scope and close range, having symbols of broad levels. With some of the most vivid and accurate descriptions of prizefight scenes in any fiction, Pollini has captured the fever and terror of all competition. By telescoping the passion of international contest within the ropes of a boxing ring, he exposes the basic fury that man has for mankind, especially when man has been systematically trained for conquest. Pollini's thesis rises above polemics with his relentless probing into the minds and psyches of the three main characters, two of whom are in the narration dramatically poised in opposition like boxers in the ring. The form of the book is therefore a figure of the action. Structurally, also, Pollini has Farn talk in the past tense, indicating his role as the creator of the protagonist, while Sheila speaks in the present tense, dramatizing her role as the threat of the present to Dave's conditioning. Symbolically, America's war policies are not only personified in the characters, but they are analyzed and judged, especially by Dave's long tirades which to the reader express Pollini himself. The author's vision of a revolutionized world excites us as he projects the future possibility of a world without violence. We are courting disaster with our war philosophy, says Pollini; and we are forcing people of integrity to destroy themselves arbitrarily.

The novel gives some specific recommendations. While warning us of our economic duplicity in producing weapons, Pollini judges and condemns the lack of quality and integrity of our writers. In convincing conversations between Dave and Sheila, this author is suggesting that we absorb the styles and contents of artists like Camus, and the European dramatists. Pollini's characters resemble Pinter's in that they are so much larger than themselves. Dave is humanity; Farn is the structured system of commerce; Sheila is beauty and the creative impulse; and the Crown is the homicidal or suicidal victory of a war society. Pollini emphasizes the dichotomy of American society, its idealism and its intrigue, in the juxtaposition of the chapters narrated by Farn and Sheila, whose qualities he gradually reverses. Sheila, the creative becomes intrigue; and Farn, the commerce-system, becomes the concerned individual. The catastrophe is the more tragic for the inevitability of Dave's final calamity.

As we recover from the blow of the book, we totter, sustained only by Pollini's conviction that, hopefully, we have the alternative of freeing people from the imposed prison of warped training. Dramatically, the book provides a catharsis for our moral duplicity. It works with the supreme function of art in wounding us while it informs us that our materialistic and prejudiced civilization begets its own destruction. Pollini identifies the Italian-American writer and the novelists of other minorities as the alternative to that art which has compounded this destruction for a price tag. Systematized success, he demonstrates, is the kind of victory that feeds the roaring, bloodthirsty crowd. Generated by hate, this victory is both dishonest and suicidal. Although Dave Stanley wears a crown in the boxing ring, he discovers the horror of his strength, the hatred that gives his fists such deadly accuracy. This hatred breeds its own ultimate defeat, since it is an undiagnosed psychosis that has driven the victor, nursed by real or imagined wounds of the past. The real crown of our achievement, therefore, is to destroy the illusions that have created the wounds, remove the distortions in our training, and open the arena to the fair and honest competition that will enhance the art of living.

Pretty Maids All In A Row

Francis Pollini deals with the split personality of duplicity with his sharpest talent in his fifth novel, *Pretty Maids All In A Row*, 1968.[5] Embodied in attractive and adulated image, the protagonist, a dichotomy of good and evil, is a monster of terror. Pollini counterpoints the progress of this para-hero with the ironic, low-keyed development of an emulative youthful admirer, a process that intensifies both characterizations.

Tiger McDrew, assistant principal, guidance counselor, stellar high school football coach, is an exciting teacher of history and an exemplary husband and father. By popular acclaim, his is the stabilizing hand of Sawyersville High School; he is the faculty advisor preferred by the students, and one of the most respected citizens of Sawyersville. Tiger is the special friend and mentor of Ponce de Leon, the dreamy, questing, and astutely intelligent pupil who is his student-assistant. Starting *in medias res*, the story opens with Ponce in the act of discovering the body of the murdered Jill Fairbunn, beloved cheer-leader and popular symbol of the student body. Ponce agonizes with the entire school family and the members of the community through this shocking introduction to a series of bizarre murders that are committed mysteriously within a few days. Developing the narrative along three parallel lines, Pollini arranges the order of the murder episodes next to the sequential "testings" in Tiger McDrew's office, interlacing these developments with Ponce de Leon's progress in his love affair with a teacher of English, Betty Smith. Supporting the progression of these events are choruses in the form of interviews programmed by the local police, discussions in all the classes, banter reverberating in the locker rooms, and individual private reactions to reading assignments. The orchestration of all these notes is syncopated in Tiger McDrew, whose internal monologues give psychic direction to the narration. In a grim parody of national events, Francis Pollini creates a steady, terrorizing momentum with the incidents of the murders, intensifying the impact of evil with the paradoxical increase of the lustful "testings" in McDrew's office. While the charismatic Tiger imprints his "stripes" on each one of his willing "maids" by appointment, only a wistful sadness tempers him briefly as the tragedies multiply. In his lectures, McDrew, the teacher, declaims his compassion for a defective world; he motivates his pupils to think. In football practice, he is a giant of

5. Francis Pollini, *Pretty Maids All In A Row* (New York: Delacorte Press, 1968).

action; at the crucial Sawyersville-Caverton game he drives the team to victory, an achievement beyond its capacity, a reflexive response to the strong hypnotism he exerts on each of the players. The members of the team suddenly play to kill; each boy is charged with the urge to vindicate the murdered girls. This paradox contains the key to the narration, the key that is suddenly revealed to the revering Ponce when he, by accident, discovers Tiger's score card on which are listed the names of the school's prettiest girls. The mysterious coding of stars after each name suddenly enlightens Ponce as to the horrendous truth.

The point of *Pretty Maids All In A Row* is that the stereotyped image of the benign American is, in truth, an exquisitely balanced dichotomy of good and evil. Pollini has explored various facets of this theme in his previous books. Marty Landi in *Night* is the sincere idealist projected against the deceptive evil of Ching; Glover is the instinctive brutal violence poised against the metaphysical, artistic projection of Lieutenant Patton; Janet Hunter in *Excursion* is the principle of creative beauty satiating itself to oblivion; Dave Stanley in *The Crown* demonstrates the corruption of hatred that can destroy the most perfectly synchronized social machine; Tiger McDrew is the monument of the contemporary principle of altruistic action operating to compensate for its own degeneration. In *Pretty Maids All In A Row,* Pollini brings the current theories of education to their logical conclusions; and the high school experience becomes an experiment of sexual relations among students with students, or students with teachers. The sexual motif has violence as its necessary vent. With the rhetoric of Tiger's lectures, Pollini indicates that America's violence is the extended outlet of her external sanctimony, that the national obsession with sex is the internal activation of this violence that sanctifies even the brutalities of war.

As Tiger is thinking about Jill Fairborn's murder, a small voice in his head sings the nursery tune, "cockle shells and silver bells," and he tries to connect the innocence of the rhyme to the problem facing the school. His perplexity is a microscopic model of the confusion of the American complex in search of a solution for national problems. The only truth Tiger admits is that things cannot be static; they are ever changing and moving. When, later in the day, he contemplates the shock of Ponce's experience, Tiger muses that life is a series of brutal discoveries, and he thinks back to his own experience in Korea and Vietnam. When Surcher, the detective, makes his series of interviews, he is impressed by Mr. Mike McDrew's credentials as the maker of amazing teams. Pollini presents these tangential glimpses of varied reflections of the theme, for example, when McDrew concludes that he has never met "a negative kid," that, above all, the pupils want to grow up and fulfill all their dreams. In this same internal monologue, Tiger thinks that it is the "spirit of the kids" that keeps him alive; and he wonders if the dead Jill ever had known about the brutal core of life. Pollini extends this thinking into a political essay when he analyzes Miss Smith's conversation with Ponce. He points out that the nation is in a "vicious cycle of heredity—social—personal—intra—and inter—personal pressures, factors, and processes, all interrelating and interacting, relentlessly" (p. 140). Integration will have to cement the "split-off" parts, but in education we must avoid the encroachment of mechanization.

Pollini expands his theme with his educational theory that the teacher-student relationship must be more intimate than it has been. Extremes in these relationships, he believes, are caused as a relief from the attempt being made to dehumanize education. When he broadens these themes to include foreign affairs, Pollini expounds that American Democracy has become undemocratic and corrupt to a point of deriding intelligence. Miss Smith tells Ponce that appreciation and understanding require a certain level of intelligence, intellect, emotional maturity, character structure. Pollini decries the fact that in our society too few reach this level. For this reason, the author caricatures our system of education in Tiger's reading *Time* magazine for information on "A Perfect Education," which outlines that to learn is to love, that students should revel in their own discovery, and that pupils should be in love with their teachers. It is Ponce who incorporates this whole theme, Ponce who disdains the "kid stuff" of "beat music," and who looks to his teachers as models. However, Ponce is the model of an extraordinary person, "backing his culture," as Tiger explains to the Negro boy, Jim. Reflecting on the indecipherable problems at Sawyersville High School, Tiger McDrew thinks that every single human being with any kind of mentality beyond that of an idiot comes to realize, sooner or later, somewhere within himself, the power of these stark, fearful paradoxes. Pollini dramatically crystallizes this thinking later, as he has Tiger reading the book *The Human Vagina* and concluding that "orgasm cannot be separated from primal socio-psychological factors" (p. 285).

Pollini expounds the theme of sex-violence as a problem that cuts across every stratum of American life. In this land of extremes, Tiger ponders that there is the highest percentage of churchgoers in the entire civilized world, and the highest crime rate. This paradox filters through to the person, as it does to Ponce, who finds himself in a bewildering "spectrum of emotions" between his being appalled at the murders and excited over the football team. The paradox intensifies as he discusses with Miss Smith the lyrical ecstasies of Donne's poems, which are both sacred and profane, the supreme reflection of the eternal ever-present conflict between the flesh and the spirit. At the core of this conflict, Pollini writes, are the corpses of the victims. "The worst crimes perpetrated by mankind," he argues, "on vast national, international scales were wrapped in pious, righteous phrases" (p. 398). Mankind acts out the tragedy of reparation, amelioration, and restoration.

Tiger McDrew and Ponce de Leon are the two sides of the moral dilemma in a world paradox. Tiger is so integrally the personification of the theme that he barely escapes being typed. The reader commends the images McDrew enjoys, admiring his initiative in organizing the investigation of the murders and respecting his concern over the school's involvement. Furthermore, McDrew is a formidable figure of efficiency as he programs a course of "probability or distribution" to solve the murders, but the reader is made uneasy as Tiger prolongs his reflection on "that magnificently formed girl." The "list" he keeps is mystifying, but we forget this and appreciate his concern with Ponce, whom he calls "the most psychologically astute" youngster he has encountered and whom he sees as a future teacher at the school and his assistant football coach. When Tiger becomes the principal, as he expects, Ponce will be his chief aid, exercising his idealism by teaching literature. We learn that Tiger has his ambitions and his prejudices; he will, for example, get rid of Crispwell, whom he calls an "ultra respectable," a hawk, a quasi-John Bircher. The reader tolerates this prejudice and actively approves Tiger's warm and healthy relationship with his wife, "Looby-Loo." There is a wistful appeal in Tiger's introspection over his genuine involvement with the school "kids." As Pollini describes every erotic detail of the lustful encounter with which Tiger "tests" his "maids," the reader is simultaneously outraged and fascinated. There is a disturbing amount of egotism in Tiger's warm grins as he evaluates himself as holding the winning record of all the high-school coaches in the country. His amazing abandonment to activity plunges him obsessively into helping Surcher find the murderer; in doing so, he can with deadly accuracy make the despised homosexual, Mummer, at least a target whose presence will be removed. Ironically, one of his clearest decisions comes as he is discussing with the cast of players the feasibility of presenting Pirandello's *Six Characters in Search of a Play.* Like a puppeteer, Tiger types each pupil on the basis of fixed physical presentation. With complete detachment, as though he were directing a play, he agrees to pay respects to the murdered girl who "must look beautiful, like a princess, sleeping in her casket." With the same dramatic empathy, he is filled with sorrow. At home, Tiger is the gentle, playful Daddy and the ideal lover and husband. He helps his Junie with her homework, and watches television with Looby-Loo, whom he calls his "only one." Later, he studies *The Human Vagina* with the same absorption with which he had once studied military strategy. After a period of concentration, he comes to no conclusion on primal mysteries, and, in his bafflement, goes to make love to his wife. The next day, in the Teachers' Conference Room, again with detachment as the decision is made to dismiss Mummer, Tiger concerns himself only with checking his watch, because he must not disrupt his time schedules for interviewing the "young maids." Later in the day, after his "testing," he reflects that two of the "most divine and sublime" are gone forever from life; he stares at his list, which is shrinking, and he feels like crying, as though he were a spectator at a theatrical performance. Sighing, he turns his thoughts to his appointment with Barbara Brook, with whom he might "find paradise," since they had such a rapport with each other. As he waits, he thinks about the school problems and then the "deeper waters" of America, "his only, and her problem with crime." At this point, he melds completely with Pollini's theme. Abstracting himself from human involvement, Tiger McDrew reflects on America's "core"; patriotism is good for "wayward kids"; religion has its place. Coming to specifics, he decides to suggest to Surcher that he keep school open and all activities normal; there should be no knuckling under to intimidation or adversity. At this point, Pollini has placed his protagonist in a supremely ironic role. The dramatization is at its height when Poldoski, the Chief of Police, discovers Tiger with Jeannie Bonni in his car in the school yard. Pollini builds momentum with Tiger's action. The only emotion Tiger feels is increasing "sadness," remorse. As he talks to Poldoski, he feels that he is an accident of the "forces that govern all destiny," forces constituting a process that is irreversible, and that he can do absolutely nothing about it. As he reflects that all human activity falls into an inevitable pattern of converging directions, he strikes Poldoski with the karate blow. Then he is mournful as he leaves his victim. The next day, when Miss June Craymire seeks his advice over her resignation, he scientifically leads her to the conclusion that violence and love are inevitably driven by the complexities of sex. He uses the strategy of playing football as an example. To channel this violence into victory is everyone's concern, a national malaise. With this, Tiger pushes the team beyond its real strength. He is, according to Pollini, the raging animal at the core of a nation that masks itself with a Puritanical benign face.

Ponce is Tiger's alter ego, his youthful idealism that may succeed in the future, with the significant name of the legendary seeker of the fountain of youth. But Ponce has dimensions of which Tiger is incapable. Apparently, the young hero embodies Pollini's concept of the American character, which has absorbed additional, constructive qualities, such as have been contributed by the Italians to American civilization. Ponce burns with the shock of having found the murdered body of a beautiful classmate. He knows that the experience will "stay inside" for the rest of his life. In his unfolding growth in sex and love, all the women he knows become beautiful: Miss Smith, Miss Nectar, his mother; and they all move toward one another and become part of each other. His trust of the older generation has a degree of pathos, but it determines his decisions that enrich his experiences with them, especially with Tiger and Betty Smith. His salvation is his natural intelligence and astuteness. Tiger knows that Ponce is the most superior "youngster" he has encountered, and he plans his future with vision. Tiger's own success would be ensured by the help of this kind of boy. Pollini's deft irony juxtaposes the activities of the two, progressing to the inevitable resolution—that Ponce's very quality of knowledgeability and human perception is the key to exposing the malaise of Tiger's character. A lesser mind could not have perceived the meaning of Tiger's "list." It is Ponce who has been able to understand that the police are wrong about the Negro students; it is Ponce who really feels "rotten" about the tragedies and all the ensuing actions. It is Ponce who calculates the winning strategy with which Tiger's bullying tactics force the team. Furthermore, Ponce is capable of great misgiving and fear of injustice in condemning Mummer's activities. The boy is a young humanist, and what he admires in the Coach is Tiger "internalized," the morale-booster, the confidence-inspirer. He has genuine love, which he reflects in his warmth for his mother, his father, his younger brother, and even his cat, Peppy. His sexual experience with Betty Smith is rendered poetical by their discussions of Milton, Donne, and the Romantic writers. In practice, his sex is an aesthetic dimension of his love; and he dreams of coming back to teach at Sawyersville and marrying Betty Smith. His real ambition to be a writer is Pollini's large brush-stroke emphasizing the abstract motif of the boy's creativity. Like some poetic natures, Ponce is not responsive to trigonometry, but he is entirely fascinated by music. Pollini writes that Ponce remembers that from very early childhood he been exposed to opera, which both his father and mother enjoyed, especially Italian opera. Ponce reflects that it must be the "Southern European" origins of his father's family that have made him so vulnerable to the "sheer beauty" of music. In an internal monologue, he experiences a crescendo of tunes, a "whole torrent of operas" around him, and he steadies himself with the historical fact of the power of *The Teatles,* which he calls "kid stuff." These cultural tastes, inbred in Ponce, have developed the warmth of personality that makes him one of the most-admired student heroes in the school. When he falls in love, he does so "hopelessly," and he knows he always will be "with that dream."

Italian-Americanism is an integral part of established values in *Pretty Maids All In A Row.* Starting with the obvious, Pollini pictures the schoolboys enjoying the famous ravioli and spaghetti at Selmo's. A boy's name that ends in a vowel, furthermore, meets with only approval, as when the football captain spells "A-L-M-O." From this level, Pollini goes to the other ends of the spectrum as he portrays Miss Smith, the teacher of English, who knows Italian and goes into ecstasy over the marvels of Florence. Not to make the reference too academic, Miss Smith also comments that the apples in Italy are incomparable, while we remember that the apple is a legendary culture-symbol in frontier America. Ponce responds to her comments as much as he revels over his identification with Italian music, which he considers permanent and eclectic. This eclecticism has permeated many things in the community, the natural acceptance, for example, of Sam Roto's poolroom, which in another generation would have been shunned. Italianisms have become so absorbed that even Tiger, when he thinks of his youth, remembers his father in California as an expert in the garden, tying up the tomato plants as his immigrant neighbors had instructed him. The absorption of all these lesser levels of ethnic contribution is most notable, however, in the mentality of the young Ponce de Leon, the new seeker for the fountain of truth. To him the future lies in his facing this truth when he finds it, and in having the courage and discipline to cope with the truth. This conclusion is both spiritual and practical, the only constructive direction for hope.

The novel is dramatic, serious, and apocalyptic. Without humorous relief, Pollini challenges the smugness of our righteousness and wins our respect by exposing the paradoxes in human rationalization. An expert at theatrics, Pollini engages the reader in his tale of planted suspicion that grows relentlessly into monstrous fact. His protagonist becomes a terrifying mirror, catching with increased clarity the outlines of our own ambiguity; he is a model, picturing the horror of universal evil and common hyprocrisy. Pollini warns us that the true quality of life lies in the amalgam of its ideals and its facts as they are demonstrated in humanity.

As a novelist, he handles his narration with a triple focus, his dialogue with onomatopoeia to accompany the action. But Pollini's greatest achievement in this book is the introspective dimension, which, as in his previous novels, is found in the dreamlike musings of the main characters. In the composite creation of Ponce de Leon the author has personified his theory of a positive plan for the future. He persuades us that sex and violence must no longer be the inevitable, objectivized areas of inhibited civilized behavior. We are to remove the pious mask from repressed sadism. In absorbing the cultures of recent immigrants, our traditional code of morality may become more humanistic, like Ponce, as he decides to do "the right thing" to rectify the crimes of his beloved Tiger. With this book, Pollini brings to culmination his conviction that the Italian-American, with his astute perception and ancient-hewn humanity, is helping the nation amalgamate, and is helping it reduce the extremes of its dichotomy.

14

MARIO PUZO (1920-   )

For the average reader, the Italian-American novel has arrived with Mario Puzo. His books definitely and dramatically document the thesis that the Italian-American novelist has identified himself with what has been professionally and socially inimical to him, the national American culture. Meanwhile, the erstwhile hostile environment has finally accepted and absorbed him. Puzo demonstrates some violent dynamics of this contemporary Italian-Americanism in three books: *The Dark Arena* (1953); *The Fortunate Pilgrim* (1964); and *The Godfather* (1969).

Despite, or perhaps because of, contemporary America's psychic obsessions, Puzo's novels have achieved recognition, since he deals aggressively with areas of Italian-American experience to which the mass media have given national notoriety. Although racisim has obstructed each successive immigrant group as it moved upward to economic stability, the Italians, especially, have had to confront not only a language barrier, but the increased efficiency with which communications operate with propaganda. With the historical national tradition of piratical enterprise in the accruement of wealth now stabilized before them, the Italians in America have been able to share in the formidable economic structure, often at the price of being labeled associates of organized crime. Furthermore, they have felt that the pejorative genocidal stamp on the image of the Italian in fictional treatments in books, periodicals, newspapers, and in broadcasting has continued to be unopposed. Much has been written to document this phenomenon, but it is sufficient to note that there is evidence in the Italian-American Press that this negative propaganda was able to continue without challenge, ironically because of the very human characteristics with which the immigrants clustered, obeyed the laws, and formed no united protest groups beyond their own society. Meanwhile, they became convenient scapegoats as criminal stereotypes for the writers of fiction.

Because of the recent widespread and organized violence in the nation, the reading public responds instantly to works that reflect this criminal aspect of society. Furthermore, the distributors of reading material are not always concerned with the possibility that criminality may be only a fractional aberration from the normal behavior of the members of a minority whose own literary output, reflecting genuine predominant characteristics, goes systematically out of print. Ironically, however, Mario Puzo's protagonists command both our respect and sympathy, stirring us with a wistful desire that genius be put to better use. Such talent should handle the more extended human affairs within our national complex.

Puzo has gathered his materials from authentic sources. A native of New York City, he was educated at the City College of New York, Columbia University, and the New School for Social Research. He lives in Bayshore, Long Island, with his wife and five children. Although his first two books were praised by the critics, he had to continue to write literary reviews until he composed *The Godfather*, which became the fastest-selling book in American literary history.

The Dark Arena

Mario Puzo's first novel, *The Dark Arena*,[1] is about the occupation of Germany after World War II. He explores the extremes to which military occupation leads both the conquered and the conquerors. Walter Mosca, a twentieth-century centurion who has lost his idealism as a soldier in World War II, seeks compensation for its loss in the intricacies of the black-market activities with which the Army of Occupation allies itself to the German people. Puzo depicts the personal problem of this one soldier as a microscopic model of our entire national military machinery. In this story, the author introduces his basic idea that American idealism has fallen into sin. Subsequent to our error, we seek salvation, hoping for maturation by identifying ourselves with the enemy. Puzo shows that we have made a full circle back to the old ethical theme of the conflict between good and evil that occupied Hawthorne and Melville.

Walter Mosca, a psychically wounded ex-G.I., can no longer adjust to the warmth and intimacy of his Italian-American home and family. Stripped of emotion, his responses to his prewar fiancée are mechanically brutal; furthermore, he is not able to accept either his brother's challenge or his mother's tearful pleadings. Therefore, he returns to Germany and to Hella, whom he is not free to marry because she is German. Walter basks in the companionship of the men at the billet, enjoying a degree of friendship with several of them, one of whom is

1. Mario Puzo, *The Dark Arena* (New York: Random House, 1953). References here are to reprint edition, Dell Publishing Company, Inc., 1969.

Eddie Cassin, an accomplished realist. Drained of compassion, Walter brutally obeys his own instincts in any situation, whether it be in the showing of respect to a superior, the sympathy for a child, bare loyalty to another man, or some consideration for the woman with whom he lives. Against regulations, he moves into rented rooms with Hella, and only eventually requests official permission to marry her. Meanwhile, consequences grow rapidly in his activities with Wolf, who has a plan to earn large sums of money with black-market scrip. In the extension of this enterprise, Mosca confronts Yergen, who needs money without delay to hospitalize his crippled child. When Hella develops a tooth infection that requires penicillin, Walter goes to Yergen for the medicine, because drugs are not allowed to Germans. Yergen, feeling no compunction for Walter, who had shown no sympathy for his child, knowingly sells Walter some defective penicillin. As a result, Hella dies; and Mosca, outlawing himself, pursues Yergen to kill him.

The point of the story is that our national politico-military machine has brutalized men to respond automatically in an imposed, approved pattern. When they respond the same way in the more enlightened civil environment, there is not approval but charge of illegality; their acts are classified as crime. The brutalized Walter Mosca laughs at the picture he shows his mother of the German bazooka man crumpled in the snow. He is trying to joke as he says, "My first victim" (p. 17). Then, as he is leaving her, Walter regrets that he, too, had not been killed in the war and thus have avoided "this festering sorrow, this knowledge that he was irrevocably gone, that if he died, she could never weep over his body, bury him, bring flowers to his grave" (p. 26). When he arrives in Bremen, he is drawn into the sinister atmosphere, noticing the "sharpers," the black-market operators, the children laying their traps for unwary G.I.'s. Some of this seduction is in Hella, too, as she readily succumbs to him in the campaign to make him not want to leave her, and to make him stay in the land of the enemy with her, the enemy. When she explains to him her loss of a previous baby, she feels she must have him read the official documents, "knowing," as Puzo writes, "that in the world and time in which they lived, she had to give proof, that there was no absolute trust" (p. 52).

A German says to Walter, "People like you and me meet face to face and kill each other. Our enemies are behind us . . . and commit the crimes for which we die" (p. 79), therewith encapsulating the whole situation. The thing behind them is the same inimical darkness which appears in another German's eyes, the man whose face was smashed because he had dared to leave camp. Puzo writes, "It was a look of horror, as if he had seen some terrible and shameful thing in which he had never believed" (p. 79). That night, as Walter reaches for Hella, he remembers the German's face, and he recalls a former battle scene, the time he had suffered the first violation of his flesh and bone and had come to know the meaning and the terror of annihilation. This dark terror has other levels. When George Middleton, the Marxist, points out Walter Mosca to his friend, a professor, the latter sees Walter as a tall, dark boy, not older than his own son, but that this boy has serious brown eyes and a grave, almost sullen face that just misses being ugly. Mario Puzo portrays the professor as "afraid of all young men—the hard, sullen German youths with their years of warfare and defeat—but even more of all these young, drunken Americans who would beat or kill without provocation" (p. 90). These Americans, however, find no comfort in this land they occupy. Puzo writes that Gordon Middleton feels "the alien atmosphere of the requisitioned home, living with belongings which had no memories, no associations, not knowing who had picked out the pictures on the wall, the furniture scattered through the rooms, who had played the piano which rested against the far wall" (p. 93). This dehumanization underlies even the theme of the opera in Bremen. Eddie Cassin, incapable of any emotion tenderer than contentment, reflects that the physical world around him is as ridiculous as the make-believe world he has seen on the stage. Eddie has no illusions; he knows, for example, that Wolf and Mosca go out nights to trade in the black market. As for Mosca, the only emotion he feels is an occasional fear, which he usually obliterates with anger. He hates the Germans who try to ingratiate themselves with him. Their behavior puts him on the defensive for enjoying the sight of the ruined city around him. Just as he cannot go home because he has no feeling for his mother and brother, he cannot leave "the ragged and torn sky line as if a great jagged ax had chopped off the city's skull. That when he was home the solid, unending, wall-like streets, unmarred, secure, had made him angry, uneasy" (p. 128).

Thus, Mosca stands "out-of-place" in the duplicity of the world's morality. Each day he lives, he breaks the law; having Hella in the billet, buying clothes with Middleton's Army card. He may be sent to jail for loving Hella and will not accept any rationalization that he should be ashamed. Mario Puzo writes, "He couldn't stand reading the newspapers, they made him puke. They said this is good today and tomorrow they said you're evil, a murderer, a wild animal, and they made you believe it so much you helped hunt yourself down. He could get away with murdering Fritz but go to jail for taking care of a woman he wanted" (p. 131). Having watched the shooting of some Poles the week before, Mosca, says Puzo, reflects that the "Polacks had made a mistake; they murdered a few days after the occupation had begun instead of a few days before, and instead of receiving their medals from the general as brave guerrillas, the top half of their bodies had been shrouded in brown cord sacks . . . and the firing squad stood almost on top of them, shooting down into the slumped bodies a few feet away" (p. 132).

The shooting of the Poles, however, does not interfere with Mosca's breakfast. Despite this obvious passivity, when he accompanies Honny and Wolf to the basement room filled with headless corpses, he feels a sudden release, and for the first time can think with emotion of his mother and brother, knowing that the safety they know they do not really have. At this point, Puzo universalizes his theme, applying the darkness of fear to everyone. He writes, "they dreamed in their own terror. Suddenly he felt they were all in danger, everyone that he knew, and that there was nothing he could do about it" (p. 143).

After this cosmic application, Puzo intensifies the theme by interrelating it with different people. When Middleton leaves, Walter Mosca must get other people's commissary cards to trade out in the country "like real Germans." He stays awake with the strange feeling that this has been the purpose behind everything, and that he was living as one of the enemy. This progressive degradation is thematically personified in others. In Contrescarpe Park a man lectures on sin and guilt, excoriating his audience for the condition of the land in ruins and for the triumph of evil. He says that Satan sees "the death of man and everything man has done since the beginning of time" (p. 155). This evil is the dark arena. This evil, says the speaker, will ruin civilization in the future. Between Middleton's Communism and the preacher's apocalypse, Walter Mosca knows that things are wrong because he can no longer trust anybody who can force him to do something, no matter what the reason is. That includes the Communists, he says, "because those people and you yourself are controlled by forces that you refuse to concern yourself with. You exercise no free will when you fight on your level, in your narrow circle, your little personal arena. When you do that you put those people you care about in terrible danger" (p. 161). The culmination of this evil is dramatized, however, when Mosca contemplates the dead Hella. He has faith in the defense he has built against grief and trusts that the memory of destructive years will shield him now. Then, Puzo writes, "suddenly a thousand enemies came coursing through his blood, the bile rose in his throat, a giant hand cramped the beat of his heart, drowned all light" (p. 233). This darkness surrounds Walter as others bury Hella; he feels only "a bewildered sense of loss, as if there was nothing he could ever want to do and no place in all the world he could go." Aesthetically, the death and burial of Hella are symbols of Puzo's theme of darkness. He writes that, as Walter Mosca catches the shadows of his anguish reflected in his mirror, "he saw the cruelty and evil, the black glints in the dark eyes, the firm and brutal chin" (p. 250). In the end, only when he is sure that Yergen is dead does Mosca feel release from fear and tension; then "the sickness and blackness left his body." As he becomes one with the enemy, he feels familiar with "the ruined continent he could never leave." The theme's conclusion is that the darkness of evil is such that man must implement his own justice through retribution.

Since Walter Mosca carries most of the action of *The Dark Arena,* he bears the burden of the theme when it is dramatized. While all of the incidents of the story express Puzo's theme of the evil of man's duplicity, it is Walter who holds "buried inside himself the other life" his hatred for everything his former associates believe. Although the trauma he suffers is a personal application of a global situation, the other characters in the book endure more than satellite roles in a disordered cosmos. For example, Hella humanizes for us the warm, receptive decency of trapped goodness in a propaganda-pulverized political enemy. Eddie Cassin, philandering in the sadism of detachment; Wolf, abrasive and cruel with his ambitious enterprise; Leo, fearful with his need for survival; Gordon Middleton, loquacious as the textbook philosopher-communist; Yergen, despicable as the selfish opportunist—all are characters who come into focus with both primary and blended colors. There are other scene-players who are sharply and briskly drawn like the briefly speaking personae in Shakespeare—for example, the German who pleads "*Ich hab eine Frau und Kinder*" (p. 85). What equates all these personalities is their trained reaction to a ring of malignant violence; their behavior demonstrates a rigid automatism in response to an environment.

With this first book, Mario Puzo has brought a renewed historical excitement to American literature. Responsible critics have recognized in *The Dark Arena* the emergence of a masterful talent of power, precision, and verisimilitude. There is enough of creative inventiveness, sincere meaning, and evocation of mood and place to give the novel solid substance, while the style is refreshingly controlled and versatile, sounding the action of the situations, the intensities of emotional pressures, and the speech habits of the characters. It is an impressive, informative, and illuminating book. The reader may agree with Maxwell Geismar that Puzo has written "in the only new language to emerge in our literature since the stylistic innovations of Hemingway." Acclaimed as one of the finest novels to come out of America's occupation of Germany, the story involves the reader totally and then continues to haunt him. The action never stands still, often engaging the reader in a rhythmic mounting of terror, as in the incident when Walter Mosca pursues Yergen. In content, the author informs America of the postwar occupation as Francis Pollini informs us of the Korean mind-controlling of our prisoners of war. Puzo is professionally expert, and when he uses brutalities and obscenities, it is as barometers of the speech and behavior of real people in authentic situations. He has the sure talent of piercing to the core of a situation and thrusting its exposition directly at the reader with tense momentum leading to an inevitable conclusion. This talent orchestrates the subject matter with clearly resonant modulations of theme in the minor actions and in the aesthetic representation of ideas through symbols. The rubble and the bodies in the square, for example, are tragically counterpointed in Mosca's dream of white flowers that wither and die. Again, when he plays dice with his friends, the scene of the game symbolizes the situation of the man as T. S. Eliot's "Game of Chess" dramatizes human struggle in a wasted environment. Scenes of action are dramatizations of ideas, as, for example, the meetings at Frau Vlavern's house, the headquarters of the black-marketeers, where Germans and Americans are equal; there are no national conquerors in criminal traffic. Occasionally, the symbols are evocative. Prepared for any type of departure, Walter Mosca always carries the blue gymnasium bag his mother had forced him to take with him, a symbol of his tie with his past, a remnant of a time of innocence. One of the most powerful symbols, however, is the basement room filled with headless bodies, a brutal externalization of man's harvest of his own evil. When Mosca leaves the basement, he sees the moon—another symbol, since it appears "as if it were a light shed by some lifeless and metal instrument, mirroring its own image in the earth, its own arid craters and lifeless scars" (p. 143). With this particular reflection, Puzo hands the mirror to Walter Mosca, who, while he personifies the situation of his nation, is as well the symbol of every citizen of that nation.

The Dark Arena conveys a formula for the contemporary Italian-American novel, symbolized in the person and situation of the protagonist. As the Italian-American has been a fragmented individual caught between the extremes of a dual society, and as the ethnic writer has been isolated from an established literary tradition, so Walter Mosca stands between the early, circumscribed security of his family at home and his ambiguous position in the land of the enemy. The environment of the home he has left parallels all ethnic inner-directed structures, exemplified pathetically in his former fiancée's toast, "To our family." Then, crushed by his war experiences, and finding that he does not relate any longer to his family, Mosca withdraws into the state of emotional paralysis that is his personal isolation. Eventually, he descends to compromise in order to make an adjustment, and joins the enemy through unlawful channels.

In a discussion about the civilization of pioneers, Wolf says that some people do not fight, not because they are cowards, but because they are too civilized. "Terror and force are great weapons. Organizations in every country use them and never underestimate their power" (p. 69). When Mosca relies on them to solve his personal problem, he becomes a symbolic protagonist for the literature that Mario Puzo "contracts" and "registers into" the American literary mainstream.

The Fortunate Pilgrim

In his second novel, *The Fortunate Pilgrim*,[2] Mario Puzo explores the stresses of Italian-American life on New York's Tenth Avenue during

2. Mario Puzo, *The Fortunate Pilgrim* (New York: Atheneum, 1964).

the nineteen-thirties. He lifts the story of one tenacious immigrant, Lucia Santa Angeluzzi-Corbo, to the broad American theme of the struggle of an ethnic minority to survive and achieve what social scientists call upward mobility. All the members of Maria Santa's family attempt in their own ways to achieve economic solvency for the family while she holds a tight control over each. Puzo dramatizes this theme with evocative power. Covering two decades preceding the Japanese attack on Pearl Harbor, the writer penetrates thoroughly one of the fragmented groups of America, and exposes a skeletal pattern of endemic genesis: American success is implemented by the compromise of ideals through the use of illegality, which may lead to organized protective pressure or to competitive violence. The reader may conclude that material success in any area operates on the same dark principle.

The characters in this story illustrate the author's idea with varying degrees of success. Puzo does luxuriate in polemics about the American Dream, but his rhetoric effectively intensifies the meaning of the situations in which he moves his characters. His intimate knowledge of them and of their behavior engages the reader into the crises of their actions so that even coarse liberties with language become acceptable. With the legendary magic of the once-in-a-generation unsurpassed story-teller, Puzo drills his message of sinister realities into the reader's consciousness, and subconscious.

The scope of the book is ethnically specific and socially inclusive. While Puzo evokes the environment of a first-generation Italian family in America, his story is memorable because of his portrayal of a human being, Lucia Santa, who forges a place for her family. As a representative unit of an ethnic minority, Lucia is a formidable matriarch, twice widowed but undefeated by circumstances. Fanatically dedicated to her six children, she resists the temptation of keeping her mentally disintegrating husband at home; she has him committed to an institution where he may have suitable care while he waits to die. With the same protective instinct for the children, she refuses to have the boy Vincenzo adopted by the wealthy Philomena, but coerces the older children into contributing to the support of the younger ones. Larry, the oldest, becomes a "dummy-boy," guiding the New York Central through the streets of New York, dreaming of becoming a romantic hero, but succumbing to the seduction of an easier and more remunerative career. This decision gradually implicates him with a syndicated protective organization operating through coercion. Octavia, the oldest daughter in the Corbo family, is a counterpoint to Larry in her integrity. The prototype of the second-generation Italian-American girl, she relinquishes her ambition of going to college. To help the family, she becomes a supervisor in a garment factory, where she meets Norman Bergeron, a Jewish employee who dreams of writing poetry. Their eventual wedding supplies an exuberant chapter of Italian-Americana. In contrast to the wedding is the funeral of Vincenzo, who meets a tragic, accidental death that cannot be compensated. In time, also, the death and funeral of Frank Corbo provide occasion for detailed descriptions of Italian-American rituals.

While these episodes entrench Lucia Santa's position in her family, the resisting Gino, inheritor of Frank Corbo's rebellious nature, complicates her strategy for facing the future. Although he cooperates temporarily, he escapes to the Army to serve in World War II. Eventually, Lucia Santa rides with her family in Larry's limousine to their new home on Long Island, and reflects on her good fortune and looks for a better life to come.

The Fortunate Pilgrim explores the agitation on the home front during the war years. In it the compromise of ethics with necessity generates the domestic problems that tighten the restrictions of an already limited social environment. Assurance of success or happiness is lessened. Maria Santa's enemy is life itself; her only weapons are her shrewd invincibility and her strategy of functioning with the basic instinct of self-preservation. She is one of those country women from the farms of Italy of whom Puzo writes,

> Audacity had liberated them: They were pioneers, though they never walked an American plain and never felt real soil beneath their feet. They moved in a sadder wilderness, where the language was strange, where their children became members of a different race. It was a price that must be paid. (p. 8)

Describing these immigrants, Puzo presents the case of the Italian-American writer whose very identity has been obliterated before he acquired the basic tools of language, but who nevertheless forged through the unsympathetic social structure to professional recognition. The protagonist is healthy, courageous, and fearless, without being foolhardy and reckless. In the beginning of this story, Puzo equips Lucia Santa with everything she needs for the responsibility of bringing a large family to adulthood and freedom; but at this time she lacks the cunning that does more for people than virtue. Against her better judgment, she allows Octavia to prevail upon her to lessen her pressure on Larry, who becomes entangled with the Le Cinglatas, the bootleggers in the neighborhood. This atypical permissiveness is the slip that lets loose the dogs of war with the law. Some of the general reaction to the law enforcement figures is exemplified even in the quiet and sensitive younger brother, who cavorts with Joey on box cars and taunts the police. When the officer hesitates to frighten the boys by drawing his gun because he is afraid that the Italian laborers in the "yard gangs" might see him and he would then be a marked man, the action forecasts the author's subsequent development of coercive gangster tactics. Puzo depicts this type of action, however, as a release from the tensions created by the frustrations in just surviving, his pervasive theme. Boys who grow up in this grim atmosphere are victimized by problems, the solutions to which are vague or thwarted for the lack of proper agents. For example, when Gino and Vincent (Vincenzo) are confused at the oppressive anguish at home over the disappearance of the father, the only consolation they have is to "sit-sleep" together on the window sill, feeling the breeze from the Hudson River. The smell of green things is something strange, from a distance beyond their reach. Receptive to the danger of their mood, Lucia Santa strikes out against Larry, and excoriates the Le Cinglatas. This action also intensifies Puzo's demonstration that those people are successful who put money above everything. Of these people, Lucia Santa says, "What animals. And yet when they have money they dare look everyone in the eye" (p. 77). Then, when the Cinglatas send an emissary, ostensibly a lawyer, to Lucia Santa, she realizes that her son's involvement is serious. But she maintains her dignity and does not quail before the man she knows to be a dangerous criminal. Later, she gives the admiring Octavia the courage to go to her work, saying that honest people like themselves never get rich. The situation has subtle implications for the rest of the family. Larry confronts Charlie, the policeman, about the boys, who have been stealing coal from railroad property. Chiding the officer for having beaten the boys, he tries to "reason" with the law. Puzo writes, "It was well done. Everyone had saved face, he hadn't been too tough and made enemies, and he hadn't backed down" (p. 83). This action depicts the thematic pattern of survival in the story. Later, the dramatic action of this theme is sharpened in the open fight between Larry and the "Bull," an incident that demonstrates to all the witnesses that neither man is a coward, and the tensions are dispelled.

This struggle for survival affects all the family's thinking. For example, when Vincent returns from his summer visit at the country home of the *Herald Tribune* Fresh Air Fund members, he overwhelms his mother with his new insights into another world with people who want him to return and who will send him presents. Lucia Santa wonders what kind of people these are who make strange children happy. She comments about how safe these people must be to "squander" love and money on a boy whom they might never see again. In the Corbo home she has learned that the stress of money problems is tragically crushing even to integrity. When Octavia is fired, for example, because she cannot with a clear conscience convince poverty-stricken women that they should buy gadget-loaded sewing machines, she learns that to get ahead in the world means despoiling her fellow-human beings. Her illusions disappear as she realizes that her former teachers have "tricked her with their compliments with their urgings to find a better life. . . . They had sold her an ideal too expensive for her world" (p. 115). Her disenchantment gives her greater understanding of her mother, for whom money is the equivalent of the new homeland. She is, therefore, proportionately surprised that her mother, paradoxically, is careless with money, buying the best olive oil, the most expensive cheese, and only imported prosciutto, while she systematically hoards money to buy a house in Long Island. Octavia is ethnically oriented enough to realize that her "people" do not compromise on the quality of the basics for survival, but she is educated sufficiently to know that it is the pressure of the need to succeed that destroys some immigrants. Frank Corbo is only one of the many Italian men in America to break under this pressure, as if, as Puzo writes, in leaving their homeland they had torn a vital root from both body and mind. A broken man, he finally cries out against the policemen's collaboration with the lawbreakers and personally defies their power to overcome him. Only the strong Lucia Santa can control him. Her deft strategy is particularly effective when Zí Pasquale, the most successful of the lawbreakers, loses his money in the bank, and she comments that nothing ever "goes right," no matter what you do. No one believes her, because everyone knows that she is pessimistic only in speech; but her sympathy is a necessary balm. Puzo writes, "Yet she lived like a true believer in good fortune" (p. 167). Only the daughter, Octavia, really shares with her mother the disturbance and wreckage with which the Depression unsettles the home. Octavia is particularly concerned about the young Gino and Sal, whom she sees growing up to be stupid laborers, loutish, coarse, living in slums, and breeding children into the same poverty.

Despite the poverty, optimism persists. Octavia reassures her mother, for example, that she is not having a baby without a husband, that she is still a "good Italian girl." She spurns and curses at the condescending welfare agent, who, courting her, flaunts his token knowledge of the heroines of nineteenth-century American novels. He is unaware of the fact that she is an avid reader, has seen many plays, and holds in contempt "those generous, witless maidens who exposed themselves to shame while serving pleasure to men who flouted their wealth as bait" (p. 194). Puzo portrays the agent as the Italian-American who exploits his own people, who are, in turn, rescued by Anglo-Saxon Americans of integrity. The author is creating at this point a correlative of the Italian-American writers who have been obsequious to publishers and readers by writing novels with characters in stereotyped roles that are ingratiating and despicable. Puzo, in selecting the materials he uses, is doing what Octavia does to clear the atmosphere of that "treatment accorded to the sick," the treatment that Lucia Santa, the conventional Italian, has accepted only because everyone must pay to stay alive. Larry, on the other hand, seeks a way out of the trap of a relentless environment. The reader feels the pathos of Larry's submission when Zí Pasquale asks, "Do you respect me as a man? Do you accept me as a tribal chief, as a second father, as an honorary godfather?" (p. 201). These questions have overtones about the kind of job being offered. In Larry's classically Italian answer, "It would be a pleasure to work for you," lies the entire commitment of the socioeconomic morality that Puzo examines here and, later, more extensively in *The Godfather.* He is dramatizing the Italian-American who is compelled to accept organized pressure in order to survive, but who must hold this relationship in respect, protecting it by silence and cementing it with unalterable loyalty. In this way, the future is assured.

This theme is supported by other characters in the neighborhood, who pay their dues "as befitted people who in the old country gave eggs to a priest for reading a letter and wine to a village clerk for telling them what the laws were" (p. 207). Observing that the police support this cooperation, Larry sees the "whole majesty of the law" crumble before his eyes, especially when the German baker is coerced into submission. Mr. di Lucca tries to assure Larry that poor people cannot live by all the laws and stay alive. His arguments for compromise in order to survive sustain even Lucia Santa, who appreciates her good fortune that she will not die alone. She can rationalize saving money by buying stolen goods by believing that the people who sell these goods are no different from the more affluent shopkeepers. As she dozes, thinking of her children, Puzo says of her, "America, America, what different bones and flesh grow in your name" (p. 242). She pities the wistful Vincent, and Larry, who has fallen from the standard of the real men of Italy who were "husbands, protectors of children . . . creators of their own world, acceptors of life and fate who let themselves be turned into stones to provide the rock on which their family stood" (p. 243). With these words, Puzo emphasizes the general degradation of the Italian-American in his alien environment. The writer does not place the fault on America alone, because he asks, "Where were those wretches who cursed America and its dream?" (p. 257).

With the war, these people earned money and made plans to buy houses. They have even developed personal power, illustrated in Larry's being able to force Lefty Fay to tell the truth about Vinnie's accident. Vinnie, the writer insists, did not survive because of his gentle, vulnerable kindness and his fatal awareness of defeat.Gino, on the other hand, all perception and cognizance, is contemptuous even of his mother, who pretends at the funeral that all these curious people are Vinnie's friends. Lucia Santa, however, dismisses Gino's arrogance because she realizes what he does not know of the terrible need that she has had for shields against the blows of fate. When in the end, like a Greek chorus, the old women of Tenth Avenue chant Lucia Santa's woes, she measures the extent of her good fortune: her children are busy, healthy, strong, and handsome; she runs her house like a signora; she reaps courage from the anticipation of moving; and she has proved that in America you can "escape your destiny."

The theme of survival is, therefore, personified and fulfilled in Lucia

Santa, surrounded by the old women who are, as Puzo writes, "ready to murder anyone who stood in the way of so much as a crust of bread for themselves or for their children, implacable enemies of death. They were alive. The stones of the city, steel and glass, the blue-slate sidewalks, the cobblestoned streets, would all turn to dust and they would be alive" (p. 286). As Lucia Santa looks around her on the last day in the apartment, she weeps for her past and for her father, thinking that she had never meant to be a pilgrim; but here she is, like the others, leaving for a strange place, the El Dorado of her dreams. The truth of a dream, she realizes, is that no achievement is perfect. Puzo then concludes that preservation is not enough. When he writes, "America, blasphemous dream," he is emphasizing what his protagonist has learned that she has wanted all she has without guilt, without sorrow, without the fear of death and the terror of judgment, all of which is impossible. Although bread and shelter are not enough for happiness, America holds the opportunity for further possibilities. As Lucia Santa looks into the future on Gino's return from the war, possibly hating her as she had her father, she knows that he, too, will be a pilgrim and will search for another America. Puzo's theme of survival, therefore, transcends necessity and its incriminatory operations, and looks to a future of a humanity made more expansive in a better environment.

In this story Mario Puzo has explored many Italian-Americanisms with which to expand his theme. When the women talk about the morals of America, which their children are absorbing, they make their judgments with the criteria of the mountain villages in southern Italy that they have left. They confront their children's insolence and defiance with the application of Italian discipline, a razor strap or a *tackeril*, a small club. They cry out with common Italian terms: *Figlio disgraziato* and *Mannaggia America!* In maintaining their old mores they have a slyness that renders them exceedingly effective. Actually, they have assimilated more of America than they pretend: Lucia Santa, for example, speaks idiomatic English when she mimics her children. As a shield against their children's increasing sophistication, they repeat the scandals of their mother country. Lucia Santa makes her compromises, however, even consenting to call her baby Aileen because it is "time to be American"—but she abbreviates the name to "Lena." At times, she, too, is overwhelmed, for example, by the attitude of Octavia who is contemptuous of marrying an Italian because she feels that an Italian wants a woman he can treat like a dog. Puzo portrays Octavia as the typical older sister in the Italian-American household, who shares her mother's responsibility to support and shape the family. The violence with which the mother sometimes strikes her sons to enforce discipline is a behavioral trait of which the daughter does not approve, but she agrees that they all must work hard together. Puzo emphasizes this Italian insistence that the boys be useful in terms of contributing work; he describes Vinnie (Vincent, Vincenzo) as the extreme who has "strange lines of fatigue and tension." This preoccupation with work intensifies with the adults. The men, for example, rarely take the family on pleasure outings. Puzo writes, "These Italians had never stretched idle on a beach. They suffered the sun all week working on the tracks of the railroad. On Sunday, they wanted the cool of a house or garden, they wanted their minds occupied and alert over a deck of cards, they wanted to sip wine, or listen to the gossip of women who would not let them move a finger" (p. 69). In their way of life, they are constantly strengthening the family ties to make every member feel that there is no obligation more sacred than blood. Brothers must defend each other at all costs. This is the power that compels Larry to fight the Bull over Vinnie. With his victory, Larry earns the respect that comes of protecting not only his brother, but his family honor. In practical terms, this inner-directedness of the family enables them all to function with extreme thrift, the kind that buys "thousands of houses" on Long Island. Lucia Santa is atypical in that, while she saves, she spends some of her money. Generally, the clannishness of the people extends even to spiritual dimensions: Roman Catholicism, for example, is as much a part of their "blood" as their family relationship, and, when Frank Corbo is persuaded to join the Literal Baptist Church, this action is an uprooting that precipitates his insanity. This Italian-American group's use of language is a status symbol. When Lucia Santa attempts to impress on the physician that she feels that her husband's illness is largely physical, he responds in accurate, academic Italian, which labels him as her enemy, the class of people who exploit the poor. On the other hand, there are happier dimensions of ethnical attitudes, as when, for example, the crates of grapes are delivered in the fall for wine-making. Furthermore, most of the immigrants have an obsession about improving themselves through education. "Otherwise," writes Puzo, "you'll be just a slob down on the docks or in the railroad" (p. 151). Education, however, is only a means; the supreme accomplishment is respectability. When Lucia Santa investigates the Marconozzi, the family of her future daughter-in-law, her single concern is that the girl have a good reputation. Articulating another Italian attitude, Zia Louche, her friend, assures Lucia Santa that philandering men like her son marry only girls who are irreproachable. The most characteristic Italian reaction to an American condition, however, is implicit in Zí Pasquale's remark when, having lost his money, he says, "They stole it from me without a gun, without a knife, in broad daylight. How is it possible?" (p. 164). However, writes Puzo, since in this land there has been hope, they all will start again. Although difficult to comply with, this constructive attitude pervades the environment, in which even Lucia Santa, as she pampers the welfare worker, feels no resentment for having to pay tribute. Much of the protection offered is extended with the rhetoric of affection; but, as

Puzo writes, "Underneath the affection there was iron" (p. 206). This iron clamps them heavily to their past and present, while moves to the future are constrained. Symbolically, when Lucia Santa is about to leave her old rooms, she is engulfed wearily by nostalgia. Puzo is demonstrating that this is the common nostalgia that all immigrants have for their former life and origins; but the change must be made; and when Lucia Santa complains, Octavia calls her a "phony." The daughter knows that her mother's traits are indelible, especially in her attitudes toward her family and their relationships with members of other ethnic groups. Whatever racism Lucia Santa shows is usually an attempt at humor or a snide characterizing, as in her son's going with the "Irish tramp from Ninth Avenue," or her daughter's marrying the "only Jew in the world who does not know how to make money." Lucia Santa is that type of Italian-American, who, in a show of respect to others, suffers self-recrimination. In any event, she is prepared to follow her "buona fortuna" to a more spacious house, which will more lavishly contain the problems of more people.

Mario Puzo uses the protagonist of *The Fortunate Pilgrim* to control his story. For this reason, a cursory reader may miss the really penetrating delineations of the other characters, who give proportion to the progressive action of the book. Lucia Santa is a woman of power, a goddess of her bit of earth, as she watches the family playing, studying, maturing, marrying, departing, dying, and paying tribute by their respect for her. Puzo says that she is "like the legend of God peering out of a cloud at human children too engrossed to glance upward and catch him" (p. 81). Although she is illiterate and uneducated in any profession, she is competent emotionally and mentally and her decisions relate to others. For example, because she knows that her husband will be a liability to the family and that she has a duty to her children, she dismisses her personal feelings in order to preserve the honorable unity of the family. She has a special relationship with Gino, who resists her in his own determined fashion to rise above her stated conviction that the family should be satisfied with merely staying alive. The tension between mother and son is aggravated dramatically by the mounting, unforgiving anger that Lucia Santa nurses over Gino's failure to attend his father's funeral. With a vengeance, she eventually humiliates this willful son at the rituals of Vinnie's death. Usually, however, her behavior is either intensified or contradicted by Octavia's response to it. Octavia, poised tragically between her mother and the needs of the other children, possesses both a superior intellect and a creative imagination, but she is trapped by an environment that crushes her potential and bends her to work in a garment factory. With a vengeful irony, Puzo has this literate victim retaliate with blasphemous and obscene language; her curses frighten the children into submission, but the reader feels that her imprecations are aimed at a hateful fate. She assumes her mother's sense of duty and honor by surrendering any ideas she has about teaching in order to work to help the boys go to college, sublimating her ambition by helping the children with their homework, taking them to the dental clinic, and planning how to save her mother's money. Her stay at a sanatorium proves to be a brief oasis that gives her a taste of another life, the mannerisms of which she pathetically imitates for a few weeks, but then must drop to conform to her situation. Not without some bitterness has she earned her mother's pronouncement that she is the best of the children. Lucia Santa appreciates not only Octavia's wholehearted moral support, but her honest appraisal of the relationships within the family and Octavia is as happy when she lightens the look of "suffering and loneliness" on her young brother's face as when she enjoys the gentle, comfortable companionship of her husband, Norman. She finds it rewarding, also, that Larry's success is due in part to his gracious manners and willingness to cooperate. In Larry the reader recognizes the young prototype of Don Vito Corleone in *The Godfather.* It is a mark of Puzo's sure competence that the people in *The Fortunate Pilgrim* have vigorous life, motivated action, and projected expectations. Even the old women of the neighborhood, though they may be buried, will, as he says, instantly come alive, chanting the entrance hymn of Lucia Santa's service of fortune.

Mario Puzo has said that *The Fortunate Pilgrim* is one of his better books.[3] The reader is impressed by the author's masterful ability to tell a gripping story that is illuminated by recognizable people. Puzo depicts Lucia Santa's quest for stability with authentic details and intensely dramatic episodes. He argues eloquently against accepting the frontier theory that American civilization has come about through colonization by Anglo-Saxon people exclusively. Lucia Santa symbolizes other immigrants whose linguistic and cultural compromises are in proportion to their intelligence and will to make a change. With a sure sense of drama, Puzo portrays his group with a whole spectrum of emotional experiences from farcical comedy to lacerating tragedy, avoiding sentimental extravagance. He handles his scenes with authority and force, whether it be a wedding, a funeral, a family quarrel, or a detective's subtle acceptance of a legal infraction. His familiarity with and sensitivity to his metier give precision and verity to his portrayals, without either social overtones, condescension or reactive defensiveness. At times he uses colloquial diction with ethnic overtones, intensifying his characterizations. Generally, he avoids embellishments and literary mannerisms. *The Fortunate Pilgrim,* in its legend, force, insight, language, authenticity, and persuasion, is good enough to be the classic Italian-American novel and an important milestone in the mainstream of American literature.

3. Tom Buckley, "The Mafia Tries A New Tune," *Harper's Magazine* (August 1971), p. 55.

The Godfather

The history of the United States has recorded the rise of the Robber Barons in the nineteenth century. In fiction, writers like William Dean Howells and Theodore Dreiser differed in their presentation of the moguls of American enterprise. In the twentieth century, fired by legends and reports of unprecedented rags-to-riches achievements, immigrants followed the dream of easy success in America. Therefore, exploring the methods by which to make use of the opportunity here, the newcomers gradually developed forms of organized effort to help themselves. In time entrepreneurs arrived, marking the succession of ethnic groups: the Germans, the Scandinavians, the Irish, the Italians, the Jews, the Slavs, the mobilized Blacks. As each group in turn became assimilated, its members occasionally fortified themselves with dynastic policies in politics in order to rally, solidify, and perpetuate useful working factions in our party system of government. Although this power at times may have been implemented by coercive or even illegal methods, once the power was galvanized it continued to maintain itself by legitimate means while simultaneously intercepting threatening competition by obliterating the competitor, illegally if necessary.

Daniel Bell, in an essay entitled "Crime As an American Way of Life," affirms that crime has been a ladder of upward social mobility from the beginning of our nation's history. He agrees with the frequently asserted statement that many of our great fortunes have been acquired by methodically bribing public officials, padding public contracts, organizing violence, price-fixing, and exercising the despotic generalship attributed to the mid-twentieth-century mobster. It is beyond the province of this discussion to present the available research materials that expose the man who makes his fortune by running contraband goods in one generation in order to leave a legacy that in two or three generations entangles national policy. The coterie of such a man supplies an abundance of raw material for literature in characters, real or created, who are familiar with the intricate machinery of factional structure and who will use any method to eliminate competition. The frontier skirmishes may appear ruthlessly clannish or brutally combative. When the nation was reading about the "changing of the guard," as it is sometimes called, in the St. Valentine's Day Massacre in Chicago, for instance, it became dramatically aware of the ethnical character of some local revolutions. A "Bugs" Moran who is overcome by an Al Capone may seem to be a far cry from Nelson over Napoleon, but the contemporary conscience is becoming increasingly cognizant of their sinister similarity.

Crime has convenient and, sometimes, paradoxical definitions. The Nuremberg Trials inaugurated an international controversy that is still raging, over the legality of killing the enemy, which has the sanction of governmental decision, as against the illegality of killing a personal enemy. When conquest by violence is promoted as protective of the nation, it is recognized as patriotic and heroic; when a killing is perpetrated by a self-directed syndicate for the protection of only its own members, it is classified as organized crime. There are increasingly vociferous groups, however, that insist that killing for any purpose is a crime. In any event, the theme of crime continues to fascinate the American reading public. Furthermore, our citizenry responds to violent themes in political terms, seeking constantly to relate them to the functioning government in which politicians must have the means with which to operate. The judgment of whether or not a practice is a crime is confusing to a people who observe, for example, that while gambling as a private enterprise may be classified as syndicated crime, it may be a sanctioned means for a state to raise funds to make its government solvent. Likewise, while extortion is admittedly a criminal activity, there are many taxpayers who consider our national submission to what they term taxation without representation a synonym for a coercion made possible by our fear of governmental bankruptcy. In consequence, personalities in crime and in government have at times become diffused in image.

From the nineteen-twenties to the sixties, the members of the Italian-American Press worked assiduously to demonstrate what they considered the constructive and admirable qualities of a predominantly sober, thrifty, conservative, and self-respecting minority. Newspapers like *Il Popolo*, *Il Progresso*, and *Il Corriere d'America*, along with others of more regional interests, encouraged their readership to cease their defensiveness and to take pride in the wealth of documentation of their historic cultural past. In time, after a long, tenacious campaign to promote the delicate machinery of assimilation in sensitive and critical human areas, a point was reached when even in local politics contestants were careful to avoid hyphenated ethnic terms. Then, suddenly, at the beginning of the sixties, politicians reverted ruthlessly to the exploitation of factions in religious, economic, and ethnic blocs. With this resurgence of factionalism, there emerged militant organizations by which minorities have sought not only to protect themselves, but to promote their welfare within the national structure. Because the Italian-Americans have been predominantly inner-directed as a group, they have not waged wholehearted campaigns in ethnic competitions. Recently, however, as demonstrated by various organizations like the Italian-American Civil Rights League, they have been stirred to unite against what they have termed the unchallenged tendency of the communications media to present factual or fictional stories of crime in almost exclusively Italian ethnic terms. In his essay, "The Mafia and the Web of Kinship," Francis A. J. Ianni writes,

> The strict diffusionist approach that sees only Mafia in Italo-American crime syndicates must therefore assume that the concept of Mafia lay dormant among southern Italian immigrants for

> decades and then suddenly emerged as a model to organize Italo-American involvement in crime. Further, it must assume nothing was happening in the acculturative experience of Italo-Americans that allowed them to find better and already proven models in the native American setting. These assumptions do not bear up under analysis.

Historically, the native American setting has nurtured certain endemic culture-heroes in its literature. In a country whose educational system pervasively offers as one of its several classics of fiction, and sometimes the only one, the anti-establishment and appealing *Huckleberry Finn*, it is a foregone conclusion that the writers of novels should increasingly deal with an anti-hero. In the 1957 Freshman English first-semester course in a large university in the East, there were listed three books for required reading other than the composition texts: *Huckleberry Finn*, Turgenev's *Fathers and Sons*, and *The Great Dialogues of Plato*. For many students this list comprised the total reading assignment in creative American literature during their college years. Since this vital area of education in the humanities is thus limited, and recently has come to require even less student reading, there is reason to believe that even the quasi-educated reading public may be receptive to a matured Huck Finn and able to identify with the multifaceted and solid attractions of a Don Vito Corleone.

Emerging out of our contemporary disposition, Mario Puzo's *The Godfather* is more than a controversial book. Phenomenally, it is a work that grips the reader's imagination, becomes one of the fastest-selling novels in literary history, and sets in motion a host of imitators. There are already numerous books dealing with coercive syndicates, and they cover a whole spectrum of treatment, from Jimmy Breslin's farcical *The Gang That Couldn't Shoot Straight* to Charles Durbin's brutal *Vendetta*. Furthermore, there are various "authentic" works exposing the hierarchical structure of "family" syndicates, one of which is Ovid Demaris's *Captive City*. Coincidentally, the shooting of Joseph Colombo in New York City on June 28, 1971, during the celebration of Italian-American Unity Day, an episode similar to what happens to Don Vito Corleone in *The Godfather*, has heightened public interest, not only in coercive syndicates, but in the drama of Puzo's novel. This interest has spread to a wide variety of articles in periodicals, from Tom Buckley's "The Mafia Tries a New Tune" in *Harper's Magazine* (August 1971) to Nicholas Gage's "How Organized Crime Invades the Home" in *Good Housekeeping* (August 1971).

Tom Buckley makes the point that

> the Italian-American syndicates comprise only one layer, which they share, in many parts of the country, with syndicates of other or mixed ethnic derivation, in what is essentially a vertical struc-

> ture. Without the ready compliance of corrupt police and public officials, such enterprises as bookmaking, policy, loan-sharking, and the importation and distribution of narcotics could not be carried out on a continuing basis, just as without the connivance of corrupt bankers, stock brokers, and realtors, illicit funds could not be transferred into ostensibly legal enterprises.[4]

Buckley also makes the significant observation that Italian-Americans no longer have the brazen, street-wise ghetto youngsters who would profit from such enterprises.

In any event, Mario Puzo, fleshing the skeleton of a contemporary socioeconomic ethnic image, has sculptured an ice-coated snowball and hurled it directly into the face of American duplicity. He definitively explodes Van Wyck Brooks's thesis of the dichotomy of the American literary mind polarized between the overt holiness of Puritan idealism and the covert claptrap of technical materialism. Puzo says: "I was looking to present a myth. That's what real fiction is about. A legend. That's why *The Godfather* takes place twenty or twenty-five years ago. If I really knew more about it I wouldn't have written so popular a book. To me *The Godfather* isn't an exposé; it's a romantic novel."[5] He also says that he did not intend the book as a defacement of Italian-Americans. Apparently, in writing this book, Mr. Puzo has aimed to show that the type of syndicate he portrays is one of the only ways in which the Italian-American could survive in the nation. He says that "It's an environmental thing. Certain animals take on a certain coloring over the generations because of the terrain." Puzo brings together the various themes of Italian-American writers —"out-of-place," isolation, fragmentation, recall, frontier necessity, benevolent villainy, polite segregation, not-so-polite confrontation— all the constituents that perpetuate the basic dichotomy of human nature in the struggle between the constructive and the destructive. With great sweep, hurtling pace, and electrifying suspense, he constructs an inimitable story.

Don Vito Corleone, the benevolent under-establishment despot, rules the Sicilian-American "gangster" world from his post of command in Long Island. The "family" mall supplies the opening scene, where, in full swing, all the members are celebrating the wedding of Costanza Corleone and Carlo Rizzi ("half-breed"—half Sicilian, half Italian). During the festivities, the Godfather is approached by an assortment of favor-seekers and petitioners for interviews by members of his own and others' syndicated "families." Puzo immediately sets in motion the plot and subplots that make the novel massive, turbulent, and vibrating with progressive tensions: the starting point is the

4. Tom Buckley, "The Mafia Tries a New Tune," *Harper's Magazine* (August 1971), p. 56.

5. *Ibid.*, p. 54.

proposition made by the emissary of the Sallozzo-Barzini family to exchange the Don's political connections for impending profits in the narcotics traffic. Meanwhile we witness the beginning of the Sonny Corleone-Lucy Mancini sexual relationship, the solidification of the positions of the sons in the family, the exposition of the connection to the Don of singer Johnny Fontane, and the Don's briefing of *consigliere*, Tom Hagen, on the family's strategy. Hagen is a German-American who has been reared in the Corleone family since boyhood.

The narrative begins with the Godfather's refusal to cooperate with the competing families who insist on planning to trade in narcotics. An attempt is made on his life and, based on an authentic incident, a gang war follows. Moving with breathtaking speed, scene follows scene to recreate the smell, sound, and feeling of every conceivable type of brutal murder. Observing the time-honored code of Sicilian tribal customs, hierarchies, and pacts, the Corleone family systematically exterminates its enemies, including its own members who have demonstrated their treachery. In the course of this relentless bloodbath the subplots are developed. Connie Corleone Rizzi is repeatedly beaten brutally by her husband, who is disgruntled at his slow advancement in the family business. Then, one day, as Sonny Corleone is on the way to defend his sister, he is murdered. The Don forbids any reference to this in the future, but it becomes the dramatic device and motive for the outcome of the story. When the Don survives the attempt on his life, his exquisite strategy leads the son Michael, the thoroughly Americanized Dartmouth student in love with the more thoroughly American Yankee Kay Adams, to avenge the father's assault by murdering Sallozzo and the cooperating police officer, Captain McCluskey. The Don's long arm reaches to Sicily, where Michael is harbored until he receives the news of Sonny's death. During his stay in Sicily, Michael, convinced that Kay Adams must know the truth about him and his family, marries the exotic Appolonia, who is soon afterwards killed by a bomb intended for her husband. The Sallozzo-Barzini connection having obviously ferreted out his whereabouts, Michael's reasons for returning home are compounded. Meanwhile, through the legal functioning of Tom Hagen, the Don has held a visibly peaceable hold on his empire, indicating no further ambitions for power, informing everyone that his intentions are to concentrate on investments in Las Vegas. He has set in motion the machinery for insuring the success in Hollywood of his godson, Johnny Fontane, by a gruesome subjugation of producer Jack Woltz. In this detail, Puzo exposes the sadistic mores and opportunism of the success code in the world of entertainment. The progression of events then leads to Las Vegas, where Freddie Corleone is a hotel manager, and where Lucy Mancini has been settled by the Corleone family. Lucy meets and eventually marries Dr. Jules Segal. When Michael Corleone returns, only his father, the astute and perceptive Don, appreciates him as the potential Godfather. Michael, accepting his destiny, assumes the power designated to him by his father, and, following his father's death, immediately executes his father's plan of exterminating all his enemies and emerging as the undisputed Don. He marries Kay Adams, who reluctantly but philosophically accepts the truth about the Corleones. Ironically, this New England Puritan turned Sicilian becomes the new Don's loyal wife, bears him two sons, embraces his ancestral religion and family loyalties, becomes absorbed in his life, and unites with his mother in praying for his soul.

The Godfather is a story dealing with the contemporary strategy of gaining and securing power. While Niccolo di Bernardo Machiavelli wrote a handbook to guide a prince in expediently establishing his forces in a political world of contending monarchies, Mario Puzo has fictionalized the code for the gaining of control over others in the competition of outlawed enterprises. While the prince had to create and promote warfare, mobilizing armies of mercenaries to seize power from vulnerable monarchies, the American gang leader builds an economic empire in which he attains power by personal warfare, the killing of competitors in the contexts of loyalty or treachery. Both contenders must operate in a vacuum, constantly circling in the absence of popularly ratified and enforced law and order. Puzo's theme is that gangsterism in America thrives as the result of the cooperation of elected government agents.

This theme is dramatized by the struggles of the competitive forces in the novel. Amerigo Bonasera, seeking vindication for the assault on his daughter by two young men who go unpunished because of the corruption of the courts, decides "They have made fools of us. . . . For justice we must go on our knees to Don Corleone."[6] With this statement, Puzo's theme is triggered into action. The Don, responding to the quest, demonstrates that when a man is generous, he must show the generosity to be personal. He asks, "Why did you go to the police? Why didn't you come to me at the beginning of the affair?" (p. 30). Using the strategy of operating from a personal basis, the Don shows that justice is built on the debts incurred through friendship. He emphasizes the hypocrisy of the law, saying that when the judge rules, America rules, and accepting his judgment is approving the ethics of a judge "who sells himself like the worst whore in the streets" (p. 32). The Don knows that the courts are sheltered by higher powers; even the Senator shows him this, since, as Puzo writes, he is one of the great stones in the Don's power structure, and his generous gift at the wedding is a reaffirmation of loyalty. This kind of power is not visible to the uninitiated. Kay Adams, Michael's Yankee sweetheart, sees the Don as a good-hearted and generous business man whose methods are perhaps not exactly constitutional. It is not possible for her to perceive

6. Mario Puzo, *The Godfather* (New York: G. P. Putnam's Sons, 1969), p. 17.

the nuances of the Don's statement as he promises Johnny Fontane the movie role he wants: "I say to you: you shall have it" (p. 44). This kind of disposal power generates from a firm, hierarchical structure with an internal complexity that can only baffle Kay's Anglo-Saxon mind. As Puzo writes, "Between the head of the family, Don Corleone, who dictated policy, and the operating level of men who actually carried out the orders of the Don, there were three layers, or buffers. In that way nothing could be traced to the top. Unless the *Consigliere* turned traitor" (p. 50). The author assures us that no *Consigliere* has ever betrayed any of the powerful Sicilian families that have established themselves in America. The *consigliere* is not only the advisor but also the tactician. For example, it is Tom Hagen's role to call on Jack Woltz, the producer, to inform him that if the interview concerning Johnny Fontane is not a happy one, there could be a labor strike at the movie studio. Hagen has learned the art of negotiation from the Don himself. One never gets angry or makes a threat; rather, one should "reason with people." The art of reasoning is to ignore all insults. Hagen, however, has the courage to express himself when the Don asks his advice, as he does about the Sollozzo proposition to engage in the drug traffic. The lawyer feels that the other "family" will amass so much revenue that they may become a threat, but he cannot convince the Don, who will not negotiate with men who traffic in drugs and sex. The Don's ethics in this matter prove to be a tragic flaw, because his decision tempts defections from his power structure.

Eventually, particular incidents of violence must lead to negotiation. After the Don survives the attack on him, Solozzo, observing the strategy of traditional warfare, uses a tactic of delay to earn time to win allies and "avert a big war which hurts everybody and brings the papers and government into the act. Also, Sollozzo wiill give them a piece of action" (p. 115). When Sonny wants to solve everything by simply killing Sollozzo, Hagen advises him that "this is not a personal thing, this is business," a statement that introduces a corollary theme. Tensions are increased by the interpretations of action; Sonny cannot concede that the shooting of his father was business, not personal. Puzo uses much of the following action to demonstrate the causes of warfare and how abstract economics reduces to the personal factor. For example, when Michael, the student, visits his father in the hospital, he no longer feels that he is negotiating a business transaction; he does feel a furious anger rising in him, and a cold hatred for his father's enemies. Learning that the police captain, McCluskey, has been paid an extraordinary sum to remove the official guard detectives from the Don's door, and that McCluskey is going to get a "piece of the drug operation," Michael is not so certain that matters can be settled without a major war.

Negotiations among warring syndicates are impossible without police protection. Puzo draws McCluskey as the catalyst of bribery in a deliberately ignorant society. He writes, "He never confided in his wife on anything. She thought they lived the way they did on his policeman's salary." McCluskey, says Puzo, has been "a brave cop"; he has obeyed the system, taking "only clean graft," and has sent his four sons to Fordham University. Making it his policy "never to show that he understood what other people were up to," he asks a price because he knows that Sollozzo is after "one of the biggest Mafia men in the country" (p. 139). It never occurs to him that he might be in danger, and he needs money to send to his uncles and aunts in Ireland so that they may keep their potato farms. In this thinking is a diffusion of law, business, and personal interest. Michael's strategy, however, involves more of the personal element. Planning to avenge his father, he arranges with Tom Hagen to send emissaries to Sicily to prepare a hiding place for him. His act of personal revenge will precipitate the war among the "Families," a type of war always fought only by the persons involved. As his *caporegime* (lieutenant), Clemenza, says, "These things have to happen every ten years or so. It gets rid of the bad blood. And then if we let them push us around on the little things they want to take over everything. You gotta stop them at the beginning. Like they shoulda stopped Hitler at Munich" (p. 142). Michael remembers that the Don said in 1939 that if the Families had been running the State Department, there would never have been a World War II.

Once the personal decision is made, then the strategy for acquiring power extends to group action. A "family" war depends upon timing and on "how well we can plant stories with the newsmen. How much the Police Department wants to cover up. How violently the other Families react" (p. 145). All these factors, however, are external projections of the personal. Michael tells Tom Hagen, "It's all personal, every bit of business. Every piece . . . every man has to eat every day of his life is personal. . . . The Great Don. He takes everything personal. Like God. He knows every feather that falls from the tail of a sparrow. . . . Accidents don't happen to people who take accidents as a personal insult" (p. 147).

In Book III, Puzo interrupts his story to give a biographical history of Don Vito Corleone, tracing the development of his power from its beginning in Hell's Kitchen. In his first involvement with the neighborhood extortionist, he learns that a man with great connections does not inform to the police; therefore, he has no choice other than to kill Fanucci. From this experience, Vito Corleone derives one of his personal beliefs, that every man has only one destiny, that Fanucci has set him on the path to become a Don. Later, when he is advising Sonny to study law because "Lawyers can steal more money with a briefcase than a thousand men with guns and masks" (p. 221), he shrugs his shoulders at the information that Sonny has witnessed Fanucci's murder, an admission that now seals Sonny's own destiny. As the Don's power becomes entrenched, he weighs the facts that all the great cities of Amerca are torn by underworld strife, and that guerrilla wars might lead to stricter laws. Puzo makes the significant point that "He foresaw that public indignation might even lead to a suspension of democratic procedures which could be fatal to him and his people" (p. 222). Like other lawgivers in history, Don Corleone decides to reduce the warring factions to a manageable number; after three years he brings peace to New York and becomes the national underworld's apostle for peace. Ironically, he achieves a working agreement that Puzo describes as being like the Constitution of the United States, respecting fully the internal authority of each member in his state or city. The agreement covered only spheres of influence and the cooperation to enforce peace in the underworld. This is the vast power the Don achieves and his son emulates. Sonny (Santino) has observed the operations of the confidence men at Long Beach. Impressed by the legality of sales swindlers, the Don decides to have a place where his talents can be used in a world other than that of his "honest youth." He is brought to bed, however, by Sollozzo's ambition.

Family wars use a strategy based on fixed codes. Sonny Corleone's bloodthirstiness, for example, is condemned as barbaric and lacking in sound business sense. Paradoxically, Sonny's ruthlessness does not allow him any personal violence toward women, children, or helpless creatures. This tenderness proves to be the flaw that tricks him to his death. All the Dons are good listeners, patient men. As Puzo describes them, he writes, "They had one other thing in common. They were those rarities, men who had refused to accept the rule of organized society, men who refused the dominion of other men. There was no force, no mortal man who could bend them to their will unless they wished it. They were men who guarded their free will with wiles and murder. Their wills could be subverted only by death. Or the utmost reasonableness" (p. 287). When these men go about their business, their lives and their fortunes depend upon their doing each other services. Puzo explains that the denial of a favor asked by a friend was an act of aggression. Since these favors were not asked lightly, they could not be lightly refused. In this context, Don Corleone assumes the posture of being at peace before his competitors until the safe return of his son. He formally agrees to disregard the drug traffic and to give his consent to the Families' assisting one another in technical matters like the bribing of jurors.

The family absorption in personal matters includes only those areas which are strictly Sicilian. Don Corleone, in "making his peace" with the other Dons, emphasizes that not one finger will be lifted against a man among them without the utmost justification. Enlightening the reader about the Sicilian code, he says:

"As for our own deeds, we are not responsible to the .90 calibers, the *pezzonovantis* who take it upon themselves to decide what we shall do with our lives, who declare wars they wish us to fight in to protect what they own. Who is to say we should obey the laws they make for their own interest and to our hurt? And who are they then to meddle when we look after our own interests? . . . these are our own affairs. We will manage our world for ourselves because it is our world. . . . And so we have to stick together to guard against outside meddlers. Otherwise they will put the ring in our nose as they have put the ring in the nose of all the millions of Neapolitans and other Italians in this country" (p. 293).

Trying to translate this code to Kay, Michael rationalizes that his father has been a businessman who has worked to provide for his family and friends. The Don has not accepted the codes of America because the rules would have condemned an Italian man of extraordinary force and character. He says,

> What you have to understand is that he considers himself the equal of all those great men like Presidents and Prime Ministers and Supreme Court Justices and Governors of the States. He refuses to live by rules set by others, rules which condemn him to a defeated life. But his ultimate aim is to enter that society with a certain power since society doesn't really protect its members who do not have their own individual power. In the meantime he operates on a code of ethics he considers far superior to the legal structures of society. (p. 365)

Then, when Michael agrees to the adoption of this code, he explains that he believes in Kay and the family they will have together. However, he does not trust society to protect them. He warns, "I have no intention of placing my fate in the hands of men whose only qualification is that they managed to con a block of people to vote for them" (p. 365). He admits that his father's time is over, that the Corleone Family must join society, but he insists that he will join it with plenty of power of his own.

To secure this possibility Michael's strategy is as efficient as he can make it by imitating the Don, operating with an astutely hidden force, "a man jealously guarding his true strength from public gaze, following the Don's precept that a friend should always underestimate your virtues and an enemy overestimate your faults" (p. 399). When the strategy succeeds, Michael becomes the Italian-American who is respected in general society. Remembering that the Don's last words are "Life is so beautiful," he decides that power is only a means of enhancing human values. With this conviction, he is free to improve on the course of his father, who had lived in a world of warfare. With his full membership in the executive council of men, he may care for his children, his family, his world. Puzo writes, "But his children would grow in a different world. They would be doctors, artists, scientists,

Governors, Presidents. Anything at all. He would see to it that they joined the general family of humanity, but he, as a powerful and prudent parent would most certainly keep a wary eye on that general family" (p. 410).

Puzo pursues his themes through the actions of the characters, especially of the protagonists in the novels: Walter Mosca succumbing to the degeneration of a militarily imposed environment, Lucia Santa compromising for survival against hostile obstacles, and Don Vito Corleone overcoming a society by exploiting its weaknesses.

Admittedly, there is some ophidian quality about Don Vito Corleone. To the wary reader, however, the Godfather is not a cobra, coiled and ready to spring. He is, rather, more closely related to the serpent in the Garden of Eden, exposing by knowledge the inevitable conclusions. Motivated by a tragic wisdom restricted by circumstances, he functions by disciplined, cold reasoning. Created with what he accepts as a God-invested power, the Don is the knowing agent of a force forbidden to flourish because it operates within a structure fouled by human decadence. He is the archetype of the highly endowed man born into a minority group, who thereby is consigned to limited freedom within pre-established boundaries largely controlled by piratical men. In his exclusive world, the Don reigns as supreme arbiter and benefactor. Puzo demonstrates that many people owe their good fortune in life to the Don and that, on intimate occasions like a wedding, they are free to call him "Godfather." Even the entertainers and service people are his friends. He, in turn, receives everyone—powerful, humble, rich, and poor—with an equal show of warmth. He slights no one; nor is he ever angry with anyone. "He had long ago learned that society imposes insults that must be borne, comforted by the knowledge that in this world there comes a time when the most humble of men, if he keeps his eyes open can take his revenge on the most powerful" (p. 19).

With all his humility, the Don has other qualities that contribute to his superiority. At Costanza's wedding, it is Don Vito Corleone who senses that something is amiss between Johnny Fontane and Nino Valenti; it is he, therefore, who plans the ensuing action. Furthermore, he is honest with Fontane, excoriating him for his disruptive behavior. He warns Fontane to be loyal to Nino, because, says the Don, "Friendship is everything. Friendship is more than talent. It is more than government. It is almost the equal of family" (p. 38). Don Corleone's benign philsophy, however, is an outgrowth of his earlier violence. He had won Fontane's first contract by "putting a pistol to the forehead of the band leader and assuring him with the utmost seriousness that either his signature or his brains would rest on the document in exactly one minute" (p. 43). Power by threat of violence has its limitations, however, although the Don's friends do attribute divine power to him. It is not divinity, but ruthlessness that gives the Don such power. When he has Jack Woltz's six-hundred-thousand-dollar horse killed, the shock intimidates the producer. To the Don, this kind of action is the swift implementation of business, but his code has other restrictions. He will not cooperate with the Sollozzo traffic in drugs and prostitution because he is straitlaced in matters of sex. Nor does he approve of flaunting one's power. Of the eight houses in the mall where the various members of the "family" live, the Don occupies the smallest and least ostentatious home. The harmless-looking compound, however, is an impregnable fortress. Between functional violence and practiced humility, the Don operates with sensitive balance and delicate management. He can assure Fontane's Academy Award because "he controls, or controls the people who control, all the labor unions in the industry, all the people or nearly all the people who vote." This power, however, is propelled by his personal qualities: "to be good, you have to be in contention on your own merits. And your Godfather has more brains than Jack Woltz" (p. 171), says Hagen.

Some of this persuasive power is endemic with Sicilian-Americans, as is demonstrated in this book. Whereas the Mafia in Sicily had been a second government, its escapees in America have extorted money from families and storekeepers by threat of physical violence. From the beginning, the Don has observed an adaptation of this historic precedent in his environment on Tenth Avenue, but he does not submit to the criminal Fanucci. In his initiation into a career of violence, Vito Corleone commits himself with a voice that is reasonable and without anger: "It was courteous, as befitted a young man speaking to an older man of Fanucci's eminence" (p. 200). The phrase "I'll reason with him" becomes the warning rattle before a deadly strike, as Puzo describes it, the final opportunity to resolve an affair without bloodshed. With the Fanucci incident, Mrs. Corleone sees her husband change before her eyes; she feels him radiate a dangerous force. Gradually, with the mounting of this force, he punctuates negotiations with a characteristic smile that is chilling because it attempts no menace. As more people turn to members of the Corleone family for help, Vito Corleone becomes their savior; it is he who is able to prevent Mrs. Colombo's losing her home; he manipulates the landlord. Gradually establishing his image as that of a "man of respect," the Don rises in a traditional pattern. In the "olive-oil war," the men who are not amenable to his reasoning find their warehouses burned. None of the Don's fellow-Sicilians breaks the "ten-century-old law of *omertà* (silence)." All this power might easily remain tribal, but, as Puzo shows, the established government nourishes the powers within and against it. Prohibition rockets Vito Corleone into a star of great power from a quite ordinary, sometime ruthless businessman to a "great Don" in the world of criminal enterprise. Puzo details the structure of the organization, making a convincing argument that "the Don got the idea that he ran his world far better than his enemies ran the greater world which continually obstructed his path" (p. 216). He overcomes his competitors, solidifies his forces, and by 1941 controls some of the industries of a booming America, which industries included black-market OPA food stamps, gasoline stamps, travel priorities, war contracts, black-market materials for clothing firms, and draft exemptions for the men in his organization.

Having thus established the strength of his organization, the Don constantly exerts his power, even to the most intimate detail, over the personalities of the members within it. Puzo illustrates this point in the relationship between the Don and his son-in-law, Carlo Rizzi. The reader has a terrifying suspicion of the facts behind the Don's ostensible equanimity over Rizzi's connection with Sonny's murder. The subtle line between personal interest and structural power tightens when, after he has been told of his son's murder, the Don says, "None of you are to concern yourself with this affair. None of you are to commit any acts of vengeance, none of you are to make any inquiries to track down the murderers of my son without my express command. There will be no further acts of war against the Five Families without my express and personal wish" (p. 273). The reader is instantly aware that all subsequent conflict in the story will be personal. Tension tightens in the dramatic process Puzo uses, picturing the Don as acquiescent and peaceful. We are reminded, however, that Don Corleone is a man who has made only a few mistakes in his career and that he has learned from every one of them. The reader, therefore, is sympathetically engaged in the Don's fate, and finds himself approving and advocating the carnage that is inevitable in the Godfather's personal retribution.

The other characters in the novel support the themes with symbolic differences. Sonny (Santino) has an uncontrollable temper, which his enemies exploit, and a visible intransigence that weakens his strategy. His anger is the flaw that sets in motion the central conflict in the story. As he beats Carlo, his fury creates one of the novel's most brutal scenes. With fatal results, his impetuosity overcomes his reason as he leaves the mall to rush to his sister's defense. While Sonny's reputation for violence makes him thus a marked man, Michael's suave exterior serves as most protective armor for the emerging Don. His deliberately nurtured appearance of detachment from the family business, his Dartmouth education, and his alliance with Kay Adams succeed in deceiving the Corleone enemies into believing that the Don's young son is a weakling. Puzo portrays him, however, with the same quiet reasoning and chilling strategy that marked the Don, but with finer precision. Michael Corleone emerges as a legitimate American corporation man, whose exercise of power, having "made its bones" in the blood of violence, will continue in the national industry. Meanwhile, his family of the future will engage both in politics and in the mainstream of society.

Puzo also shows that this social structure has stratifications according to personal ability, as in the example of the almost anonymous brother Frederico, who finds a suitable niche as a hotel-keeper in Las Vegas. The Las Vegas enterprises bind the Corleone power to the area of entertainment. In this field Johnny Fontane personifies another level of the Godfather's person-oriented, syndicated power, since it is the Don's strength that makes Fontane's fame and fortune.Johnny knows that his relationship with the Don makes him as close to a royal patron as it was possible to be in America. Although he feels that he is a master of his particular type of music, he has learned that success depends on more than talent, that tactics must be the yeast of rising activity. The supreme tactician of the Don's strategy is, of course, the educated and supremely trained Tom Hagen, whom the Don has coached into a working machine for himself. Despite the contempt of the Sicilian families, who have never known of a non-Sicilian *consigliere*, Hagen has been nursed into thinking and acting like a Sicilian to the extent that he can nearly always anticipate his Don's moves. He is completely the Don's man, and is the device for keeping the Don's power in unceasing motion while the Godfather is incapacitated. He is the instrument of detection of and reconciliation with Kay that enables her to understand Michael and accept him dutifully as a husband. In time, Kay becomes as Sicilian as her mother-in-law, submitting herself to this world of men for whom the women pray. We know that these women, like the old women of Tenth Avenue in *The Fortunate Pilgrim*, will survive, for Puzo has warned us of their wisdom, demonstrated in Mrs. Vito Corleone's detachment from the arena of violence and her motherly condescension to the Don in his final years. We also realize that Ginny Fontane, the patient wife to whom Johnny continually returns, will inherit his world and rule his children. All the surviving characters in the story, therefore, are issues of the novel's contained world of power. When Tom Hagen assures Kay that "you and the children are the only people on this earth he couldn't harm," he is implying that the world of violence must dissipate before the rise of the new generation.

In my discussion of the specifics that define the Italian-American novel, *The Godfather* was used as an example of literary material created in order to force attention. Reason supports the conclusion that the feudal world of mobsters and syndicates is atypical of any minority, especially that of the Italian-Americans. Mario Puzo, however, like William Faulkner before he wrote *Sanctuary*, was not appreciated for the masterful novels he had published prior to *The Godfather*. Therefore, he wrote this novel with the avowed intention of producing a best seller. For this reason, the story's presentation of Italian-Americans has the restrictions of a cluster-cultural area. The book's point of view of Italian-American life is therefore simultaneously confined and exaggerated. There are, for example, numerous references to Sicilian customs, such as that by tradition no Sicilian can refuse a request on his daughter's wedding day, and that no Sicilian ever misses such a chance. This inner-directedness intensifies the sensitivity to insulting racial references by other groups, as in the episode when Michael endures Captain McCluskey's tirade outside the hospital, "I thought I got all you guinea hoods locked up" (p. 126). At another time Puzo writes that it never occurs to Johnny Fontane to desert his family and children, that he is too much of an old-style Italian. Not only must the sacredness of the family supersede the needs of any member in it, but the family mores demand certain indispensable obligations. When Kay visits Mrs. Vito Corleone for the first time, the older woman is concerned only with her obligation to make sure that her guest has something to eat. Obligation is the ritual flame of the family altar. It is Sonny's inbred sense of the obligation of a Sicilian brother to protect his sister that moves him against Carlo Rizzi. It is Mama Corleone's obligation as a dutiful wife that binds her, in her wisdom, not to perceive what is going on that pains the men. Systematically, she continues to boil coffee, prepare food, and pray. Tying all the family members together is the closely knit structure of blood relationships; they are a society where family loyalty preempts loyalty to a wife. In a late chapter Puzo describes the detailed background of the Sicilian world to which Michael returns for refuge, where he learns about the roots from which his father grew. This is a world of feudal history and of the struggle of a people faced with the savagery of absolute power, where the historical Mafia has become "the illegal arm of the rich and even the auxiliary police of the legal and political structure. It had become a degenerate capitalist structure, anti-communist, anti-liberal, placing its own taxes on every form of business endeavor no matter how small" (p. 328). There are appealing descriptions of Sicily's pastoral beauty, and of the traditionally humanized interiors of the homes. Puzo emphasizes the Italians' need for living with appointments of beauty, often camouflaged by a stern exterior. When Michael returns to New York, he takes Kay to the decrepit brownstone house in the deteriorated neighborhood on Mulberry Street. Inside, Kay is stunned to find that it is as expensively and comfortably furnished as a millionaire's town house.

Michael's Italianism and Kay's Puritan Americanism are integrated with their marriage. At home, as Kay watches Michael's face when he receives Clemenza, "he reminded her of statues in Rome, statues of those Roman emperors of antiquity, who, by divine right, held the power of life and death over their fellow men" (p. 438). Kay is able to attribute this quality to Michael because she is heiress of an intellectual culture, the American transcendentalism that emerged from classical education with the discipline of Roman ideals. Her acceptance of her husband lies not only in her educated evaluation of his people, but in the identity of the genesis of their common culture.

As a novel, *The Godfather* has been called everything from a staggering literary triumph to a package for best-sellerdom. Admittedly it has all the formulaic requirements of sensationalism in the treatment of sex, sadism, shock, and fear; it also has authenticity, validity, artistry, and power. Puzo himself says: "I wished . . . I'd written it better. . . . It has energy and I lucked out by creating a central character that was popularly accepted as genuinely mythic. But I wrote below my gifts in that book."[7] However, exposing a real dimension of the American ethnic-societal structure, he has succeeded in writing convincing fiction. While he has created a valid social document, he relies more on symbolic action than on metaphysical exposition. Aesthetically, he carries the reader with hurtling momentum, not embellishing the raw events with literary mannerisms. He is a master story-teller who renders the most intolerable episode entirely plausible and natural. Dramatizing in relentlessly detailed action several forms of human slaughter, he electrifies the reader into making some effort to reform law and order in society. Puzo is thus a social historian of American civilization, informing the reader of the nation's sinister and powerful fraternity of crime, and warning that the power of such a fraternity can operate only in a democracy whose law enforcement is corrupt. Puzo's genius has created extravagant characters who are so convincing that they seem both possible and appealing. Thematically, the book challenges America's racial categories, dynastic tendencies, and social prejudices, demanding that before we rent out rooms we had better set our house in order. Structurally, the book abounds with evil incident, debased sex, and primitive terror, and realistically records the solecisms and colloquialisms of the Italian-American characters. Puzo has written in *The Godfather* a novel of power that nearly paralyzes the emotions and the intellect with the terror of a dark evil which must be checked. The wisdom of the serpent should be utilized for its truth. This book has the content and force to change a direction in our civilization.

As an Italian-American novelist, Mario Puzo has pried open the box that has secreted the sacred blackballs of the American literary club. In making his hit, he has exposed once more the password to the inner sanctum of the governing board room. There, where the guardians of American literary conscience are still uniformed in the livery of our dichotomous maturity, the transcendentalism and the materialism decried by Van Wyck Brooks, they stand with the weapons that trigger the old conflict between good and evil. When Michael Corleone commits his first murder, he "makes his bones," and becomes a man to be respected with fear; and he gives a new nomenclature to the American dreamer who identifies with the enemy. Here is another symbol for

7. Mario Puzo, *The Godfather Papers* and Other Confessions (New York: G. R. Putnam's Sons, 1972), p. 41.

our literary lexicon. As writers, Italian-Americans have now made their bones in their acquiescence to the brutal themes of contemporary fiction—the depravities, crime, lust, sex aberrations, violence, bigotry, racism, and hate. By using all these elements to assault the reader in *The Godfather*, Mario Puzo has won acceptance for his two previous books, which are important works of art and valid documents of American civilization. Those who control the machinery of critical support and sales distribution may eventually make an honest and empirical evaluation of all those Italian-American novels that have quietly and systematically gone out of print. In due time we may all discover that the Italian-American writer, who has been with us right along, has had to make a marriage with American tradition. Corleone breeds his children through an Adams; we return to the great, vast themes of America's past—the conflicts of Ahab, the search for our integrity after having sinned, The Marble Faun salvaging himself from Vietnam, the reality of putting aside the weapon that has enjoyed the sanction of power.

Like its author, the Italian-American novel has come of age. Its baptism into our faith has required a sponsor who had to be supreme in envisioning our own evil; but, surviving this initiating exaggeration, we have the fairness to accept all the other human themes that are, after all, more predominant. Meanwhile, the Italian-American novelist has survived his trauma and outgrown the defensiveness of biographical, racial, and self-conscious themes; his books are now making a dent in American fiction. By confronting either inadequacy or corruption, the contemporary hero, socially registered or assimilated, "bones" his way to salvation. As our traditional themes have demonstrated that man must know sin to save his soul, so art distorts creation in order to re-create. In the context of the novels of America the former distortion of the Italian-American was, at least, a recognition of his presence. It was up to the Italian-American writer himself to accept the challenge of this distortion. Now, like Puzo's Michael Corleone, he joins the general family, but he must keep a wary eye on its humanity. In this way, his art is evaluated on equal terms with that of other writers.

15

EPILOGUE. PROJECTIONS INTO THE 70S

In the nineteen-seventies a number of critics have been wailing that the novel is dead. With increasing insistence they allege that the contemporary novel does not appreciably or materially augment our understanding of either ourselves or our place and time. There are, of course, reliable judges who disagree. One Englishman, for example, Tony Tanner, in his book *City of Words*,[1] affirms that American novelists have created a literature of wonder with adolescent narrators, retreats, open roads, green lights, and a diminishing frontier. Significantly, he omits any reference to the direction of life in the circumscribed areas of ethnicity.

Tanner indicates that the great fault of American writers lies in another direction. While not losing their sense of wonder, writers of fiction in America have been content to move between two points: the nonidentity of pure fluidity and the contrasting "fixity" of definitions. Any new direction toward "flexibility" has been limited to the development of a flexible style—disrupting language, parodying it, and inventing what one professor calls a new hieroglyph that an old poetics can not decipher. The protagonist of this microcosm has learned all the ways to avoid expending energy, choosing to recline and soliloquize while he composes fictions about fictions.

What Tanner says about Thomas Pyncheon may be easily applied to Francis Pollini; the pursuit theme in *V* may validly be compared with the odyssey in *Excursion*. It is significant that this English critic's evaluations are objective and sympathetic; he asserts that America's sense of inferiority about its fiction of the last two decades is unwar-

1. Tony Tanner, *City of Words: American Fiction 1950–1970* (New York: Harper and Row, 1971).

ranted. Therefore, while one critic like Clifford A. Ridley[2] may dismiss Updike's *Bech: A Book* as merely a picaresque odyssey of a writer who suggests Bellow—a fact that he may find irrelevant to time and place, another critic may find significance in the embodiment of a writer-gone-dry as a man frozen in the frightening, demoralizing, paralyzing, and exceedingly human predicament of impotence in creativity, nonproduction, and loss of working ability. It is encouraging to find that Tanner admires Updike's symbology, for the author of *The Centaur* has demonstrated his mastery not only of metaphor, but of felicitous phrase and appropriate myth-making.

There is validity in this critic's stress on common themes, such as the fear of enslavement to systems and media, and in his pointing out that this fear has engendered a formula for the contemporary American novel in which the protagonist is an archetype who flees from conformity, isolates himself, and then conforms to his own unpatterned isolation. It matters not if one figure shouts and another whines; they both protest. While Professor F. Dick of Fairleigh Dickinson University points out that Flannery O'Connor has found freedom within a seemingly rigid theology, and Joyce Carol Oates within the strictures of chronology, we might note that it is the ethnic writer who has the real freedom. He is moving outside the shadows of sameness that darken the lexical city. The Italian-American novelist, for example, moving into the seventies, is constantly improving his own image and that of his fellow ethnics, who were almost unknown in earlier literary circles.

At this point it is pertinent to explore the reason in America for lack of faith in fiction as a form of art. A battle wages as to whether a novel should have a function or whether it is sufficient that it exist in itself as a work of art—an artistic expression, complete and whole in and of itself, rich in multiple levels of meaning and universal values. One suspects that for most people art exists in direct relation to the lives of those who experience it; novels, therefore, should relate to human events that are vitally contemporary and urgent to the interests of most people. The Italian-American writer is as much engaged in fulfilling this purpose as are other writers of fiction. In an age proliferous in an overabundance of nonbooks and anti-stories, the story-teller is working with an art that, according to Malcolm Cowley, has a tarnished image. Cowley says that the "idea has gotten around that story-telling is a primitive skill, a little easy, a little to be despised; that a book or a long poem that tells a story is not quite 'serious,' does not 'speak to the age;' and that plot, which is the story element, is a shameful concession to the audience."[3] In the anti-stories, some of the

2. Clifford A. Ridley, "The Expanding Arts," *The National Observer* (November 2, 1970), p. 21.

3. Malcolm Cowley, "Storytelling's Tarnished Image," *Saturday Review* (September 25, 1971), p. 25.

books have no characters except the author himself, whose subject or theme is often the extreme difficulty the author finds in writing fiction. He knows a great deal about technique but has little else to offer the reader. Some authors make collections or albums of meaningless events without the connection of cause and effect, with the obvious philosophy that life is meaningless, absurd, and without order.

Cowley emphasizes that we live in a world of time that is filled with events and that we are less moved by conceptual thinking than by the story-teller who says, "After this happened, this happened; in the end, this happened." Narrative, therefore, deals effectively with events in sequence; that is, with what is becoming—a process, rather than a pattern. Furthermore, the modern mind is conditioned to process thinking. Therefore, those writers who depict the world as a spatial concept only, a stasis instead of a progress, are giving an irresponsible picture of the world in which we live. The writer, in order fully to realize his art, might provide more than a microcosm of the macrocosmic chaos implied when he presents unrelated events or perceptions. The interest in story-telling has declined, therefore, because the authors themselves have not kept faith with American society, which contains the reading audience. With his usual critical acumen, Cowley shows the wide loss of faith of most writers in the future of the country, in humanity, and in the sincerity and good sense of officials and leaders who try to control the situation. Writers stress the absurd and the unjust. Further, many of these writers are NOW people, characters in their books, who can not tell stories. A story depends on the past and looks to the future. There is intrinsic order in the structured novel; this novel tells a good story, is intelligible and lasting, with a shape carved out of time.

The phases of development of the Italian-American novel as I have analyzed them demonstrate that the ethnic novel has a shape carved out of time. The Italian-American novel is not like the Negro novel, for example, in which the conflict is more intense between race and art. Robert Bone, in *The Negro Novel in America,* contends that "Art-as-Weapon" is a fallacy, referring to Nick Aaron Ford of Morgan State College and Lloyd Brown, associate editor of *Masses and Mainstream,* both of whom assume that art is primarily a function, a weapon in the racial or class structure. Ford points to the art of Tolstoy and Whitman, with its overtones of ethnicity and its conscious goal of fostering human brotherhood. Social propaganda, he says, requires skillful handling not to be recognized as such by the intelligent reader; and symbolism is an indispensable device for disguising propaganda. Brown frankly states that the pen is the essential weapon in the fight for liberation.

But art is not politics. I agree with Bone that the obliteration of the color line, with all its racial overtones, is a political, not a literary task. I agree, also, that some equality of persons is gained when ethnic writers segregate themselves in a cultural ghetto. However, it seems that for the ethnic writer, especially for the Italian-American novelist, the direction should now be toward a raceless participation in the general American field. As Richard Gibson has written in the *Kenyon Review*,[4] black writers have beeen coerced into commitment to the propaganda novel. This has been true, to a degree, of Italian-American writers, who have also been at the mercy of publishers who traffic in racial sensationalism, and of the professional liberals who carry attention-getting banners for popular causes. Therefore the ethnic writer has not been allowed to transcend his category, especially if his materials are specifically identifiable with a walled-in cluster of society. On the other hand, the writer need not consciously avoid his ethnicity; to do this would condemn him to an inverted bondage. The successful ethnic writer should have both immediacy within and distance from his personal cultural environment.

The Italian-American novelist finds that if he confines himself to immediacy, as do the writers who concentrate on autobiographical materials, both his audience and his choice of publisher are limited. Furthermore, to demonstrate his contribution to attitudes in extended human relationships, he is more effective if he selects his material not only from his intimate knowledge, but from less familiar subjects that are pertinent to universal contemporary social problems. As Italian-Americans are becoming an integral part of the national society, their experiences are those of all other assimilated Americans; their difference lies only in their personal, subtle, and almost unconscious attitude toward many of these experiences. In the end, the quality of their writing and its acceptance by readers are in direct proportion to their elimination of antagonizing ethnical themes and in their success in integrating their constructive ideas into American thinking.

In the present movement of American ideas, the involvement of the Italian-American writer is following two lines of direction, both in content and in form. In content, one group of writers is engaged in fictionalizing social problems as material for creative imagery, while aother group is creating images forged from authentic experiences in a specific profession. To understand the first group, in which is most of the writing, one must appreciate what has happened in the general progress of American ideas. Happily, in his recent *The Age of Energy*, [5] Howard Mumford Jones supplies a convenient history of these ideas along with a compendium of cultural flashbacks in which he clarifies contrary intellectual movements. He contrasts the optimism of the theologians' *Progressive Orthodoxy* to the pessimism of Brook Adams's *Law of Civilization and Decay;* William Dean Howells's attack on sentimentality and romanticism in American fiction to the naturalist school's counterattack on Howells's definition of realism; the increas-

4. Richard Gibson, "A No to Nothing," *Kenyon Review* 13 (Spring 1951).
5. Howard Mumford Jones, *The Age of Energy* (New York: Viking, 1971).

ing reverence for the Supreme Court and the Constitution to the growing attacks on Congressional and judiciary corruption; the cult and worship of American technology to the threat to respect for human life that science seemes to engender. Jones's book is only the latest on a substantial list of reliable references on the development of American culture, but his book has a particular fascination because of its enormous range and objective treatment. What is singularly pertinent to this discussion is Jones's technique in exposing the stereotyped references to the activities of a period. As Professor D. E. Fortuna of the State University of New York has pointed out,[6] the Robber Barons pillaged, but in their humanitarianism they appear like the merchant-prince patrons of the arts of the Renaissance. However, as Professor Fortuna indicates in her criticism, and I agree, Jones does not attempt to analyze the dichotomy of American civilization, the idealism and the materialism (which Van Wyck Brooks defined so carefully), into mainstreams or cross currents of American ideas. Comparing the post-Civil War period with that of the incipient nineteen seventies, Jones indicates that the blatant oratory, the reckless propaganda, the bitter denunciation, and the strident reform movements of both times are similar.

The Materials in the Latest Italian-American Fiction

The first line of direction, the telling of a story that illustrates a social problem, is now bringing most of the latest Italian-American novelists to a broadened consideration of the former theme of fragmentation. Within the scope of human relationships, however, the two objects of concentration remain the same: self or humanity in general. While in earlier novels Italian-Americans were to a large degree concerned with self-exploration in a search for their ancestral roots, they now appear to be analyzing their own experiences in the treatment of self—a lawyer in how he reacts to his cases, a psychiatrist in how he treates his patients.

In the search for true identity involved in social problems, the Italian-American writer is in a very select company. Returning to the scene a decade after he appeared in John Updike's *Rabbit Run.* Harry Angstrom (Rabbit) is advised by his estranged wife, Janice, that in the year nineteen sixty-nine two mature people have no reason to smother each other to death out of simple inertia. Eventually, Rabbit returns from the experiences detailed in the book as the universal contemporary man in search of his valid identity. With his particular sensitivity and understanding executed brilliantly with wit and restraint, Updike explores precisely the relationship of experience to his place and moment in time--the Black militants, the Vietnam war, sex, drugs, and

6. *Saturday Review* (December 4, 1971), p. 39.

violence. With one of America's best writers of fiction, therefore, a good story relates to the social conditions of the moment. Likewise, at the beginning of the seventies we find that the Italian-American writers are expanding beyond their ethnic world to the more interactive America of today; they, too, are sharing Updike's place and moment in time.

It would serve no purpose to list all the books of this category that are being published, or have recently gone out of print. To authenticate these materials, it suffices to analyze representative writers of the first category—those who fictionalize general social problems—as examples also of writers of the well-made novel. At this point, we note the author who emerges from a specific profession, Richard D'Ambrosio, for example, a practicing psychoanalyst and an Adjunct Professor at Long Island University, who uses the conventions of the novel to give a factual account. As he tells the story of the twelve-year-old Laura in *No Language But A Cry*,[7] he totally engages himself in compassion, tenderness, and dedicated devotion to transform a neglected, broken piece of "human refuse" into a functioning human being.

At the beginning of the story, after surviving acute tragedy, Laura has never spoken a word since, brutally abused and burned by her parents to a horrifying deformity, she has withdrawn from the world around her. The nuns with whom she has lived for seven years are sincere and resourceful, but they have neither the facilities nor the professional training to help her. The young psychiatrist who accepts this challenge tells the story, narrating the progress of the psychoanalysis with every absorbing detail, forcing the reader into the inner life of both Laura and her physician. D'Ambrosio succeeds in writing an effective story with imaginative depth and full range. Although the author lacks the masterful rhetorical art of Updike, he does write with energy and communicates the need to be heard with warmth. D'Ambrosio's absorption in Laura's desperate case, which demands all his skill, patience, and imagination, is the kind of valid identification that gives the book a place in our time.

Similar identification coming from professional experience is more imaginatively treated by John Nicholas Iannuzzi in two books, *What's Happening* and *Part 35*. An active trial lawyer in partnership with his father, Iannuzzi has defended a number of men and women on charges of murder in the first degree. *Part 35*,[8] is a long, rapidly paced novel about the defense of two Puerto Rican drug addicts who are accused of killing a policeman on the rooftop of a New York tenement. Iannuzzi explores the connections of hundreds of people to this murder trail, including the defendents, their families, the detectives, the neigh-

7. Richard D'Ambrosio, *No Language But A Cry* (Garden City, N. Y.: Doubleday and Company, 1970).
8. John Nicholas Iannuzzi, *Part 35* (New York: Richard W. Baron, 1970).

bors, the prosecution, the defense counsel, the judge, and the various people who happened to be at some significant place on the particular afternoon when the policeman was shot. The lawyer, Sandro Luca, stubbornly contests the legal structure of the state to ensure justice. A young, ambitious attorney, Luca is the product of New York's "Little Italy," who must contend with Sam Bemer, a seasoned criminal lawyer who believes that only one percent of all defendents are not guilty. In addition to the merciless district attorney, Vincent Ellis, there are Ramon Hernandez, who committed burglary in El Barrio on the day he was apprehended for murder, and Luis Alvarado, a black who has a narcotics record. The novel gets its title from the court sections numbered Part 30 or higher, where homicide trials are held in the Supreme Court of the State of New York.

While the pursuit of evidence and the course of the trial intensify the action, the theme of the book is one of particular relevance today. Fully engaged, Sandro Luca is faced with his human responsibility of a man's life in the palm of his hand. This responsibility reaches its climax at the trial, when Sandro declares that he is bothered when people in the street, people on television and in newspaper accounts, and even law-enforcement people say that the rights of the ordinary citizens are being stepped on, that the courts are letting criminals get away with murder. Iannuzzi writes,

> When the rights of a defendent, a man on trial, are being protected, the rights of citizens *are* being protected. For criminals are citizens before they are criminals. . . . What happens the night, God forbid, when you are coming home from the movies, a newspaper under your arm, and you find yourself looking into the business end of a .38 caliber Police Special. You are innocent, but you are arrested nonetheless. Would you want to lose your rights at the moment you are arrested? Should you? And if *you* shouldn't, why should any one else?" (p. 497)

Although his experience, even with the men he is defending, is less than satisfactory, Sandro Luca presents a thoroughly researched and eloquently delivered case. Rewarded by fatigue, he has at least the satisfaction of knowing that he has put everything he had into this trial, and that no matter what the others think, he has done his job the best he knows how. In the end, when he answers Mike's taunt about some other "colored guy" with the weary response that he'll talk about it later, all the racial implications of the case are suggested in Mike's supposedly facetious remark: "You guinea bastard, just because these guys are spics, you don't give a damn about them, is that it?" (p. 517).

Sandro Luca's special kind of idealistic sacrifice of self continues to fire other novels like *Part 35.* Meanwhile, there continues to stay alive the type of story that exercises the kind of ethnical introspection that is incorporated objectively in the character of Tommy Martana in *What the Ancients Said,*[9] by Lou D'Angelo. A contributor to the "Phoenix Nest" in *Saturday Review,* D'Angelo is a New Yorker, a graduate of the College of the City of New York (1954), who earns his living by writing book advertising. His first book, *How to be an Italian*, contains a series of comic photographs with captions, and has attracted appreciable good-humored attention. *What the Ancients Said* explores the rearing and training, the confinement and liberation, and the gradual Americanization of a Sicilian-American of the contemporary period. The book is socially relevant to our place and time, and is an appropriate reminder that the process of assimilation at its frontier stage is always with us as new immigrants join the populace. To comfort the newcomers, Italian-American writers like Lou D'Angelo continue to recall the ethnic past and identify it with the new audience as well as with the memory that is fading in the assimilated second and third generations. D'Angelo's narrative has a comic treatment with overtones of the stern discipline of the older Sicilian immigrants; and what the ancients said, primarily in maxims and proverbs, remains pertinent today. Significantly, the boy Tommy has been soothed by his mother's "The good have to suffer but they will prevail. All evil does not come to harm" (p. 43). After World War II he returns home and hears the far-fetched interpretations of his father of the war and its leaders, especially of President Roosevelt, whom they call "The Green Rose" (everyone has a nickname). It is symbolic of the assimilation of generations that the returning soldier and his father go to celebrate in Times Square, where they "silent and smiling, held on to one another and submitted to the crowd" (p. 208).

Mass Media Genesis

Among the writers who are oriented to social problems are those who have developed creatively from the assigned labors of the mass media, especially in the field of journalism. There are two, especially, who have a promising future: Gay Talese and Julia Savarese.

Since the works of Gay Talese are based on authentic rather than on imaginative materials, his are what the critics call nonnovels, yet are works that have the power of novels. In this discussion, therefore, it suffices to refer to Talese as an example of the trend toward the creative presentation of nonfictional material. His works include *New York—A Serendipeter's Journey*, *The Overreachers*, *The Bridge*, *The Kingdom and the Power*, and *Honor Thy Father.* A former reporter for the *New York Times,* Talese draws a candid portrait of life inside the institution of the New York newspaper in *The Kingdom and the Power.* The book classifies the author as one of the first and, now, possibly the best, of

9. Lou D'Angleo, *What the Ancients Said* (Garden City, N. Y.: Doubleday and Company, Inc., 1971).

the "New Journalists," who, as Paul F. Levy has written, "immerse themselves so thoroughly in the life of their subjects that they are able to recreate it, not in the relatively staccato form of the daily newspapers, but in the broader sweep of the novel."[10] In *Honor Thy Father,*[11] Talese has surpassed his effort with regard to the *New York Times* and has written an important and brilliant book about a person. In this novel the author authenticates what Mario Puzo created imaginatively in *The Godfather.* He has delineated a clear and compelling portrait of Bill Bonanno, the son of Joe Bonanno, who is the alleged leader of the five New York "Mafia" families. The book is especially fascinating to readers not only because of its frightening authenticity, but because it satisfies readers who are preoccupied with crime and violence. Writing the inside story of a significant and bizarre sector of the American scene, Talese has a sympathetic attitude toward his protagonist; he does not judge the character, but immerses himself in Bonanno's everyday life with his devoted family.

Julia Savarese, on the other hand, writes a conventional novel about the magazine business in *Final Proof.*[12] A native New Yorker who has published poetry and short stories in literary and popular magazines, she has worked as a magazine writer for several years. After her first book, *The Weak and the Strong,* she decided to use her personal experience for the material in *Final Proof.* The plot centers around a struggle for power within a large publishing empire that, bankrupt, is about to dissolve. While the action involves many people in key positions around the protagonist, Paula Jericho, she tries to avoid, without success, the corporate intrigues around her. Loyalties are diffused, and honesty compromised. In the structure of the plot, Miss Savarese has Paula fall in love with the leader of the opposition, with whom she identifies because he has come up from poverty in much the same way as she has. Making this choice, she must confront several layers of betrayal, and some of the characters are symbols of universal life. In the end, Paula discovers her identity; she learns that she, too, has several dimensions and that her motives have not been, nor would they ever be, the open, obvious ones she has professed. Miss Savarese writes, "And in many ways I hated this knowledge of myself. Because it seemed that, understanding yourself, you were never freed from the understanding of other people, too" (p. 310).

Directions in the Form of the Novel

Italian-American novelists are like other writers of American fiction in that they are taking two directions in form, writing either the nonnovel, or the novel of structure. The larger number of them are

10. In *The Sunday Bulletin* (Philadelphia) (October 10, 1971), VB 3, Sec. 2.
11. Gay Talese, *Honor Thy Father* (New York: The World Publishing Company, 1971).
12. Julia Savarese, *Final Proof* (New York: W. W. Norton and Company, Inc., 1971).

adhering to narrative structure than to the nonnovel. One of the more outstanding writers of unstructured form is Gilbert Sorrentino.

Sorrentino, who now lives in Manhattan, grew up in the neighborhood in Brooklyn that he describes in his second novel, *Steelwork.*[13] He has also written *The Sky Changes* (1966), *The Perfect Fiction* (Poetry) (1968), and the recent *Imaginative Qualities of Actual Things* (1971). *Steelwork* aptly illustrates the author's talent at the unstructured novel. Setting his word-pictures in Brooklyn, and ranging in time between 1935 and 1951, he covers the Depression, World War II, the Cold War, and the Korean War. In ninety-six separate but interlocking episodes, sometimes only vignettes of people, he details life in an underprivileged white neighborhood. Although poor, the people start out as honest and decent; but they degenerate into a tangled, greedy, and less-than-honorable conglomeration of characters who are corrupted by the inflated profits of the war economy.

The reader is aware that Sorrentino is controlling his "formless" form, and that he has dispensed with chronology, jumbling his episodes in no visible order. He moves back, forth, and around in the way memory does, destroying the usual pattern of coherence in time and circumstance to create a senselessness. The reader, as well as the characters, slips from episode to episode, and becomes immersed in the author's theme and mood. The vision of senselessness through artlessness is not, of course, original, and there is a narrative discernible in Sorrentino's kaleidoscope—the progressive change in this particular neighborhood, this section of America. Evocative of the past, the titles of certain vignettes invite the reader: "Queen of Wands," "Carminootch," "Chicky's House," "The Sailors," "Red's Grandma," "The Poolroom," "Movie Houses," "The Lot," and many more.

Arbitrary arrangement of incidents is an "art" form that Sorrentino continues to develop in *Imaginative Qualities of Actual Things.*[14] In this novel he creates scenes, situations, time, and atmosphere as deftly as an Updike or a Cozzens, and sets himself not only to report or recreate, but—in theme like William Carlos Williams—to see actual things in such a light that their truly imaginative qualities are revealed. He fabricates eight lives, six men and two women, and demonstrates how art and life feed and starve each other intermittently. The episodes center on characters like Guy Lewis, who is defeated in his efforts. The theme of the book is climaxed in Bart, who might have become a painter or sculptor but became instead a wealthy decorator, pleasing people and compromising with his critics. The characters represent the life-styles of contemporary Americans, especially of those in the world of the arts. Although the book is a bitter indictment of our materialistic values, Sorrentino succeeds in being comic and

13. Gilbert Sorrentino, *Steelwork* (New York: Pantheon Books, 1969).
14. Gilbert Sorrentino, *Imaginative Qualities of Actual Things* (New York: Pantheon Books, 1971).

engaging. His technique is self-conscious, but so are the efforts of his characters. The style is the story; the ritualistic clichés and ordinary responses are the tired mannerisms of our behavior, and the creative spirit is in a turmoil trying to focus on the identity of humanity. Again with his kaleidoscope, Sorrentino demonstrates that the failure to create is the failure of the imagination to abstract the meaning from our time and place. Since *Imaginative Qualities of Actual Things* has no plot at all, it is simply an attestation of the author's ability to be imaginative and engaging. Sorrentino's talent creates a world that has little function. His book works, however, because of the writing charged with questions to the reader: for example, what is entailed in suspending belief when nothing is believable? It is the author's good-natured indifference to his own work that conveys to the reader the real need of values to sustain life.

Novels of Structure

In the ratio of four to one, Italian-Americans write novels that have plots "carved out of time." In contrast to Gilbert Sorrentino's non-novel, straight narratives have been created by Joseph Pillitteri, Don De Lillo, Bill Pronzini, and the ever-fecund Paul Gallico.

These writers are telling new stories in new ways. Since the image of the story-teller's classic art has been tarnished by reactions to the well-made novel, there have been continued attempts to extend Joyce's epiphanies and to experiment with such extremes as deleting characters, reality, subject, event, meaning, and analysis, whereupon the story-teller risks the danger of losing his audience. Word-making as a technique would then reign supreme in a private world of traumatic sensations. But the novelists who have faith in their place and its humanity adhere tenaciously to the traditional principles of art. Non-representational or meaningless materials impede the writers of well-made novels who insist on controlling a situation with sincerity and good sense. These authors continue to produce new structures, fitting the design to a world appointed with all the contemporary improvements. In the writing of fiction, the appointments include an awareness of the democratic principle functioning with a view toward improved relationships among all people, not merely satisfaction with what Cowley calls the "NOW people's desire for instant stimulus, instant perception, instant euphoria."

Among these new writers is Don DeLillo, a native New Yorker, who has written a novel significantly entitled *Americana,*[15] in which he renews the American myth of innocence and vitality. David Bell, a young and successful television executive in New York, attempts to discover himself by making a movie. The plot involves the reality of and accounts of the war in Southeast Asia, mystifying reports in the

15. Don DeLillo, *Americana* (Boston: Houghton Mifflin Company, 1971).

office, and the internal struggle for leadership in communication. Since there are patterns in this electrifying world, David decides to externalize them in a film. He therefore goes West with three friends, a sculptress, a former fighter pilot, and an inebriate. In a small western town he starts to index his memories "not in terms of good or bad memories, childhood or adult, innocent or guilty, but rather in two very broad and simple categories. Cooperative and uncooperative" (p. 310).

DeLillo's theme develops through the analysis of memory. Responding to David Bell, for example, Sullivan gives a detailed account of the incident involving her Uncle Malcolm. "And I knew then that the war is not between North or South, black or white, young and old, rich and poor, crusader and heathen, warhawk and pacifist, God and the devil. The war is between Uncle Malcolm and Uncle Malcolm" (p. 342). Bell, however, puts both memory and awareness into action as he takes off on the first stage of the second journey into the "depths of America, wilderness dream of all poets and scoutmasters, westward to our manifest destiny, to sovereign red timber and painted sands, to the gold-transfigured hills, westward to match the shadows of my image and myself" (p. 352). In due time, his experiences exhaust all emotion, climaxing in the total abandonment to physical sensation generated by liquor and sex in the scene with Clevenger, Lump, and Dowd, and the Mexican women. In the end, hitch-hiking to Dallas, his encounters with the philosophizing, one-armed homosexual, and with an assortment of strangers, all bring him to the conclusion that "I felt it was literature I had been confronting these past days, the archetypes of the dismal mystery, sons and daughters of the archetypes, images that could not be certain which of two confusions held less terror, their own or what their own might become if it ever faced the truth" (p. 388).

Almost circular in form, the novel begins in New York and ends on the way back. In this movement, DeLillo depicts the coastal towns, the small villages, and the wilderness of America—all places that American traditional writers have filled with innocence and myth. The protagonist grows with the process of his film-making, and the novel, as a result, is like a panoramic screen with an overwhelming wide angle. David Bell is contemporary youth seeking to explore himself, and he does so with a determined plan. His flight on the plane is symbolic of his direct route to the core of action in which he will have an emphatic part.

Joseph Pillitteri, who lives with his wife and family in Buffalo, New York, has demonstrated a natural gift for the narrative art, working his materials into neat, tightly written books, of which he has written two: *When The Giraffe Runs Down* (1970) and *Two Hours On Sunday* (1971).

The first novel, *When the Giraffe Runs Down,*[16] is the story of three people united by interrelated action in the course of one day: Claude,

16. Joseph Pillitteri, *When the Griaffe Runs Down* (New York: The Dial Press, 1970).

a student of medicine; the Reverend Mr. Abraham, his father; and Dr. Robert Collier, a young intern suffering from a bad head cold and an unhappy marriage. Claude is in a dilemma of several dimensions: his sweetheart has jilted him; a terminal case wants to die; his scholastic schedule is making heavy demands; his father is making further demands; his unmarried pregnant sister is a problem; and several other harassments find their way to him at every turn. The minister has problems in that he has lost his faith, along with any happiness with his family, and he is battling a guilty conscience. There is no comfort for him, with a dead son and a dying friend. As for Dr. Collier, who is beginning to doubt his capacity and skill in his profession, problems are compounded in his private life, all the more distressing because of his indisposition, fatigue, ennui, and fear. It is the prevailing fear of death that unites the three, who come together on the sixth floor of the hospital, isolated when the hospital gets on fire.

Pillitteri portrays his characters as good men, intent on solving their problems with dignity and integrity. In the end the survival of the spirit is more essential than physical mortality. As the author illustrates his theme, we, although feeling the intensity of the plot, are given grace by the modulated style in which there is the relief of sufficient humor. Finally, as we are informed that Eleanor Higgins has passed away, and that Dr. Abraham is pocketing his prayer cross that is to comfort his son, we are convinced that the story-teller has succeeded in resolving the plot through release of tension.

In his second novel, *Two Hours on Sunday*,[17] Joseph Pillitteri shifts his scene to professional football. A second-string quarterback with the Normandy Hawks, Alex Lincoln plays with a surgically spliced knee. Placed on the "active injured" list, he feels his insecurity increasing. He is already oppressed by the facts that his brother, an obstetrician, needs money, his father needs help, and his wife needs his attention along with his sixteen-year-old stepson and his thirteen-year-old son by a previous marriage. His personal problems counterpoint the sequence of the Hawks' plays, and they aggravate Lincoln's nervous stomach. He is the incarnation of the man at work as part of a team in an intensely competitive area. He could be one of a sales group in a business corporation, a junior member of the American corporate system. Here, again, Pillitteri tells an uncomplicated story of American life, limning a portrait of Everyman in the contemporary scene of which the Italian-American is so much an integral part that he identifies without self-coloration.

Bill Pronzini, one of the most recent to join the group of contemporary novelists, has been a prolific writer of short stories; since 1966, he

17. Joseph Pillitteri, *Two Hours on Sunday* (New York: The Dial Press, 1971).

has sold over thirty-five on a wide range of subjects. Born in Petaluma, California, and a resident of San Francisco, he spends a great deal of time in Majorca, where he writes. His novel *The Stalker*[18] illustrates the Italian-American novelist's penchant for a well-structured novel, preferably centered on the high drama often best generated from themes of crime. The plot is built on the events that follow the execution of an apparently perfect and unpunishable crime. Steve Kilduff, Larry Drexel, Jim Conradin, and three other ex-servicemen, who in 1959 had robbed an armored car of $750,000, were never caught or even suspected by the police. Each man has waited out the cut-off date provided by the Statute of Limitations in the state in which the crime was committed to eliminate any subsequent legal prosecution; then each man goes his separate way. To all appearances, no one of them has been in communication with any other for eleven years, and the robbery is buried and forgotten in the files of unsolved crime. Then, three of the six die in successive mysterious accidents in their home towns. Alarmed by the unaccountable coincidence of the three "accidents," Drexel, the cautious, reticent, self-appointed leader of the group, who has kept a file on the other five, warns Kilduff and Conradin, who refuse to budge from the "simple accident" theory. When a fourth member of the group dies suddenly, without explanation, there is no doubt that some nameless, faceless stalker has been pursuing the men. Obviously this stalker has plotted his murders with calculated precision; he must be a man who knows his victims better than they do themselves; nor does he care how many people are injured or killed while he pursues his quarry. Meanwhile, the reader learns of the other human problems in which the men are engaged. The story is brought into focus by the increasing tension of inner conflict and decision of the man at war with his own weakness. As Pronzini writes, "Marik had to have somebody to blame for what had happened to him" (p. 234). The protagonist indicates at the end of the story that he expects to be prosecuted and condemned for his share of the crime, but that "it's going to be all right." Pronzini has constructed a novel firmly founded on the past and looking toward the future without loss of faith. Above all, he tells a superb story.

A felicitous contribution to the art of the novel through well-structured narration is Paul Gallico's latest work, *The Zoo Gang.*[19] The earlier discussion of Gallico's eclectric writing has established that in his production of some forty books, this one-time sports-page writer brings his own special zest and polish to celebrate the average man who aims for higher sights. Other diverting stories include *The Snow*

18. Bill Pronzini, *The Stalker* (New York: Random House, 1971).
19. Paul Gallico, *The Zoo Gang* (New York: Coward-McCann, Inc., 1971).

Goose (1941), *The Small Miracle* (1951), and *Thomasina* (1959). Obviously, we may always depend on his books for engrossing reading, but in *The Zoo Gang* there is a new Gallico.

The five members of the bizarre menagerie that makes up the Zoo Gang fight crime along the Côte d'Azur on the French Riviera, where Gallico lives at the present time. These contemporary Robin Hoods are survivors of a French Resistance group who plagued the Nazis thirty years ago. A tightly knit unit, they have individual pseudonyms that belie their personalities: Le Leopard, Gaston Rive, an obese and slothful electrical contractor, formerly an expert in communications; L'Elephant, Jean Coleau, a slight figure trafficking in garlic and onions, once an expert in sabotage; Le Loup, Alphonse Cousin, bar owner and part-time aviator and expert locksmith; Le Tigre, Antoine Petit-pierre, sad and gentle carnation-grower, an expert assassin with a stiletto; and their leader, Le Renard, Colonel Pierre Roquebrun, blue-eyed and polished antiques dealer, the contact with the Riviera underground. The group advises, pursues, and avenges in giving assistance to Captain Claude Scoubide, the Chief of Detectives, in four separate cases. The episodes involve the theft of twelve Renoir paintings from a local museum (having the outcome of a new hospital with free beds for the poor); a hypothetical jewel robbery in which the group, finding themselves unwitting advisers of the local security men, as a result help forestall a real robbery plan that they had presaged and preenacted; a double kidnaping involving an auto tycoon's child and the child of the kidnaper; and a battle with a drug syndicate that is smuggling narcotics into the Riviera. The drugs are transported during the Mardi Gras carnival on a float called "Snow White and the Seven Dwarfs," and are stored on the stage of an abandoned theater. In an old-time gang-style climax, the Zoo Gang shoots it out with the seven "dwarfs" of the narcotics ring, and the bodies are removed in the fashion of a "Dutch" Schultz melodrama.

With this book, Paul Gallico keeps pace with current themes. A careful researcher who reads from thirty to a hundred books on any subject he treats, he makes personal visits to the locales of his stories to give them verisimilitude; then he becomes one of the characters in both time and place. He moves with the stream, his fixed point being his concern with the "little people" whom he considers the giants of this world, and who have a lasting innocence that enables them, as he says, "to continue to love each other." With practiced skill he injects this innocence entertainingly into the current themes of violence and personal human involvement; love is the catalyst that knits together both the people and the telling of their story. He wrote in his *Confessions* that he hoped in the future, with "a joy and an excitement and a throbbing of the pulses, to sit down and once more set forth toward the unreachable goal, the great story." He continues to write like the great story-teller he is.

The Future of the Italian-American Writer

The future of the Italian-American writer of fiction lies, therefore, in his writing great stories. The conflicts of a minority's struggle for upward mobility have so far engendered appealing and exciting materials for the creative representation of anguished experiences. No longer do literary artists need defensive histrionics and offensive polemics. The time has come for the writer of Italian ancestry not to be concerned that his books may no longer appeal to the strictly Italian-American community, as Jerre Mangione indicated in his "violent diatribe against the Italian-American press" at the conference of the American Italian Historical Association on "The Italian-American Novel" on October 25, 1969. Mangione contended that the Italian-American Press has failed to educate its readers about other groups, which would give them a sense of American community. The other Italian-American novelists at this conference, Joseph Caruso, Ralph Corsel, and Joseph Vergara, made the same complaint, that publishers are convinced that novels about Italian-Americans are not likely to sell. While the point was made that one reason for the absence of this market lies in Italian-American preference for achieving material success and prestige over reading books, the conclusion appeared valid that the present third-generation Italian-Americans no longer consider themselves a separate group whose inner-directedness needs emphasis in literary efforts having strictly ethnic themes. In the final analysis, these themes must relate to the general structure of American culture in order to be a valid part of its literary record. In their contribution to this literature, Italian-American writers will be judged as Americans with a certain advantage in having come of Italian ancestry.

There are two points of view about a national Italian-American community at which writers and publishers might aim. The Reverend Paul J. Asciolla, C.S., Associate Editor of *Fra Noi* in Chicago, has stated that writers and publishers should no longer aim at a community that exists "only biologically." He poses the question of where the audience may be for themes dealing with sex, violence, the Mafia, and priests. Many Italian-Americans regard the old themes as exploitative, and they are weary of them. Father Asciolla, as a reviewer of Italian-American books, has found that the response to themes of crime is: "we don't need this garbage, because we already know about these creeps." He remarks that Italian-Americans, predominantly members of the working white middle-class, have not been reading because they have not had the time or energy to do so. This Italian-American middle class, however, is moving to the suburbs. Yet Robert Critchton says[20] that the new Italian-American culture from which its writers will have

20. In a letter in response to the invitation to attend the conference on The Italian-American Novel.

to spring is presently encapsulated for the most part in lower-middle-class conformity, with a combination of anti-intellectualism and conservatism, with a disappearance of the old colorful neighborhoods. Critchton adjudges that suburban Italian-America, on the edges of the city, is a smothering society from which the writer runs.

On the other hand, the Italian-American community is seen as gathering strength in such articles as "The Italians are Coming!" by Gaeton Fonzi in *Philadelphia Magazine.*[21] Fonzi writes that there is a resurgence of ethnicity not only among the political activists and the young intellectuals, but among the working class as well. A good deal of the new ethnic militancy as exhibited by the Italians in Philadelphia is in reaction to the rise of Black power. Much current writing is concerned with the rise of the white ethnic in general, as illustrated, for example, in Michael Novak's[22] article "White Ethnic" in *Harper's* Magazine (September 1971), in which he decries the plight of the Poles, Italians, Greeks, and Slavs (PIGS) as having neither status nor political voice, whose silence burns like hidden coals in the chest. The relevant point that Novak makes is that America has not confronted squarely the problem of preserving diversity, despite the Bill of Rights and a current culture that permits everyone to do his own thing. He insists that to be critical and intelligent is not to be less ethnic.

The solution seems to lie in how the ethnic novel reflects the evolving social situation. Most writers who represent the white ethnics will find audiences among people whose coals of burning silence are igniting into words. These ethnics, as Michael Novak points out, resist the organized pressure of radicalism, with its optimism about human anarchic tendencies. They do not share, as a whole, a liberalism freighted with emotions, sentiments, and coercive convictions. Nor do they feel that institutions are repressive in any meaningful way; they find the "state of nature" emotionally far less liberating, far more undifferentiated and confining. As Novak says, the intellectual life has a great deal to like in it, and it takes effort to discern the flaws. He writes, "My emotions and values seem to run in affirmative patterns."[23]

The reference to affirmative patterns brings us back to the theme of this discussion, that Italian-American writers have absorbed both the material and transcendental values of traditional American literature, and have, in turn, contributed to it their confirmation of American aspirations with a constructive view and optimism for the future. That the Italian-American novel has finally made its existence apparent to general readers through books of violence like *The Godfather* testifies

21. (December 1971), p. 98.
22. Also Michael Novak's, *The Rise of the Unmeltable Ethnics* (New York: The Macmillan Company, 1971).
23. Michael Novak, "White Ethnic," *Harper's Magazine* (September 1971), p. 50.

to a basic American disposition that crime is an accepted method for achieving power, even as transgression is the occasion of the salvation of the soul from sin. The American novelist of Italian ancestry, conditioned by a long tradition of constructive order, demonstrates a preference for the well-made story. As he expands his erstwhile limited subjects to more extensive, contemporary themes, he will find his audience responding to the excellence of his performance. In sum, in addition to his characteristic constructive, humanistic optimism, he will find that it is the quality of his work that admits him to the American literary mainstream.

APPENDIX

TABLE I

The Number of Immigrants Who Entered the United States
(1822–1922)[1]

Italians	4,476,739
Irish	4,449,596
English	2,635,709
Germans	5,793,209
Poles	196,549
Russians	3,004,588

TABLE II

Foreign Born White Prisoners and Juvenile Delinquents[2]

Nationality	Population	Total number of prisoners per 100,000 of its own population	Total number imprisoned for drunkenness and disorderly conduct
Swiss	124,834	313.2	167.4
Germans	2,311,085	383.4	218.9
Italians	1,343,070	527.3	158.1
Poles	937,884	537.2	306.5

1. Antonio Stella. *Some Aspects of Italian Immigration to the United States.* New York: G. P. Putnam's Sons, 1924. This is a definitive collection of statistical data based upon the figures of the United States Census and other official publication
2. Tables 138 and 104, United States Government Census Report, 1910.

English and Welsh	958,934	727.4	488.5
Scotch	261,034	1,196.0	836.3
Irish	1,352,155	1,983.4	1,540.1
Mexicans	219,802	2,336.2	1,379.0

TABLE III

Drunkenness in the United States[1]

Country of Birth	Number of arrests for drunkenness and disorderly conduct, per 100,000.	Number of deaths from alcoholism (1900 census) per 100,000
American born (white, Negro)	285.9	2.4
Italians	158.1	0.7
English	488.5	8.3
German	218.9	6.1
Irish	1,540.1	17.7

1. United States Census of 1910, Department of Commerce, Bureau of Census, p. 415.

BIBLIOGRAPHY

I
PRIMARY SOURCES: CREATIVE BOOKS WRITTEN BY AMERICANS OF ITALIAN ORIGIN

Angelo, Valenti. *Nino.* New York: The Viking Press, Inc., 1938.

———. *Golden Gate,* a sequel to *Nino.* Illustrated by the author. New York: The Viking Press, Inc., 1939.

———. *Paradise Valley.* Lithographs by the author. New York: The Viking Press, Inc., 1940.

———. *Hill of Little Miracles.* Illustrated by the author. New York: The Viking Press, Inc., 1942.

———. *Look Out Yonder.* Illustrated by the author. New York: The Viking Press, Inc., 1943.

———. *The Rooster Club.* Further adventures of Nino. Illustrated by the author. New York: The Viking Press, Inc., 1944.

———. *The Acorn Tree.* Illustrated by the author. New York: The Viking Press, Inc., 1958.

———. *The Honey Boat.* Illustrated by the author. New York: The Viking Press, Inc., 1959.

———. *Angelino and the Barefoot Saint.* Illustrated by the author. New York: The Viking Press, Inc., 1961.

———. *The Merry Marcos.* Illustrated by the author. New York: The Viking Press, Inc., 1963.

———. *The Tale of a Donkey.* Illustrated by the author. New York: The Viking Press, Inc., 1966.

Arleo, Joseph. *The Grand Street Collector.* New York: Walker and Company, 1970.

Arrighi, Antonio A. *The Story of Antonio, the Galley Slave.* New York: F. H. Revell Company, 1911.

Basso, Hamilton. *Relics and Angels.* New York: Macaulay Company, 1929.

______. *Beauregard: The Great Creole.* New York: Charles Scribner's Sons, 1933.

______. *Cinnamon Seed.* New York: Charles Scribner's Sons. 1934.

______. *In Their Own Image.* New York: Charles Scribner's Sons, 1935.

______. *Courthouse Square.* New York: Charles Scribner's Sons, 1936.

______. *Days before Lent.* New York: Charles Scribner's Sons, 1939.

______. *Wine of the Country.* New York: Charles Scribner's Sons, 1941.

______. *Sun in Capricorn.* New York: Charles Scribner's Sons, 1942.

______. *Mainstream.* New York: Charles Scribner's Sons, 1943.

______. *The View From Pompey's Head.* Garden City, N. Y.: Doubleday & Company, Inc., 1954.

______. *The Light Infantry Ball.* Garden City, N. Y.: Doubleday & Company, Inc., 1959.

______. *A Quota of Seaweed.* Illustrated by Tom Frank. Garden City, N. Y.: Doubleday & Company, Inc., 1960.

______. *A Touch of the Dragon.* New York: The Viking Press, 1964.

Benasutti, Marion. *No Steady Job For Papa.* New York: The Vanguard Press, Inc., 1966.

Buranelli, Prosper. *You Gotta Be Rough.* Garden City, N. Y.: Doubleday, Doran & Company, 1930. London: Selwyn & Blount, 1928.

______. *Maggie of the Suicide Fleet.* Illustrated with line drawings by Herb Roth. Garden City, N. Y.: Doubleday, Doran & Company, 1930.

______. *Big Nick.* Garden City, N. Y.: Doubleday, Doran & Company, 1931.

______. *News Reel Murder.* New York: Wilfred Funk, Inc., 1940.

Calitri, Charles. *Rickey.* New York: Charles Scribner's Sons, 1952.

______. *Strike Heaven on the Face.* New York: Crown Publishers, Inc., 1958.

______. *Father.* New York: Crown Publishers, Inc., 1962.

Canizio, Frank. *A Man Against Fate* (As Told to Robert Markel). New York: Frederick Fell, Inc., 1958.

Canzoneri, Robert. *I Do So Politely.* Boston: Houghton Mifflin Company, 1965.

______. *Men With Little Hammers.* New York: The Dial Press, 1969.

______. *Barbed Wire and Other Stories.* New York: The Dial Press, 1970.

Caruso, Joseph. *The Priest.* New York: The Macmillan Company, 1956.

Cautela, Giuseppe. *Moon Harvest.* New York: Lincoln MacVeagh, The Dial Press, Inc., 1925.

Cenedella, Robert. *A Little To The East.* New York: G. P. Putnam's Sons, 1963.

Ciambelli, Bernardino. *I Misteri Di Mulberry.* New York: Frugone & Balletto, 1893.

______. *I Drammi Dell' Emigrazione, Sequito ai Misteri.* New York: Frugone & Balletto, 1893.

______. *I Misteri Della Polizia, Il Delitto Di Water Street.* New York: Frugone & Balletto, 1895.

______. *I Misteri di Bleeker Street.* New York: Frugone & Balletto, 1899.

______. *I Sotterranei di New York.* New York: Società Libreria Italiana, 1915.

______. *La Trovatella di Mulberry Street;* ovvero *La Stella dei Cinque Punti.* New York: Società Libreria Italiana, 1919.

Corsel, Ralph. *Up There The Stars.* New York: Citadel Press, 1968.

Covello, Leonard (with Guido D'Agostino). *The Heart Is The Teacher.* New York: McGraw Hill, 1958. Later Title, *The Teacher In The Community.* Littlefield Adams, 1958.

Creatore, Luigi. *This World is Mine.* New York: Rinehart & Company, 1942.

Cuomo, George. *Jack Be Nimble.* Garden City, N. Y.: Doubleday & Company, Inc., 1963.

______. *Bright Day, Dark Runner.* Garden City, N. Y.: Doubleday & Company, Inc., 1964.

______. *Among Thieves.* Garden City, N. Y.: Doubleday & Company, Inc., 1968.

______. *Sing, Choirs of Angels* (Short Stories). Garden City, N. Y.: Doubleday & Company, Inc., 1969.

D'Agostino, Guido. *Olives on the Apple Tree.* New York: Doubleday, Doran & Company, 1940.

______. *Hills Beyond Manhattan.* New York: Doubleday, Doran & Company, 1942.

______. *My Enemy the World.* New York: The Dial Press, 1947.

______. *The Barking of a Lonely Fox.* New York: McGraw Hill, 1952.

D'Ambrosio, Richard. *No Language But A Cry.* Garden City, N. Y.: Doubleday & Company, Inc., 1970.

D'Angelo, Lou. *What the Ancients Said.* New York: Doubleday & Company, Inc., 1971.

D'Angelo, Pascal. *Son of Italy.* New York: The Macmillan Company, 1924.

De Capite, Michael. *Maria.* New York: The John Day Company, Inc., 1943.

______. *No Bright Banner.* New York: The John Day Company, Inc., 1944.

———. *The Bennett Place.* New York: The John Day Company, Inc., 1948.

DeCapite, Raymond. *The Coming of Fabrizze.* New York: David McKay Company, Inc., 1960.

———. *A Lost King.* New York: David McKay Company, Inc., 1961.

De Lillo, Don. *Americana.* Boston: Houghton, Mifflin Company, 1971.

———. *End Zone.* Boston: Houghton, Mifflin Company, 1972.

DeVoto, Bernard Augustine. *The Crooked Mile.* New York: Minton, Balch & Company, 1924.

———. *The Chariot of Fire.* New York: The Macmillan Company, 1926.

———. *The House of Sun-Goes-Down.* New York: The Macmillan Company, 1928.

———. *We Accept With Pleasure.* Boston: Little, Brown & Company, 1934.

———. John August [pseud.]. *Troubled Star.* Boston: Little, Brown & Company, 1939.

———. *Rain Before Seven.* Boston: Little, Brown & Company, 1940.

———. *Advanced Agent.* Boston: Little, Brown & Company, 1942.

———. *The Woman in the Picture.* Boston: Little, Brown & Company, 1944.

———. *Mountain Time.* Boston: Little, Brown & Company, 1947.

DiDonato, Pietro. *Christ in Concrete.* Indianapolis: Bobbs-Merrill Company, 1939.

———. *This Woman.* New York: Ballantine Books, Inc., 1959.

———. *Three Circles of Light.* New York: Julian Messner, Inc., 1960.

———. *Naked Author* (Short Stories). New York: Phaedra, Inc., 1970.

Fante, John. *Wait Until Spring, Bandini.* New York: Stackpole Sons, 1938.

———. *Ask the Dust.* New York: Stackpole Sons, 1939.

———. *Dago Red* (Short Stories). Illustrated by Valenti Angelo. New York: The Viking Press, Inc., 1940.

———. *Full of Life.* Boston: Little, Brown & Company, 1952.

Ficarra, Bernard J. *I Zappatori.* Boston: Christopher Publishing House, 1953.

Forgione, Louis. *Reamer Lou.* New York: E. P. Dutton & Company, 1924.

———. *The Men of Silence.* Introduction by Walter Littlefield. New York: E. P. Dutton & Company, 1928.

———. *The River Between.* New York: E. P. Dutton & Company, 1928.

Fumento, Rocco. *Devil By the Tail.* New York: Alfred A. Knopf, 1954.

———. *Tree of Dark Reflection.* New York: Alfred A. Knopf, 1962.

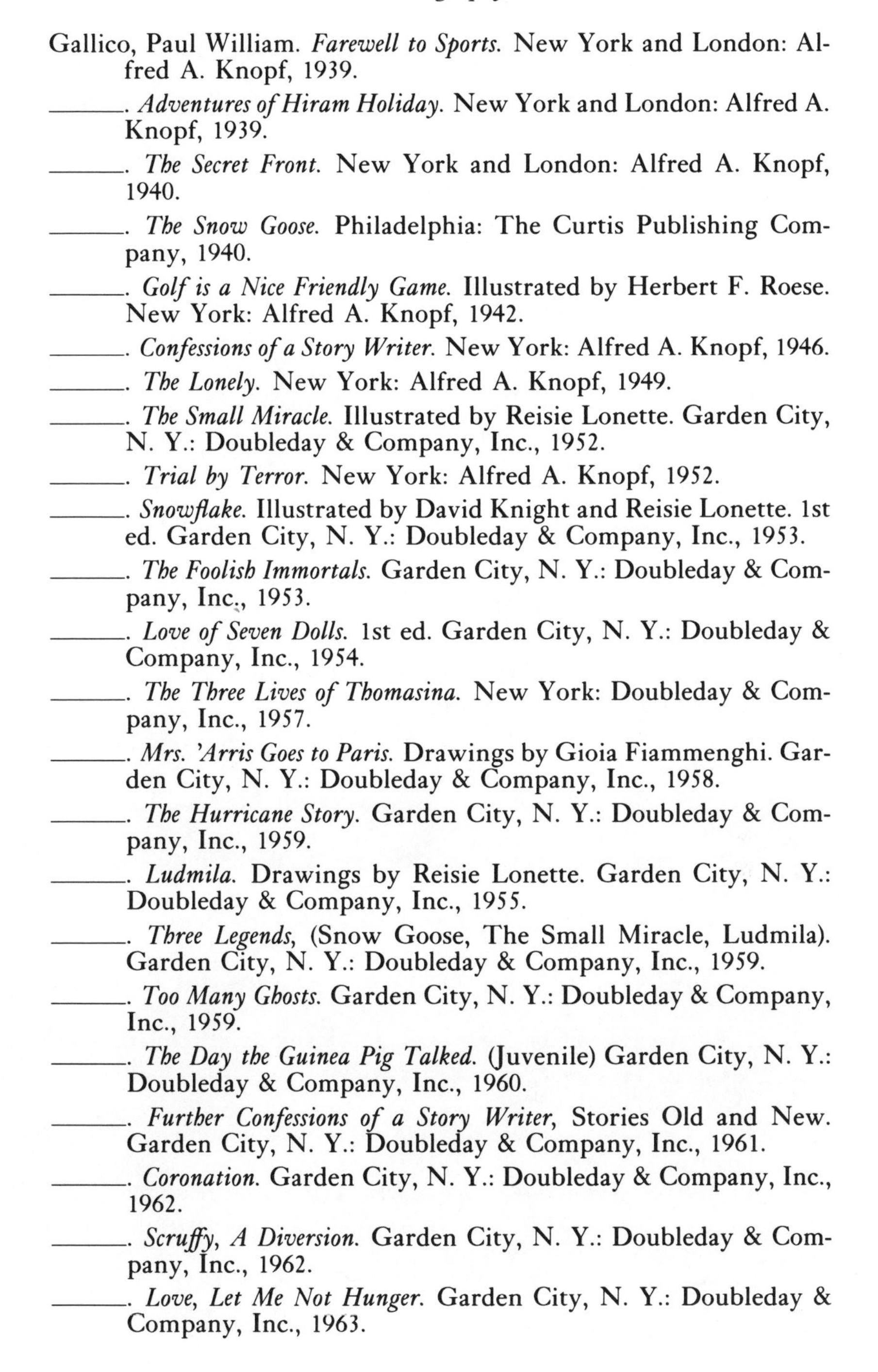

Gallico, Paul William. *Farewell to Sports.* New York and London: Alfred A. Knopf, 1939.

———. *Adventures of Hiram Holiday.* New York and London: Alfred A. Knopf, 1939.

———. *The Secret Front.* New York and London: Alfred A. Knopf, 1940.

———. *The Snow Goose.* Philadelphia: The Curtis Publishing Company, 1940.

———. *Golf is a Nice Friendly Game.* Illustrated by Herbert F. Roese. New York: Alfred A. Knopf, 1942.

———. *Confessions of a Story Writer.* New York: Alfred A. Knopf, 1946.

———. *The Lonely.* New York: Alfred A. Knopf, 1949.

———. *The Small Miracle.* Illustrated by Reisie Lonette. Garden City, N. Y.: Doubleday & Company, Inc., 1952.

———. *Trial by Terror.* New York: Alfred A. Knopf, 1952.

———. *Snowflake.* Illustrated by David Knight and Reisie Lonette. 1st ed. Garden City, N. Y.: Doubleday & Company, Inc., 1953.

———. *The Foolish Immortals.* Garden City, N. Y.: Doubleday & Company, Inc., 1953.

———. *Love of Seven Dolls.* 1st ed. Garden City, N. Y.: Doubleday & Company, Inc., 1954.

———. *The Three Lives of Thomasina.* New York: Doubleday & Company, Inc., 1957.

———. *Mrs. 'Arris Goes to Paris.* Drawings by Gioia Fiammenghi. Garden City, N. Y.: Doubleday & Company, Inc., 1958.

———. *The Hurricane Story.* Garden City, N. Y.: Doubleday & Company, Inc., 1959.

———. *Ludmila.* Drawings by Reisie Lonette. Garden City, N. Y.: Doubleday & Company, Inc., 1955.

———. *Three Legends,* (Snow Goose, The Small Miracle, Ludmila). Garden City, N. Y.: Doubleday & Company, Inc., 1959.

———. *Too Many Ghosts.* Garden City, N. Y.: Doubleday & Company, Inc., 1959.

———. *The Day the Guinea Pig Talked.* (Juvenile) Garden City, N. Y.: Doubleday & Company, Inc., 1960.

———. *Further Confessions of a Story Writer,* Stories Old and New. Garden City, N. Y.: Doubleday & Company, Inc., 1961.

———. *Coronation.* Garden City, N. Y.: Doubleday & Company, Inc., 1962.

———. *Scruffy, A Diversion.* Garden City, N. Y.: Doubleday & Company, Inc., 1962.

———. *Love, Let Me Not Hunger.* Garden City, N. Y.: Doubleday & Company, Inc., 1963.

______. *The Abandoned.* The Story of Jennie. New York: Alfred A. Knopf, 1964.

______. *The Hand of Mary Constable.* Garden City, N. Y.: Doubleday & Company, Inc., 1964.

______. *The Day Jean-Pierre was Pignapped.* (Juvenile). Garden City, N. Y.: Doubleday & Company, Inc., 1964.

______. *Mrs. 'Arris Goes to Parliament.* Drawings by Gioia Fiammenghi. Garden City, N. Y.: Doubleday & Company, Inc., 1965.

______. *The Golden People.* Garden City, N. Y.: Doubleday & Company, Inc., 1965.

______. *The Man Who Was Magic,* a Fable of Innocence. Garden City, N. Y.: Doubleday & Company, Inc., 1966.

______. *The Story of Silent Night.* New York: Crown Publishers, 1967.

______. *Manxmouse,* The Mouse Who Knew No Fear. Illustrated by Janet and Anne Graham-Johnstone. New York: Coward-McCann, Inc., 1968.

______. *The Poseidon Adventure.* New York: Coward-McCann, Inc., 1969.

______. *The Day Jean-Pierre Joined the Circus* (Juvenile). New York: Franklin Watts, Inc., 1970.

______. *Matilda.* New York: Coward-McCann, Inc., 1970.

______. *The Zoo Game.* New York: Coward-McCann, Inc., 1971.

______. *Honorable Cat.* New York: Crown Publishers, Inc., 1972.

Gillette, Paul. *Carmela.* New York: Arbor House Publishing Co., Inc., 1972.

Iannuzzi, John Nicholas. *Part 35.* New York: Richard W. Baron Publishing Company, Inc., 1970.

______. *Sicilian Defense.* New York: Richard W. Baron Publishing Co., Inc., 1972.

Lapolla, Garibaldi Marto. *The Fire in the Flesh.* New York: The Vanguard Press, Inc., 1931.

______. *Miss Rollins in Love.* New York: The Vanguard Press, Inc., 1932.

______. *The Grand Gennaro.* New York: The Vanguard Press, Inc., 1935.

Longo, Lucas. *The Family on Vendetta Street.* New York: Doubleday & Company, Inc., 1968.

Madalena, Lawrence. *Confetti for Gino.* New York: Doubleday & Company, Inc., 1959.

Maggio, Joe. *Company Man.* New York: G. P. Putnam's Sons, 1972.

Mangione, Jerre. *Mount Allegro.* Illustrated by Peggy Bacon. Boston: Houghton Mifflin Company, 1942.

______. *The Ship and the Flame.* New York: A. A. Wyn, Inc., 1948.

______. *Night Search.* New York: Crown Publishing, Inc., 1965.

Marchiello, Maurice R. *Crossing the Tracks.* New York: Vantage Press, 1969.

Maresca, James V. *My Flag is Down.* New York: Dutton & Company, 1948.

Miceli, Frank. *The Seventh Month.* New York: Frederick Fell, Inc., 1969.

Mirabelli, Eugene. *The Burning Air.* Boston: Houghton Mifflin Company, 1959.

———. *The Way In.* New York: The Viking Press, Inc., 1968.

———. *No Resting Place.* New York: The Viking Press, Inc., 1972.

Moroso, John Antonio. *The Quarry.* Illustrated by L. Thomas Fogarty. Boston: Little, Brown & Company, 1913.

———. *The People Against Nancy Preston.* New York: Henry Holt & Company, 1921.

———. *The Stumbling Herd.* Frontispiece by Harvey Dunn. New York: The Macaulay Company, 1923.

———. *Cap Fallon, Firefighter.* New York and London: D. Appleton & Company, 1923.

———. *The Listening Man.* New York: D. Appleton & Company, 1924.

———. *Bread Eaten in Secret.* New York: The Macaulay Company, 1931.

———. *Poor Passionate Fool.* New York: The Macaulay Company, 1932.

———. *Love in Her Heart.* New York: The Macaulay Company, 1934.

———. *Black Chalice.* New York: The Macaulay Company, 1934.

Paese, Robert. *The Associate Professor.* New York: Simon & Schuster, 1967.

Pagano, Jo. *The Paesanos.* Boston: (Atlantic Monthly Press) Little, Brown & Company, 1940.

———. *Golden Wedding.* New York: Random House, Inc., 1943.

———. *The Condemned.* New York: Prentice-Hall, Inc., 1947.

Panetta, George. *We Ride a White Donkey.* New York: Harcourt Brace & Company, 1944.

———. *Jimmy Potts Gets a Haircut.* Illustrated by Reisie Lonette. Garden City, N. Y.: Doubleday & Company, Inc., 1947.

———. *Viva Madison Avenue!* New York: Harcourt, Brace & Company, 1957.

———. *The Sea Beach Express.* New York: Harper & Row, 1966.

Panunzio, Constantine M. *The Soul of An Immigrant.* New York: The Macmillan Company, 1924.

Papaleo, Joseph. *All The Comforts.* Boston: Little, Brown & Company, 1967.

———. *Out of Place.* Boston: Little, Brown & Company, 1970.

Pasinetti, P.M. *Venetian Red.* New York: Random House, 1960.

______. *The Smile on the Face of the Lion.* New York: Random House, 1965.

______. *From the Academy Bridge.* New York: Random House, 1970.

Patri, Angelo. *A Schoolmaster of the Great City.* New York: The Macmillan Company, 1917.

Pei, Mario A. *Swords of Anjou.* New York: The John Day Company, 1953.

______. *The Sparrows of Paris.* New York: The Philosophical Library, 1958.

______. *Tales of the Natural and Supernatural.* Old Greenwich, Conn.: The Devin-Adair Company, 1971.

Pellegrini, Angelo M. *Americans By Choice.* New York: The Macmillan Company, 1956.

Petracca, Joseph. *Come Back To Sorrento.* Boston: Little, Brown & Company, 1952.

Piazza, Ben. *The Exact and Very Strange Truth.* New York: Farrar, Straus & Company, 1964.

Pillitteri, Joseph. *When the Giraffe Runs Down.* New York: The Dial Press, 1970.

______. *Two Hours On Sunday.* New York: The Dial Press, 1971.

Pollini, Francis. *Night.* New York: G. P. Putnam's Sons, 1961.

______. *Glover.* New York: G. P. Putnam's Sons, 1965.

______. *Excursion.* New York: G. P. Putnam's Sons, 1965.

______. *The Crown.* New York: G. P. Putnam's Sons, 1967.

______. *Pretty Maids All In a Row.* New York: Delacorte Press, and Dell Publishing Company, 1968.

Pronzini, Bill. *The Stalker.* New York: Random House, Inc., 1971.

______. *The Snatch.* New York: Random House, Inc., 1971.

Puzo, Mario. *The Dark Arena.* New York: Random House, 1955.

______. *The Fortunate Pilgrim.* New York: Atheneum, 1964.

______. *The Godfather.* New York: G. P. Putnam's Sons, 1969.

______. *The Godfather Papers* and Other Confessions. New York: G. P. Putnam's Sons, 1972.

Radano, Gene. *Walking the Beat.* New York: World Publishing Company, 1968.

Savarese, Julia. *The Weak and The Strong.* New York: Putnam Publishing Company, 1952.

______. *Final Proof.* New York: W. W. Norton & Company, Inc., 1971.

Savo, Jimmy. *Little World "Hello!"* Illustrated by A. Birnbaum. New York: Simon & Schuster, Inc., 1947.

Siciliano, Vincent. *Unless They Kill Me First.* New York: Hawthorn Books, Inc., 1970.

Sorrentino, Gilbert. *The Sky Changes.* New York: Hill & Wang, 1966.

______. *Steelwork.* New York: Pantheon, Random House, Inc., 1969.

______. *Imaginative Qualities of Actual Things.* New York: Pantheon, Random House, 1971.

Sorrentino, Joseph. *Up From Never.* New Jersey: Prentice-Hall, 1971.

Stefano, Joseph. *The Black Orchid* (Novelized by Edward Ronns). New York: Almat Publishing Corp., 1959.

Talese, Gay. *The Overreachers.* Illustrated by Stanislav Zagorski. New York: Harper & Row, 1965.

______. *The Kingdom and the Power.* New York: The World Publishing Company, 1969.

______. *Fame and Obscurity.* Includes Short Stories and Reprints of *A Serendipiter's Journey* (1961) and *The Bridge* (1964). New York: The World Publishing Company, 1970.

______. *Honor Thy Father.* New York: The World Publishing Company, 1971.

Tomasi, Mari. *Deep Grow the Roots.* Philadelphia: J. B. Lippincott Company, 1940.

______. *Like Lesser Gods.* Milwaukee: Bruce Publishing Company, 1949.

Trocchi, Alexander. *Cain's Book.* New York: Grove Press, Incorporated, 1960.

______. *The Outsiders* (Young Adam). New York: Heineman, 1961.

Tucci, Niccolò. *Before My Time.* New York: Simon and Schuster, 1962.

______. *Unfinished Funeral.* New York: Simon and Schuster, 1964.

Ventresca, Francesco. *Personal Reminiscences of a Nuturalized American.* New York: Daniel Ryerson, Inc., 1937.

Ventura, Luigi Donato. *Peppino.* Translated into French, with introduction and vocabulary. New York: William R. Jenkins Company, 1913.

Vergara, Joseph. *Love E Pasta.* New York: Harper and Row, 1968.

Villa, Silvio. *Claudio Graziani, an Episode of War.* New York: Brentano's (privately printed), 1919.

______. *The Unbidden Guest.* Illustrated by Carlo Beuf. New York: The Macmillan Company, 1922.

______. *Ultraviolet Rays.* New York: The Macmillan Company, 1927.

Vivante, Arturo. *A Goodly Babe.* Boston: Little, Brown & Company, 1959.

______. *The French Girls of Killini* (Short Stories). Boston: Little, Brown & Company, 1958–1967.

______. *Doctor Giovanni.* Boston: Little, Brown & Company, 1959, 1966, 1969.

Winwar, Frances [Francesca Vinciguerra]. *The Ardent Flame.* New York: The Century Company, 1927.

———. [Francesca Vinciguerra]. *The Golden Round.* New York and London: The Century Company, 1928.

——— [Francesca Vinciguerra]. *Pagan Interval.* Indianapolis: Bobbs-Merrill Company, 1929.

——— [Francesca Vinciguerra]. *Gallows Hill.* New York: Henry Holt and Company, 1937.

——— [Francesca Vinciguerra]. *The Sentimentalist.* New York: Harper & Brothers, 1943.

——— [Francesca Vinciguerra]. *The Eagle and the Rock.* New York: Harper & Brothers, 1953.

——— [Francesca Vinciguerra]. *The Last Love of Camille.* London: Alvin Redman, 1955.

II. SECONDARY SOURCES (SELECTED): BOOKS RELATED TO ITALIAN IMMIGRATION AND ITALIAN-AMERICAN WRITING

Albini, Joseph L. *The American Mafia: Genesis of a Legend.* New York: Appleton-Century-Crofts, 1971.

Bailey, Harry and Katz, Ellis. *Ethnic Group Politics.* Columbus: Merrill Publishing Company, 1969.

Barzini, Luigi. *The Italians.* New York: Atheneum, 1965.

———. *From Caesar To The Mafia.* New York: The Library Press, 1971.

Biagi, Ernest L. *Italian Name-Places in the United States with Historical and Descriptive Annotations and Information.* Philadelphia: Adams Press, 1970.

Brandenburg, Broughton. *Imported Americans.* New York: Fred Stokes Company, Publishers, 1904.

Bromwell, William J. *History of Immigration to the United States 1819–1855.* New York: Augustus M. Kelley, Publishers, 1970.

Carlevale, Joseph William. *Americans of Italian Descent in Philadelphia.* Philadelphia: George S. Ferguson Company, 1954.

Child, Irwin. *Italian or American?* New Haven: Yale University Press, 1943.

Cordasco, Francesco. *Italians in the United States.* A Bibliography of Reports, Texts, Critical Studies and Related Materials. New York: Oriole Edition, 1972.

Covello, Leonard. *The Social Background of the Italo American School Child.* Leiden: E. J. Brill, 1967.

De Conde, Alexander. *Half Bitter, Half Sweet.* An Excursion Into Italian-American History. New York: Charles Scribner's Sons, 1972.

De Voto, Bernard Augustine. *The Literary Fallacy.* Boston: Little, Brown & Company, 1944.

Di Donato, Pietro. *Immigrant Saint. The Life of Mother Cabrini.* New York: McGraw Hill Book Company, Incorporated, 1960.

Dinnerstein, Leonard and Frederick C. Jaher. *The Aliens: A History of Ethnic Minorities in America.* New York: Appleton-Century-Crofts, 1970.

Eiseman, Alberta. *From Many Lands.* New York: Atheneum Publishers, 1970.

Faderman, Lillian and Barbara Bradshaw. *Speaking For Ourselves.* (American Ethnic Writing). Glenview, Ill.: Scott, Foresman and Company, 1969.

Fairchild, Henry Pratt. *Immigration: A World Movement and Its American Significance.* New York: The Macmillan Company, 1933.

Felici, I. *Father To the Immigrants. The Life of John Baptist Scalabrini (1839–1905).* Staten Island, N. Y.: Center For Migration Studies, 1971.

Fleming, Thomas J. *The Golden Door. The Story of American Immigration.* New York: Grosset & Dunlap, Inc., 1970.

Foerster, Norman. *Image of America: Our Literature From Puritanism to the Space Age.* Notre Dame Ind.: Notre Dame University Press, 1962.

Foerster, Robert Franz. *The Italian Emigration of Our Times.* Cambridge, Mass.: Harvard University Press, 1919.

Fuchs, Lawrence, ed. *American Ethnic Problems.* New York: Harper & Row, 1968.

Fusco, Jeremiah N. *Diplomatic Relations between Italy and the United States 1913–1917.* New York: Carlton Press, Inc., 1970.

Garlick, Richard C., Jr., & Associates. *Italy and the Italians in Washington's Time.* New York: The Italian Publishing Company and Casa Italiana, 1933.

Gerson, Louis. *The Hyphenate in Recent American Politics and Diplomacy.* Lawrence, Kan.: University of Kansas Press, 1964.

Gifford, Edward S., M.D. *The Evil Eye.* New York: The Macmillan Company, 1958.

Glanz, Rudolf. *Jews and Italians.* New York: KTAV Publishing House, Inc., 1971.

Glazer, Nathan & Moynihan, Daniel F. *Beyond the Melting Pot.* Cambridge, Mass.: Harvard University Press, 1963.

Gordon, Milton. *Assimilation in American Life.* New York: Oxford University Press, 1964.

Greeley, Andrew. *Why Can't They Be Like Us?* New York: E. P. Dutton & Company, 1971.

Greenleaf, Barbara Kaye. *American Fever: The Story of American Immigration.* New York: Four Winds Press, 1970.

Handlin, Oscar. *The Uprooted.* Boston: Little, Brown & Company, 1951.

———. *Race and Nationality in American Life.* Boston: Little, Brown & Company, 1957.

———. *Immigration As a Factor in American History.* Englewood Cliffs, N. J.: Prentice-Hall, Inc., 1959.

———. *Boston's Immigrants. A Study in Acculturation.* Cambridge, Mass.: Harvard University Press, 1959.

Hansen, Marcus Lee. *The Immigrant in American History.* Cambridge: Harvard University Press, 1940.

Hapgood, Hutchins. *The Spirit of the Ghetto.* New York: Schocken Books, 1966.

Haslam, Gerald W., ed. *Forgotten Pages of American Literature.* Boston: Houghton Mifflin, 1970.

Higham, John. *Strangers in the Land.* New Brunswick: Rutgers University Press, 1959.

Hutchinson, E. P. *Immigrants and Their Children: 1850–1950.* New York: Wiley Publishers, 1956.

Iorizzo, Luciano J. and Mondello, Salvatore. *The Italian-Americans.* New York: Twayne Publishers, Inc., 1971.

Italian-American Who's Who. New York: Vigo Press, 1952.

The Italians of New York. A Survey Prepared by Workers of the Federal Writer's Project, Works Progress Administration in the City of New York. New York: Random House, 1938.

Jones, Howard Mumford. *The Age of Energy.* New York: Viking, 1971.

Kahl, Joseph A. *The American Class Structure.* New York: Rinehart & Company, Inc., 1953.

Kane, Michael B. *Minorities in Textbooks.* A Study of Their Treatment in Social Studies Texts. Chicago: Quadrangle Books, 1970.

Kobler, John: *Capone. The Life and World of Al Capone.* New York: G. P. Putnam's Sons, 1971.

Kogan, Norman. *A Political History of Postwar Italy.* New York: Praeger, 1966.

Kurokawa, Minako, *Minority Responses.* New York: Random House, Inc., 1970.

La Guardia, Fiorello H. *The Making of an Insurgent: An Autobiography: 1882–1919.* New York: J. B. Lippincott Company, 1948.

La Gumina, Salvatore J. *Vito Marcantonio, the People's Politician.* Dubuque, Iowa: Kendall, Hunt Publishing Co., 1969.

Levy, Mark R. and Michael S. Kramer. *The Ethnic Factor.* New York: Simon and Schuster, 1972.

Litt, Edgar. *Beyond Pluralism—Ethnic Politics in America.* Glenview, Ill.: Scott, Foresman College Division, 1970.

Lodge, David. *The Novelist At the Crossroads.* Ithaca, N. Y.: Cornell University Press, 1972.

Lopreato, Joseph. *Peasants No More.* Calif.: Chandler Press, 1967.

———. *Italian Americans (Ethnic Groups in Comparative Perspective* series). New York: Random House, 1970.

Lord, John J., Eliot, D. Trevor, and Barrows, S.J. *The Italian in America.* New York: B. F. Buck & Company, 1906.

Lowitt, Richard, Gen. Ed. *The Novel as American Social History.* Lexington, Ky.: University of Kentucky Press, 1970.

Makers of America. A Survey of 400 Years of ethnic diversity in the United States. Encyclopaedia Britannica Educational Corporation, 1971.

Mangano, Antonio. *Sons of Italy; a Social and Religious Study of the Italians in America.* New York: Missionary Education Movement of the United States and Canada, 1917.

Mangione, Jerre. *Reunion in Sicily.* Boston: Houghton Mifflin Company, 1950.

———. *America is Also Italian.* New York: G. P. Putnam's Sons, 1969.

Mariano, John Horace. *The Italian Contribution to American Democracy,* with an introduction by Hon. F. H. LaGuardia. Boston: Christopher Publishing House, 1921.

———. *The Italian Immigrant and Our Courts.* Boston: Christopher Publishing House, 1925.

Marinacci, Barbara. *They Came From Italy, The Stories of Famous Italian-Americans.* Illustrated. New York: Dodd, Mead & Company, 1967.

McAvoy, Thomas T. (O.S.C.), ed. *Roman Catholicism and The American Way of Life.* Notre Dame, Ind.: The University of Notre Dame Press, 1960.

McLaughlin, V. Y. *Like the Fingers of the Hand: The Family and Community Life of First Generation Italian-Americans in Buffalo, New York, 1880–1930.* Ph.D. Dissertation, University of New York at Buffalo. June, 1970.

Merrill, John C. *et al. The Foreign Press.* Baton Rouge, La.: Louisiana State University Press, 1970.

Musmanno, Michael A. *Verdict!* New York: MacFadden Bartell Corporation, 1963.

———. *The Story of the Italians in America.* Garden City, N. Y.: Doubleday Company, Inc., 1965.

Nagourney, Peter J. and Steiner, Susan G. *Growing Up American.* Belmont, Calif.: Wadsworth Publishing Company, Inc., 1972.

Nelli, Humbert S. *The Italians in Chicago, 1880–1930. A Study in Ethnic Mobility.* New York: Oxford University Press, 1970.

Novak, Michael. *The Rise of the Unmeltable Ethnics.* New York: The Macmillan Company, 1972.

Odencrantz, Louise Christine. *Italian Women in Industry.* New York: Russell Sage Foundation, 1919.

Pareto, Vilfredo. *The Mind and Society.* New York: Harcourt Brace and Company, Inc., 1935.

Park, Robert E. and Herbert A. Miller. *Old World Traits Transplanted.* New York: Harper & Brothers, 1921.

Patri, Angelo. *Child Training.* New York: D. Appleton & Company, 1922.

Paulson, Belden and Athos Ricci. *The Searchers.* Chicago: Quadrangle Books, 1966.

Pei, Mario. *The America We Lost.* Cleveland: New American Library, Incorporated, associated with The World Publishing Company, 1968.

Pellegrini, Angelo M. *Immigrant's Return.* New York: The Macmillan Company, 1951.

Peragallo, Olga. *Italian-American Authors and Their Contribution to American Literature.* New York: S. F. Vanni, 1949.

Pisani, Lawrence Frank. *The Italian in America.* New York: Exposition Press, 1957.

Potter, David M. *People of Plenty.* Chicago: Phoenix Books, The University of Chicago Press, 1954.

Rose, Philip M. *The Italians in America.* New York: George H. Doran Company, 1922.

Sartorio, Henry Charles. *Social and Religious Life of Italians in America,* with an introduction by Dean George Hodges. Boston: Christopher Publishing House, 1918.

Schermerhorn, R. A. *Comparative Ethnic Relations. A Framework for Theory and Research.* New York: Random House, 1970.

Schiavo, Giovanni E. *Four Centuries of Italian-American History.* New York: Vigo Press, 1952.

———. *Italian-American History.* 2 vols. New York: Vigo Press, 1947 and 1949.

———. *The Italians in America Before The Civil War.* New York: Vigo Press, 1934.

———. *The Italians in Chicago.* Chicago: The Italian American Publishing Company, 1928.

———. *The Italians in Missouri.* Chicago: The Italian American Publishing Co., 1929.

Schiro, George. *Americans by Choice, History of the Italians in Utica.* Utica, 1940.

Schrag, Peter. *The Decline of the Wasp.* New York: Simon & Schuster, 1971.

Shibutani, Tomatsu and Kiav Kwan. *Ethnic Stratification.* New York: The Macmillan Company, 1965.

Smith, Dennis Mack. *Italy: A Modern History.* Ann Arbor: University of Michigan Press, 1969.

Spiller, Robert E., Willard Thorp, Thomas H. Johnson, Henry Seidel Canby, eds. *Literary History of the United States.* 3 Vols. New York: The Macmillan Company, 1948.

______, Harold Blodgett, eds. *The Roots of National Culture: To 1830.* rev. ed. New York: The Macmillan Company, 1949.

Stein, Rita F. *Disturbed Youth and Ethnic Family Patterns.* Albany, New York: State University Press, 1971.

Steinfield, Melvin. *Cracks In the Melting Pot.* Beverly Hills, Calif.: Glencoe Press, 1970.

Stella, Antonio. *Some Aspects of Italian Immigration to the United States.* Preface by Nicholas Murray Butler. New York: G. P. Putnam's Sons, The Knickerbocker Press, 1924.

Strafile, Alfonso. *Vita Coloniale degli Italiani nel Nord America.* 3 vols. Philadelphia: Mastro Paolo Printing House, 1910.

Tanner, Tony. *City of Words: American Fiction 1950–1970.* New York: Harper and Rowe, 1971.

Tomasi, Sylvan M. and Engel, Madeline H., eds. *The Italian Experience in the United States.* Staten Island, N. Y.: Center For Migration Studies, 1971.

Van den Berghe, Pierre. *Race and Ethnicity. Essays in Comparative Sociology.* New York: Basic Books, Inc., 1970.

Vecoli, Rudolph J. *The People of New Jersey.* Princeton, N. J.: 1965.

Villari, Luigi. *Gli Stati Uniti D'America e l'emigrazione Italiana.* Milan: Frat. Treves, 1912.

Warner, W. Lloyd *et al. Social Class in America.* New York: Harper and Brothers Torchbooks, 1960.

Warner, W. Lloyd and Srole, Leo. *The Social Systems of American Ethnic Groups.* New Haven: Yale University Press, 1945.

Wheeler, Thomas C. (ed.) *The Immigrant Experience.* New York: The Dial Press, 1971.

Whyte, William. *Street Corner Society.* Chicago: University of Chicago Press, 1943.

Williams, Phyliss H. *South Italian Folkways in Europe and America.* New Haven: Yale University Press, 1938.

Williams, Robin M., Jr. *Stranger Next Door.* Englewood Cliffs, N. J.: Prentice-Hall, Inc., 1964.

COMPREHENSIVE COLLECTION

The American Immigration Library. 30 vols. reprinted in facsimile. New York: Jerome S. Ozer, Publisher, Inc., 1971.

III
SECONDARY SOURCES (SELECTED): ARTICLES IN AMERICAN PERIODICALS

Abramson, H. J. "Inter-ethnic Marriage Among Catholic Americans and Changes in Religious Behavior." *Sociological Analysis* 32, no. 1 (Spring 1971): 31–44.

Adams, Charlotte. "Italian Life in New York." *Harper's New Monthly Magazine* 62 (April 1881): 676–84.

"Aliens?" *The Nation* (June 25, 1924), p. 7256.

Appel, John. "American Negro and Immigrant Experiences. Similarities and Differences." *American Quarterly* (1968).

Barker, Folger. "What of the Italian Immigrant." *Arena* 34 (August 1905): 174–76.

Bennett, Alice. "Italian-American Farmers." *The Survey* 22 (May 1, 1909): 172–75.

Bernard, William S., "New Directions in Integration and Ethnicity." *International Migration Review* 5 (Winter 1971): 464–73.

Campisi, Paul J. "Ethnic Family Patterns: The Italian Family in the United States." *American Journal of Sociology* 53 (1948): 443–49.

Carr, John Foster. "The Coming of the Italians." New York Liberal Immigration League (1906). Reprint from *Outlook* (February 24, 1906).

Carter, Hugh, ed. "Reappraising our Immigration Policy." *The Annals* (of the American Academy of Political and Social Science) 262 (March 1949), entire issue.

Castiglione, G. E. De Palma. "Italian Immigration into the United States." *The American Journal of Sociology* 2 (September 1905): 183–206.

Colajanni, Napoleone. "Homicide and the Italians." *The Forum* 31 (March 1901): 62–68.

Cometti, Elizabeth. "Trends in Italian Emigration." *Western Political Quarterly* 11 (December 1958): 820–34.

Corresca, Rocco. "Biography of a Bootblack." *Independent* (December 4, 1902), pp. 2863–7.

Cowley, Malcolm. "Storytelling's Tarnished Image." *Saturday Review* (September 25, 1971), p. 25.

D'Amato, Gaetano. "The Black Hand Myth." *North American Review* 187 (April 1908): 543–49.

Darroch, Gordon and Marsten, Wilfred G. "Ethnic Differentiation: Ecological Aspects of a Multidimensional Concept." *International Migration Review* 4, no. 1 (Fall 1963): 71.

Duncan, Otis and Lieberson, Stan. "Ethnic Segregation and Assimilation." *American Journal of Sociology* (January 1959).

Etzioni, Amitai. "The Ghetto: a Re-evaluation." *Social Forces* (March 1959), pp. 255–62.

Feminella, Frances X. "The Impact of Italian Migration and American Catholicism." *The American Catholic Sociological Review* (Fall 1961).

Foerster, Robert F. "A Statistical Survey of Italian Emigration." *Quarterly Journal of Economics* 23 (November 1909): 66–103.

Fonzi, Gaeton. "The Italians Are Coming! The Italians Are Coming." *Philadelphia Magazine* 62 no. 12 (December 1971): 98–103, 171–81.

Franklin, Lawrence. "The Italian in America: What He Has Been, What He Shall Be." *The Catholic World* 71 (April 1900): 67–80.

Gambino, Richard. "Twenty Million Italian-Americans Can't Be Wrong." *The New York Times Magazine* (April 30, 1972), pp. 20, 21, 26, 30–40.

Gibson, Richard. "A No to Nothing." *Kenyon Review* 13 (Spring 1951).

Golino, Carlo L. "On the Italian 'Myth' of America." *Italian Quarterly* 3 (Spring 1959): 19–33.

Grabo, Carl H. "Americanizing the Immigrants." *The Dial* 66 (May 31, 1919).

Greeley, A., "The Alienation of the White Ethnic Groups." *Sign* 50, no. 10 (May 1971): 16–21.

Handlin, Oscar. "Preface" and "Historical Perspectives on the American Ethnic Group" in "Ethnic Groups In American Life." *Daedalus,* Journal of the American Academy of Arts and Sciences (Spring 1961), entire issue.

Hapgood, Hutchins. "The Foreign Stage in New York." *The Bookman* (August 1900), pp. 545–53.

Hawkins, Gordon. "God and the Mafia." *The Public Interest* (Winter 1969), pp. 24–51.

Heller, Celia. "Class As an Expression of Ethnic Differences in Mobility Aspirations." *International Migration Review* (Fall 1967).

Howells, William Dean. "Our Italian Assimilators." *Harpers Weekly* (April 10, 1909), p. 28.

Hutchinson, E. P., ed. "The New Immigration." *The Annals* 367 (September 1966), entire issue.

Ianni, Francis. "The Italo-American Teenager." *The Annals* (November 1961).

Irwin, Grace. "Michelangelo in Newark." *Harpers* (September, 1921), pp. 446–54.

"Italian Future in America." *Review of Reviews* (April 1900), pp. 486–87.

Jansen, Clifford. "Leadership in the Toronto Italian Ethnic Group." *International Migration Review* 4, no. 1 (Fall 1966): 25.

Kallen, Horace M. "Democracy Versus the Melting-Pot." *The Nation* 100 (February 18 and 25, 1915): 190–94, 217–20.

Karlin, J. A. "The Italo-American Incident of 1891 and the Road to Reunion." *The Journal of Southern History* 8 (May 1942): 242–46.

Keniston, Kenneth. "Alienation and the Decline of Utopia." *American Scholar* (Spring 1960)

Kraus, Albert L. "Equal But Separate." *New York Times* (July 17, 1968), pp. 55, 61.

Lodge, Henry Cabot. "Efforts to Restrict Undesirable Immigration." *The Century Magazine* 67 (January 1904): 466–69.

La Gumina, Salvatore J. "The New Deal, The Immigrants and the Congressman Vito Marcantonio." *The International Migration Review* 4, no. 2: 57.

Lipari, Marie. "The Padrone System: An Aspect of American Economic History." *Italy-America Monthly* 2 (April 1935): 4–10.

MacDonell, Ann. "Italian Spirit in D'Annunzio." *New Republic* (July 3, 1915), pp. 229–30.

Mailey, Hugo. "The Italian Vote In Philadelphia, 1928–46." *Public Opinion Quarterly* (Spring 1950).

Mangano, Antonio. "The Associated Life of the Italians in New York City." *Charities* 12 (May 7, 1904): 476–82.

Marraro, Howard R. "Italo Americans in Pennsylvania in the Eighteenth Century." *Pennsylvania History* 7 (July 1940): 159–66.

———. "Lincoln's Italian Volunteers from New York." *New York History* 24 (January 1943): 56–67.

Merlino, S. "Italian Immigrants and Their Enslavement." *The Forum* (April 1893): 183–90.

Mikulski, B. A. "Who Speaks for Ethnic America?" *The New York Times* (September 29, 1970), p. 43.

Mondello, Salvatore. "Italian Migration to the U.S. as Reported in American Magazines, 1880–1920." *Social Science* 39 (June 1964): 131–42.

———. "Protestant Proselytism Among the Italians in the U.S.A. as Reported in American Magazines." *Social Science* 41 (April 1966): 84–90.

———. "The Magazine *Charities* and the Italian Immigrants, 1903–14." *Journalism Quarterly* 44 (Spring 1967): 91–98.

Monticelli, Giuseppe Lucrezio. "Italian Emigration: Basic Characteristics and Trends with Special Reference to the Last Twenty Years." *The International Migration Review* 1 (Summer 1967): 10–24.

Moorhead, Elizabeth. "A School for Italian Laborers." *The Outlook* 88 (February 29, 1908): 499–504.

Moss, Leonard and Thompson, Walter. "The South Italian Family: Literature and Observation." *Human Organization* (Spring 1969).

Nam, C. B. "Nationality Groups and Social Stratification in America." *Social Forces* (May 1959).

Nelli, Humbert S. "Italians in Urban America: A Study in Ethnic Adjustment." *International Migration Review* (Summer 1967), pp. 38–55.

Novak, Michael. "White Ethnic." *Harper's Magazine* (September 1971), pp. 44–50.

Palisi, B. J. "Patterns of Socio Participation in Two Generations of Italian Americans." *Sociological Quarterly* (Spring 1966).

Palmieri, F. Aurelio, Order of St. Augustine, D.D. "Italian Protestantism in the United States." *Catholic World* (May 1908), pp. 177–89.

Panunzio, Constantine. "Italian Americans, Fascism and the War." *The Yale Review* 31 (June 1942): 771–82.

Parenti, Michael. "Ethnic Politics and the Persistence of Ethnic Identification." *The American Political Science Review* 61 (September 1967): 717–26.

Pecorini, Alberto. "The Italians in the United States." *The Forum* (January 1911), pp. 15–29.

Peixotto, Ernest. "Italy in California." *Scribner's Magazine* 48 (July 1910): 75–84.

Puzo, Mario. "The Italians, American Style." *The New York Times Magazine* (August 6, 1967), pp. 7, 14, 18, 25–30.

Richardson, Alan. "A Theory and a Method for the Psychological Study of Assimilation." *International Migration Review* (Fall 1967).

Ridley, Clifford A. "The Expanding Arts." *The National Observer* (November 2, 1970), p. 21.

Riis, Jacob A. "Feast Days in Little Italy." *The Century Magazine* 58 (August 1899): 491–99.

"The Rise of the 'New' American." *The New Republic* (May 10, 1922), pp. 301–2.

Rodgers, A. "Migration and Industrial Development: The Southern Italian Experience." *Economic Geography* 46, no. 2 (April 1970): 111–35.

Rodino, Peter W., Jr. "Today's Need for Immigration Revision." *The International Migration Review* 4, no. 3: 11.

Roseboro, Viola. "The Italians of New York." *The Cosmopolitan* 4 (January 1888): 396–406.

Roselli, Bruno. "An Arkansas Epic." *The Century* (January 1920), pp. 377–86.

Ross, Anne. "Books." New York *Herald Tribune* (December 31, 1961), p. 7.

Russo, Nicholas. "Three Generations of Italians in New York City:

Their Religious Acculturation." *The International Review* (Spring 1969).

Salomone, A. William. "The Nineteenth-Century Discovery of Italy: An Essay in American Cultural History. Prolegomena to a Historiographical Problem." *The American Historical Review* 73 (June 1968): 1359–91.

Schuyler, Eugene. "Italian Immigration into the United States." *Political Science Quarterly* 4 (September 1889): 480–95.

Scudder, Vida D. "Experiments in Fellowship, Work with Italians in Boston." *The Survey* 22 (April 3, 1909): 47–51.

Senner, Joseph H. "Immigration from Italy." *North American Review* 162 (June 1896): 649–57.

Sherwood, Herbert Francis. "Whence Came They." *The Outlook* 88 (February 22, 1908): 407–15.

Silverman, Sydel. "Prestige in a Central Italian Community." *American Anthropologist* (August 1966).

Singer, Caroline. "An Italian Saturday." *The Century* 101 (March 1921): 591–600.

Smith, Sandy. "The Mob." *Life* 63 (September 1,8,1967): 15–22, 42B–45, 91–104.

Smith, Timothy L. "Immigrant Social Aspirations and American Education, 1880–1930." *American Quarterly* 21 (Fall 1969): 523–43.

Speare, Charles F. "What America Pays Europe for Immigrant Labor." *North American Review* 188 (January 1908): 106–16.

Speranza, C. L. "The Italians in the United States." *The Chautauquan* 9 (March 1889): 346–49.

Speranza, Gino C. "How It Feels to Be a Problem. A Consideration of Certain Causes Which Prevent or Retard Assimilation." *Charities* 12 (May 7, 1904): 457–63.

______"Petrosino and the Black Hand." *The Survey* 22 (April 3, 1909): 11–14.

Swanson, Evadene B. "Italians in Cortland, New York." *New York History* 44 (July 1963): 258–73.

Swierenga, R. P., "Ethnocultural Political Analysis: A New Approach to American Ethnic Studies." *Journal of American Studies* 5, no. 1 (April 1971): 59–79.

Tortora, Vincent R. "Italian Americans, Their Swing to G.O.P." *The Nation* 177 (October 22, 1953): 330–32.

Tosti, Gustavo. "The Agricultural Possibilities of Italian Immigration." *Charities* 12 (May 7, 1904): 472–76.

Train, Arthur. "Imported Crime. The Story of the Camorra in America." *McClure's Magazine* 34 (May 1912): 82–94.

Turano, Anthony M. "An Immigrant Father." *The American Mercury* 27 (October 1932): 221–29.

———"The Speech of Little Italy." *The American Mercury* 26 (July 1932): 356–59.

Vecoli, Rudolph J. "Contadini in Chicago: A Critique of *The Uprooted.*" *Journal of American History* 51 (December 1964): 404–17.

———"Prelates and Peasants." *Journal of Social History* 2 (Spring 1969): 217–68.

Velikonja, Joseph. "Italian Immigrants in the United States in the Mid-Sixties." *The International Migration Review* 1 (Summer 1967): 25–38.

Walsh, James J. "An Apostle of the Italians." *The Catholic World* 107 (April 1918): 64–71.

Watson, Barbara M. "Immigration Today." *The International Migration Review* 4, no. 3: 47.

Watson, Charles H. "Need of Federal Legislation in Respect to Mob Violence in Cases of Lynchings of Aliens." *Yale Law Journal* 25 (May 1916): 560–81.

Whitehill, Walter Muir. "Who Rules Here? Random Reflections on the National Origins of Those Set in Authority Over Us." *New England Quarterly* 43 (September 1970): 434–49.

Wiley, Norbert F. "The Ethnic Mobility Trap and Stratification Theory." *Social Problems* 15 (Fall 1967): 147–59.

INDEX